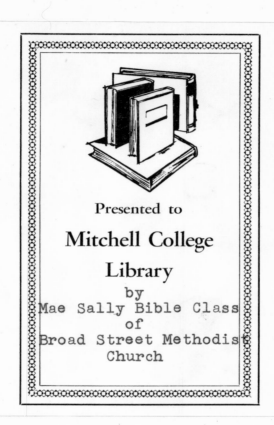

THE FAILURES OF CRITICISM

BY THE SAME AUTHOR

Louis Ménard. New Haven: Yale University Press, 1932.

Bibliographie critique de l'Héllenisme en France de 1843 à 1870. New Haven: Yale University Press, 1932.

Shelley et la France: Lyrisme anglais et lyrisme français au XIXᵉ siècle. Le Caire, Université, 1935.

Hommes et Œuvres du vingtième siècle. Corrêa, 1938.

L'Influence des littératures antiques sur la littérature française moderne. New Haven: Yale University Press, 1941.

Problèmes français de demain. New York: Brentano's, 1943.

Les Générations littéraires. Boivin-Hatier, 1948.

Connaissance de Baudelaire. Corti, 1951.

Pensées de Baudelaire. Corti, 1951.

The Contemporary French Novel. New York: Oxford University Press, 1955.

Observations on Life, Literature and Learning in America. Carbondale: Southern Illinois University Press, 1960.

Literature and Sincerity. New Haven: Yale University Press, 1963.

Contemporary French Literature: A Critical Anthology. New York: Harper and Row, 1964.

Qu'est-ce le Classicisme? Nizet, 1965.

Essais de Méthode, de Critique et d'histoire littéraire de Gustave Lanson. Hachette, 1965.

The Literature of France. (Princeton Studies on Humanistic Scholarship in America.) New York: Prentice Hall, 1966.

French Novelists of Today. New York: Oxford University Press, 1967.

THE FAILURES
OF CRITICISM

Emended edition of *Writers and Their Critics*

By HENRI PEYRE

Sterling Professor of French
Yale University

Cornell University Press

ITHACA, NEW YORK

First edition entitled *Writers and Their Critics: A Study of Misunderstanding* copyright 1944, emended edition entitled *The Failures of Criticism* copyright © 1967, by Cornell University

Library of Congress Catalog Card Number: 67-19473

PRINTED IN THE UNITED STATES OF AMERICA
BY VAIL-BALLOU PRESS, INC., BINGHAMTON, N. Y.

Acknowledgments

PERMISSION to reprint copyright matter has been courteously granted by the following:

Harcourt, Brace and Co., for two quotations from T. S. Eliot, *East Coker*, in Chapter IV.

The Macmillan Company, for a quotation made in the last chapter from W. B. Yeats's brief poem "The Scholars," from Yeats's *Collected Poems* (1940).

The American Academy of Arts and Sciences, for the article "What Is Wrong with American Book-Reviewing," originally published in *Daedalus*, XC (1961), 128–144.

Contents

THE FAILURES OF CRITICISM

Introduction

THE present volume, or the larger part of it, first appeared in 1944, published by Cornell University Press, under the title *Writers and Their Critics: A Study in Misunderstanding*. A number of readers then found fault with the title for being too narrow, since artists and musicians provided almost as many illustrations as writers and had been, over the ages, treated by reviewers with even worse obtuseness. They also objected to the title as too timid, since the purpose of the volume was, and has remained in the present revision, to warn readers against the preposterous, and allegedly most damaging, overweening pretentiousness of much criticism today, French and American in particular. It appeared to me that "The Failures of Criticism," if too sensational, would convey more accurately the author's intent.

The author is an academic critic himself and a student of the past, the exciting liveliness and permanent greatness of which he has attempted to convey to generations of students and to varied audiences in the United States and abroad. He has also endeavored to remain open to the present and to innovations effected in several arts and in several branches of scholarship in the present age. Some of the hazards of literary and artistic creativeness that result from the predominance of critics over imaginative creators around us have always appeared to him a threat to the enjoyment of beauty. The insolent dogmatism of many contemporary critics, their assumption, or affectation, of a pedantic language (it hardly can be called style), their ferocious insistence on searching, and therefore finding, one key to open all the locks of infinitely variegated works (a key manufactured by linguists, stylisticians, structuralists, phenomenologists, sociologists, or one of the other academic guilds) have aroused the ire of many novelists, poets, painters, and composers. Worse still, at a time when critics had practically monopolized the space in our so-called literary magazines and, of course, in our learned journals, when they were generally heard and seen on the air and on television, when they had, as captive audiences at their feet, millions of students and thousands of adults in lecture rooms and alumni seminars, it was questionable whether they had fulfilled the function expected from them: to enhance the public's interest in contemporary art and letters, to help it understand or enjoy it, to refine its taste, and to stimulate its potential passion for beauty.

Communication is an inelegant term, but one which is bandied about today in all discussions of art, of mass media, and of politics. It is often submitted that, in the welter of complexities which dims our minds at present, with 90 per cent of all the scientists who ever lived being now alive (what proportion of the very great, however, is not calculated so easily), scientists can no longer communicate with each other, even inside one broad province such as physics, medicine, or sociology. Humanists, as critics used to be called, have just as signally ceased to communicate among themselves, or with the authors of the very works which justify their own existence as commentators, or with the public. The one concern which animates this member of the critical and academic profession is an undying love for literature, carrying with it the conviction that criticism is and should remain secondary to imaginative inventions, should serve as the handmaid to creation and, at all times, strive for humility. A Russian writer is supposed to have hinted, probably with his tongue in his cheek, that a great poet ought to be "un peu bête," an adjective inadequately rendered by "foolish," "silly," or "stupid" and, in French, occasionally a gentle term of endearment. A number of poets indeed have been just that. Critics might also well prefer to be "un peu bêtes" rather than too clever, too complacently profound, or, to use the other favorite adjective of the French, too intelligent.

There has never been much love lost between writers and critics, still less between artists and art critics or between musicians or actors and the reviewers on whose pens their fate sometimes rests. The responsibility for that age-long divorce clearly does not lie just with one side. It is probably natural that creators, as they are clumsily called, should be endowed, not with the equanimity and impartiality of the supreme Maker, but with the virtues of both sexes, necessary to any fruitful creation. Theirs is the power of imaginative synthesis, the capacity for abstract composition with which men generously credit themselves alone. Male spirits take naïve pride in repeating that no woman has ever succeeded as architect, dramatist or musical composer, in planning a truly elaborate meal or a really artistic dress. But creators are also endowed with the charming frailties of the once-called weaker sex: they like to be liked, and they love even more to be loved. They readily take at face value any hyperbolic compliments and words of praise; none the less readily they resent any reservations on their originality or greatness, and they cast a suspicious eye on young rivals bold enough to side with views or techniques different from theirs. "At my age, sir, one no longer reads; one rereads," declared old Royer-Collard to Alfred de Vigny, who was paying him a deferential visit as a candidate to the French Academy. In the feminine sensitiveness of writers Anatole France saw the source of that beneficial custom which has always included an imposing number of marshals, cardinals, ambassadors, and statesmen among the forty Immortals of the Academy. Every self-respecting Academician will hasten to cast his vote for those respectable dignitaries who have the good sense not to write books, and hence the good taste not to compare themselves with him. But he will frown on any revolutionary youngster who dares, before he has reached the noble age of threescore years and ten, to solicit a seat in the august assembly on the strength of his literary prowess and thus shove his predecessors into an untimely grave.

Writers, to be sure, are seldom Olympian enough to resist glancing at critical articles concerning their productions. They will, at no mean cost, subscribe to a clipping bureau and diligently paste in a scrapbook the inglorious comments that arrive in the morning mail. Seldom, however, do they condescend to profit by the praise or the blame lavished upon them. The story of every literature has at all times echoed the mutual misunderstanding and the exchange of eloquent abuse which characterize relations between critics and writers.

This peevishness of writers, often of the greatest talents if not of the loftiest spirits among them, is not necessarily unjustified. They hold themselves neglected or unrecognized, and they have a good deal or reason for feeling so. The mistakes made by criticism are numberless; and if I am here attempting to list and if possible to redress some of them, let me, at once, grant extenuating circumstances to those who practice that most difficult of all the literary arts. It is natural, that is to say human, for a critic to eye with envy the creators who are able to translate their sorrows and joys into words, who give free rein to their roaming fancy, who imagine and depict the most sublime heroes or the most passionate heroines, while the unfortunate censor can only drily carp at the productions of others and dissect technical minutiae. Authors awake one morning and find themselves famous; thousands of copies of their novels are sold in a week; their dramas are acclaimed by an uncritical and enthusiastic audience; their verse smiles on the glowing lips of young women; their most burning sentences are generously borrowed by the adolescent, laboriously composing his first love letter. The critic's posthumous life will be restricted to a few quotations made by some impersonal teacher, a few judgments extracted from his works, to be discussed on examination day by students who will inwardly curse his name. Worse still, his successors will unmercifully point out his mistakes and sneer at the unfulfilled prophecies. Few books are as uniformly dreary as histories of criticism, even when written with the knowledge and gusto of a Saintsbury. Yet the men whose pages we turn over with a smile or a yawn, a Brunetière, a Lemaître, a Sarcey, a Matthew Arnold, a Macaulay, a La Harpe, or even greater ones, a Samuel Johnson or a Sainte-Beuve, could in their day kill a book with one sentence or, with three words of high praise, grant it success, wealth, and fame.

This long and probably inevitable misunderstanding is apparently destined to go on. It is needless to hope that the duel may end with the voluntary surrender of either of the contestants. In vain did exasperated artists like Whistler wish that art might be received in silence. There will always be critics; there will be more and more of them in the future. The public seems to have become in the field of arts and letters all the more obedient as it has won wider rights in political and social life. Its obliging alacrity to follow its favorite lecturers or commentators is as admirable in its meekness as it is disconcerting. Even those of us who would never dream of buying a certain brand of coffee, cigar, or toothpaste solely on the strength of an enticing advertisement joyfully bow before the latest book-of-the-month selected by a self-appointed body of critics, or religiously repeat, without the encumbrance of quotation marks, what the fashionable lecturer or the renowned musical expert has pronounced on Joyce, Miró, or Berg. We are not content with asking the critic to sift out a few good books among a production which we find overwhelming; we want him to elucidate for us works which we find difficult, to tell us what we should think of them and what we should in turn repeat to our neighbor at the dinner table, to our partner in the ballroom or on the golf course.

There have been fortunate ages in which critics were an unborn or rare species. Their place as occupied, it is true, by slanderous gazetteers, by ingenious distillers of pungent satires and inane poetical arts, or by grammarians and professors of rhetoric. Those ages are no more. America, long a privileged land in that respect, is today afflicted by a veritable epidemic of criticism; its vanguard reviews are encumbered by pedantic disquisitions in which several disciplines are marshalled to succor, if not to elucidate, literature: esthetics, sociology, muscular physiology, psychology as modern laboratories understand it (i.e., the study of the behavior of rats, mice, guinea pigs, apes, never of the soul of man), pre-embryonic pathology, psychoanalysis, and the latest born but not the loveliest of these goddesses, structural anthropology. Feeling poetry was a permissible ideal for our naïve grandparents. We have changed all that: understanding it is the motto of the day, and we are being scientifically informed that only a critic trained in three or four disciplines, including logic and the "new" psychology, knows how to read a book or how to read a page.

Let us not mock too harshly those repeated pangs of childbirth which, even in the case of arid and austere mountains such as I. A. Richards and L. Goldmann, have thus far brought forth only infinitesimal mice. Modern criticism is still groping for its method and enthusiastically experimenting with several techniques. It has not yet outgrown the primitive stage in which physics similarly fumbled before Bacon and Descartes, chemistry before Lavoisier, sociology before Auguste Comte, and physiology before Claude Bernard. Scornful of the vulgar language and loose statements of the illogical human herd, it has taken refuge in university laboratories, where it feeds on acid abstractions. To journalists and occasional book reviewers it has surrendered the accounts of current literature, the rash utterance of value-judgments, and even the naïve perception of beauty. It prefers to fathom, weigh, and dissect the connotations, denotations, and ambiguities of Joyce, Donne, and Mallarmé, or elucidate Aristotle once more. These modern critics, who shrink from all esthetic emotion and literary enjoyment, have not unjustly been called "the uninfluentials."

Criticism might well display more ambition. Its function might be as beneficent today as it repeatedly proved to be in the past. The final chapters of this book will endeavor to define some of the tasks which literary criticism has consistently refused to face or failed to fulfil in our century. Critics have abdicated their three-fold duty to the writers, to the public, and to future generations. No one will deny the impossibility of artificially fostering or producing geniuses, least of all through criticism. But many talents might have been aided and encouraged if they had blossomed in a more favorable climate; and the duty of critics is, through discussion and appreciation, to create an atmosphere in which "mute inglorious Miltons" and lonely Cézannes will be inspired to write or to paint—sometimes encouraged by contradiction, spurred on by anger or defiance. Somewhat dramatically a French writer on the subject announced: "We are dying for lack of a philosophy of criticism." [1]

We are, alas, dying from many other causes, while our literature remains very much alive. But it is true that the generation of Auden and Spender, even of Surrealism, of Giono and Malraux, did not find its critics, even in France, where criticism is a national art and a highly esteemed profession. The corresponding absence of a Sainte-Beuve among the young romantics, of a Baudelaire as an interpreter of Delacroix, of a Remy de Gourmont as a champion of the Symbolists, would have meant for those artists or writers an incalculable loss. The number of readers has grown immensely in the last century, at least that of potential readers of literary works and actual readers of comic strips and detective stories. The number of books published every year has grown also, although not as much as we fondly imagine considering the increase in the total population. Book reviewers and readers complain of the bewildering burden; cynics like Anatole France pile up the new productions in a bathtub and display them as the surest deterrent to a literary career to visitors who respectfully question them on "how to become a great writer." The obscurity of modern literature and art is supposed to have become an unpassable barrier for the layman, unless he is assisted by a diligent squad of guides, interpreters, and clarifiers. The critic is thus more sadly needed than he ever was. But the good critic remains what he always was, as rare, said Schopenhauer, "as the phoenix, which appears only once in five hundred years." Time has belied the famous pronouncement of James Russell Lowell: "Before we can have an American literature, we must have an American criticism." Twentieth-century America can easily boast of ten important

[1] Maurice Rouzaud, *Où va la Critique?* (Éditions Saint-Michel, 1929), p. 9.

novelists, read and translated all over the world, of almost as many poets and dramatists fervently admired, but not perhaps of a single critic of very eminent stature.[2]

That long misunderstanding which has consistently driven creators and critics apart has also impoverished them. It has been no less serious for the public and for all those who, in the universities, in the lecture-rooms of their clubs, in picture galleries, or in the wide world, are eager to acquire and complete a cultural education. No better or more concise formulation of the purpose of a broad education has been offered than Matthew Arnold's definition of the aim of the French schoolboy: "to understand himself, and the world." Literature and the arts of a country or of an age are, if rightly interpreted, the most faithful mirror— distorting and magnifying, to be sure, but not unreliable—to that country and that age. For artists and authors are gifted, or afflicted, with keener insight, more nervous sensitiveness, and more prophetic intuition than ordinary human beings.

Yet most of us pass among contemporary artists and writers without even reaching for the golden key held out to us in vain. Before 1929, anyone who interpreted the America of the years of prosperity and wild speculation, not from the statistics of economists, the curves of the stock market, and the figures of automobile salesmen, but from the bitter literature of discontent and revolt of the Twenties, would probably have foretold some of the subsequent events which struck the complacent professional prophets like a bolt from the blue. The true soul of England, suddenly laid bare by the perils of Dunkirk and the challenge of a tragic threat, surprised political commentators, economic experts, and the never-wearied prophets of the decline of Britain; it had not, however, remained unobserved by the few who, between 1932 and 1940, had read in the poetry of young rebels clamoring for a heroic cause and thinking "continually of those who were

2 The greatest—Edmund Wilson, Lionel Trilling, Alfred Kazin—are not any more likely to be read in 1980 than the greatest European ones—Georg Lukacs, T. S. Eliot, Jean Starobinski, Gaëtan Picon.

truly great" a message far different from that which Aldous Huxley, Noel Coward, Somerset Maugham, P. G. Wodehouse had
offered to disillusioned cynics and London high-brows a few
years earlier. The true heart of France, in the same decade, did
not beat in the debates of the Chamber of Deputies, in the political scandals, or in the easy and all-too-clear literature with which
academic writers and Academicians pandered to the taste of a
reading public, complacently looking for what conformed to
their set habits and accepting only a carefully limited share of
conventional innovation. It throbbed in the imaginative courage
and the uncompromising fearlessness of the more difficult art and
literature, and above all in the new poetry. Woe to the country which, at the very moment when the world looks to it with
fervent expectation, does not bring forth a Balzac, a Dickens, a
Tolstoi to interpret its soul and symbolize its image for the times
to come! Hundreds of journalists and scores of economists and
social inquirers visited Russia between 1920 and 1940; dozens of
hurried observers flew across the South American continent in
the same era and revealed the "inside" of half a hemisphere to
readers of good will, whose docile patience is one of the marvels
of the modern world. In series of articles subsequently collected
in big volumes, the new influentials of our day, the reporters,
have compiled trade statistics, psychoanalyzed dictators and generals, described hospitals, factories, insane asylums, and women's
clubs. Yet the Russia of Lenin and Stalin, the Argentina of the
same era have never come to life in their pages. Soviet Russia,
indeed, will never seem real to our descendants until a Gogol or a
Tolstoi expresses it and re-creates it in immortal literature. South
America will perhaps some day cease being alternately patronized
and courted by the northern hemisphere—when she translates all
her latent greatness and her mute originality into one great work
of music, painting, or literature which will impose its vision upon
us. Two hundred volumes of so-called revelations on the French
defeat of 1940, crammed with all the best-contrived thrills of the
most vulgar mystery story, will weigh far less in the scales of
Time than the only masterpieces thus far inspired by the Aeschy-

lean disaster of France: Saint-Exupéry's *Flight to Arras* and
Aragon's *Le Crève-Coeur*. Not all our present wealth of photo-
graphic technique, radio commentary, and first-hand reporting
has enabled us to see, to live, and to understand the greatest war
in history as will some day a literary masterpiece of a Stendhal or
a Tolstoi yet unknown or unborn. American sensibility and attitudes could, in 1965–1967, have been profoundly altered by one
great novel on the suffering of Vietnam.

In order to turn thus to literature and art as the most faithful
and prophetic image of a civilization, one must first be aware of
the best productions of one's age, discriminating between the
works which look to the future and express the deeper part of
the present and those which are merely pleasing and insipid imitations of former models, skillful rehashings of familiar platitudes.
The task is hard—so hard, indeed, that mankind has seldom accomplished it creditably. Criticism has often proved deaf and
blind, or blunt and dull, in the presence of the most original
creations of contemporary authors. It has perversely accumulated
instances of unbelievable blundering.

It may be that it will continue accumulating them. I shall not
attempt here impudently to discover a safe method or an infallible recipe for the right appraisal of our contemporaries, still less
to solve the impossible problem of the criteria of esthetic judgment or to enumerate the unmistakable features of the beautiful.
Impressionism and relativism must always play a considerable
part in any critical appreciation. Taste, flair, and intuition remain,
after all, the least fallible asset of any appraiser of art and literature. Even more than poets, critics are born, not made. But they
are more scarce than poets.

Must we, then, despair of ever advancing? Literary and artistic
critics have, compared to rhetoricians and estheticians of two
centuries ago, developed and improved their technique as re-
markably as history and psychology have in the same length of
time.[3] Obviously such progress is neither continuous nor inevit-

[3] The progress in scope and variety, if not always in depth, has been told
in one of the important histories of our age: René Wellek's *History of
Modern Criticism* (New Haven: Yale University Press, 1955–1968).

able. We occasionally go through stages of retrogression or suffer from epidemics of obstinate aberration. Coleridge, Sainte-Beuve, De Sanctis have probably thrown as much insight as we may ever hope to possess into the understanding of some great writers of the past. Yet a boundless future opens before present-day criticism. Virgin soil is as vast there as in any realm of knowledge. To record the mistakes of past critics merely for the pleasure of smiling at them would be a childish pastime. The game of opposing the opinions of critics to one another to prove once more the uncertainty of all human judgments requires nothing but a retentive memory, some skepticism, and a little cheap irony. It is not even worthy of a Ph.D. apprentice at a loss for a thesis subject and short of original ideas.

But it may be a helpful task to collect a number of examples of clear-cut mistakes made by our predecessors when appraising the work of their contemporaries, provided we draw from it positive lessons. If we must err in the future as we did in the past, let it be with full consciousness of errors committed by our predecessors and with keen awareness of the causes which misled them. Through diligent study of history, the human species will obviously never succeed in solving its impossible problems; indeed, much of our renewed delight in living would be blunted if children could ever benefit by the accumulated experience of their parents and inherit their wisdom. As it is, each generation is entitled to its own formulation and its own provisional solution of eternal riddles.

In order to make a fair and representative selection of instances of misunderstanding between writers and critics, a few rules must be followed. Examples should be as varied as possible, and chosen, not from one literature alone, but from several, and, for the most part, from the last two centuries, since literary criticism hardly existed before 1700 as an autonomous province and a systematic genre. A few illustrations, drawn from music and the fine arts, will occasionally show that unacknowledged talents were not limited to literature. We should also bear in mind that fairness is a prerequisite for such an inquiry and avoid quoting only the partisan charges which were brought against a great talent, while dismissing or ignoring the few clear-sighted contemporaries who perceived and revealed the brilliance of the ascending star. Lastly, one should attempt this fragmentary survey of the mistakes of criticism without any scorn or condescension for our predecessors. None of us can boast of being, at this very moment, less guilty than those who ignored Milton and Bach, who ridiculed Baudelaire and Rodin. Above all, the study of the past should make us humble, but determined to avoid the most obvious pitfalls into which others have sunk.

If the failures of criticism which this book attempts to expose and, in a modest way, to help to remedy are as regrettable as I believe them to be, some steady reflection on them might perhaps lead us to a reconsideration of the teaching of literature and the arts in our colleges and to a drastic reorientation of the professional training for the Ph.D. degree in those fields. Familiarity with vigorous works of literature in our own language and perhaps in one or two others, not the ability to discuss theoretically and often verbosely on esthetics and on symbols unperceived by the scorned unsophisticated layman, should be the aim of a humanistic education. The writing of better poetry, of more mature fiction and drama, the composition of significant works of music, painting, sculpture, architecture by native Americans could, it seems, reasonably be expected from a country of nearly two hundred million people, which, a century and a quarter ago, did enjoy an "American renaissance" when it could only draw its talents from a mere thirty million people.[4] Critics, it is true, have since multiplied in a manner altogether out of proportion to the number of writers or to the population; that is a tribute to the enormous progress of scholarship in America and to the power and influence of the universities, comparable today in their predominance, wealth, and spiritual authority to the churches, mon-

---

[4] A survey of the most original painters, sculptors, musicians and even architects (the latter from Finland, Germany, Japan, Italy) who were born abroad, while it testifies to America's power as a center of cultural attraction and to her generosity, would be disquieting. Since 1950, however, the "brain drain" has drawn scientists, technicians, engineers to this country, but few artists and even fewer writers.

asteries, convents, and charitable institutions of the Middle Ages. But the gulf separating imaginative writers from critics is, if anything, deeper today. The bitterness of the writers against that criticocracy is more intense. It is expressed with a resentment which almost matches the satirical denunciations of English and French writers in centuries when literary satire had not yet lost its pungency.

Academic critics of today delight at lecturing on some of those invectives against reviewers and critics of the past, and they invariably side with the sharp-tongued and talented writers who dipped their pens in gall with more zest than their descendants, bitten by the bug of universal kindliness and insipid tolerance (even of the ugly and the base), summon up today. Bacon called the critics "only brushers of noblemen's clothes"; Swift inveighed against them in *The Tale of a Tub* and *The Battle of the Books;* Charles Churchill denounced their treachery:

> Conscious of guilt and fearful of the light,
> They lurk enshrouded in the veil of night,
> Safe from detection, seize the unwary prey,
> And stab, like bravoes, all who come that way.

Before Churchill and in the same country, Congreve had railed in *The Way of the World* at those self-appointed judges of literature, "on no pretence for judgment fit"; and in the prologue to *The Conquest of Granada*, Dryden had ascribed to them, as Corneille, Molière, and Racine had done to their petty and envious adversaries, incompetence and even impotence and spite:

> They who write ill, and they who ne'er durst write,
> Turn critics out of mere revenge and spite.

Addison, soon after, and then in a later century, Carlyle (scathingly scornful of those "flesh-flies of literature"), Whistler maligned by Ruskin, and almost all the authors of originality of the Victorian era felt likewise unfairly condemned by the pompous Zoiluses of the solemn magazines, not unworthy of the fourth-century Greek sophist whose name became synonymous with carping and cantankerous criticism.

Nor is the record of French critics less blemished, or the hostility they aroused in all the writers of great talent less fierce. The enumeration, not solely of the writers' indignant cries of anger and of scorn, but of their pathetic pleas for a more understanding attitude, would fill a volume; and such a volume should some day be compiled. It would enlighten us on how the creators in several arts wish to be judged, not only and in fact not usually with leniency, but with close attention and a modicum of fairness. Agrippa d'Aubigné, in a biting quatrain published in 1629, begged those who would "correct" him to try first to understand him and to read him more than once therefor. In the romantic age, Hugo in his preface to *Les Orientales,* Théophile Gautier in his preface to *Mademoiselle de Maupin*, Vigny, and then Leconte de Lisle, Flaubert in his letters from 1846 to 1876 and in his preface to Bouilhet's *Dernières Chansons*, and the Goncourt brothers (or the one of the pair who survived and expressed himself on the subject in the *Journals* in November 1890), all took issue with the mediocrity of their judges.

Maupassant and Zola never lacked readers, even during their lifetimes. But they found them among the "masses," which were fortunately untouched by the articles and reviews of the critics, regularly ready to blame them. The former, in his preface to *Pierre et Jean,* retorted to those dogmatists who claim to decide, against the authors, that a new book is or is not a novel. "An intelligent critic should, on the contrary, look for all that least resembles the novels already in existence, and urge the young to strike new paths." Zola ridiculed Sainte-Beuve's obtuse praise of Xavier de Maistre above Stendhal and Eugène Sue above Balzac, and in his *Documents littéraires*, written for a Russian paper, he courageously deplored the bankruptcy of French criticism and the disadvantages under which a literary movement or a generation which fails to find its critic must labor. The painter Manet, whom Zola alone appreciated during his struggling years, was so demoralized by the unanimous attacks of the critics that he no longer dared ask anyone to pose for him; he saw his friends looking sedulously away from him on the street so that they would not have to offer their condolences on his paintings' lack of success. Claude Monet, at the very time (in the early 1870's) when he painted his most radiant pictures of boatmen on the Seine, was so discouraged by the hostile derision of critics and the threat of starvation that he twice was tempted by thoughts of suicide.

Nor have the writers and painters of our own century been understood more sympathetically by critics during their struggling years, when intelligent interpreters of the novelty of their works were most needed. Proust's anger at Sainte-Beuve and at his descendants who proved incapable of sharing the vision or of heeding the music of an innovating artist is repeatedly vented in the course of his long novel. Gide for years fared no better. Mauriac, long after his consecration with academic honors, unable to refrain from reading critics and always hoping to learn from them something about himself, begged critics to attempt to understand before passing judgment. "What critics brand and reject in us is precisely what is most truly ourselves . . . what differentiates us thereby from our great predecessors"; let them instead ask whether the author knew how to remain true to the laws of his own inner world, he insisted. To be judged and, if need be, condemned would not irk an author, if he is condemned according to his own law or standard. Paul Claudel, atrociously mishandled by critics for some thirty years, calmly outlined for them a program through which they could become "more scientific," explaining the work under discussion and explaining themselves, instead of rushing into personal lyrical explosions of praise or blame. Paul Valéry, apparently for no personal motive, for he was lauded in his lifetime as no other poet had been since Hugo and raised on an official pedestal by his country's authorities, recurred more than twenty times to the glaring inadequacies of criticism: he upbraided critics for seizing only, like the psychologists, "the outside of the inside," stressing influences, sources, biography, implicit ideas, and hidden symbols, but having never the faintest inkling of what is in truth involved in an art work.[5] In his view, the genuine merit of a work (different from its value to a reader) lies in the relationship between the author and his project, in the appraisal of the author's achievement relative to what he had planned to achieve. "A mind should only be judged according to its own laws."

What have most of the critics in our century done which has turned more and more authors against them and impressed upon the public the notion that modern literature is not for it, indeed that only hyper-sophisticated minds can learn how to read a book or a page with due attention to its paradoxes, symbols, images, and structural arcana?

Many of them have evinced a conservatism in matters of taste, but also of ethics and even of politics, which has made them appear as supporters of "the Establishment," the new ugly monster for the youth in and just out of college at which they aim their arrows as they once did against Wall Street, the robber barons, and Madison Avenue. They have gone to literature, looking in it for a substitute for religion. Criticism has become the successor to theology. Much of it recalls to historians of ideas the so-called Byzantine quarrels of the pedants who argued while their culture was being threatened and engulfed by barbarians, or the councils of the second century after Christ where displays of vain subtlety were the order of the day and rivalled the Talmudic disquisitions. A great historian of religion, Ernest Renan, wrote in *L'Église chrétienne* words which apply just as aptly to the old Alexandrian rhetoric and to those of today:

To insist upon finding everything in a text is also to force oneself to childish "tours de force." When the natural meaning is exhausted, one seeks mystical meanings; then one counts the letters, weighs them as if

---

[5] See François Mauriac, "Critique de la critique," *Journal ii* (Grasset, 1937); Paul Claudel in Frédéric Lefèvre, *Les Sources de Claudel* (Lemercier, 1927), pp. 143–144; Paul Valéry, *passim*, especially *Choses tues* (Gallimard, 1932) and *Cahiers*, Vol. VII, covering the years 1918–1921 (no date of publication).

they were numbers. . . . There was evidence of an ardent religious faith in those controversies heaped up over the best manner of obeying the law, but also an intellectual game and an entertainment. Ingenious and active men, condemned to a sedentary life, divorced from the general spirit of the time, endeavored to amuse their boredom through the application of dialectics to legal texts.

Scaffoldings of sophistry are thus erected over *Measure for Measure*, *A Winter's Tale*, *Lycidas*, and, after D. H. Lawrence had been almost unanimously banned as an immoral pornographer for thirty years and Joyce treated with equal contempt, over *Women in Love* and *Ulysses*. Inordinate amounts of subtlety and paraphernalia of linguistic analysis and of rhetorical terminology are brought into the analysis of a writer's effects. Poems which any teenager used naïvely to recite to himself with joy (Herrick's "Corinna's Going a-Maying," Wordsworth's solemn "immortality ode, Tennyson's flabby "Tears, Idle Tears") are now approached only with awe. Intense, if barren, cogitation is expended by teenagers so as to eschew the plainest and obvious meaning and to resist any appeal to the senses or to sensibility, any recourse to the student's own experience. The relevance of poetry, and even of fiction, to everyday life is branded as a defacement of the nobility of "literature as such." As one of the practitioners of the art asserted, a poem must not mean, but be. The distinction, which had been clumsily interpreted by mediocre pedagogues, between content and form is derided by austere judges. "What is called 'fond' ['subject matter' is a poor rendering] is but a poor form," submitted the Frenchman who most steadily preached that form and music are everything in poetry: Paul Valéry.

Some poetry, it is true, can work its magic without resting on thought, sentiment, or imaginative experience: songs of Shakespeare or Fletcher, though hardly the greatest, nursery rhymes, carols. But what a paltry affair poetry would be if reduced to those! There is a substance and a wealth of suggestions in "Kubla Khan" and in "La Belle Dame sans Merci," even in Keats's 1818 ballad on Meg Merrilies, in some early lyrics by Yeats; fortunately that poetry is, and lives, in part because it also means. How much meaning is embedded in Lucretius and Dante and Goethe and Baudelaire and Rilke! And that content of poetry, to use an unfashionable term, is often most moving and arouses in us the most durable response when it also is the simplest, the least ambiguous, and untainted by irony. The remarks lent to Shakespeare by Henry Fielding in a fantasy which depicts the author visiting the underworld after his death (*A Journey from This World to the Next*, chapter 8) may appear too unsophisticated to specialists in symbolic subtlety, but they are far more sensible and more likely to enhance our insight into Shakespeare:

I marvel nothing so much as that men will gird themselves at discovering obscure beauties in an author. Certainly the greatest and most pregnant beauties are ever the plainest and most evidently striking; and when two meanings of a passage can in the least balance our judgments which to prefer, I hold it matter of unquestionable certainty that neither of them is worth a farthing.

The balance sheet of the laborious undertaking of I. A. Richards and of Kenneth Burke and their followers does not impress some of us today as a richly positive one. The movement once called "new criticism" has rendered services to teaching and focused a sane attention to the text itself. But it has also and perilously offered to epigoni a series of easy devices and led them to believe in their dogmatic infallibility. The gusto of earlier critics who loved literature and fired their readers and students with that love is sadly missed in all but a few of our contemporaries on the campuses of this continent: Northrop Frye, Harry Levin, Lionel Trilling are those fortunate exceptions, not unequal to the best literary interpreters of the past. But one may well miss, among the innumerable others, the ebullience of H. L. Mencken, the candid freshness of Dahlberg, the adventurousness and the flamboyant verve of James G. Huneker (who was the first to discover Joyce's originality, as early as 1917, in a review of *The Portrait of the Artist* for the *Sun*). Two or three of the most sharply discriminating and most broadly cultured talents in mid-century America stand among those who have deplored the misunderstanding between writers and critics and the insolent imperialism of academic critics since 1950 or 1960. One is the late Randall Jarrell, in an excellent volume of essays, *Poetry and the Age* (New York: Knopf, 1953), who compared a great deal of modern American criticism to material "written by a syndicate of encyclopedias for an audience of International Business Machines." He added further: "Many bad critics are bad because they have spent their life in card-indexes . . . we become good critics by reading poems and stories and by living; it is reading criticism which is secondary." Another, no less vehement and no less talented, is Saul Bellow. He implored us to prefer naïvety to culture-idolatry, feeling to meaning, and to recover the value of flesh and bone.[6] Both voiced their fear of the practice now current to call upon authors to reside on a university campus and, through a process of mysterious osmosis, to instil into young people some of their creativeness. "They will be comfortably turned in upon themselves. They may catch the academic dread of the crime of risk. . . . They may learn an unnatural hostility to vulgarity. . . . Many a creative writer will turn to indifferent criticism in these circumstances, because it is safe, and thereby lose the creative habit."

Underlying the whole trend of resorting to needlessly abstract jargon and of evolving theories to imprison and emasculate the free impulses of creative artists is the urge to reach some definitive security in critical judgments and to ape the precision and the neatness of science. The prestige of science is universal in our time, and it already appeared so when Comte, Taine, Zola, and Brunetière himself looked up to it for objective criteria of judg-

[6] Saul Bellow, in the *New York Times Book Review* of February 15, 1959, and again in the same publication of July 10, 1966, in even more earnest tones and in bitterer hostility to the academics and to the university-sponsored quarterlies. Stephen Spender has fought the same battle in the same periodical of January 15, 1956: "Are Critics Too Much with Us?" So has another Englishman, V. S. Pritchett, *ibid.*, November 28, 1954, and an Australian, A. D. Hope, in "Literature versus the Universities," *The Cave and the Spring* (Adelaide: Rigly, 1966).

ment and in order to flee from the ephemeral subjectivity of their impressions and opinions. That noble experiment proved a failure. The wisest of French literary historians, and as discerning a critic as any since in his country, Gustave Lanson, rightly remarked, opposing the Tainian determinism: one thing alone can safely be borrowed by literature and by criticism from science, its conscience. Divergencies among critics have in no way been made less sharp by their resorting to techniques or to terminology borrowed from linguistics, from psychoanalysis, or from the systematic inclusion of varied literary temperaments into one key concept borrowed from the philosopher Bachelard, or from Georges Poulet's obsession with time or with interior distance. The greatness of literature and art, and the secret of their permanent appeal for scientists, among others, and for men who work in severe statistics and struggle against ineluctable laws during the day, lie in that indeterminacy which scientists have recently discovered in their own pursuits. It would be easy to be a critic or a politician if only one could apply safe standards and measure unpredictable temperaments according to set rules. But it would entail the sure death of literature, of art, of the humanities, and of all progress in politics. The more pseudo-scientific the humanities have attempted to become, the more surely they have alienated the very practitioners of the sciences of which they offer ludicrous caricatures and the more they have misunderstood the scientists themselves, who are fundamentally just as impatient of measurements, standards, rules, and quantitative data in the inventors and the discoveries as are artists and imaginative critics.

George Meredith is credited with the saying that, while a silly Briton is just disarmingly plain silly, a stupid Frenchman is a stupid man who reasons. There has not been overmuch stupidity of the humble and touching sort in French criticism since 1930 or so; but there has been such an overdose of sophisticated intellectuality, such a passion for philosophical theories impeding freshness of perception and the healthy vagaries of taste, such an insolence on the part of the critics in Paris (and even more in

Geneva or Zurich) congratulating each other like Molière's characters ("Peste! où prend *son* esprit toutes ces gentillesses?") that it is a miracle that all creative inventiveness in literature has not been stifled under those bombardments of words and doctrines. Stendhal noted, in his *Life of Napoleon*, that every thirty years the terms concerning war change; the vulgar (the unhappy many) thus believe they have effected some progress in their ideas while they have merely changed the words. He added in a note: "such is also the case in the art of curing diseases." It is even truer of criticism, which today has caught up with strategy and the art of love in the sense that the amateurs are proving more exciting at it than the professionals; the latter are bogged down in quarrels about words and language.

Polemics revels in those quarrels, and all the more lustily since 1958 or so, as the French seem to have lost their passion for battles of words in the realms of politics and of religion. Against the dullness of their lives henceforth lived in the midst of security, governmental stability, and economic prosperity, and since no storm is any longer aroused by successors of Diaghilev and Stravinsky in music, of Cézanne and Rodin in art, of Surrealism in letters, the French have fallen back upon wars among the critics. The academicians, far from being reducible to one school carrying the faded banner of Lanson, have exchanged scornful and murderous arrows: Lucien Febvre against Lefranc's ideas on Rabelais and Henri Lefebvre against both; Jean Pommier against René Jasinski on Racine and against J.-P. Richard on later novelists and poets; professors at the Sorbonne against those of the École des Hautes Études which they shelter; younger talents drawn to phenomenology or structuralism, unable to write a page without resorting four times to the magical adjective "existential," aligned against the older masters. The year 1966 witnessed a genuine battle of the books by critics: Barthes versus Picard; Sartre versus the cadavers of Flaubert and of Titian, but raising Mallarmé and Tintoretto as the idols of atheistic existentialism; Bonnefoy, Mauron, Doubrovsky gleefully jumping into the fray. The old linguist De Saussure, the psychologist and physician Lacan, the anthropologist Lévi-Strauss have become the new untouchables whose every word, much to their dismay, is carried over from their discipline into the evaluation of literature. Writers of the past, even those who had remained unperturbed by anxiety, were reinterpreted as tragically anguished by human time or constrained to spin into the whirling and mystical metamorphosis of a circle—or else their careers had been governed by incidents occurring before their fourth or fifth year which conditioned the development of their imaginations. Maurice Blanchot, who had started out to become our most profound mid-century critic, became a monotonous prophet of despair and a worshipper of silence, perpetually wondering why authors write at all when literature is only "the right to die." A critic of the 1960's in Paris or Geneva would deem himself, or deem any writer, unworthy of the superior status to which his pursuit entitles him if he did not, as the phrase goes, "contest language" at every page and turn all literature into a meditation on language. If the result of so much controversy were to foment discussion and active thought on contemporary literature, the result might be beneficial. Unfortunately literary creativeness has been almost as little affected by those debates as it has in the United States. If anything, it has been deprived of potential talents who chose to go into heated discussions on language, structure, and what criticism should be, instead of trusting their own imagination. The quality of novels, plays, short stories, and poetry has declined. Many a young man, repelled by the inhuman dryness of critical reviews like *Critique* or *Tel quel*, has turned away from a literary vocation toward the social sciences or to law and administration. The few who have not sunk into pompous obscurity or into the comfortable security of a system and who have persisted in serving literature seem almost embarrassed by their obstinacy in thinking freely, in feeling intensely, and in writing clearly: Gaëtan Picon, Jean Starobinski, Manuel de Diéguez, Robert Kanters. Textual analysis is not without its virtues in an academic seminar and the intellectual agility which it helps develop is a valuable tool. But art is not primarily an intellectual affair; it also demands

an emotional acceptance and an excited response. David Cecil has
had the courage to say so to his compatriots, who once used to be
derided as the Puritans fearful of cakes and ale and of the word
"pleasure" introduced into art. With the second half of our century, the French seemed to have become the dour fanatics of a
new austerity in art and culture and the apostles of systematic
boredom in their "new" novels. Their neighbors across the Channel are now those who are being charged with decadence and
laziness; gay London has replaced sulking Paris. It had to be an
Oxford professor who is also the scion of an old family who
exclaimed:

Art is not like mathematics or philosophy. It is a subjective, sensual
and highly personal activity in which facts and ideas are the servants
of fancy and feeling; and the artist's first aim is not truth, but delight.
. . . The primary object of a student of literature is to be delighted.
His duty is to enjoy himself; his efforts should be directed to develop-
ing his faculty of appreciation.[7]

Dryden, if he came back to life in these days of "mésentente
cordiale," would probably no longer endorse the two-edged compliment he paid to the French in his "Dedication of the *Aeneis*":
"The French are as much better critics than the English as they
are worse poets."

The inelegance of their style and their blatant preference for
their own self-enclosed systems over the work of art in whose
beginning their end should be are, in my opinion, the unredeem-
able faults of those French critics, justifying the title which this
book bears. Several of them have been marked by the impact of
Sartrian existentialism (although none of them can match Sartre
in critical power and even in emotional force), but they have not
rid themselves of the "bad faith" which Sartre hunted out in the
bourgeois, in the believers and the moralists. The most blatant
instance is that of Lucien Goldmann, dubbed a follower of
Lukacs by many and a master in the technique of striking
hammer-blows of pontifical assertions on his readers. A Marxist,

[7] Lord David Cecil, *The Fine Art of Reading and Other Literary Studies*
(London: Constable, and New York: Bobbs-Merrill, 1957).

he intoxicates himself with statements in which the novel is defined as a mere reflection of the contradictions of capitalism and of economic and social forces crushing the authors. His long essay on Malraux in *Sociologie du Roman* and scattered critiques, such as one on Genet's *Le Balcon* in *Les Temps Modernes* of June 1960 which explains the play as "a didactic work stemming from the essential transformations of industrial society in the first half of the twentieth century," are the lucubrations of a doctrinaire insensitive to literature.

Roland Barthes has greater breadth and occasional flashes of intuition into the psychology of Michelet and into the poetry of Racine; more commonplace and often tedious are his introduction to La Bruyère's *Caractères* and most of his *Essais critiques*, in which Racinian tragedy, Hegelian motives, Brecht's dramas, *Zazie dans le Métro*, the abbé Pierre, and the *Guides bleus* are ground into a uniform paste. His claim to create a third category, "l'écriture," intermediate between language and style and to evolve "a metalanguage" for criticism is a hollow boast. The search for structures to underlie a work of art and act as patterns of mysteriously interlocked and coherent meanings may be a grandiose philosophical attempt. It appears to me to rest on false premises: that in any work, any mind, or even any organism there lies a fundamental unity, and that, ultimately, the laws of the world and those of human thought are identical. The assumption may be a seductive one for all monists, intent upon hitting upon one explanation and upon erecting one all-embracing system; those critics are the true compatriots of Descartes, Laplace, and Auguste Comte. In literature, when they condescend to step down from their doctrinaire tripod and to discuss specific works, they emit a few maxims ("Racine is an impure author . . . in whose plays germs of the future bourgeois theatre are already lurking. . . . He offers the very type of the work of transition, in which life and death are at odds. . . ."—Roland Barthes), ignore diversity and the contradictions of the artists, reconstruct those artists and authors arbitrarily, and disregard the changes brought into their inspiration by crises in their lives and in their times and the contingency of all sublunar phenomena.[8] Chronology, history, biography are thrown overboard. Enjoyment of literature is out of the question. The saddest feature of those new Jansenists or Puritans of letters is their basic hatred of literature. While they argue back and forth with as much cantankerous obstinacy to prove the unique validity of their own terminology as the Talmudic commentators and the medieval theologians ever poured into their controversies, they concur in only one feature of their attitudes: their neglect to heed the literature now being produced around them and often against them. The novel, the drama, the essay, new art forms emerging today are altogether neglected by those obstinate exegetes of Racine, Baudelaire, and Mallarmé. All their endeavors seem to be centered on elaborating oracular theories on poetry which they force upon the poets of the past. Helen Gardner of Oxford voiced what is the conviction of those who have the independence and originality of contemporary literature at heart and watch its role among the youth of today declining: "The true critic does not extend a sceptre over the poet; he raises a torch to illumine the poem," and he should then have the modesty to know when to withdraw gracefully.

[8] To the titles by Barthes, De Diéguez, Doubrovsky, and Picard listed in the bibliographical notice at the end of this volume, referring to the debates on criticism which shook a few circles in France in 1963–1966, the following may be added: Roland Barthes, "L'activité structuraliste," in *Les Lettres nouvelles* (Julliard, 1964); Barthes, "Criticism as Language," *Times Literary Supplement* (London), September 27, 1963; De Diéguez, "J.-P. Richard et la critique thématique," *Critique*, no. 193 (July 1964), pp. 517–535; De Diéguez, *Essai sur l'Avenir poétique de Dieu* (Plon, 1966); Aline Fialkowski, "Structuralisme et Herméneutique," *Esprit*, July–August 1966, pp. 16–30; Lucien Sebag, "Méthode structurale et idéologies structuralistes," *Critique*, no. 210 (November 1964), pp. 963–978; *Times Literary Supplement* (London), September 30, 1965, and June 23, 1966; Martin Turnell, "The Criticism of Roland Barthes," *Encounter*, XXVI, no.2 (February 1966), 30–36; Center of Cérisy la Salle, *Entretiens sur les Notions de Genèse et Structure* (The Hague: Mouton, 1965). See also Jean Piel, "La Fonction sociale du critique," *Critique*, no. 80 (January 1954), pp. 3–13; Paul de Man, "Impasse de la critique formaliste," *Critique*, no. 109 (June 1956), pp. 483–500; and a long, rambling, but refreshingly humorous attack against the pretentious claims of new critics and novelists, *Pour Sganarelle* (Gallimard, 1965) by the novelist Romain Gary.

PART ONE

HOW IT STRIKES A CONTEMPORARY

CHAPTER I

From the Ancients to the English Moderns

EXAMPLES drawn from antiquity are too remote, too few, and too fragmentary to be truly significant. Our knowledge of Greek criticism is very scant, yet sufficient to make us deplore our lack of information. Some of the moderns, whom the ingenious and monotonous minutiae of Cicero's *De Oratore* or of Quintilian's treatise repelled in their youth, have remained prejudiced against the rhetoric of the ancients and convinced that those declamations and recipes by professors of speech were the sole and dubious achievement of Greco-Roman criticism. Rhetoric reached indeed its supreme development among the Greeks. Joined with sophistry, it constituted perhaps the only grave sin of Greek literature; even those who, like the author of *Gorgias* and of *Protagoras*, condemned it were not immune from it. But the Greeks must also be credited with inventing hermeneutics, or the science of explanation and interpretation of texts. Their most systematic philosopher, Aristotle, practiced the strictest kind of objective and analytical criticism in his *Didascalia*, unfortunately lost. Aristarchus understood, two thousand years before Taine, that a work of art must be explained and judged according to its time and its environment. Above all, we owe to Aristotle and to the pseudo-Longinus perhaps the two finest works of critical and esthetic theory ever written: the *Poetics* and the *Treatise on the Sublime.*

If by literary criticism, however, we understand a judgment on a work of art, past or present, together with the impressions and reasons upon which this judgment rests ("This book is good or bad, to me and in general: here are my reasons and my point of views"), there was little systematic criticism among the ancients. The old Attic comedy delighted in informal criticism of that

29

kind, as the *Frogs* and the titles of many a lost play may recall to
us. In the first century B.C. lived the most typical literary critic of
antiquity, Dionysius of Halicarnassus: he could discuss sources,
dates, the comparative value of orators and writers, and, above
all, style, with competence, if not with the insight of genius.
After him, Dio Chrysostom in the first century after Christ, the
pseudo-Demetrius, Plutarch, even the incisive Lucian disappoint
the modern who looks among the Greeks for any systematic
appraisal of Plato, Sophocles, Thucydides, or Virgil.

From the darkness which shrouds most of the literary judgments of antiquity, two groups of facts may nevertheless be
brought to light. First, our whole perspective of Greek and Latin
literature must remain fragmentary and probably erroneous or
misleading, for the works which have come down to us are mere
shreds and random vestiges. Many of them are certainly not
those which antiquity admired, and our traditional reverence,
inherited from sixteenth-century humanists, for many fourth-rate
Greek and Latin writers would doubtless have bewildered the
critical opinion of their day. Almost all the Greek tragedians
have been lost; of the larger number of the five hundred comic
writers and the five or six hundred historians of whom the
Greeks boasted, not even the names have survived. Corinna and
Simonides, often praised in their time above Sappho and Pindar,
are mere legendary figures for us. So are many of the Latin poets,
like Gallus and Varius, or even Ennius, who were often lauded
more warmly than Lucretius or Virgil.

Moreover, the Greeks, "that nation of aristocrats, that people
wholly composed of connoisseurs," as Renan called them, often
judged the masterpieces of their own times in a manner worthy
of the Boeotians, altogether wrongly, since to be right in those
matters means forestalling the decree of posterity. Aeschylus
seems to have been crowned with the victor's laurel for five out
of the seven tragedies of his which have survived (we have no
information on *The Suppliants* and *Prometheus*). But the most
perfect tragedy of Sophocles, and perhaps the most perfect ever
written, *Oedipus Rex,* was ranked after a play by Philocles. On

Euripides' *Hecuba* and *The Phoenician Women* the Greeks seem to us to have lavished excessive admiration; but the moving *Alcestis* by the same dramatist did not win the prize (Sophocles was then the victor, and the judges may have had good reasons for their decision). And we can only grudgingly admit that two poets who are mere names for us, Xenocles and Euphorion, should have had their plays preferred to the beautiful *Medea*. Aristophanes won the first prize for his *Acharnians*, his *Knights*, his *Wasps*, and even for his *Frogs*, which moderns are inclined to overestimate, but not for the more admirable *Clouds* (Cratinos and Ameipsias were preferred to him that year), not for *Peace* (Eupolis carried off the prize), nor for the original and poetical *Birds*.

We may disregard Zoilus and his like, who flourished at all periods of ancient literature, as well as the countless grammarians and scholiasts who dissected masterpieces with an ingenious patience equalled only by their ingenuous naïvety. But it is difficult not to marvel at the excessive praise lavished by the ancients on orators like Isocrates and Hyperides, and not to regret that Menander did not remain for us a mere name, for his much-vaunted spareness and bareness seem to us akin to poverty. We cannot help feeling disconcerted by many literary pronouncements of the credulous Plutarch and even by the decrees of the shrewd rhetor Dionysius of Halicarnassus. We are even more grievously disappointed when discovering that neither Aristophanes nor perhaps Aristotle really appreciated Euripides, to us "the most tragic" (that superlative can hardly have been a word of praise under Aristotle's pen) and the most human of the Greek dramatists; that the sublimity of Aeschylus was defined by Sophocles (according to Plutarch's treatise on *Progress in Virtue*) as "ostentatious pomp"; and that Horace characterized the author of the *Oresteia* as "speaking in lofty tone and strutting in the buskin."

Did Horace, at least, understand Virgil and the stately grandeur of the *Aeneid*? It would be adventurous to assert it, from the odes which he devoted to "the half of his soul" and which hardly echo the mysterious and suggestive quality of the great Roman bard. We may also doubt whether the author of the *Odes* and *Epodes* ever yielded to the spell of those elegiac poets, more original and more tenderly exquisite than himself, if less popular with schoolmasters and retired magistrates: Lucretius, Catullus, Propertius. Modern scholars have, in particular, been more than once puzzled by the disquieting and almost unanimous silence in which his contemporaries seem to have shrouded Lucretius' splendid philosophical poem. Except for a celebrated invocation in the *Georgics* and for a hyperbolic couplet in Ovid's *Amores*, Roman writers were apparently little struck by the originality of their only philosophical poet. Cicero, whom an unreliable statement by St. Jerome presented as the editor of the *De Rerum Natura* and who should have read the poem of his contemporary, were it but to refute it as he did the writings of the Epicureans, hardly seems to have glanced at it.[1] He mentions the work only once in an obscure and controversial sentence in a letter to his brother and certainly remained unmoved, if touched at all, by an achievement unparalleled in ancient literature.

It is scarcely easier to determine precisely how their contemporaries received the writers of the seventeenth and eighteenth centuries whom we regard today as the greatest. Systematic appreciation of new productions only began, in a timid and tentative way, in 1665, with the foundation of the *Journal des Savants*. For many decades criticism remained primitive and naïve in its methods, little skilled in stating its motives and reasons or in analyzing and justifying its impressions. If we have improved considerably on those humble beginnings, we have also acquired a vain sophistication and become tainted with an unenviable mercantile spirit. More valuable than the pronouncements of the amateurish critics of two and three centuries ago would be the history of the reception of literary masterpieces and of their shifting fortunes with public taste. Unfortunately, the study of

[1] See an article on the subject by William A. Merrill, *University of California Publications in Classical Philology*, September 8, 1909.

the sources and genesis of literary works has engrossed the attention and efforts of most historians. The story of the gradual or capricious diffusion of those works among the reading public, while of secondary interest, would be worth writing and would be a welcome contribution to a history of taste which must some day be undertaken. The scarcity of materials, the extreme prudence with which every fragment of information should be weighed, and the inadequacy of a purely quantitative method (twenty enthusiastic and proselytizing readers of Rousseau, Marx, and Nietzsche count more heavily than a million passive buyers of the latest bestseller) have thus far discouraged scholars from writing the history of the reputation of Bacon, Donne, Pope, Dickens through the succeeding generations.

What fame Shakespeare and the other Elizabethan dramatists enjoyed among their contemporaries and during the following century or two is very imperfectly known. At what precise moment, thanks to whom, and for what reasons did the glory of Shakespeare, of Donne, of Milton outstrip that of other poets long acclaimed by the public and suddenly thrown into obscurity or oblivion? We are not in a position to answer such a question very definitely. The written evidence which has survived and which has been compiled in learned "Allusion-books" is often attributable to paltry grammarians, envious pedagogues, or personal enemies of a writer. Other witnesses, including perhaps the neutral or the impartial ones, have been forgotten or buried by time. Goethe has uttered a warning which all historians of literature and all students of the past should bear in mind: "Literature is a fragment of fragments; of all that was done and was said, only the smallest part was ever written; of what was written, only the smallest portion has survived." [2]

The history of Shakespearean criticism has not yet been written with the accuracy and amplitude that the subject deserves.[3] It

[2] Goethe's works, German ed. (Stuttgart and Berlin), XXXVIII, 270. A similar aphorism is to be found *ibid.*, p. 260.

[3] Our remark holds true in spite of Mr. Augustus Ralli's painstaking if not altogether satisfying attempt and Mr. Agappar Pillai's survey of the first

is well known, however, that the praise bestowed on the greatest of all dramatists by his contemporaries sounds inadequate and often hollow to our ears. Gentle and honey-tongued were the favorite epithets applied to the author of *Macbeth;* fancy and grace were mentioned as his chief qualities. Even the affectionate homage prefixed by Ben Jonson to the First Folio of 1623 seems disappointing to us. Others, even tragic Webster and, as early as 1598, Francis Mere, were struck above all, as not a few modern readers are today, by the prodigious verbal gift of the poet and his inexhaustible invention of images.

But on the whole in the hundred and fifty years which followed Shakespeare's death England was more than chary of praise and more than slow in her recognition of genius (even in the guarded and moderate appreciations of Shakespeare's excellence written by Dryden and, in 1711, by John Dennis). Several ingenious and impartial critical minds (Ben Jonson in his *Discoveries,* Sir John Denham, Cartwright, Rymer) preferred one of his contemporaries (Fletcher, or Ben Jonson himself) to Shakespeare. Milton hardly admired Shakespeare as a tragic writer and ranked him below the Greeks. Dryden thought fit to rewrite *Antony and Cleopatra* and *Troilus and Cressida.* Davenant rewrote *Macbeth* and, together with Dryden, *The Tempest.* Nahum Tate cut up and "arranged" *King Lear.* Samuel Pepys saw nothing but insipid foolishness in *Twelfth Night* and called *A Midsummer Night's Dream* "the most insipid ridiculous play that I ever saw in my life." *Romeo and Juliet* again is condemned by him as "a play of itself the worst I ever heard in my life." He preferred some cheap contemporary comedy to *Othello* and declared *The Silent Woman* (by Ben Jonson) "the best comedy, I think, that was ever wrote." In the middle of the eighteenth century, Blair, David Hume, and Chesterfield were very severe on Shakespeare's extravagances and unclassical license. Even

one hundred and seventy years. Shakespearean criticism in the eighteenth century has received a good deal of attention from Professor David Nichol Smith, Herbert S. Robinson, and Robert W. Babcock. A combination of scholarly research and breadth of view would be desirable.

Johnson pitilessly, though in beautiful sentences, scores Shakespeare's faults. Only in the late eighteenth century, with Farmer, Mrs. Montagu, Garrick, did Shakespearean "idolatry" begin, soon to be followed by the enthusiastic and illuminating criticism of the English, German, and even French romantics.

No modern should feel foolishly superior and condescending toward Shakespeare's contemporaries, who did not discover in *Antony and Cleopatra*, in *Richard II*, in *Measure for Measure* the subtle beauty that Coleridge, Hazlitt, and Walter Pater have admired and taught us to admire in those plays. To any dutiful worshipper of Shakespeare inclined to remain this side of idolatry, the obvious question will nevertheless occur: were Shakespeare's contemporaries and successors completely devoid of critical sense and of discriminating taste when they ranked Shakespeare with other dramatists of his age or only slightly above them? or have we not, since the romantics, unduly altered the perspective and grossly exaggerated the difference which divides Shakespeare from Ford or Middleton, Fletcher, Massinger, or Webster? To what extent are we perfectly sincere and open-minded in our estimate of past writers?

The literary customs of our ancestors, often sharply at variance with ours, must be borne in mind whenever we study "the chronicle of wasted time" and the literary reputations of two or three hundred years ago. Much of the excessive praise in verse or in stilted prose which lauded a writer loved or feared by his friends (such praise as has been diligently collected in the *Johnson Allusion-book*, for instance, or quoted in Walton's delightful *Lives*) should hardly be taken more seriously than the wreaths of sonnets or the "tombeaux" of elegies which mourned Ronsard, Théophile Gautier, and Mallarmé; not even more seriously than the elaborate ceremonies of official apotheosis which more recently accompanied the centenaries of Goethe, Victor Hugo, and Pushkin. The surprising glory enjoyed for a time by Abraham Cowley or Edmund Waller can easily be accounted for by a perilously prompt and unanimous agreement between them and the average reader of their times. To some competent or fashionable critics of the 1930's, the fame of Pope in the eighteenth century may even appear to have been justified. Such recurrences in the varied history of taste, sometimes degenerating into similar epidemics of bad taste, are frequent and normal happenings. They betray the secret undercurrent of spiritual affinity which often links generations decades or centuries apart. A series of curves, running roughly parallel with wide deviations, which would follow through periods of twenty or thirty years each the shifting fortunes of Chaucer, Spenser, Milton, Dryden, Pope, Scott, Wordsworth, Tennyson, Dickens, should be drawn some day by a conscientious scholar; it would be a useful contribution to that history of literary taste which our contemporaries, enamored of social values and aware of the potent social action of literature, should undertake to write.[4]

Among those imaginary curves, that symbolizing the varied fortunes of John Donne would be one of the most revealing. Our contemporaries often believe that they alone have discovered and truly enjoyed that strange poet, whose acute intellectuality, condensed and enigmatic thoughts, startling images, and broken rhythm seem, indeed, to have been purposely calculated to attract the devotees of Gerard Manley Hopkins, Mallarmé, and T. S. Eliot. But a few other men had already understood and loved Donne: Browning, for instance, and in the America of the middle of the last century, Emerson, Thoreau, Melville, and Lowell. As many allusions, and in particular Carew's "Elegy" upon the death of Donne, bear witness, the youth of 1620–1650 hailed the poet and Dean of Saint Paul's as the leader of a reaction against Elizabethan lyricism. Even if Donne was not an unrecognized genius, it is doubtful whether his contemporaries appreciated him for the same reasons that we do today. Donne's subsequent eclipse through the eighteenth century and most of the romantic period (Coleridge and a few acute and omnivorous

---

[4] The early history of Chaucer's fortune should be excepted, since a proper appreciation of the fourteenth-century poet depended upon the establishment of a correct text, one which did not betray the spelling, pronunciation, and versification of the original.

readers excepted) remains one of the most strangely disconcerting phases in the posthumous history of great writers.

The seventeenth century in English literature is to most of us the age of Milton. Yet the poems of Milton which today seem to us the most evidently beautiful, the lines which are engraved in our memories and in our hearts, made so little impression upon his contemporaries that they never mentioned them and probably hardly read them. "L'Allegro" and "Il Penseroso" did not receive the humble honor of one allusion in any text printed in Milton's lifetime. The *Sonnets* found admirers (chiefly Wordsworth, who owes them much, and Hazlitt) only in the early nineteenth century. Not a single contemporary apparently praised or even mentioned *Lycidas.* A century later, Samuel Johnson, who barely alludes, and then in lukewarm or even icy tones, to "L'Allegro" and "Il Penseroso," is more than severe with *Lycidas* and harshly, though perhaps justly, denounces the lack of dramatic force in *Comus.* The few contemporaries who meted out any praise to Milton ranked him below Cowley (the Duke of Buckingham in 1682) and on the same plane as Waller (*The Athenian Mercury* in 1691). Only a handful of clear-sighted readers showed more warmth in their applause: Dryden, Prior, Addison, John Dennis.

Even so, *Samson Agonistes*, that Promethean epic drama, and *Paradise Regained* remained buried in silence: in the opinion of all but a few connoisseurs, the latter has ever since been unjustly sacrificed to its more glorious predecessor. Of *Paradise Lost* itself, only thirteen hundred copies had been sold eighteen months after its publication, and four thousand in all in the first thirteen years (1667–1680).[5] The great Christian epic was so little appreciated that, twenty-five years after Milton's death, a certain John Hopkins thought he added flavor to the poem by giving a rhymed version of it; Dryden himself, about the time of Milton's death, had turned it into a poor drama, *The State of Innocence and Fall of Man.* Of *Paradise Lost*, Waller, the most highly ac-

[5] We have no accurate means of ascertaining how large was then the English reading public, in a country of probably seven million inhabitants.

claimed poet of the age, declared: "If its length be not considered
a merit, it hath no other." Much later, Samuel Johnson did not
hesitate, after some words of praise, to characterize the greatest
epic in the English language as "one of the books which the
reader admires and lays down and forgets to take up again. . . .
The want of human interest is always felt. . . . None ever
wished it longer than it is. Its perusal is a duty rather than a
pleasure." A sophomore of the present day might share the opinion of the famous lexicographer, but would not dare express it in
the face of a century and a half of critical and professorial
tributes to Milton's greatness.[6]

Let it be readily granted that Milton's fiery personality, his
violent religious and political polemics, his defence of divorce
and almost of polygamy, his justification of regicide may explain
the hostility of some contemporaries, unable to separate the poet
in him from the man. But the reverse should have been equally
true: Milton's partisans should have proved all the more eager to
recognize and to celebrate his greatness. More disturbing than
some partisan hostility is the almost unanimous silence of
seventeenth-century readers and critics about Milton's shorter
poems and the complete absence—so far as we know—of any
commentary on or allusion to *Paradise Lost* (except for Edward
Phillips, Marvell, and Barrow) for seven years (1667–1674) after
the appearance of that masterpiece.

The same disquieting conclusion might be drawn from a careful study of the reception given the great poets of the following
generations, and probably those of our own times. I shall omit
from this survey William Blake, whose most admirable works
were in his lifetime accessible, if at all, to only a very limited
public. I shall likewise omit poets who happened to be, from the
very first, in harmony with their public and who seem to more

---

[6] The history of Milton's contemporary fame has been thoroughly studied
and told by Raymond D. Havens in two articles published in 1909 in *Eng-
lische Studien*, and again by William Riley Parker in *Milton's Contemporary Reputation* (Columbus: Ohio State University Press, 1940). I have utilized some of the precise data provided by these two scholars. For Johnson's
criticism, see the *Lives of the English Poets*.

dispassionate readers to have been ranked unduly high (Campbell, Rogers, Thomas Moore) or to have been celebrated for extraliterary reasons (Walter Scott, Byron). Burns himself should be placed among the latter, for the story of his humble condition and the flavor of the Scottish dialect greatly helped his success. He was generally acclaimed by critics, from 1786 on, as a new and robust genius (a volume by John D. Ross published in Glasgow in 1900 has collected the early critical reviews of Burns), and the prevailing tone of official magazines, including the *Edinburgh Review,* in which Carlyle's famous article appeared in December 1829, was one of affectionate admiration for the naïve and untamed poet, of pity and leniency for the moral weaknesses of a man who was not born a gentleman.

If there be one poet who expressed the England of his times while embodying the immortal soul of England, a poet fit to be cherished alike by the British family religiously gathered around the tea table, by the spinster ecstatic over fields of daffodils and daisies, by the country gentleman listening to the cuckoo or watching the celandines, by the officer nostalgic for the lakes and the meadows of his native island while serving in India or in the African wilds, a poet whom the traditional critics of the grave and solid reviews should have acclaimed—even more than Tennyson, that poet is Wordsworth. Moreover, he led an exemplary life (at least for his contemporaries, to whom the youthful liaison with Annette Vallon, carefully excluded from Wordsworth's autobiographical poems, remained unknown); his style is not marred by artifice or pretentious obscurity; he did not resort to strange technical devices, to far-fetched metaphors, or to prosodic innovations. He never sided with the enemies of England or with revolutionary prophets. His verse is both austere and chaste, offering the moral "message" dear to the descendants of the Puritans—a message which the Britain of Pitt, of Wellington, and of Castlereagh had every reason to find conforting and "uplifting."

Yet for nearly twenty years British criticism displayed little but cold reserve or bitter contempt for Wordsworth's poetry. Only a very few contemporaries (Crabb Robinson, Coleridge, Southey, Lamb, Hazlitt, Shelley) assigned the poet to his rightful place in English literature, and chiefly in private conversations or in letters which remained unpublished or passed unnoticed. In the great majority of carefully considered and influential judgments which appeared in print on the *Lyrical Ballads* (1798 and 1800), the *Poems* (1807), and *The Excursion* (1814), one finds a marked lack of understanding or a stubborn refusal to understand. "Childish," "infantile," "silly," "affected," "drivelling," "difficult of comprehension," "unintelligible," "bombastic," "obscure," "absurd," "nauseating": such are the choice epithets with which contemporary critics characterized Wordsworth's poetry.

Carefully collected in a large volume are the book reviews and articles which commented, upon their publication, on Wordsworth's successive volumes of verse.[7] Its reading affords ample evidence that, while the esteem and admiration of such men as Crabb Robinson, Southey, Shelley, or Keats hardly reached the public, professional criticism was overwhelmingly hostile and, which is much more disturbing, congenitally and hopelessly obtuse.

As early as October 1793, the *Monthly Review* begged the youthful author of *Descriptive Sketches*, found guilty of obscurity, to examine his thoughts till he himself understood them before throwing them hastily into rhyme. The same magazine, in June 1799, saw a return to barbarousness in the *Lyrical Ballads*, dismissed "We are seven" as "innocent and pretty infantine prattle," and criticized "Tintern Abbey" as "tinctured with gloomy, narrow, and unsociable ideas of seclusion from the commerce of the world, as if men were born to live in woods and wilds, unconnected with each other!" Not one word on the dazzling originality of Wordsworth's blank verse, on the precise and bold psy-

---

[7] Elsie Smith, *An Estimate of Wordsworth by His Contemporaries, 1793–1822* (Oxford: Blackwell, 1932). I have also made use of two earlier collections of critical articles by John Louis Haney, *Early Reviews of English Poets* (Philadelphia: The Egerton Press, 1904), and by E. Stevenson, *Early Reviews of Great Writers, 1786–1832* (London: W. Scott, 1890).

chological description of a mystical ecstasy in the presence of nature, on the gravity of the philosophical message. The sale of the first edition of the *Lyrical Ballads,* which marks for us today the beginning of the splendid lyrical flowering of English Romanticism, was consequently slow and discouraged author and publisher.

In 1807, Wordsworth published his *Poems* in two volumes, which contained some of his most regular and revered masterpieces, "The Daffodils," the odes to the cuckoo and the skylark, the "Ode to Duty," and the celebrated "Ode on Intimations of Immortality." Here is a sample of the gracious compliments paid the volume by contemporary critics:

A silly book is a serious evil, but it becomes absolutely insupportable when written by a man of sense. . . . We have, at different times, employed ridicule with a view of making this gentleman ashamed of himself, and bringing him back to his senses. But, unfortunately, he is only one of a tribe who keep each other in countenance by mutual applause and flattery, who having dubbed themselves by the names of poets, imagine they have a right to direct the taste of the nation, and thus, infinitely to their own satisfaction, abuse the good sense and weary out the patience of mankind with their fantastical mummeries. [*Critical Review,* August 1807.]

Mr. Wordsworth, continues the critic, had, to be sure, given some promise a few years ago. He has not fulfilled it. (How often we shall find the same original sentence under the pen of critics!) "Alas! we fear that the mind of Mr. Wordsworth has been too long accustomed to the enervating debauchery of taste for us to entertain much hope of his recovery." There he is, in his riper years, drivelling to the redbreast and to a common pilewort, "pouring out his nauseous and nauseating sensibilities to weeds and insects."

In October of the same year, 1807, in the *Edinburgh Review,* Jeffrey displayed an even more perfect incapacity to understand or to feel Wordsworth's poetry. "Childishness, conceit and affectation . . . disgusting absurdities" were his first exclamations. The "Ode to the Daisy" is "very flat, feeble and affected." The

"Ode to Duty," "in which the lofty vein is very unsuccessfully attempted," was even less to Jeffrey's taste, and he found the last two lines "utterly without meaning." In the "Ode to the Cuckoo," "in which the author, striving after force and originality, produces nothing but absurdity," the Scottish reviewer was utterly baffled by the meaningless mysticism of an English bard who saw in a mere cuckoo

> No bird, but an invisible thing,
> A voice, a mystery.

Other poems were even worse, such as "Foresight," characterized as "the quintessence of unmeaningness." The critic's indignation rose to the boiling point when he reached the "Ode on Intimations of Immortality": "This is, beyond all doubt, the most illegible and unintelligible part of the publication. We can pretend to give no analysis or explanation of it."

The same adjectives, "incomprehensible," "difficult," recur in the *Annual Review and History of Literature* of 1807 and the *Eclectic Review* for January 1808. "A more rash and injudicious speculation on the weakness or the depravity of the public taste," concluded the latter, "has seldom been made, and we trust that its inevitable failure will bring back Mr. Wordsworth to a sense of his own dignity as well as of the respect due to his readers." The ode on immortality was again singled out for special blame: "The reader is turned loose into a wilderness of sublimity, tenderness, bombast and absurdity, to find out the object as well as he can."

When in 1814 Wordsworth published *The Excursion*, which his friends had eagerly awaited, the general impression was one of disappointment and dismay. Lamb and Hazlitt (the latter in three articles in the *Examiner*) had some warm praise for the long poem. But the far more influential Jeffrey opened his comments in the *Edinburgh Review* for November 1814 with the famous verdict: "This will never do." The legal dismissal was also a medical diagnosis: "The case of Mr. Wordsworth, we perceive, is now manifestly hopeless; and we give him up as altogether incur-

able and beyond the power of criticism." And the grave Whig
nodded his head in lament over Wordsworth's perverse obstinacy
in preferring the company of dalesmen and cottagers, when he
might have associated with serious men of letters, who would
have helped him improve and refine himself. As to the new poem,
it was branded as

a tissue of moral and devotional ravings, in which innumerable
changes are rung upon a few very simple and familiar ideas . . . with
such a hubbub of strained raptures and fantastical sublimities, that it is
often difficult for the most skilful and attentive student to obtain a
glimpse of the author's meaning, and altogether impossible for an ordinary reader to conjecture what he is about.[8]

Such were typical comments on Wordsworth's poems by the
most influential critics of the times. The fame of the poet, to be
sure, depended only in part upon reviews: it spread among an
elite between 1815 and 1820. Even making allowance for the
often tart and sanctimonious tone of esthetic revelation in
Wordsworth's prefaces, which may have annoyed some critics,
we must bear in mind that the *Prelude*, probably the finest long
poem of the century, though completed as early as 1805, was not

[8] The *Monthly Review* for February 1815 and the *British Critic* for May
1815 also castigated *The Excursion,* while the *Eclectic Review* praised it
with insight and discernment in January 1815. Coleridge was disappointed
by the poem, but in a chapter of his *Biographia Literaria* protested against
Jeffrey's brutal attack. Keats praised the poem in a private letter to Haydon
on January 10, 1818. Attempts have been recently made to justify Jeffrey's
severe strictures on Wordsworth, or to weigh against them more favorable
utterances in which Jeffrey is supposed to have indulged in private conversation, See Robert Daniel, "Jeffrey and Wordsworth," *Sewanee Review*
(April 1942), 195–202. It may be that Jeffrey's damning criticism overstated
his sincere opinion, because a hostile and ironical review makes more entertaining reading than a mild and fair balancing of merits and faults. It may
be also that Jeffrey proved more appreciative of Wordsworth in oral and
private criticism. But a critic must be judged, not by his mental reservations,
but by what he prints for the contemporary public which takes him at his
word. More examples of Jeffrey's inability to understand whatever greatness
lay in new writers, and of the exalted prestige which he enjoyed in his lifetime, are found in an excellent essay by Lewis E. Gates in *Three Studies in
Literature* (New York: Macmillan, 1899).

published until after Wordsworth's death in 1850. The disturbing fact is that the charges most commonly brought against the clearest and sanest of English Romantic poets were those of difficulty, obscurity, absurdity, mannerism.

Coleridge, who had not ventured with Wordsworth into prosaic excesses nor (at the time of his poetical inspiration) indulged in ambitious theorizing on poetic diction, was somewhat less roughly handled by critics. Yet in October 1798 *The Ancient Mariner*, the poem of his which, above all others, seems invested with inevitable magic and obvious charm, was characterized in the *Critical Review* by Coleridge's own brother-in-law Southey as "a Dutch attempt at German sublimity. . . . We do not sufficiently understand the story to analyze it." Wordsworth was not more enthusiastic, for, in the second edition of their joint venture, the *Lyrical Ballads*, he elaborately listed four main defects in the poem of his friend. The critic of the *Monthly Review* in June 1799 was likewise baffled by that masterpiece, which today a child of twelve has no difficulty in grasping at the first reading.

The Rime of the Ancient Mariner . . . is the strangest story of a cock and bull that we ever saw on paper; yet, though it seems a rhapsody of unintelligible wildness and incoherence (of which we do not perceive the drift, unless the joke lies in depriving the wedding-guest of his share of the feast), there are in it poetical touches of an exquisite kind.

The same note was struck in the *British Critic* (October 1799), which criticized the confusion of images "which lose all effect from not being quite intelligible." *Christabel*, which appeared in 1816 with the enchanted fragment, "Kubla Khan," was no better received; it horrified the critic of the *Monthly Review* (January 1817) by its monstrous effort "to teach the human ear a new and discordant system of harmony." To the *Edinburgh Review*, the new volume of verse appeared as "utterly destitute of value" and "a most notable piece of impertinence," since it could obviously not aim at being understood by the public. Finally, the following year, the prose volume which Arthur Symons has called, perhaps with some exaggeration, "the greatest book of criticism in English," *Biographia Literaria*, was contemptuously ignored by the

Quarterly and bitterly attacked by Hazlitt in the *Edinburgh* and in *Blackwood's* by Wilson, who heaped upon it such gracious adjectives as "execrable," "rambling," "ignorant," "indolent," "obscure," "conceited," "arrogant."

The case of Wordsworth and Coleridge did not remain exceptional. Great Britain in the early years of the last century regularly begrudged her recognition of the great writers who, in our opinion, did the country as much credit as her statesmen and her generals. She extolled a Southey, a Thomas Moore to the skies; she lauded Kirke White, Hogg, Felicia Hemans, and of course Byron, but Jane Austen, Landor, John Clare, Beddoes passed almost unnoticed while Shelley and Keats were scorned and ridiculed. We smile complacently today at so much incredible and voluntary blindness in critics and readers of the past. It is easier to smile with condescension at our predecessors than to prove clear-sighted toward our own contemporaries.

Reasons, good or bad, were not lacking to antagonize the traditional opinion of a prudish England and turn it angrily against Shelley the man, and hence, though unjustly, against Shelley the poet. His early revolutionary and atheistic writings, his youthful declamations on free love, on D'Holbach's materialism, and on Godwin's political system, appeared as so many challenges to the self-righteous public of 1812–1822, and were taken up as such. Even those who, like Peacock and Keats, were in a position to appreciate the real Shelley and should have known better failed to view him with sympathy. Lamb and Wordsworth were even less discerning, and Hazlitt, in a chapter of his *Table Talk,* did himself little honor by drawing a harsh picture of the poet as a "philosophical fanatic," a seeker after notoriety, and a dizzy Ixion reaching for unsubstantial clouds.

A perusal of the contemporary critics of Shelley is most disheartening.[9] We feel no undue surprise at the vitriolic sentence

[9] Mr. Newman I. White has very ably and very conveniently collected the contemporary criticism of Shelley in a volume entitled *The Unextinguished Hearth* (Durham: Duke University Press, 1938). Many of my quotations have been borrowed from his carefully reprinted extracts.

passed upon the *Revolt of Islam* by a former schoolmate of Shelley's at Eton (*Quarterly Review*, April 1819), although the outrageous tone was hardly in keeping with the lofty moral and religious motives which were supposed to have prompted the scurrilous article. It is not difficult to understand that the *Cenci* was received, along with a few halting words of admiration, with frightened and doubtless sincere qualms. Some invectives, nevertheless, leapt beyond all the bounds of decency: the article in the *Literary Gazette* of April 1, 1820, which opened thus:

Of all the abominations which intellectual perversion, and political atheism have produced in our times, this tragedy appears to us to be the most abominable. . . . It seemed to be the production of a fiend, and calculated for the entertainment of devils in hell. . . . This is the dish of carrion, seasoned with sulphur as spice.

The modern devotee of the most ethereal and disembodied poem of Shelley, *Epipsychidion*, grateful to the few contemporary periodicals which took notice of that strange rhapsody (four in all, and one, very favorable, an English magazine published in Paris),[10] readily forgives the reviewers who dwelt ponderously on the "immorality" and the obscurity of the poem. "I take it to be an endeavour to set aside the divine prohibition, that a man may not marry his own sister," perfidiously hinted Christopher North in *Blackwood's* in February 1822.

Let us not dwell too long on the scornful silence which enshrouded *Alastor* in 1816. "Madness," "profound stupidity," "morbid jargon" were among the choice delicacies then offered by the critics to describe a new poetical masterpiece. Let us not even argue too easily from *Prometheus Unbound*. A few reviewers felt compelled to pronounce the word "genius," qualifying it with the adjectives "irregular," "immoral," or "misguided." They felt or scented its strange beauty. Others, and by far the majority among them, confessed to being utterly at a loss to understand its meaning. The *Literary Gazette* of September 9,

---

[10] The *Paris Monthly Review*, March 1822. See H. Peyre, *Shelley et la France* (Le Caire, Université, 1935), pp. 114–115.

1820, could commend it only to readers of rebuses, charades, and riddles.

To our apprehension, *Prometheus* is little else but absolute raving; and were we not assured to the contrary, we should take it for granted that the author was lunatic—as his principles are ludicrously wicked, and his poetry a melange of nonsense, cockneyism, poverty and pedantry, . . . the stupid trash of a delirious dreamer, . . . maniacal raving.

And the sublime cosmic hymns of the fourth act of *Prometheus*, probably unexcelled in the range of English lyricism, having been duly read by the critic, who quotes from them at length, are summarily dismissed: "Did ever the walls of Bedlam display more insane stuff than this?"

Other critics likewise balked at the very real difficulty of *Prometheus*. "The mind, fatigued and perplexed, is mortified by the consciousness that its labor has not been rewarded by the acquisition of a single distinct conception," remarked the *Quarterly* of October 1821. How often will the same mercantile balance sheet of profits and losses be drawn by the judge of sovereign masterpieces! Let it be granted that Shelley's lyrical flights are ineffectual indeed, and hardly repay the critic seated behind his counter and eager for substantial profit. At least, a few contemporary readers read as far as the last act of *Prometheus Unbound* and realized that the work was important enough to be ridiculed.

With the *Prometheus* volume of 1820, however, Shelley's publisher, Ollier, had included several shorter poems: none other than the "Ode to the West Wind," "The Cloud," "The Skylark," and "The Sensitive Plant." Few lyrical masterpieces lay claim to a higher and richer harmony, a more classical perfection. Few are more easily understood today by any reader in his teens. Yet these poems were received with an icy silence. Such a brutal reception is not merely revolting to our sense of justice, but constitutes one of the most inexplicable blunders of British criticism. Only one contemporary critic mentioned the "Ode to the West Wind": in *Blackwood's*, September 1820, he praised the ode as "abounding in richest melody of versification and great tenderness of feeling." The same reviewer admired the ode "To a Skylark." In Shelley's lifetime, only one other reviewer (*Dublin Magazine*, November 1820) took any notice of "To a Skylark" and that in the course of a rather unfavorable article. "The Cloud" was mentioned twice before Shelley died: first, by the same *Dublin Magazine* which quoted the title of the poem in a perfectly noncommittal way and with the solemn warning that "Mr. Shelley appears in his poetry like a man speaking a foreign language, . . . writing under the inspiration of ambition rather than of genius or feeling." Again in the *Quarterly* of October 1821 "The Cloud," if anything too easy and too clear for us today, was quoted as a model of "galimatias" worse than simple nonsense.

The "Ode to Liberty" was praised warmly in one review in the year 1820, and severely taken to task by three others as dangerous and subversive political poetry. It is natural for conservative reviewers to have been prejudiced against that poem. It is, however, more disturbing to observe that "The Sensitive Plant," that marvel of delicate and tender description of nature, followed by the most restrained and touching statement of philosophical idealism in the conclusion, passed unnoticed by all but two contemporary reviewers. *Blackwood's* condescended to devote three lines to "the most affecting" poem in the volume, "which is the history of a beautiful garden." The critic of the *Quarterly* (October 1821) merely dismissed it as devoid of meaning: he could not appreciate lines, today famous, on the hyacinth whose music "was felt like an odor within the sense," and branded them as "quaint and affected . . . the tricks of a mere poetical harlequin." On the whole of the admirable volume of 1820, the same critic summarized his verdict thus: "In short, it is not too much to affirm that in the whole volume there is not one original image of nature, one simple expression of human feeling, or one new association of the appearances of the moral with those of the material world."

Adonais, probably the most perfect poem of its type and

length in the English language, first appeared in Pisa in 1821, then in London and Paris in 1829. *Blackwood's* reviewed it in 1821. In what tone, the following quotation will show:

Locke says that the most resolute liar cannot lie more than once in every three sentences. Folly is more engrossing; for we could prove, from the present Elegy, that it is possible to write two sentences of pure nonsense out of every three. A more faithful calculation would bring us to ninety-nine out of every hundred, . . . leaving about five readable lines in the entire poem [of 495 lines].

Examples were given to prove that Shelley had merely conglomerated epithets pirated from a lexicon and flung them like pebbles from a sack. The *Literary Gazette* of December 8, 1821, likewise denounced the "incurable absurdity" of those "unconnected, interjectional and nonsensical stanzas," and even "atrocities to be found in this poem quite enough to make us caution our readers against its pages." The critic took pains to classify six kinds of nonsense to be found in the poem (pastoral, physical, vermicular, pathetic, nondescript, and personal). And, declaring that *Adonais* is "as miserable in point of authorship as in point of principle," he concludes:

The poetry of the work is *contemptible;* a mere collection of bloated words heaped on each other without order, harmony, or meaning; the refuse of a schoolboy's commonplace book. . . . It is so far a fortunate thing that this piece of impious and utter absurdity can have little circulation in Britain.

Two years after the tragic death of Shelley in the gulf of Spezia, his *Posthumous Poems*, edited by his wife, appeared in England. They received no more recognition than the earlier volumes, although they contained such incomparable jewels as "Mont Blanc," "Stanzas Written in Dejection near Naples," "The Indian Serenade," "On the Medusa of Leonardo da Vinci," "Hymn of Apollo," "Hymn of Pan," "The Question," "Autumn," "Rarely, Rarely, Comest Thou," "Evening: Ponte al Mare, Pisa," "To Jane, The Invitation," and that masterpiece of tender melancholy, "The Zucca." How much the British public and

English poetry lost by that unanimous lack of discernment on the part of the poet's contemporaries should some day be assessed in a careful study of Shelley's fame and after-fame parallel to S. C. Chew's valuable work on Byron's fortune in England.

The modern student of poetry is well aware that Keats was hardly better understood by his contemporaries than Shelley; yet nothing in Keats's private life, in his philosophical or political opinions, could give offence to the most suspicious critic. We are forced to explain the hostility of reviewers by sheer blindness or crass stupidity, by fear of originality, and not even by envy of a superior genius, which would postulate some recognition of genius.

American scholars who have carefully collected the reviews of Keats's poems published until his death have shown conclusively that, out of eighty mentions of Keats between 1817 and 1821, a large majority were not as hostile as we often imagine.[11] The truly harsh articles number only fifteen or so; but they were the most influential ones, for they appeared in the leading periodicals and were especially scathing in tone.

Endymion baffled and repelled many readers in 1818 through its luxuriance and monotonous splendor. Wordsworth could not discern the influence of his own poetry on the "Hymn to Pan," which he coldly pronounced "a pretty piece of paganism." Shelley hailed the "highest and finest gleams of poetry," but wished that the author had printed only fragments of the whole, lest few readers should follow him to the end. The *Quarterly* was notoriously blind and unjust. *Blackwood's*, the *British Critic*, and other reviews attacked the poem. Perhaps, as Andrew Lang confessed to Sidney Colvin, many a modern admirer of Keats would have been similarly severe or uncomprehending in 1817, with no "Hyperion" or "Eve of St. Agnes" or "Odes" yet written and

[11] George L. Marsh and Newman I. White, in *Modern Philology*, XXXII (August 1934), 37–53. See also an early article by Keats's devoted friend, Severn, in the *Atlantic Monthly* for April 1863, Sidney Colvin's work on Keats, and Edmund Blunden's slender volume, *Shelley and Keats as They Struck Their Contemporaries* (London: Beaumont, 1925).

only the *Endymion* volume before us. A few critics, however, especially one in the *Champion* of June 7, 1818, perceived at once the originality of the long mythological poem and ranked the "Hymn to Pan" with the *Sonnets* of Shakespeare.

Two years later, there occurred a more puzzling case of contemporary failure to recognize greatness. In the spring of 1820, Keats published a new volume of verse, undoubtedly the most priceless in the whole history of English poetry, including as it did "Lamia," "Isabella," the "Eve of St. Agnes," "Hyperion," and four great "Odes." In the stately magnificence of the "Odes" and of "Hyperion," if nowhere else, the hand of genius was unmistakable. The schoolboy wonders today how the readers of 1820, steeped in classical culture, could remain unmoved by the sculptural grandeur of the description of Saturn, the profound humanity of Oceanus' speech, the suggestive invocation of the "Ode to a Nightingale," and the nostalgic sensuousness of the "Ode to Psyche." Yet no less a critic than Charles Lamb praised the tale of "Isabella," but ignored "Hyperion" and the "Odes." Shelley found "Hyperion" a fragment worthy of Aeschylus, but said not one word on the beauty of the "Odes." Byron—never a shrewd critic—was struck by none of the poems; after scurrilous attacks against Keats, he finally turned to exaggerated praise when told by Leigh Hunt that the younger poet had expressed admiration for *Don Juan* (the first two cantos of which had appeared in 1819). Among the contemporary magazines, the most discerning one proved to be the relatively minor *Gold's London Magazine*, which, in December 1820, discovered the sublimity of "Hyperion"; it praised the poet's gift for "hitching the faculty of imagination on a single word" and, for the first time, singled out for quotation "that exquisitely imaginative line:

She stood in tears amid the alien corn."

On July 1, 1820, the *Literary Gazette* offered in quotation the two odes "To a Nightingale" and "To Autumn," without, however, going into raptures over their beauty. Its words of comment, dry and uninviting, ran: "We present by way of novelty

the following specimens from the minor productions." Although
the *Monthly Magazine* of September 1820 thought it honored
Keats highly when it ranked him along with the author of *Rimini*
and that of the *Dramatic Scenes*, the modern reader can scarcely
remember those once celebrated poets, Leigh Hunt and Barry
Cornwall.

Once again, through lack of discernment, the contemporaries
of a great poet and his immediate posterity had been deprived of
a keen esthetic pleasure and the revelation of a new kind of
literary beauty. These poems by Keats, like those of Shelley, had
to wait twenty years to be recognized and to influence English
poetry and sensibility. No separate reprint appeared until 1840.
The general public was steeped in mediocre productions, though
it was fully capable of enjoying "Adonais" and "Hyperion" if it
had been introduced to them by clear-sighted critics. Only a few
brother-poets proved more discerning and more courageous:
Browning, an adolescent composing *Pauline*, read Shelley with
raptures; Tennyson admired Keats; FitzGerald, Rossetti, and
Swinburne soon followed them in the worship of those two
neglected titans of English verse. The fame of the two "inheritors
of unfulfilled renown" was launched and created, not by critics,
but by a small troop of young enthusiasts. In 1829, three Cambridge undergraduates (Tennyson's friend Hallam, Sunderland,
and Monckton Milnes) went as a deputation to the Oxford
Union to uphold, in a debate, the superiority of Oxford's scion
and outcast, Shelley, over the Cantabrigian, Byron. Before the
expedition, Monckton Milnes (later Lord Houghton), applying
for an *exeat* to the Master of Trinity (then Dr. Wordsworth, a
brother of the poet), had to imply, in a pious lie, that Wordsworth, and not Shelley, was the poet whom he was going to
defend at the rival university. Shelley had then been dead seven
years.

We would gladly believe that these blatant mistakes of partisan
or ignorant critics were solely a feature of the romantic period,
and a disease peculiar to the pompous and dogmatic reviews of

the early nineteenth century. The disease has, however, remained chronic, and the evil has never been far from us. Many instances could be cited. The list of misunderstood writers, who were charged with obscurity, madness, decadence, and immorality, would include practically all the great English writers whom we admire today. To be sure, not all their contemporaries were equally blind or mistaken: there have been a few voices crying in the wilderness, proclaiming the originality of new talents. But the more dignified and respectable the periodicals and the more imposing the critics, the more preposterous the misjudgments, the more influential the mistakes.

We are apt to forget that, while Jane Austen and Thackeray were kept in the background, praise and fame went for years to novelists once universally read: Mary Meeke, Kitty Cuthbertson, Marie Corelli, and the poet Owen Meredith. Dickens had an enormous popular following: yet, when a collected edition of his novels appeared, one of the literary periodicals which commanded most respect in England, the *Saturday Review*, prophesied on May 8, 1858, that he was doomed to oblivion and that in fifty years his humor would not be understood. "We do not believe in the permanence of his reputation. . . . Fifty years hence, most of his wit will be harder to understand than the allusions in *The Dunciad*, and our children will wonder what their ancestors could have meant by putting Mr. Dickens at the head of the novelists of his day." The novels of the Brontë sisters were (as will be recorded in a later chapter) as indignantly denounced in the Forties as *Ulysses* and *Lady Chatterley's Lover* were in the present century. Carlyle fared roughly at the hands of the *Athenaeum* (May 20, 1837) and not for his unbearable *Sartor Resartus*, but for his *French Revolution:* "three long volumes of misplaced persiflage and flippant pseudo-philosophy, . . . whimsical coxcombry, . . . extravagance and absurdity," declared the critic, who attributed Carlyle's far-fetched mannerisms to "an imperfection of intellect, an incapacity for feeling truth and beauty," and branded the work as a misplaced attempt "to transfuse the vague verbiage and affected sentimentality of a sect of Germans into our simple and intelligible philosophy."

George Meredith's reputation with his contemporaries has been studied in monographs by Maurice Buxton Forman (in 1909) and René Galland (in 1923), the latter volume giving a far more representative selection of British criticism of Meredith. The poetry of George Meredith, which, unless we are mistaken, will remain the more lastingly beautiful part of his work, was hardly understood between 1851 and 1880, with the result that splendid pieces like "Hymn to Color" or even humbler jewels like "The Thrush in February," far superior to anything Matthew Arnold, William Morris, or Arthur Hugh Clough ever wrote, have not yet won the recognition they deserve among lovers of English poetry. Meredith's early *Poems* (1851) were granted some praise, although with grave reservations on what some termed its "coarse sensuality," others its "sensuousness." The *Guardian* of July 9, 1851, uttered this warning: "Shelley, whom he studies carefully, will show him that the utmost luxuriance of language is consistent with spotless purity of thought." Twenty years earlier, the same critic would doubtless have dispensed the same advice to Shelley, proposing Wordsworth as a model, and forty years earlier, he would have reproved Wordsworth and appealed to Gray. On May 24, 1862, the staid *Spectator* suggested that a more accurate title for *Modern Love* would be "Modern Lust"; and the injustice of the *Athenaeum*, on May 31, 1862, was so flagrant that Swinburne felt impelled to protest openly. The novel *Richard Feverel*, today required reading in English literature courses, was guardedly appreciated in the *Times* (October 14, 1859) and censured for its obscurity and lax morality. Everywhere else, it was denounced as impure and dangerous, preached against from the pulpit, banned from circulating libraries. Meredith, who was highly sensitive to blame, was deeply wounded; the book had to wait nineteen years for a second edition. The author of *The Egoist* was about fifty when, in 1878, he finally found a more sympathetic critical appreciation; that was due to a new generation of writers who championed and almost imposed his poems and his novels alike: Swinburne, W. M.

Rossetti, Henley, Stevenson, James Thomson (B. V.), H. D. Traill. Success with the general public came only in 1884 with the much-discussed and long-overrated *Diana of the Crossways*.

The English estimate of the contemporary French novel had, in the same years 1820–1860, displayed none of that detachment which is often the privilege of foreign critics. In their stubborn refusal to accept their continental contemporaries, the British critics cut the figure of insular Pharisees and even rabid fanatics. Mrs. Trollope, in 1835, in a book on *Paris and the Parisians*, is typical of a score of her compatriots, astounded by the unbridled indecencies of Victor Hugo's dramas and apparently forgetting that England had had an Elizabethan drama of murder and incest and a Restoration comedy of witty lewdness. George Sand's romantic novel, *Lélia*, was likened by the *Athenaeum* of September 28, 1833, to "a mire of blood and dirt." The reviewer added in sadness: "Something of his melancholy theory, which represents all things as false, virtue and vice as indifferent, . . . has always been interwoven with the indecencies and characters of the fashionable French novels."

Two long articles in the *Quarterly* (March–June 1834, pp. 177–212, and April 1836, pp. 65–131) undertook to warn the British public against the corruption of French plays and novels and, if possible, to cure the seemingly incurable French nation of its immorality. They are one long abusive tirade against Balzac, George Sand, Victor Hugo, Dumas. The central argument is that such a literature affords conclusive "evidence of the state of moral feeling and social life in France." Long quotations from the crime columns in French newspapers "prove" that crimes and vices, adultery, incest, and murder occur daily in Paris, as they do in French novels and plays. Many women are apparently "either adulteresses or prostitutes," most men "bastards or foundlings." The incident which fascinates all the novelists must be a daily occurrence in French life: "a lapse of female chastity." Indeed, the English moralist quotes from the reports of trials in the Paris Assizes which are proof to him that the French writers merely reproduce the depraved manners of their land. *Le Père Goriot*,

La Peau de Chagrin are the record of daily occurrences. So is *La Cousine Bette*, that "mass of nauseating depravity." George Sand can hardly be expected to be true to the discreet reserve of her sex since, according to the fantastic explanation of her pseudonym seriously offered by the critic, she deliberately adopted the name of "a German fanatic who astounded the world with that practical scene of enthusiastic and bloody romance: the assassination of Kotzebue." In a word, let the King of France put a stop to such a profligate literature; in the meanwhile, concludes the *Quarterly* reviewer, let the British banish such examples of perverse cynicism and Gallic indecency or sell them only with red labels duly warning the normal English reader against these poisonous imports.

Virtuous indignation is, unfortunately, a ready peril to critical clear-sightedness. British commentators apparently saw no difference in literary merit between Hugo and Dumas, Balzac and Paul de Kock. Macaulay delighted in the latter. Eugène Sue appeared to many English readers as unequalled among the new French novelists. Thackeray in his *Paris Sketch-Book* found Charles de Bernard more refined and truer to life than Balzac. Frédéric Soulié and Jules Janin were commonly ranked as at least equal to the author of *La Comédie humaine*. Matthew Arnold, like George Eliot, seems to have preferred George Sand to all other French novelists and visited her at Nohant in 1846. Recognition was granted to Balzac's genius only very slowly in England. Elizabeth Barrett, whose literary tastes were often more virile than her poetical creations, was among the first to hail Balzac as a genius (in a letter dated April 27, 1846, to Robert Browning) and to sacrifice all the English novelists to his pre-eminence. Later on, George Moore, recalling the youthful memories of his life in Paris, was to celebrate "that vast immemorial mind" above all other French novelists.[12]

[12] The fame and influence of Balzac in England deserve a careful study. Much valuable information has been gathered, for the early period, by Marcel Moraud in *Le Romantisme français en Angleterre* (Champion, 1933), from which I have drawn a few data.

It would be tedious to recall at length that the great poets who followed the romantic generation suffered from the same neglect or the same blind prejudices of the British public as their elders. Tennyson's silence between 1833 and 1842 is commonly attributed to the hostile outcry which followed his *Poems* of 1833 and to the bitter animosity of reviewers. Later on, the poet of "Maud," "Enoch Arden," and the *Idylls of the King* was complacently admired for those works where he is least original; while the robust terseness of some of his later poems ("The Ancient Sage," "The Higher Pantheism") remained, and remains to this day, unsuspected by too many readers. Browning, for once, was not accused of immorality. It seemed so utterly out of the question that he could ever be understood that no one dared even assert that *Sordello* or *Men and Women* could contain dangerous crudities or fleshly descriptions. Victorian wits screamed with laughter over *Sordello,* of which two lines alone, the first and the last, made sense:

> Who will, may hear Sordello's story told. . . .
> Who would has heard Sordello's story told.

A typical reaction to *Men and Women,* Browning's masterpiece in subtle dramatic psychology and in delicate music, was that of the *Saturday Review* in 1855. It opened: "There is another book of madness and mysticism, another melancholy specimen of power wantonly wasted, and talent deliberately perverted." The critic then confessed with ponderous irony his inability to understand the so-called poems, "even after prolonged study." Quoting the four stanzas from "By the Fireside" which begin with "My perfect wife, my Leonor," he challenged any reader to "pierce" the obscurity of such "stuff" and offered "a gold medal in the department of hermeneutical science to the ingenious individual who, after any length of study, can succeed in unriddling" a passage from "Master Hugues of Saxe-Gotha." The reviewer's final condemnation, which excepted only "The Statue and the Bust," was unambiguous: "We can find nothing but a set purpose to be obscure, and an idiot captivity to the jingle of Hudibrastic phrase."

Such narrow and unfair attacks, unworthy of the name of criticism (which should imply severe but helpful and constructive censuring), entail grave consequences. They have more than once driven gifted writers into discouraged silence: Wordsworth after *The Excursion,* Tennyson after his early poems, Hardy after *Jude the Obscure* are famous instances, and there are many more in which the promising writer ceased to write for his contemporaries and even ceased to write at all. Such undiscerning criticism throws young talents into bitterness and isolation, stiffens their youthful harshness, or leads them to emphasize their tendency to mannerism and obscurity. It deprives the public of the early understanding of the writers of its own generation and distorts the course of criticism and of literary reputation, often for scores of years. For it is likely that a subsequent wave of opinion will reverse either the praise lavished upon conventional talents or the blind condemnation of innovating geniuses by an earlier generation. Scott and Dickens have suffered in the valuation of a sophisticated elite from having been too widely acclaimed by the general public. Tennyson paid for his official success in the mid-Victorian era with undue neglect of his later poems. Browning had, for many years, encountered banter and scorn: a new generation then repaid him with excessive admiration and, between 1880 and 1920, worshipped the Browning of the later poems, when his message had degenerated into shallow optimism, his tricks of psychology and versification had grown effete. It will then take a further period of disfavor and of comparative neglect (we are apparently going through it now) for Browning to be rediscovered anew and for his fame after extreme oscillations to reach a balanced estimate.

It would not be difficult to follow up this long series of mistakes, due either to hostile prejudices or to exaggerated and superficial praise, with those of more recent critics. To indict the countless errors of contemporary criticism might, however, be deemed libellous; to quote samples of what we consider their grossest mistakes might be judged either unfair caricature or a mark of overweening insolence. A foreign observer of literature, moreover, though he may claim unprejudiced detachment and serene relativity, loses too much in breadth of knowledge, discrimination for the finer shades, and warmth of feeling. Let me leave to others the task of thorough and fearless revaluation of which contemporary English literature stands in dire need. The mysterious and frigid female sphinx called posterity is already relentlessly performing her duty. *Of Human Bondage* and *The Five Towns* appear, in spite of their honorable workmanship, no more likely to endure than *Esther Waters* or the sad stories of George Gissing. The novels of Virginia Woolf, with all their evanescent charm and their frail, dazzling grace, will age as quickly as did Stevenson's subtly wrought tales; her feminist pleas for matrons with three guineas and for spinsters with a room of their own have already worn as thin as the precious artistry of *Virginibus Puerisque*. Her *Common Reader* may outlast Orlando's metamorphoses and Mrs. Dalloway's peregrinations as surely as Katherine Mansfield's moving *Letters* will outlast her slender and too feminine short stories. Maurice Baring with all his cosmopolitan charm and Charles Morgan, except for a few inspired chapters in the second part of *The Fountain*, may soon appear as pleasing and ephemeral as a hundred subtle and conventional technicians of the novel have proved in the last hundred years. After the disappointing attempts of *Eyeless in Gaza* and *After Many a Summer*, it seems all too clear today, as it was to a few discerning eyes ten or fifteen years ago when *Point Counterpoint* was extravagantly lauded, that Aldous Huxley will survive, if at all, as a clever essayist or an English and fourth-rate Anatole France, if not a twentieth-century Thomas Love Peacock. In fact, it is distressing to ponder over the probable fate which most of the English novels of the last hundred years may meet at the hands of Time: *The Return of the Native*, probably a few terse stories by Kipling, perhaps *The Man of Property* and the *Indian Summer of a Forsyte*, one or two novels of the sea by Conrad,

Ulysses and a few pages of *The Portrait of the Artist as a Young Man*, probably some novels and a dozen long-short stories by D. H. Lawrence, may alone be rescued from the shipwreck of so many illusory values.

The legacy of modern English poetry may be similarly re-appraised. The undisputed pre-eminence which English lyricism enjoyed over European poetry from Blake to Swinburne seems to have been broken off with the latter, whose fame has suffered a decline in our century (a decline which would be excessive if it were to underrate permanently such admirable poems as "Hymn to Proserpine," "The Garden of Proserpine," "Ave atque Vale"). Baudelaire, Rimbaud, Mallarmé, and other French rebels became the most original force in the poetry of the West. Hopkins and Yeats have probably been the only two English bards of world stature born since 1840. We smile discreetly at the fantastic eulogies of *Aurora Leigh* in which our grandfathers indulged, and we discern many flaws behind the flowery and bouncing imagery of Francis Thompson. The excessive praise given by the generation of 1920–1940 to the poetry of Thomas Hardy and *The Shropshire Lad* went, it may be suspected, less to the poetical virtues of those poems (which are great but not of the greatest) than to an ironical pessimism and to a tragic cynicism in which a disillusioned post-war youth read its own moods. The same is doubtless true of the most surprising success in the Twenties and Thirties, *The Waste Land:* it soon may be opened only as a sophisticated album of the intellectual and moral fashions of souls during a new "mal du siècle" era. If T. S. Eliot has reached abiding greatness in poetry, it is more probably in "The Hollow Men," in "Gerontion," and above all in the fervor of "Ash Wednesday" and the *Four Quartets*. The strained raptures with which the most respectable critics hailed the incredibly prosaic *Family Reunion* and the stilted pompousness of *Murder in the Cathedral* will, before long, amuse and puzzle the readers of our critical reviews. Our descendants will be equally surprised that we should have revered (or, according to our age and mood, spurned) genuine poets like W. H. Auden, Louis MacNeice, and

Dylan Thomas, and weaker ones like C. Day Lewis, in "A Time to Dance" and "Overtures to Death," and Stephen Spender.

The preceding survey of cases in which great literary names remained unrecognized by contemporary criticism is not a negative enumeration of isolated exceptions; the examples quoted were not erratic and whimsical pronouncements, but represented fairly the large majority of estimates published by "competent" reviewers of Milton, Wordsworth, Shelley, and others. The most disturbing cases are those in which no contemporary observer seems to have been sensitive to the manifest and perfectly traditional and familiar beauty of a new work.

A countertest should be briefly suggested for our inquiry: it would consist of British criticism as applied not to past literature but to the living works of the time, where criticism was discovery and adventure and was not weighed down by a ponderous body of previous opinions. Such a history has never been written; its elements could be easily gathered by many a modern scholar, accustomed to compiling extensive bibliographies of other critics before venturing an opinion of his own upon a writer.

Criticism is not one of the richest provinces of English letters, as many a British and American critic has confessed or, sometimes, boasted.[13] It is even doubtful whether English literature counts a single critic of undisputed eminence or world standing. As an enviable compensation, it has had a fine group of gentlemen-scholars, well informed and leisurely, steeped in the genteel tradition, feeling with taste and writing with graceful charm, whose dearth or disappearance in recent years has left a sad gap in our cultural life. It may also boast of seven or eight vigorous critical

[13] Saintsbury argued differently but hardly convincingly in his *History of Criticism;* Irving Babbitt reproved him for it in his essay "Are the English Critical?" reprinted in 1940 in *The Spanish Character and Other Essays* (Boston: Houghton Mifflin). "Our critics are but a feeble folk," concluded Havelock Ellis at the end of an essay on "The Present Position of English Criticism," December 1888 (reprinted in *Views and Reviews,* 1922). Whether a relative independence from critics, theories, and academies is not an advantage for a literature is a different question: *sub judice licet.*

temperaments, whose originality, verve, or keenness of insight have remained alive and attractive, while ambitious philosophical structures, long histories, dramas, and novels once judged instinct with life sank into oblivion. Dr. Johnson, Coleridge, Hazlitt, Matthew Arnold, Walter Pater, and T. S. Eliot are six of the stars (with two or three candidates for the seventh place) of that critical Pleiad.

Lucid discernment of new talents among their contemporaries has not been the crowning achievement of those critics. Some of them, through prudence or through lack of inclination, have avoided jeopardizing their authority through the appreciation of new works. Walter Pater, for instance, whose *Appreciations* remain, in spite of an overwrought style, one of the finest single volumes of criticism in English, took little notice of his contemporaries. Had he done so, he would have transfigured them under a wealth of draperies and lace. He erred most signally when he inserted a disappointing eulogy of a vulgar novel, Octave Feuillet's *La Morte,* in a series of studies on great masters. Contemporary literature also played a very inconsiderable part in the volumes of essays by T. S. Eliot and in his comments in the *Criterion.* His implied or explicit estimates of Gautier, Corbière, Laforgue, and St. John Perse, his criticism of Milton, Baudelaire, Pater, Hulme, Hardy, Kipling, and D. H. Lawrence are, indeed, more uncertain than his admirable pronouncements on Seneca, Dante, the Elizabethans, and Dryden.

Others have proved greater by the suggestiveness of the critical views which they launched into the world by their discovery of new writers: such was Coleridge, who in his youth misjudged the true place of Bowles and (in his *Biographia Literaria*) Southey. Johnson's *Lives of the Poets* are rich in blunt and harsh statements that we have refused to ratify (on Donne, Milton, Swift, Gray, Collins, etc.); they will be read forever for their occasional shrewd judgment, their racy humor, and the radiation of a robust temperament, but they have certainly not drawn for us the chart of seventeenth- or eighteenth-century poetry. Johnson's lack of flair for the approaching romantic revival, which had been clearly heralded long before 1780, disqualifies him as a prophet. Hazlitt was an inconsistent bundle of prejudices, mostly political; he erred repeatedly, worst of all and almost voluntarily on Scott, Byron, Shelley, and even (in 1816) on the idol of his youth, Coleridge. When his sympathy and his gusto could have full play, however, he had perhaps the keenest intuitions, most tersely expressed, of any English critic.

As to Matthew Arnold's fame, of all the major critics of Great Britain his seems likely to be the least secure. Like Brunetière and, before him, Taine and Nisard in France, Arnold has been served by a dogmatic ponderousness which seldom fails to impose on contemporaries and, subsequently, on professors of literature in search of final decrees that no student will dare challenge. Many a teacher quotes his famous statement on the "high seriousness" infallibly characterizing a great classic, without realizing that it excludes Chaucer, Montaigne, Molière, La Fontaine, nay, Racine himself, from the restricted band of the great classics, patterned by Arnold on the model of a mutilated Goethe. His similar pronouncements on the necessity for a poet to have read much and to know a great deal ("Wordsworth," said the dutiful son of the Rugby schoolmaster, "should have read more books, among them, no doubt, those of Goethe") have misled Anglo-Saxon criticism along a path of starched Puritan morality, mistaken for the road to beauty. An orthodox enemy of the Philistines, Arnold has uttered statements about poetry as a "criticism of life" which smack of outright poetical heresy; of Goethe's poetry, he even asserted that "what is really deeply and fundamentally effective . . . is what remains of the poet when he is translated into prose." But Pope and Dryden, who should have been poets after his own heart, he hailed half ironically as "classics of our prose."

As a critic of individual writers, Arnold, with all his good will and his praise of the *Revue des Deux Mondes,* failed just as signally—least of all probably on Homer, most of all on Celtic literature. He overrated and half misrepresented to the English the pale figures of Joubert, Eugénie de Guérin, and Sénancour;

he never wearied of quoting with respect the hardly significant
Swiss critic Schérer; but he ignored the more vigorous French
writers of his day. He peremptorily asserted (*Irish Essays and
Others*, 1882) that Molière was "by far the chief name in French
poetry." In English literature, he proved incapable of enjoying
Chaucer and even Burns, for he found them devoid of "high
seriousness." In Shelley, he saw a musician seduced by poetry,
and preferred the letter writer in him to the "ineffectual" poet.
Keats's love letters horrified him, a reaction after all more under-
standable than his cool insistence on ranking Byron above both
Coleridge and Keats. Goethe had declared that Byron, whenever
he did not reflect, "must unquestionably be regarded as the greatest talent of the century," and Arnold can but endorse the Master's dictum. Yet the picture that Arnold drew of Goethe himself
and of Heine lacks critical lucidity and penetration. In the meanwhile, six important poets flourished in England in Matthew Arnold's own generation (Tennyson, Browning, Swinburne, Meredith, William Morris, and Rossetti), two at least in France
(Leconte de Lisle and Baudelaire). He ignored them. H. W. Gar-
rod, one of his successors in the Oxford chair of poetry, lecturing
in 1931 at Harvard to one of those American audiences by whom
Arnold is revered as a professor's poet and as a solemn champion
of serious culture, did not hesitate to say that Arnold

could never rid himself of the feeling that the criticism of literature
was being treated as though it were a part of the church service. . . .
He would call no man a poet until he has been baptized and confirmed. . . . His criticism is tainted with a certain snobbery and even
dandyism.

Other English critics deserve rehabilitation. There is Swinburne, who wrote excellent textual criticism of Shelley, subtle
appreciations of the Elizabethans and of Byron, courageous and
farsighted defences of Rossetti, William Morris, and Matthew
Arnold himself, delirious yet at times shrewd eulogies of Victor
Hugo. Lamb and De Quincey have occasionally possessed a magical touch; but their eccentricities of taste and whimsical oddities

of judgment have too often made them unreliable, and their keen insight lost its edge when applied to their own contemporaries. Leigh Hunt is at times a more discriminating critic, if less artistic a prose writer: in 1816, on the slender basis of a thin volume of verse by Shelley (*Alastor*) and of a few sonnets published by Keats in a newspaper, he divined the genius of those two obscure beginners. Too often, however, he lacked delicacy and depth. Macaulay's critical essays are narrow in their range, insolent in their conceit, and steer too consistently away from the pure enjoyment of literature.

It would be easy, and unfair, to insist upon the deficiencies of minor English critics who almost never appreciated contemporary greatness. One, however, still deserves mention: Jeffrey. For his very blunders afford us a valuable lesson, and he still has many imitators in our midst. Jeffrey was, in his day, a power to be reckoned with. A Whig politician and stubborn Scottish lawyer, he never claimed to understand everything, still less to forgive those whom he failed to understand. Sentiment he distrusted, and sentimentality he hated: he was consequently repelled by Wordsworth's faith in emotion and Rousseauistic worship of the lessons of nature. His personal preferences, and even more his dislikes, he expressed brutally, as when he referred to Wordsworth's "state of low and maudlin imbecility" and pronounced "The White Doe of Rylstone," in October 1815, "the very worst poem we ever saw imprinted in a quarto volume."

Four months before thus damning "The White Doe of Rylstone," Jeffrey was lavishing praise on Southey's *Roderick:*

It abounds with lofty sentiments and magnificent imagery; and contains more rich and comprehensive descriptions, more beautiful pictures of pure affection, and more impressive representations of mental agony and exaltation than we have often met with in the compass of a single volume.

Jeffrey's admiration is as disconcerting to us today as his wrath. In March 1819, he gave Rogers' *Human Life* far warmer eulogy than he was to grant, in the following year, to Keats's "Hyperion" (although it is one of Jeffrey's few felicitous intuitions to have almost understood the force and grandeur of "Hyperion," while criticizing the subject as "too far removed from all the sources of human interest"). No hyperbole was too strong to be bestowed by the Scottish critic on Thomas Campbell. But the most significant lesson to be drawn from Jeffrey's criticism is perhaps to be found in a passage written in October 1829 in the *Edinburgh Review.* The excesses of the romantic movement had then been almost sanctioned by time; its youthful impetus had been exhausted; Keats, Shelley, and Byron had been dead respectively eight, seven, and five years; Wordsworth and Coleridge, surviving their dried-up inspiration, might have been respected as classics. This is, however, the balance sheet of the poetry of his age which the much feared and still influential lawyer was giving, while trying to assess the place of Felicia Hemans among contemporary singers:

We have seen too much of the perishable nature of modern literature. . . . Since the beginning of our critical career, we have seen a vast deal of beautiful poetry pass into oblivion, in spite of our feeble efforts to recall or retain it in remembrance. The tuneful quartos of Southey are already little better than lumber;—and the rich melodies of Keats and Shelley; and the fantastical emphasis of Wordsworth,—and the plebeian pathos of Crabbe, are melting fast from the field of our vision. . . . Even the splendid strains of Moore are fading into distance and dimness, except when they have been married to immortal music. . . . The two who have the longest withstood this rapid withering of the laurel, and with the least marks of decay on their branches, are Rogers and Campbell.

To Felicia Hemans, he felt inclined to promise an enduring fame comparable to theirs, since her "tenderness and loftiness of feeling, an ethereal purity of sentiment" made her "beyond comparison, the most touching and accomplished writer of occasional verses that our literature has yet to boast of."

The wonder is that a man who was so ponderously and consistently in the wrong should have been called by Macaulay (when, late in life, Jeffrey audaciously reprinted his contributions to the *Edinburgh Review*) "taken all in all, more nearly a universal genius than any man of our own time" and that Carlyle should have asserted in his *Reminiscences:* "It is certain there has no critic appeared among us since who was worth reading beside him."

The second half of the nineteenth century was singularly deficient in critics of very high stature, Arnold, Pater, and perhaps Bagehot excepted. The present century has, on the contrary, produced a crop of critical essays uniting wide and solid knowledge, intuitive penetration, originality of views, and literary charm which no other country but France has probably equalled. Many of these critics were university scholars whom a younger generation, intoxicated with scientific jargon, intent upon murder through dissection and pigeonholing through definition, would do well to reread: George Saintsbury, A. C. Bradley, Edward Dowden, E. K. Chambers, W. P. Ker, Walter Raleigh, H. C. Grierson, Oliver Elton, Basil de Selincourt. From the work of their successors, two works of criticism remain unrivalled for their faultless taste and their felicitous insight and phrasing: the series of Virginia Woolf's *The Common Reader*, and a masterpiece of condensation and suggestion, Lytton Strachey's *Landmarks in French Literature*. A strange lack of fixity in their capricious development, accompanied by a lack of sanity, as Matthew Arnold would have called it, or of wise relativity, has marred the critical achievement of some of their most finely gifted contemporaries, John Middleton Murry, Herbert Read, and F. R. Leavis; others, like Bonamy Dobrée, F. L. Lucas, John Squire, Arthur Quiller-Couch, and even Desmond MacCarthy, have never entirely shaken off the whimsical amateurishness dear to an English gentleman touching upon literature. Their common fault and their gravest deficiencies have been too lukewarm an interest in the literature of their day, a reluctance to assist its development, to guide its ventures, and to assess its achievements. None of the important or traditionally respected British reviews has fulfilled its duty to the literature of the twentieth century;

the place allotted to literature, art, and criticism in the *Quarterly*, the *Nineteenth Century*, the *Fortnightly*, the *Contemporary Review*, the *Dublin Review*, and the now defunct *London Mercury* remains miserably small.[14] No really first-rate or comprehensive appreciation of George Moore, W. B. Yeats, James Joyce, D. H. Lawrence, Wilfred Owen, Katherine Mansfield, or Virginia Woolf was written in their lifetimes.

The usual defence of critics who are charged with ignoring their great contemporaries is that the creators themselves never prove more just or discerning. Let us not deny critics this paltry consolation. But no one should be surprised that an author or artist, engrossed in his own creation, struggling painfully to express the truest part of himself, should be jealous or contemptuous of all that may differ too sharply from himself or undermine his self-confidence. Besides, young artists must assert themselves at the expense of their immediate predecessors and shake off the weight of the past, while older writers try frantically to hold back the wave-of-the-future which would gladly engulf them.

Thus it is that Donne was ungrateful to the Elizabethans who had preceded him; grave Wordsworth found Voltaire's *Candide* "the dull product of a scoffer's pen"; worse, he remained unmoved by the music of *The Ancient Mariner*—as early as June 24, 1799, he wrote his publisher, offering to replace Coleridge's masterpiece in the second edition of the *Lyrical Ballads* "by some little things which would be more likely to suit the common taste"; he refused to understand the beauty of Keats's *Endymion* or that of Shelley's *Alastor*, a poem in which he might have recognized a passionate feeling for nature akin to his own, a majestic blank verse that his own example had fostered. In a case where no moral or esthetic divergence could be alleged as the

---

[14] Happily several younger reviews have tried or are now trying to remedy this gap: *Life and Letters, Horizon, Scrutiny*, and the fine weekly, *The New Statesman and Nation*, not to mention the late *Criterion*. Foremost among the few works of criticism which have served the younger literature of England with sympathy and discrimination is Cecil Day Lewis' *A Hope for Poetry* (Oxford: Blackwell, 1935).

secret motive of hostility, Wordsworth—so Landor informs us —proclaimed all Scott's poetry to be "not worth five shillings." Byron was even more erratic; all his utterances are tinged with prejudice, caprice, or egotism. Meredith, reader for Chapman and Hall, made some brilliant discoveries, but rejected Samuel Butler's *The Way of All Flesh* as not worth a publisher's attention. Readers of George Moore cannot forget how his entertaining but grossly unfair prejudices against Thomas Hardy and scores of writers fill his volumes of inexhaustible reminiscences; and worshippers of Shakespeare cannot forgive his ranking of Landor far above the greatest of all dramatists. Yeats's choice of the best poetry of 1892–1935, in the *Oxford Book of Modern Verse,* will draw a smile from our descendants. Shaw's famous pronouncements on the "genius" of Brieux and on several other contemporary or past writers can, at least, be saved from ridicule by that screen of prudence, dear to British and Irish, called humor.

The list might be endlessly pursued. But no one would exchange the passionate injustice and the egocentric revelations of what the French call "la critique des créateurs" for more impartiality and a more serene detachment. Our concern should be limited here to critics honestly trying, and often lamentably failing, to understand the art of their own time. Creators are second to none as critics when their revelations touch upon their own creations or general questions of esthetics. As commentators or reviewers of their contemporaries, they fully justify one of the few valid paradoxes of Oscar Wilde's *Intentions:*

That very concentration of vision that makes a man an artist limits by its sheer intensity his faculty of fine appreciation. . . . A truly great artist cannot conceive of life being shown, or beauty fashioned, under any conditions other than those he has selected. . . . It is exactly because a man cannot do a thing that he is the proper judge of it.

CHAPTER II

A Glance at Criticism in America and Germany

IF, as I claim, the inability or unwillingness of critics to under-stand their contemporaries has been a widespread occurrence in the history of culture, it should be proved conclusively by a vast array of facts. It would be tedious to enumerate all those which diligent research could bring to light. Enough examples have been quoted to show that, in modern English literature, the great writers unacknowledged, insulted, or misunderstood by their contemporary critics greatly outnumbered the few geniuses who have been immediately appraised with definitive lucidity. Do other literatures stand the test any better than that of England?

The most important literature to be considered should obvi-ously be the oldest and most continuous one, that of France. Let me, however, first examine more cursorily a few examples drawn from two more recent ones: the German (as represented by Goethe) and the youngest of all the western literatures, the American. If I can convince our readers that the criticism of a new country, eager to discard the bad-neighborliness and the mean literary rivalries of European Grubstreets, proved no more sympathetic to Poe, Melville, and Whitman than the English re-views had been to Wordsworth and Shelley; that, in its turn, the modern nation most highly renowned for its acumen, its wit, and its flair for artistic innovation behaved toward its poets, novelists, and painters just

> Like true-born Britons, who ne'er think at all,

as Dryden derisively described his compatriots, I shall have proved the problem to be a real one in its generality and shall perhaps have incited others to look for a solution. Modern schol-arship, like philosophy both ancient and modern, is too often guilty of setting up elaborate pseudo-problems in order to display its ingenuous ingenuity in solving them.

One of the stern conditions under which American writers labored in the last century was the lack of a sympathetic and guiding criticism. To this day it remains one of the dominant features of the literary atmosphere in the United States. The divorce between creative literature and the public, due not solely but in a large measure to the absence or failure of criticism, has never been anywhere so complete as in the America of 1910–1960, when all the writers of any worth have been opposed to the established order, have satirized the reigning values, or have contemptuously ignored them. The regrets of our contemporaries cannot, however, find comfort in the nostalgic contemplation of the other great age of American literature, the period from Poe to Whitman and even to Henry James. The public was not subject to the same degrading publicity it has had to endure in our more standardized era; commercial methods had not yet been applied to the production and the sale of books; an individualism which tradition has agreed to call "rugged" and a strong and austere will power seem to have been among the virtues of the Puritans of the nineteenth century in America.

Yet in no country, not even in France when Flaubert heaped up invectives upon the bourgeois or in England when Matthew Arnold assailed the Philistines, did the writers of the middle of the last century live in so bitter and tragic an isolation, harshly rejected by a narrow and moralizing criticism. The courage and the originality of those writers were doubtless hardened or sharpened by that struggle. The gain, if gain there was, was dearly bought. The loss for the public, whom critics refused to educate to read Hawthorne and Melville, was total and final. In that utter lack of sympathy between writers and their environment lies a partial explanation of the paradox which has always struck European observers of American letters: the youngest and most active country in the northern hemisphere, where optimism is even more of a religion than plumbing, sanitation, and "having a good time," produces the most consistently gloomy literature of recent centuries. Stigmas of stifling melancholy, a moral and imaginative morbidity, a haunting pessimism mark Poe, Hawthorne, Melville, Mark Twain himself, as well as Emily Dickinson, Henry Adams, Henry James, and their successors: Eugene O'Neill, Robinson Jeffers, Hart Crane, William Faulkner, the authors of *Tobacco Road* and *U.S.A.*—if they can thus be strangely paired—and even the Franco-American novelist Julien Green.

Any list of important American writers repudiated by their contemporary critics should begin with Edgar Allan Poe. The story of his posthumous fame is too well known to bear repetition here. We are prone to smile at the French, who have made Poe their own and in the translations or eulogies of three of their greatest poets, Baudelaire, Mallarmé, and Valéry, have assured him of a place among the most influential writers in the world. Examples are not lacking to remind us of the strange choices which continental Europeans, usually led by French critics, make in American or in English literature: Ossian and Byron, Fenimore Cooper and Jack London, Aldous Huxley and Sinclair Lewis. Poe is undoubtedly a second-rate poet, marred by vulgar music and cheap effects in the poems which have been most warmly admired. It was not difficult to improve upon them in translation. But one may well wonder if the relentless obstinacy of American critics in long refusing any greatness to Poe is not due in part to a lingering prejudice inherited from the Pharisaic criticism of another century. If the poet in "The Raven" and "Ulalume" is certainly not among the finest, if the critic in *Marginalia* is often superficial and subject to strange lapses in taste, Poe's esthetics of poetry is one of the most considerable in English-speaking countries, where the genre has not been too brilliantly practiced. The short story writer in Poe deserves a place, along with Balzac and the author of *Crime and Punishment,* among the few novelists who attempted to bridge the deplorable gulf between the artistic or psychological novel and the mystery story or thriller. Finally, the strange cosmogony of *Eureka,* in which profound intuitions are juxtaposed with quackish claims, is not unworthy of a niche among American attempts at philosophic imagination. If contemporaries and immediate successors of Poe had been more prompt at discerning his importance, his influence might have served as a stimulant to American criticism of poetry as it did to French Symbolism. Emerson, whose thought and style should, it seems, have found a ready public in the America of his day, had to win his way slowly and painfully. His first book, *Nature*, which was published in 1836 in an edition of five hundred copies, was not yet out of print in 1847, when a second edition appeared. Emerson himself was not exactly enthusiastic about the great writers of his time. He proved severe and even unjust to Poe—as did Whitman —and harsh toward Irving and Bryant. The two really important contemporary men of letters whom the transcendentalist philosopher appreciated were Thoreau and, strange as it may sound, Walt Whitman. But he proclaimed Alcott "the highest genius of the time"; he did not even deign to open *Moby Dick*. Of Hawthorne, he said: "I never read his books with pleasure; they are too young." Later, on September 4, 1842, he noted naïvely: "Nathaniel Hawthorne's reputation as a writer is a very pleasing fact, because his writing is not good for anything, and this is a tribute to the man."

Hawthorne, in his turn, was not a warm admirer of Emerson; but criticism was not his forte. It is more disturbing to discover how depressed he was at the lack of recognition accorded him by his contemporaries. His early works sold little or not at all, and he was humiliated when he compared his failure with the success of innumerable female writers: "a damned mob of scribbling women; . . . worse they could not be, and better they need not be, when they sell by the hundred thousand." A few good judges, however, had displayed more insight: they had used the words "talent" and even "genius" for the author of *Twice-Told Tales* (1837). They were Longfellow and Duyckinck in the *North American Review* of 1837 and 1841, Poe in *Graham's Magazine* (May 1842), and Melville, who, in the *Literary World* of 1850, begged America to read and to encourage the new literary talent, without leaving the merit of the discovery to future ages.[1] But Melville's impassioned plea met with small success.

Indeed, when *The Scarlet Letter* appeared in 1850, the few favorable articles (scholars have listed three in all) were eclipsed by the numerous and violent attacks against the immorality of a novel which is today recognized as an American classic. The subject was thought too dangerously akin to that of dreaded French writers. The influential *North American Review* advised Hawthorne to choose "a less revolting subject" and censured "the ugliness of pollution and vice," no more relieved by the author's gift of style than "the gloom of the prison is by the rose-tree at its door." *Brownson's Review* sternly reproved the novelist for treating of revolting crimes, unhallowed by any Christian remorse. "Genius perverted, or employed in perverting others, has no charms for us," declared Orestes Brownson, a recent convert to Catholicism. In the *Church Review* of 1851, a Protestant writer, Arthur C. Coxe, was even more outraged, and even less charitable in his fanatical condemnations.

Similar examples of the inability of contemporaries to understand their best writers could be selected *ad libitum* from all the finest talents of the American literary generation of 1850. The verse of a Longfellow was extolled to the skies. At the same time, Thoreau, who should have appealed to the individualism and love for nature of his New England compatriots, reveals in his *Journal* that only two hundred and nineteen copies of his book, *A Week on the Concord and Merrimac Rivers,* published in 1849, sold in four years. But Melville's is, of all these cases, the most striking. American criticism seems suddenly to have discovered him since 1919, the hundredth anniversary of his birth. In their enthusiasm which borders on delirium, his new devotees assert that, not only is Melville the supreme American novelist, but "distinctly, *Moby Dick* belongs with the *Divine Comedy* and *Hamlet* and *The Brothers Karamazov* and *War and Peace*" (Lewis Mumford).

[1] For these references and for more details, see a short volume by Bertha Faust on *Hawthorne's Contemporary Reputation* (Philadelphia: University of Pennsylvania Press, 1939).

When *Moby Dick* came out in 1851, the obtuseness of the leading critics was apparently even worse than it had been over *The Scarlet Letter*. Yet Melville was no beginner. His early novels (*Typee, Omoo, White Jacket*) had been warmly received: the public expected him to write more tales of exotic adventure among cannibals. When they opened the tale of the symbolic pursuit of the monstrous whale by the mad Captain Ahab, the critics were puzzled and thought they had been cheated. Reviewers were baffled by a volume which it was impossible to classify. Four accounts, two in America (E. Duyckinck in the *Literary World* and an anonymous one in *Harper's*) and two in Europe (the London *Leader* and E. D. Forgues in the *Revue des Deux Mondes*), guessed the real meaning of the book and attempted, as indeed a critic should, to elucidate the meaning of the allegory on human life and the problem of evil. The remainder of the literary press was content with abuse. "Trash" was the usual and by far the most lenient word of judgment. The *New Monthly Magazine* added in more picturesque language: "maniacal, . . . gibberish, screaming, like an incurable Bedlamite, reckless of keeper or strait-waistcoat." Five reviews which had regularly discussed Melville's earlier volumes were charitable enough to omit all mention of *Moby Dick*. The New England writers, on whose sympathy Melville had counted, did not raise their voices in defence. Hawthorne, whom Melville admired and worshipped, made no effort to understand his friend's work, and the two soon drifted apart; R. H. Stoddard and E. S. Stedman ranked Melville as a very minor talent, as Henry James (who felt repelled by his predecessor's morbid mysticism), Lowell, Barrett Wendell, Woodberry, and countless professors of literature were to do for over fifty years. Historians of American letters grudgingly granted him a few lines, while they reserved several dithyrambic pages for Longfellow. The British critics, in the meanwhile, had an easy explanation for the decadence of the American novel: it had exchanged the beneficent example of Scott and Dickens for that of Balzac and George Sand; given up "the smiling landscape glowing in its freshness and beauty, for the loathly atmosphere, the wretched sights and smells of a dissecting room" (*The Literary World*, August 28, 1852).

Let not the cynical optimist hint that such misunderstanding on the part of his contemporaries served Melville's glory by helping us vindicate his unrecognized genius. For, far from having acquired a truer perspective today, we probably overestimate Melville's greatness and thus prepare a new wave of reaction. Then we might have been deprived of half of Melville's novels; for the miracle is that Melville continued to create after the disappointing reception given to his masterpiece. His biographers quote the moving letter which he wrote at this time, in the bitterness of his heart, to Hawthorne: "I shall at last be worn out and perish. . . . What I feel most moved to write, that is banned,—it will not pay. Yet, altogether write the other way, I cannot." And American literature very nearly lost fine works like *Benito Cereno* or *Billy Budd;* it may indeed have lost forever others which a happier Melville might have written.[2]

Walt Whitman is undeniably the most powerful poet of America, and the most American of poets. He was thirty-six when his *Leaves of Grass* appeared in 1855. Neither Holmes nor Lowell nor Whittier was clear-sighted enough to perceive any genius or talent in those fervent poems. Indeed, the whole of contemporary American criticism (if the transcendentalists Emerson, Thoreau, and Alcott are excepted) displayed a blind and ferocious hostility. Henry E. Legler, the author of a small volume entitled *Walt Whitman, Yesterday and To-day* (Chicago, 1916), has collected some of the anathemas which then rained upon the poet. Not all of them bear quotation. Among the choice phrases coined or used by critics were: "slopbucket," "noxious weeds," "entirely bestial," "impious and obscene," "a belief in the preciousness of filth," "defilement," "broken out of Bedlam," "ithyphallic audac-

[2] Lewis Mumford's book on Melville (New York: Harcourt, Brace, 1929) and Willard Thorp's excellent introduction to *Representative Selections* (New York: American Book Company, 1938) have been drawn upon for some of the above information.

ity" "sunken sensualist," "rotten garbage of licentious thoughts," "a poet whose indecencies stink in the nostrils," "venomously malignant," "degraded helot of literature," "the mouthings of a mountebank." Among the American periodicals, the *Criterion*, *Putnam's Magazine*, and the *Christian Examiner* were the least restrained in their vituperation. The latter, published in Boston, uttered a moral warning: "The book . . . openly deifies the bodily organs, senses, and appetites in terms that admit of no double sense" (November 1856).

Even more characteristic of the critics' obtuseness were their purely literary comments in which they tried to judge *Leaves of Grass* on other grounds than those of self-righteous and indignant morality. The *Crayon*, of New York, uttered its verdict in these terms: "The book has no identity, no concentration, no purpose; it is barbarous, undisciplined, like the poetry of a half-civilized people." England might have recognized in Whitman's verse the voice of the New World, as France and Germany were to do in the last decade of the century and in the early years of the present one. Swinburne, J. A. Symonds, and Robert Louis Stevenson did, but only after 1870 and 1880. Matthew Arnold did not, and probably could not have been expected to discover a new "criticism of life" in *Leaves of Grass*. Carlyle mocked the American bard who repeated: "I am a big poet because I live in such a big country." The *London Lancet* of July 7, 1860, is typical of the British welcome given to the poet of democracy: "Of all the writers we have perused, Walt Whitman is the most silly, the most blasphemous, and the most disgusting." No less an authority than a future poet laureate of Great Britain, Alfred Austin, declared that such "grotesque, ungrammatical, repulsive rhapsodies can be compared only to the painful ravings of maniacs' dens." As late as 1876, the *Saturday Review* of London, hearing that the friends of Whitman had appealed to the public for financial help, as the American poet was sick and in distress, published a cruel retort: "The assumption that a man who sets himself to outrage public decency should be gratefully supported by public charity is certainly a very curious one." And it explained with plausible sophistry that it was a healthy sign that the public had not bought those unsalable poems, and a mark of God's providence that a poet like Whitman should fail to make a living by his writing.

Once again, our feeling in the presence of such lack of insight should be not merely one of sentimental sympathy for the neglected poet. It is clear that robust talents sometimes gain by such opposition and will not be stifled by the infested effluvia of timorous Pharisees. If it made Whitman draw a transparent veil over some of the more audacious hymns of *Calamus,* the artistic result is perhaps a gain in restraint and suggestion worth the corresponding loss in frank brutality. But the public, whom those frightened critics want to protect, ultimately suffers most. After twenty or thirty years of neglect, during which Longfellow's "Psalm of Life" was bought and recited by millions, the slighted poems of Whitman came into their own. Swinburne and Baudelaire and Zola had in the meanwhile prepared the readers of America to hail the originality of their own revolutionary bard. A new generation arrived which damaged Whitman's fame by worshipping him as a Christ, reading an ecstatic religious meaning where their predecessors had perceived only fleshly obscenity. The true appreciation of the poet as he was, neither angel nor beast, was delayed for another thirty years.[3]

It would be almost too easy to overwhelm American criticism with a catalogue of its past mistakes. The literary atmosphere in a new country was hardly conducive to the elaboration of impar-

---

[3] A volume by William Sloane Kennedy, *The Fight of a Book for the World* (West Yarmouth, Mass.: Stonecroft Press, 1926), has related the story of Whitman's changing fortunes. The worship of Whitman by some English and many French admirers came mostly after 1895. The comparison of the author of *Leaves of Grass* with Christ occurs many times. Mrs. Anne Gilchrist, typical of some pathological disciples, declared (quoted in the story of her life by her son in 1887): "Whitman is, I believe, far more closely akin to Christ than to either Homer or Shakespeare. . . . He takes up the thread where Christ left it." And Richard Le Gallienne, the English poet, declared in 1898: "I consider him the most original man, except Christ, the world has known."

tial esthetic judgments. Some Puritan rigor and moral obsession, the harassing demands of a hard material life, and the absence of any venerable intellectual tradition stood in the way of serene appreciation of art. The consequences of that divorce between the critics and public opinion in America were still felt long after the weakening of the Puritan influence.

It has been noted above that Emerson and Longfellow were far from infallible as judges of literature. James Russell Lowell, of whom Norman Foerster wrote as recently as 1928 in *American Criticism* that "in spite of his faults, he must still be regarded as our most distinguished literary critic," is a very disappointing figure when reread today. He failed to display much shrewdness as a judge either of contemporary American writers or of English authors of the nineteenth century. A poet himself, he uttered only superficial and unappreciative comments on the English romantics such as Shelley, but he saw in A. H. Clough "a man of genius" and announced that his poetry "will one day, perhaps, be found to have been the best utterance in verse of his generation." His 1865 essay on Thoreau is hesitant and only half sympathetic to the author of *Walden*. A specialist in Romance literatures, he wrote no illuminating article on the French or Italian authors of his time. In his letters, he declared Balzac inferior to Charles de Bernard in knowledge of the "great world."

Henry James, who holds an enviable place among the shrewdest critics of the novel, fell short of greatness as a critic of contemporary writers. Let us not blame him for his consistent underrating of American novelists, for instance of Hawthorne in his volume of the "English Men of Letters" series. But while he pondered long over the technical accomplishments of French authors and judged some of them with competence and wisdom, he could not rid himself of the same distaste for open-air robustness and sensuous vitality which astonished his French friends when, at one of the most celebrated gastronomic resorts of provincial France, at Bourg-en-Bresse, spurning the tempting bill of fare and the choicest wines, he once ordered "boiled eggs, bread and butter, and tea." His *French Poets and Novelists* contains a few discerning pages and many more disconcerting ones. James, a sincere admirer of Balzac, could not forgive him for having "no natural sense of morality"; he found him for that reason inferior to Thackeray, George Eliot, and George Sand, who "are haunted by a moral ideal." James, at least, while much too lenient with Charles de Bernard, discerned his weakness and superficiality more decisively than Sainte-Beuve had done. But his essay on Baudelaire betrays the same prejudices then currently displayed by French critics. "He tried to make fine verses on ignoble subjects, and in our opinion he signally failed." Baudelaire was never sincere in his verse; he had only a puerile view of evil. Besides, he admired Edgar Allan Poe! "An enthusiasm for Poe is the mark of a decidedly primitive stage of reflection. . . . Nevertheless, Poe was much the greater charlatan of the two, as well as the greater genius." Far superior to Baudelaire, in Henry James's opinion, was Théophile Gautier, "a man of genius," ranked by the American critic with Molière and Pascal among those men whom the French Academy deemed too great to be numbered among the forty Immortals. The extraordinary fame and influence of a skillful but superficial poet like Gautier in England and America (not only the Imagists, but Ezra Pound and T. S. Eliot have not remained immune from his prestige) is among the surprising cases of overestimation by foreign readers which make the comparative history of literature, if less tragic, as entertaining as the numerous misunderstandings which mark the history of international relations.

One of the least disappointing American critics of the last century is probably William Dean Howells. A self-educated man, he nevertheless acquired a wider perspective than any other critic of his country. The range of his numberless articles included Spanish and Italian writers, French and German ones. He was one of the first enthusiasts on Russian fiction and an intelligent champion of Tolstoi. More than any of his compatriots who write about literature or teach it in colleges, he avoided adopting the provincial prejudices of English writers and he understood that originality in the American novel should lie (in so far as models or precedents are needed) in profiting freely from three or four European literary traditions, and not from one alone. Howells' little book on *Criticism and Fiction* (1891) offers, in its disconnected and unpretentious way, some of the wisest advice that can be given to critics. Howells, however, wrote far too much and often too superficially. Realism was his creed, and he played a useful part in converting his public to it; but too much benevolence, a timid fear of morbidity and immorality, a genteel tone of familiar conversation prevented him, in his mature and older years, from remaining open to the literature of his contemporaries and from reaching true originality in his critical dicta, in his discoveries of the new, or in his revaluations of the old.

The faults of William Lyon Phelps are doubtless similar. This great teacher was a pioneer in his day; he created a sensation when he advocated the study of recent works as indispensable to a scholar and teacher of literature or when, to the dismay of thousands of timid souls, he announced at Yale College, in the late Nineties, a course on "modern novels." The services he rendered to literature, through a contagious love for life and for some books, have been immense. The mere mention of a new work in one of his lectures or one of his "As I Like It" columns could, and repeatedly did, make a best seller overnight. It would be easy, however, and uncharitable, to cull from W. L. Phelps's works statements and assertions which will arouse the satirical ire of iconoclasts of the future: Maeterlinck hailed as "the foremost living dramatist"; Henry James declared to be "as a novelist, quite inferior to W. D. Howells"; Hardy's *A Pair of Blue Eyes* "a greater world-drama than *The Dynasts*"; *Jude the Obscure* branded as Hardy's worst novel, "both from the moral and from the esthetic point of view"; William De Morgan and Alfred Ollivant respectfully ranked among England's good novelists.[4] H. L. Mencken has already taken the critic to task for omitting Dreiser from his *Advance of the English Novel*, while reserving his admiration for the "genius" of O. Henry. W. L. Phelps, at

---

[4] For these statements, see William Lyon Phelps, *Essays on Modern Novelists* (New York: Macmillan, 1910).

any rate, could not be accused of lacking in boldness. In *Scrib-ner's Magazine* of October 1930, he gave a list of the hundred best novels, running the risk, which more prudent and less confi-dent critics would have avoided, of including fifty fourth-rate works along with fifty masterpieces. The best English and Amer-ican novelists of 1900–1930 are indeed absent, while *Lorna Doone* and *The Bridge of San Luis Rey* are among the chosen hundred world masterpieces; Stevenson is represented by three novels, Meredith by one only. Alexandre Dumas leads all French novelists with four titles, Balzac wins two mentions, Flaubert must be satisfied with one, and not only Loti, Proust, Gide, Mauriac, but Stendhal himself are ignored altogether, while Anatole France is rewarded with one "novel," *Sylvestre Bon-nard*—a strange choice, to say the least.

The present century has witnessed a sudden and remarkable flowering of American criticism. Many hopes were aroused in the first decade by the seriousness of the Humanists and Neo-Classicists, by Spingarn's hailing of the promised land (the new criticism inspired by Croce), by high-spirited lovers of music, beer, and lively books, like Huneker, even by ponderous literary historians thoroughly trained in the most desiccating tradition of German seminars. We must confess that those hopes have been largely disappointed. W. C. Brownell hardly bears rereading to-day, either in his well-meant and superficial search for standards or in his urbane essays on French traits. (In 1909, he completely misjudged Baudelaire in his essay on Poe.) Paul Elmer More tried most touchingly to understand Nietzsche, Proust, and Joyce; he failed. Like Irving Babbitt, although more gracefully, he opposed all that was vital in his times and in his country and distrusted modern artistic innovations *in toto*. Few books have more dog-matic vigor and more resolute conviction than Babbitt's *Rousseau and Romanticism* and *Masters of Modern French Criticism*. Few propose a more deliberately distorted interpretation of modern literature than the former or a more uncritical view of criticism than the latter, which deifies Sainte-Beuve while omitting his glaring failures, takes seriously a Doudan, a Nisard, bows to the mediocrity of a Schérer, and implicitly advocates the traditional and dogmatic kind of criticism which refuses to serve and to guide the literature of its own times, preferring to assert its own infallibility.

Critical talents have abounded since 1930: Mencken, George Jean Nathan, Carl Van Doren, Ludwig Lewisohn in his serene and Goethean moods; all have loved and served literature. Others seem to have been perversely bent upon not fulfilling the even greater promises which their early careers held out: Joseph Wood Krutch, Waldo Frank, Malcolm Cowley, or Van Wyck Brooks. The list of great reinterpreters of literature in American universities, with Cleanth Brooks, Robert Penn Warren, Irving Howe, Joseph Frank, Allen Tate, and Lionel Trilling in the forefront, is an impressive one. Sociological and Marxist criticism proved as much of a blind alley for American enthusiasts as semantic and pseudo-scientific criticism proves today for others. The honor of being the foremost American critic of the third quarter of our century, which was once Edmund Wilson's, may have been won from him by a competitor who combines lucidity and depth, taste and vitality, erudition and courage—Alfred Kazin.

But few of those eminent critics have been discoverers and interpreters of the literature of their contemporaries. American authors suffer from the bitterest isolation: the book-buying public is limited; reviews, weeklies, and daily papers grant very little space, if any, to literature as such, and accept literary talents only in so far as they are willing or able to turn into journalists and reporters, to discourse on social or political problems, and to present their profession as a pompous service to the public welfare. It is taken for granted by most readers that book reviews are meretricious and unreliable, and none but naïve provincial clubwomen would go to them for a conscientious appraisal of literary works. In the serious discussion of books publishers take little interest, since it will hardly affect the sale of a new volume, once that volume has been lavishly advertised, adopted by some monthly selecting agency, or transformed and deformed for the screen. Few informed readers would rely upon the Sunday "Book Reviews" of our newspapers, apparently meant for tolerant and somnolent after-dinner reading, when any frank and severe criticism would seem like a breach of the Sabbath peace. In no great country today is literature granted such restricted space or treated so cursorily as in the leading monthly magazines of America and even in the quarterly reviews sponsored by great universities. Wealthy patrons are readily found to protect music, painting, dancing, to back any sociological experiment or any scheme for bettering the world, to support any medical theory or advance any educational venture: they will hardly ever condescend to aid a poet, a novelist, or a thinker. They will not even buy his books and create, through the powerful medium of snobbism, the encouraging and stimulating climate in which American men of letters might mature their thought or perfect their art. In no great country does one cause the same embarrassment (as if good manners were suddenly violated and the honor of the land smirched) as in provincial circles of America when one dares question the quality of a universal best seller acclaimed by newspapers and advertisers.

Yet, since 1910, and especially since the First World War, America has entered upon a literary era equalled only once in her history: in 1840–1860, when Emerson, Poe, Hawthorne, Melville, Thoreau, and Whitman gave American literature its finest claims to a world Hall of Fame. Any traveller in Europe or South America may have observed that the opinion and the picture of the United States formed by cultured classes in those countries are derived from contemporary American books even more than from films. The importance of Dreiser, Sinclair Lewis, Sherwood Anderson, Dos Passos, Hemingway, Steinbeck, Faulkner, that of O'Neill, of Robinson Jeffers, of Frost, even of an able interpreter of American and foreign cultures like Waldo Frank, has been great in the world, and cannot be measured by figures of sales. But the American elite seems to be uninterested in her writers, or to be half ashamed of them. One would have had to search minutely, and often vainly, through the American periodicals of

1925–1945 to find a comprehensive, well-balanced study of Eugene O'Neill or of Dos Passos, of William Faulkner or of Thomas Wolfe, of American poetry, architecture, painting, philosophy.

Among the writers just mentioned, some have true greatness; others are mere talents of the hour. There are doubtless others still, whom the public does not even know by name, who one day will be judged to have been the highest representatives of our civilization and perhaps its most faithful portrayers. Our utterances on *Gone with the Wind,* or on Pearl Buck's novels, our praise of *The Grapes of Wrath* or of *Manhattan Transfer* as "timeless books," "masterpieces for the ages," will make our grandchildren smile at our erratic or corrupt taste. Among the several books of any of those authors, the same sharp differences will be drawn by our successors that we make today among the works of Hawthorne, Dickens, or Hardy. Are we unable to perceive them now? Some plays by O'Neill are the best that have been written in English in the present century (*Desire under the Elms, Lazarus Laughed, Mourning Becomes Electra*); some (*Dynamo,* for instance) fall far beneath that standard. Cannot we, in spite of the deafening publicity, sift out today what posterity will have to sift out tomorrow? In 1940, a universal chorus of so-called "critical" reviews proclaimed *For Whom the Bell Tolls* far superior to Hemingway's previous works, a classic of the American novel, "written with delicacy" (the *Atlantic Monthly,* November 1940), "one of the major novels of American literature" (*The New York Times,* October 20, 1940), "a book which people are going to be reading . . . so long a time perhaps that the book may eventually be preceded by an introduction . . . recalling how this hideous Spanish curtain-raiser [of the greater drama] came about . . ." (the *Yale Review,* Winter 1941). Everyone accepted as a truism that the new novel was unquestionably superior to *A Farewell to Arms.* Was it indeed? One may surely find more psychology, a more skillfully plotted drama, more humanity, and a more natural style in the former novel of love and war published in 1929, and have a suspicion that the direct vigor of Hemingway's short stories may well outlive

For Whom the Bell Tolls. In 1939, *The Grapes of Wrath* was similarly hailed (in the *Atlantic Monthly* of May, in the *Saturday Review of Literature* of April 15) as "the summation of eighteen years of realism," "the epitome" of all the former books by Steinbeck. For a few weeks, commentators, critics, and readers were almost unanimous in glorifying a masterpiece of the American novel.[5] Such unanimity in praise is the most deceptive homage a new book can receive. Six months elapse, and no one dreams of discussing the recent masterpiece any more, or even of reading it. New masterpieces, also unanimously eulogized, have appeared in the meanwhile, and why discuss, that is to say keep alive, a work which everyone agreed was a book for posterity? Quietly, advertisers, reviewers, and readers let it sink off the list of best sellers straight into oblivion.

The best service which could be rendered authors and publishers would consist, not in vain choruses of praise which no critical reader takes at their face value, but in intelligent and discriminating comparisons with the former works of the author considered, with those of other authors, American or foreign, in a wise and relative estimate of merits and of deficiencies. A detached article on Steinbeck in one of the leading reviews, analyzing the development of the novelist in retrospect and distinguishing severely between the lamentable cheapness of *The Moon Is Down* and the moving and restrained sentimentality of *Of Mice and Men*, or the green and fragrant spontaneity of *The Pastures of Heaven* and *The Red Pony*, would have been more worthy of a novelist who might have risen to be a leading figure in his literary generation. It is regrettable, in a country where literature now has won its place among the great literatures of the world, where the public is eager for guidance and respectful of the opinion of "experts," that so few independent and clear-sighted critics should be concerned with doing their duty to contemporary productions.

[5] Two weeklies, however, protested and pointed out some of the artistic weaknesses of the novel, *The Nation* of April 15, 1939, and *The New Republic* of May 3.

Alone among the important literatures of the world, modern German literature was born of criticism. Herder, Lessing, and the Schlegel brothers are the perfect examples of critics who sowed esthetic ideas about them and created an atmosphere favorable to literary creation. Their main task was not the judgment of their contemporaries, for few existed then in Germany who were worth judging. With their advocacy of folk poetry, of Hebraic or Hellenic "primitive" literature, of Shakespeare or of Calderón, we are not concerned here. In the last hundred years, Germany has multiplied models of minute philological research or of ambitious and penetrating literary history (Friedrich Gundolf, Ernst Robert Curtius, Walter Benjamin); but criticism of individual recent works has often been stifled under ponderous scholarship or pretentious philosophical disquisition.

The greatest of German critics is probably also the greatest of German writers: Goethe. In him a century of admirers has celebrated a poet of the very first order who was also the greatest prose writer of his country, a "Faustian" and "daemonic" creator who was at the same time a critical genius. The breadth of his intelligence was unequalled in the age between Voltaire and Renan. To the very end of his long life, he retained the elasticity of youth. As late as 1830 he could burst into flame over a scientific controversy which had opposed Geoffroy Saint-Hilaire to Cuvier at the Paris Academy of Sciences; the patriarch who, fifty years earlier, had set Europe ablaze with his *Werther* was, almost on his deathbed, avidly reading the books and gazing at the portraits of the young French romantics.

Yet how often did this universal genius fail to understand the greatness which surrounded him! He refused his admiration to the German metaphysicians, Hegel, Fichte, Schelling, Schopenhauer, thanks to whom the early nineteenth century lives as one of the greatest eras of philosophical speculation. He refused to understand and, worse still, to encourage or to aid the young romantics, Novalis, Kleist, Hölderlin, who appealed to what the early Goethe had been, to the champion of the "Sturm und

Drang." In matters of art and archeology, Goethe's taste was no more discriminating than that of his contemporaries; even on the architecture and sculpture of the ancients (Roman or Sicilian, since that lover of Greece never dared face the discomfort of travel in Greece), Goethe's oft-quoted pronouncements amount to little more than trite platitudes. In music, he appreciated Glück, Mozart, and Mendelssohn; but it took him several years to accept and praise Schubert's music for his own "Erlkönig." He disliked Weber and showed it when they met in 1825. His attitude toward Beethoven, which has been described by Romain Rolland,[6] was that of a shameless Philistine. It might have been expected that Goethe would be frightened by Beethoven's stormy inspiration; it was a challenge to his serene placidity of mind and bourgeois insistence on security and hierarchy. For months he was not even interested in hearing that the composer had written the score for *Egmont,* and had produced it in Vienna. The voluminous works of Goethe contain one reference to the greatest musical genius of the century: an "honorable mention," in 1828, of a religious service celebrated in Prague in honor of Beethoven.

On the English and French writers of his age, many of Goethe's judgments are likewise disconcerting and teach us humility, if nothing more. He actually refused to appreciate Shelley, whose translation of some scenes of *Faust* is the most poetical ever given in English, and, on November 20, 1824, he spoke slightingly to Chancellor Müller of the English genius who had died two years before. He showed no interest in the English poet most closely akin to Germany, Coleridge. Crabb Robinson related in 1829 that, when he tried to read some poems of Coleridge to the author of *Faust,* "Goethe damned them with faint praise." On the other hand, he raised Byron on a pedestal with the same undiscriminating enthusiasm displayed by other continental contemporaries of the poet. *The Corsair* and *Lara* were masterpieces in his eyes; so was *Marino Faliero* (letter of June 18, 1829, to Count Reinhard); in *Don Juan,* a fine poem, no doubt, he saw

---

[6] Romain Rolland, *Goethe and Beethoven* (New York: Harper, 1931).

"the work of a boundless genius"; on October 2, 1823, he confessed to Chancellor Müller that Byron was the only poet he ranked as his equal. "What I call invention has never, in any man, seemed to me greater than in Byron," Goethe told Eckermann on February 24, 1825; and on November 8, 1826, he added: "If it were not for his hypochondriacal and negative attitude, he would be as great as Shakespeare and the ancients."

Goethe proved, on the whole, a keener judge of French than of English literature; he probably understood Molière and even Racine more fully than he did Shakespeare. (Saintsbury remarked that the author of *Wilhelm Meister* never really felt Shakespeare as *a poet*, and would not have spoken differently of Hamlet if he had read the play in translation.) Almost immediately, with more insight than most Frenchmen, he divined the genius of Victor Hugo (in his conversations with Eckermann, January 4, 1827); no one would blame the Olympian octogenarian for being dismayed by *Hernani* and by *Notre Dame de Paris*, "the most abominable work ever written" (Eckermann, June 27, 1813). The sedate courtier in Goethe had become more than timid in politics and, in the last year of his life, refused to open the *Globe*, up to then his favorite source of information about France, which had become too liberal for his taste, and placed politics above literature. As early as 1818 (in a letter to Zelter of March 8), Goethe discovered with extraordinary insight the talent of an unknown French writer, Stendhal, from a reading of an early and imperfect work, *Rome, Naples et Florence;* a few weeks before his death, the author of *Elective Affinities* was among the very few readers who appreciated *Le Rouge et le Noir*, "the best work by Stendhal, although a few feminine characters are somewhat too romantic."

Nevertheless, the same Goethe who hailed the nascent talents of Victor Hugo, Stendhal, Mérimée, lavished equally warm praise on very secondary French writers who then seemed the equals of the greatest: Casimir Delavigne for instance, a most mediocre pseudo-classical versifier, whom Goethe unhesitatingly ranked with Lamartine and Victor Hugo (to Eckermann, Janu-

ary 4, 1827); Guizot, whom he praised unweariedly (to Eckermann on April 3, 1829; again on April 6, "I know of no historian
whose views are deeper or broader than his," and once again on
February 3, 1830). Villemain and Cousin he also overrated. Of
those disconcerting mistakes, of which Goethe was just as guilty
as the most obtuse among his contemporaries, the strangest is
without any doubt his appreciation of Béranger. Eckermann's
faithful records of Goethe's words repeatedly sing the praise of
the French "chansonnier": on June 2, 1823; on January 21, 1827,
when Goethe lauds "his great talent"; on January 29, 1827, when
he adds: "His songs are perfect and the best of their kind. . . .
Béranger always reminds me of Horace and Hafiz." A French
visitor, Ampère, who called on Goethe on May 4, 1827, reported: "He knows Béranger's songs by heart." For a brief
while, after Béranger had published the fourth volume of his
Chansons (1828) and was imprisoned for nine months, the conservative in Goethe took fright and censured the French liberal
who had dared attack King and State (to Eckermann, April 2,
1829). Soon, however, on March 14, 1830, Goethe returned to his
admiration and celebrated in Béranger the rare combination of
the finest qualities "Witz, Geist, Ironie und Persiflage," to which
he added cordiality, naïvety, and grace.

Sainte-Beuve was indeed justified when, in 1865 (in the third
volume of his new series of *Lundis*, pp. 303–304), he protested
against the veneration which surrounded every utterance, however pompous or platitudinous, of the great Goethe: "His taste
was uncertain and questionable as concerned French literature."
Goethe's influence on criticism has been occasionally far from
beneficent, for example, when Matthew Arnold took a page from
Goethe's commonplace book and dismissed works of eternal
beauty with the curt Goethean pronouncement: "it can help us
no more." On the other hand, Swinburne's irritation, which made
him call Goethe "the world's worst critic," is of course ridicu-
lously unjust. My summary remarks on Goethe as a judge of
contemporary literature were meant in no way to belittle a great
genius. That a universal mind, always eager for new forms of

beauty, could have at times adopted such a disconcerting perspective when judging works by younger foreign writers of whom he had nothing to fear, was worth mentioning in an attempt to elucidate some of the baffling enigmas of criticism.

CHAPTER III

France

IF there is one province in which other nations have unhesitatingly conceded primacy to France—sometimes with a readiness which only half concealed, on their part, some contempt for an unimaginative and secondary talent—that province is literary criticism. Certainly, no country can boast, through the last four centuries, of so large a number of arbiters of taste, appraisers, and theorists. Several among those critics have risen to striking eminence in a genre which counts fewer acknowledged talents than any other: Boileau, Fénelon, Diderot, Sainte-Beuve, Baudelaire, Taine, Brunetière, Faguet, not to include their successors in the present century. The very climate of the French capital seems to incline to intellectual analysis and literary discussion. On the front page of a French daily paper, the review of a recent volume by a fashionable author, the granting of a coveted literary prize, even the particular nuances with which an actor has delivered some famous tirade, rival in interest the thrilling details of a boxing match, a sensational Hollywood divorce, or the refined French pastime called the "crime passionnel," in which a jealous woman cuts up, for instance, her murdered lover into neat fragments and ships the whole in a trunk to some provincial railway station. In the humblest bookselling establishment, one may hear the latest book discussed, often with insight and competence. No wonder that foreigners have defined the French as a public of connoisseurs, capable of perceiving subtle shades and arguing on matters of style which remain a closed book to other nations. Alas! if the French can boast of a refined taste, they are also sometimes afflicted with an emasculated or negative variety of it, called "good taste," which powerful innovations consistently repel.

It would appear that the prevalence of "salons" and literary "cénacles" in France, and the cafés bubbling with sparkling words as well as sparkling wine, should have developed not only an intense interest in letters but a close communion between French artists and their public. One would expect writers, on the banks of the Seine if nowhere else in the world, to be appraised by trained critics and assigned by unerring connoisseurs to the rank which posterity will confirm.

Such has not been the case. No great writers or artists have been so tenaciously opposed, so vehemently insulted (or, worse still, so placidly ignored), as Stendhal, Flaubert, Balzac, Baudelaire, Gobineau, Rimbaud, Valéry, Claudel, Proust, Péguy— unless it be French musicians from Berlioz to César Franck and French painters from Delacroix to Courbet and Cézanne.

Was there, at least, a blessed era when things were otherwise? French literature once went through a classical period, which has since been nostalgically mourned by all who censure the turbulence of modern times and the universal lack of standards. Most Frenchmen have at some time envied the stately unity of their country under Louis XIV, the cultivated taste of a restricted public, which knew how to encourage sane and true talents, laughed with Molière at the "précieuses," with Racine at the swaggering braggarts of the old theatre, and with Boileau at pedantry and affectation.

In thus imagining the seventeenth century in France as an era of exquisite taste, all of us may well have labored under a delusion. The refined courtier of Versailles or the well-read Parisian, in 1675 or 1690, asked to name the ten greatest literary talents of his times, would very probably have mentioned neither Pascal nor La Fontaine, neither La Rochefoucauld, Bossuet, nor La Bruyère (neither Mme de Sévigné nor Saint-Simon, whose works were then unpublished or not yet written). It is even doubtful whether he would have included in his list Molière, Racine, and Boileau. To the average well-informed Frenchman, many other names then seemed at least as eminent as those posterity has confirmed: Chapelain, for example, and Charpentier. Scarron was often preferred to Molière, Quinault to Racine, Benserade to La Fontaine, and Massillon to Bossuet. In the aristocratic seventeenth century as in the democratic twentieth, the loudest applause of audiences did not always go to the best plays. We have no precise figures of performances in France before the founding of the Comédie Française, in 1680; but we know from contemporary witnesses that, between 1650 and 1690, the most successful plays were *Timocrate* and *La Devineresse* by Thomas Corneille, *Le Mercure galant* and *Ésope à la ville* by Boursault, *Andromède* by Pierre Corneille (in the modern opinion one of his slightest plays), and Molière's *Le Malade imaginaire*. The list of plays coldly received by the same public is no less revealing: it includes such masterpieces as *L'Avare*, *Le Bourgeois Gentilhomme*, *Les Femmes savantes*, and *Le Misanthrope*, Racine's *Britannicus*, *Bajazet*, and *Phèdre*, Pierre Corneille's *Don Sanche*, far superior to his *Andromède*.[1]

It is of course dangerous to gauge merit by the number of copies sold or by box-office receipts. But even the best minds of the classical period, whose judgment carried much weight in an age when newspapers were in their infancy and critics were few,

---

[1] Remy de Gourmont has already commented on these discrepancies between the opinion of classical audiences and that of "posterity" (*Promenades littéraires*, 2nd ser. [Mercure de France, 1913]). In a scholarly treatise, *Histoire de la littérature française classique* (A. Colin, 1940), Professor Daniel Mornet has added much information on the reception of French classical writers by contemporary opinion. Quinault and Campistron, for instance, were long taken to be worthy rivals of Racine. Pradon's *Phèdre*, written in hasty and unfair competition with Racine's masterpiece, enjoyed a fair vogue and one performance was attended by the King. Toward the end of the seventeenth century one of the best English essayists, and among the best-informed on French literature—though not indeed a very shrewd literary critic—named three "great" French writers worthy of succeeding to Rabelais and Montaigne: Voiture, La Rochefoucauld, and Bussy-Rabutin (but neither Corneille nor Racine nor Molière nor Pascal). It is true that the same Sir William Temple, also in *Of Ancient and Modern Learning*, listed as the three "greatest wits" of England Sir Philip Sidney, Bacon, and Selden (a jurist and antiquarian of some renown in his times), not Spenser, Marlowe, or Shakespeare.

display the same confusion of opinion. To be sure, a few clear-sighted observers proved right from the first day, or anticipated the present judgment, which is what we call having been right. A scholar, Le Nain de Tillemont, perceived the unequalled genius of Pascal and wrote to M. Périer *jeune* on reading the *Pensées:* "This last work has surpassed what I expected from a mind which I considered the greatest in our century." On the other hand, Saint-Évremond, a keen and refined critic, who should have acquired an unusually fair perspective during his long years of exile in England, remained obstinately blind to the greatness of Racine. Mme de Sévigné, as witty and subtle a woman as ever wrote, disliked most of Racine's tragedies after *Andromaque.* The only merit of *Bajazet* seemed to her to lie in the acting of La Champmeslé; she even boldly prophesied that the vogue of those love dramas would not outlast the fashion of drinking coffee, then recently imported from Arabia, which was to be, in her opinion, a short-lived rage.

Donneau de Visé, a dramatist of some repute and a journalist whose taste was typical of the average Parisian, praised *Le Mis-anthrope*, but failed to appreciate Molière's *L'École des femmes* and Racine's *Mithridate.* Ménage, who was then considered not the pedant some readers of Molière might imagine, but a re-spectable scholar whose utterances impressed the public, saw in Perrault (his opponent in the quarrel of ancients and moderns) "one of our best poets." La Bruyère was widely attacked, by Donneau de Visé, D'Olivet, Charpentier, and, in oft-quoted and bitterly hostile lines, by Bonaventure d'Argonne. It is true that his *Caractères* were not innocent of polemics, and their technique then seemed new and provoking. A shrewd contemporary reader of *La Princesse de Clèves,* Valincour, proved far more severe to that novel than we have been since. Finally, Bayle's numerous critical blunders are well known: they affect his judgment on ancient literatures as well as his opinions on his contemporaries. Pradon's *Phèdre* he ranks on the same plane as Racine's. The abbé Montfaucon de Villars (known as the Count of Gabalis) is, in his eyes, the equal of Bossuet; *Circé,* a forgotten lyrical drama by the lesser Corneille (Thomas), is declared worthy of Racine's *Iphigénie*. Bayle's *Dictionary* is full of such surprising judgments.

Many more instances of mistaken criticism could be quoted from all periods of the seventeenth century. Scudéry's strictures on *Le Cid* are the most famous of all. But a fuller survey of such mistakes would be tedious, and it would be unfair if one left out the contrary cases, in which a contemporary displayed penetration and foresight in the presence of a new work.

Such cases of shrewd foresight were few in the classical age of France. Surprisingly little contemporary criticism of Racine, La Fontaine, Molière has any value to us moderns. Yet if one man in the whole range of the history of criticism proved well-nigh infallible in his judgment on contemporary writers, that man is Boileau (and his close rival would be Baudelaire, who, strangely enough, has also been linked with Boileau as a poet). Around 1665, Boileau, young and unknown, stepped on the literary scene in Paris, assailed the authors who were then fashionable and all-powerful, chided the public for admiring them, and with marvellous discernment announced that the true talents of the age were Molière, Racine, and La Fontaine, then little more than promising and independent but obscure writers. Boileau is a peremptory and dogmatic critic. He seldom explains on what grounds he based his literary decrees. He has come down to us as a severe schoolteacher, judging from traditional rules. In truth, he felt literature, and instinct was his safest guide. In the letters of his old age, among much of the dry and impersonal detail common to seventeenth-century epistles, one occasionally finds a terse and definitive estimate of *Télémaque* (to Brossette, November 10, 1699, or Pascal (to Brossette, May 15, 1705). Boileau proved clearsighted enough to declare to D'Olivet that "Mme de La Fayette was the Frenchwoman who had the best mind and wrote most excellently." In his ninth "Satire," he displayed extraordinary lucidity in rejecting the authors then at the height of fashion, whom we have since and, it seems, forever, ranked as Boileau taught us to. Finally at a time when the public was still very uncertain about which were Corneille's masterpieces and which his "minor" tragedies (just as many of us are uncertain today when asked to pick Mauriac's or Lawrence's "chief novels," Claudel's or O'Neill's best dramas), Boileau was enough of a prophet to decide which among the thirty or so plays by the father of French tragedy would survive. La Bruyère, as late as 1688, was less discriminating and would not choose between *Horace* and *Oedipe* or, as Voltaire puts it, between gold and lead.

Even so, it would be excessive to assert that Boileau always and infallibly predicted our present judgment on the seventeenth century or, as skeptics would say, that posterity, dazzled by Boileau's prestige, has obediently followed all his decrees. Today we should widen the gap Boileau made between the great writers of the French classical period and the secondary talents. Was he, like all contemporary observers, too lenient toward the lesser lights, or are we unfair in our neglect of them? This question, a most disturbing one for our indolent faith in the infallibility of posterity, will recur several times in the present work. Once for all, we have decided that Bourdaloue is secondary as a preacher, and thus spared ourselves the trouble of reading his *Sermons*. But Boileau (and many excellent contemporary minds with him) ranked Bourdaloue extremely high. La Fontaine seems to us to be head and shoulders above all playful, "precious," and lyrical poets of his times. Boileau admired La Fontaine and, as early as 1665, he praised his *Joconde;* yet he mentions Voiture, Sarrasin, Segrais, the Countess de La Suze in the same breath as La Fontaine in his famous letter of reconciliation to Perrault. In the same letter written in 1700, that is with a perspective of many years after the publication of their works, Boileau ranks Descartes along with Arnauld and Nicole, two moralists whom one finds scarcely original and well-nigh unreadable.

The eighteenth century was the golden age of esthetic discussion in France. From the abbé Du Bos, Fontenelle, and Trublet, to Diderot, innumerable philosophical minds stirred up theoreti-

cal ideas about feeling, taste, beauty, dramatic poetry, the bourgeois drama, tradition in literature, cosmopolitanism, and so on.
Yet, if one excepts, as one always must, the universal Diderot, in
whom Saintsbury rightly saw a great impressionist critic, true
literary criticism of outstanding value is rare in that age. The
extreme refinement of the intellect and the unequalled mental
agility of that century have not endowed judgment of contemporary literature with any clearer penetration than was possessed
by, say, the more emotional romantic period. Several of the contemporary pronouncements on *Manon Lescaut, L'Esprit des lois,
Candide, Le Barbier de Séville, La Nouvelle Héloïse, Les
Liaisons dangereuses* have been conveniently collected in a volume by J. G. Prodhomme, *Vingt Chefs-d'oeuvre jugés par leurs
contemporains* (Stock, 1930). They are marked by childish levity
(even when signed Mme du Deffand, Mme de Genlis, or Voltaire) or by polemical partisanship. Then as now, in France as
elsewhere, the charge of immorality greeted new novels: *Manon
Lescaut, Candide, La Nouvelle Héloïse.*

No useful purpose would be served by listing the varied mistakes, due to obstinacy, blindness, dogmatism, which one comes
across in Fréron and Marmontel, the abbé Batteux and La
Harpe, and the literary contributors to *L'Encyclopédie.* Few
important books of the eighteenth century went unnoticed, ex-
cepting those which, like Diderot's and Voltaire's, were published
anonymously or not published until years later. Though the
scope and significance of *Le Contrat social* were not perceived by
contemporary readers, that was not a case of unacknowledged
literary merit.

Limiting ourselves to the nimblest and most acute intellect of
the period, that of Voltaire, we are surprised at the number of
erratic judgments he expressed on his contemporaries, while he
proved, whenever prejudice or partisanship did not obscure his
vision, a splendid critic of past literature. The novelist of *La
Princesse de Babylone* and *Zadig* (realizing perhaps with some
jealousy that he could never endow a single feminine character
with life) displayed little understanding of *Manon Lescaut.* His

comments on *L'Esprit des lois* are tainted with acrimonious mean-
ness. He missed the greatness of the work and never tired of
ridiculing Montesquieu's theory of climate. He was unjust or
blind to Sedaine, Marmontel, Helvétius, Chamfort, and, which is
more deplorable, to Buffon's philosophical poetry in prose and
Diderot's metaphysical imagination.

Of course he hated Rousseau and had, or thought he had, good
reason to hate him. Even so, it is difficult to discover any sem-
blance of an excuse for the foul and foolish manner in which he
lashed *La Nouvelle Héloïse,* under the signature of Marquis de
Ximénez. On the other hand, the modern critic is bewildered by
Voltaire's high praise of Saint-Lambert's *Les Saisons,* not to mention his hyperbolic eulogy of Delille, whom he seems, quite sincerely, to have admired as a very great poet. On March 4, 1771,
eager to serve "the French Virgil," he wrote to his colleagues of
the French Academy: "The poem of the *Seasons* and the translation of the *Georgics* are in my opinion the two best poems which
have honored France since Boileau's *Art poétique.*" Several times
(writing to La Touraille on January 19, 1767, to D'Argental on
December 30, 1773, to La Harpe himself on April 23, 1770),
Voltaire bestowed upon La Harpe such praise as must make us
suspicious of the quality of Voltairian taste. Indeed, the universal
admiration which for decades surrounded Voltaire's tragedies,
the unpoetical platitudes of his *Discours sur l'homme* and Delille's
Georgics [2] must fill us with anxious doubts on the validity of
universal contemporary agreement in questions of taste. Our
irresistible reaction as moderns is that, even for its own time and
with due allowance for changing esthetic values, those works
were bad poetry and extolling them was poor criticism.

In the nineteenth century, literary quarrels grew in number
and in fierceness. The shattering of the structure of rules and
conventions built by Classicism favored free esthetic discussion.

[2] Even in the early nineteenth century, Joubert, much lauded by Matthew Arnold and alternately a very keen and a partial or blind critic,
ranked Delille far above Milton.

Freedom in art was proclaimed the only law; personality was considered the most valuable asset of an artist, and originality, often strained or farfetched, was praised above all other merits. After the French Revolution, the romantic revolt and the rapid growth of the reading public made it customary for authors deliberately to antagonize a considerable portion of their audience. They repeatedly and openly professed their contempt for buyers and readers of their books. Critics, however, jumped to the rescue of the public, and every self-respecting French author or artist has had the honor of being called criminal, poisoner of souls, murderer of morality, corrupter of youth, demoralizer of society, bolshevik of art.

Such abuse should not be taken too tragically, at least in Latin countries, or even in Ibsen's Scandinavia or in the England of Shaw, Joyce, and D. H. Lawrence. A review of a few typical cases of French misjudgment on important modern works will complete the historical foundation on which we hope to establish our conclusions.

In 1820 Lamartine's *Méditations* were, after Chateaubriand's *Génie du christianisme*, the second huge literary success of the century. Of all the romantic volumes of poetry, they were the least revolutionary, the least objectionable, in theme and manner, to readers steeped in classical or pseudo-classical tradition. The general public was more enthusiastically responsive to that poetry than the critics. Gustave Lanson, who studied the genesis, history, and fortune of the *Méditations* with scholarly thoroughness, proved the point beyond doubt. More disconcertingly still, the critics who then praised the new volume praised it as religious or royalist poetry almost exclusively, and not at all for the qualities that we find in it today; when they ventured to be more precise and picked a few pieces for special eulogy, they hit upon the least original in the volume. To "L'Isolement," a favorite of all anthologies of French verse today, the contemporaries preferred "Le Golfe de Baïa." Several critics of repute bestowed their warmest compliments on the "Ode à la gloire," dedicated to the Portuguese poet Manoël, probably the most conventional in the whole volume. Modern readers opening the book will fix instinctively on "Le Vallon," "Le Lac," "L'Automne." When the *Méditations* appeared, a very precocious young poet and lover of poetry chose six titles for especial praise; they are the very ones we should pick today as the worst: "Le Souvenir," "L'Homme," "Dieu," "La Poésie sacrée," "La Semaine sainte," "L'Invocation." The name of that young man was Victor Hugo. Stendhal, to be sure, was no expert on poetry since verse was for him, according to one of his sallies in *De l'Amour*, a mnemonic device; on December 29, 1821, he inserted a short dialogue in a letter to Romain Colomb. In the course of a conversation with an imaginary American he listed, apparently on the same plane, five French poets worthy of being mentioned next to Béranger. They were Baour-Lormian, Lamartine, Chênedollé, Géraud, De Vigny. Even a few years later, in the *Globe* of 1825, a respected and discerning critic, Charles de Rémusat, expressed the general contemporary opinion of connoisseurs on "the present state of French poetry": "Three poets are in the forefront today: Lamartine, Béranger, and Casimir Delavigne." Of the three, he added, the last-named is the most promising for the future.

A tradition, which will bear challenging, presents Alfred de Vigny as the most philosophical of the French romantic poets, hence as a deep and obscure writer. It is true that he lived in a proud isolation, and may therefore have been unfairly treated by contemporary critics. But we shall choose Victor Hugo as a more representative example. Few geniuses were happier and healthier, few were more in sympathy with their countrymen and with the great democratic and humanitarian hopes of their century. Yet Hugo, the "sonorous echo" of his century, was among the most bitterly attacked and the most widely misunderstood of writers. It took no less than fifty years for critics and anthologists to reverse the judgment of his contemporaries and to hail the later Hugo (in his works written after 1843, in his visionary poems and novels, or in his epic fragments) as vastly superior to the early dramatist and novelist and to the poet of the first six volumes of verse. Scores of eminent critics, from Sainte-Beuve to

Jules Lemaître, who were ready to praise *Les Orientales* or *Les Rayons et les ombres,* smiled condescendingly at Hugo's claims to be a philosophical poet and scoffed at the later *Contemplations* as at a madman's lucubrations.

The history of Hugo's reception by the critics and the public has not yet been systematically written.[3] Many of Hugo's opponents, in his lifetime, were men of striking personality (Armand Carrel, Gustave Planche, Veuillot, Barbey d'Aurevilly), whose attacks make an entertaining record. Their blindness can be explained, if not excused, by political and religious prejudice. Other adversaries of Hugo's early works were established writers, academicians, or successful dramatists whose position was suddenly endangered by romantic innovations. Those critics of Hugo's tempestuous compositions were all the more sincere in their outraged outbursts as their material interests and their literary faith were simultaneously challenged. They appealed to the shades of Boileau and Racine to silence the young iconoclast, and one of them, Baour-Lormian, pathetically exclaimed:

Avec impunité les Hugo font des vers!

These same critics (Viennet, Jay, Alexandre Duval were among the most influential) and many younger ones were especially hurt in their conventional tastes by Hugo's technical and stylistic innovations. It is well known that such matters, like those of grammar and spelling, have always been taken by the French with the same fierce seriousness as they bring to their political and religious quarrels. The young dramatist was threatened with death (and, it seems, was actually though vainly shot at) if he did not withdraw his play *Hernani* from the stage. "Quack," "raving maniac," "carnivorous beast," "Vandal," "Visigoth" were among the compliments then heaped upon him. Worse still, he was accused, along with several young romantics, of being anti-French,

[3] There is a hasty article on the subject by Henri Houssaye in *Les Hommes et les idées* (C. Lévy, 1886); a volume by Albert de Bersaucourt, *Les Pamphlets contre Victor Hugo* (Mercure de France, 1912), provides a few useful details. Remy de Gourmont has a few pages on the subject in the fifth series of his *Promenades littéraires* (Mercure de France, 1913).

of betraying the land of Corneille, Voltaire, and Delille by his praise of the English drama, when the English (said the champions of tradition) were the enemies of yesterday and the rivals of today.

Let it be added that Hugo's powerful personality antagonized many judges; that others were repelled by his private life or his egotism, or nursed a personal grudge against him (Planche, Jules Janin, Sainte-Beuve); finally that a majority of critics praised him, either out of partisanship (the young romantics) or out of sincere admiration for his genius. Whatever the causes may have been, I believe that an impartial study of Hugo's critics would lead to the following conclusions.

As usual, Hugo's contemporaries did not discriminate (and perhaps did not try to discriminate) among the numerous works of the poet, dramatist, and novelist; their preferences, when they ventured to perceive the unequal value of different works, seldom tally with ours. Thus, Hugo's prose-dramas (*Lucrèce Borgia, Marie Tudor, Angelo*) were generally ranked above his verse-dramas, while the latter, redeemed by splendid poetical flights, alone have survived; of all his plays, *Ruy Blas*, the one which we should declare the best, was the most violently attacked by critics and branded as false and insane.

A common charge flung against all his volumes of poetry from the second one on was a familiar one with critics of all times: the author is on the decline, he has not fulfilled the promises of his preceding volume. As early as 1829, with *Les Orientales* (which, while fiercely ridiculed and parodied, enjoyed a great vogue), Hugo was declared to be on the downgrade. The same old story was told by malignant judges when *Les Feuilles d'automne* came out (Hugo is lost; his inspiration has run dry; he has nothing more to say). Again with the *Voix intérieures:* the poet, it was hinted, short of breath and hard pressed for a subject, can now sing only of himself.

When *Les Contemplations* was published, in 1856, after Hugo's long silence, broken only by his satirical wrath against Napoleon III, at least half the critics of repute were seized with Homeric laughter. "This last work calls only for compassion and contempt," wrote Chaudesaigues, a critic who then enjoyed some fame. It was worse than a decline, it was "a case of monstrous dotage," remarked another charitable observer. Hugo reminds one, said a third, "of those drinkers of absinth who have reached the stage where they can swallow pure alcohol." Ever since his youthful *Odes*, he has sunk lower and lower into literary infirmity. Duranty, a champion of realism, wrote a ferocious and complacently foolish article in his periodical, *Le Réalisme* (January 15, 1857). Barbey d'Aurevilly, no mean critic and stylist, opened his commentary on Hugo's lyrical masterpiece, *Les Contemplations*, with the following words:

One must lose no time in discussing *Les Contemplations*, for it is one of those books which must quickly be buried in oblivion. . . . The book is a crushing blow to M. Hugo's memory. . . . From this volume on, M. Hugo exists no more. We must mention his name as that of a dead man. . . . Like Ronsard, within two generations, he will have become unreadable! Nay! after *Les Contemplations*, he is unreadable already, but for some political partisans and a few persons curious of contemporary fame.

Three years later, when *La Légende des siècles* bore witness to Hugo's splendid versatility, a critic described the epic poems as "the pranks of a clown performing his antics." Another one remarked that "a foreigner, even if well advanced in the study of French, will never understand such poems." The huge popular success of *Les Misérables* likewise antagonized envious or hostile men of letters. One of them, pronouncing the novel to be worthless, condescended to praise Hugo as "the benefactor of French paper makers." He diligently calculated how much paper the first edition of the novel had used, and reached the figure of 124,095 meters per copy.

Finally, the modern critic, who delights in deploring the obscurity of twentieth-century poetry, will be mildly surprised to hear that Hugo, like most other romantic poets, was in his time censured for needless obscurity. I shall discuss that topic in a separate chapter. Suffice it to mention that not only "Ce que dit la bouche d'ombre" in *Les Contemplations* (by no means an easy poem) but "Les Pauvres Gens" in *La Légende des siècles* and several poems in *Les Feuilles d'automne* and *Les Orientales* were deemed too obscure for comprehension. As usual, the charge of obscurity was linked with that of decadent madness. Not only *Les Contemplations* but *Les Travailleurs de la mer*, even *Les Orientales*, were branded as violating the most elementary literary morality, and *Hernani* appeared to Armand Carrel as a drama "suitable for the inmates of Bedlam and Charenton"—the latter a famous insane asylum near Paris or, according to our more courteous modern euphemism, a resting-home for the mentally tired.

It is regrettable that no one should yet have undertaken to write a history of Stendhal's reputation and influence. Such a work would be not merely an important achievement of scholarly research, but a revealing chapter in the history of manners. It would trace the slow formation of a cult and of a noble mental attitude, called by the French "le beylisme," which Léon Blum has analyzed with brilliant mastery. The innumerable devotees of Stendhal have preferred minutely exploring the incidents of his private life and sifting the true from the false in the confessions of a man who mixed the two as inextricably as Rousseau and Casanova did in theirs.[4]

Painstaking research among the French periodicals of the first half of the last century would doubtless show that Stendhal was never *entirely* neglected: no writer, not even Shelley, Keats, or Rimbaud, ever was. A few contemporaries even used the words "genius" or "talent" to describe him. But those clearsighted judges were a very small minority, and won little or no attention. The riddle of Stendhal's lack of contemporary reputation remains a baffling one: why did pages such as the battle of Waterloo, the love scenes between Mme de Rênal and Julien Sorel and those, still more original, between Mlle de La Mole and the young up-

---

[4] I acknowledge my debt to a volume by Jean Mélia, *Stendhal et ses commentateurs* (1911), which, while incomplete and somewhat amateurish, provides information about several of Stendhal's critics.

start, the keen analysis of crystallization in *De l'Amour,* produce so little impression on readers who lacked neither independence of mind nor refinement of taste—Mérimée (on the whole more than reserved in his writings on his friend), Hugo, Sainte-Beuve, Flaubert, Doudan, Barbey d'Aurevilly, Brunetière? Are modern readers more attuned to Stendhal's psychology and style? or are they the victims of a collective suggestion when (often perfectly unaware of the Stendhalian cult of Taine, Sarcey, Bourget, Léon Blum, and other devotees) they sincerely and naïvely relish his novels and his numerous autobiographical or critical works?

The scorn or the silence of many contemporary judges is, in this case, all the more disconcerting, as Stendhal was not a brutal or morbid writer, challenging current morality or treating new and bold themes (as Balzac, Baudelaire, Flaubert, and Zola may have seemed to be in their age). His very technique ought not to have surprised readers of Choderlos de Laclos or De Brosses. The man passed as slightly eccentric, but he was liked and he knew how to please. His theme, in *Le Rouge et le Noir* or *Lucien Leuwen,* was the most natural and the most common: the ironical or cynical picture of manners during the French Restoration, with many allusions to political events and a keen psychological analysis reminiscent of both Marivaux and Condillac. Far from being an anti-romantic in a romantic era, Stendhal had taken a leading part in the literary quarrels over Racine and Shakespeare. It was easy to discover, behind his pose, a sentimental dreamer and an idealist in love with love, who should hardly have repelled the readers of Chateaubriand and Alfred de Musset.

The very early works of Stendhal, which are not his most personal, were perhaps the most warmly praised by critics: *Histoire de la peinture en Italie* and *Rome, Naples et Florence.* Then a much more original volume, *De l'Amour,* fell in dead silence. The philosopher Destutt de Tracy, whom at that time Beyle revered as his master, tried to read it and confessed to the author his inability to understand it. *Armance* confounded all the reviewers, with some degree of reason perhaps, since the hero's attitude can be explained only by some secret sexual anomaly. *Le*

Rouge et le Noir was warmly praised by the *Revue de Paris,* and less warmly by Mérimée and Jules Janin; but even the most favorable critics (like Jules Janin in the *Revue Encyclopédique*) were convinced that the success of the volume would be "more brilliant than widespread and lasting." Some years later, at least two great men of letters, Alfred de Vigny and Balzac, acclaimed *La Chartreuse de Parme.*

But in comparison the adverse criticism was overwhelming. Doudan, whose subtle mind sharpened several barren witticisms, wrote to Mme du Parquet on August 23, 1841, about "the stupid novel of *La Chartreuse.* I use the word stupid on trust, for I have never opened it, but the author and other books by him are not unknown to me." He thought Mme Riccoboni far superior to Stendhal. Much later, Victor Hugo replied to Henri Rochefort, who had tried, during his years of exile, to introduce him to *Le Rouge et le Noir:* "I have tried to read it. . . . But how were you ever able to continue beyond the fourth page? you must understand the *patois.* . . . Whenever I try to decipher one sentence in your favorite work, it is as if I were having a tooth pulled." [5] Indeed, to this day, one of the accepted and hackneyed criticisms has been the ridiculous charge that Stendhal could not write or, as professors put it, "had no style"!

As to Sainte-Beuve, few of his *Lundis* are as disappointing as those which he devoted to Stendhal (January 2 and 9, 1854, and a third one, August 18, 1862, which discusses him apropos of Delécluze). To be sure, there were many men of letters on whom Sainte-Beuve vented his venom, either out of personal grudge or sincere dislike; those he could not be expected to judge impartially. There were others who, on account of their romantic frenzy or their declamatory intemperance, offended Sainte-Beuve's taste after he had become a champion of classicism. Rhetoric and bombast, however, were not Stendhal's faults. The man in him appealed to Sainte-Beuve. The truth is that the great critic was incapable of admiring Stendhal; as late as 1857, in his *Causeries du lundi* (XIII, 276), relying on his own direct acquaintance

[5] Henri Rochefort, *Les Aventures de ma vie* (Dupont, 1896), II, 55.

with the novelist of *La Chartreuse de Parme,* he firmly rejected Taine's outspoken admiration for him, which was then spreading among the younger generation.

Sainte-Beuve's inability to appreciate Stendhal has been shared by many conservative critics: Caro, Monselet, Barbey d'Aurevilly, Cuvillier-Fleury, for example. In 1906, Brunetière called *La Chartreuse* "a masterpiece of pretentious boredom," and Augustin Filon said of "that sempiternal and tedious *Chartreuse*": "I do not want the penance of having to read it inflicted on even my worst enemies." Such bitter hostility to a novel over sixty years old is doubtless a proof of its vitality. The obstinate blindness of such critics had the paradoxical but usual consequence: young and independent spirits cherished Stendhal's novels all the more. A literary cult grew up about his name in France, Germany, Italy.[6] Around 1900 and since, Stendhal's fame rose very high, to a level that, it seemed, could hardly be expected to hold much longer. His influence was not, in my opinion, always a beneficent one on novelists who cultivated an ironical and desultory tone copied on his (Jean Giono, Roger Vailland, Claude Roy, Louis Aragon). The correspondence, the journals, and even the autobiographical works of the famous "egotist" were absurdly overrated. A few spirits have remained allergic to Beylism: Victor Hugo was one of them, declaring *Le Rouge et le Noir* poorly written; Paul Claudel, always closer in temperament to Hugo than he would confess, is another anti-Stendhalian, who protested violently against the neglect shrouding Hugo's novels, Alexandre Dumas, and especially Eugène Sue, while preposterous praise hailed "insipid, very foolish and paltry works, such as the pharmaceutical disquisitions of Stendhal and of *L'Éducation sentimentale*" (*Oeuvres Complètes,* Vol. XVIII). But the poetical

---

[6] Stendhal's fame had long failed to spread to the same extent in English-speaking countries. American college students resisted him as "dry" and "cynical." In November 1943, the Modern Library dropped *The Charterhouse of Parma* from its list because of poor sales. Suddenly his novels have become the favorites of undergraduates and the object of remarkable, and always favorable, studies by English and American critics: F. C. Green, William Troy, Robert M. Adams, Victor Brombert, F. W. Hemmings.

vision of Stendhal, his Proteus-like and often tragic desire to hide himself from himself, his attempt to wed the novel and politics have been admired, in the middle of our century, as never before.

It is impossible to enumerate all the important literary works which were ignored, jeered at, or savagely slashed by critics in the nineteenth century, "the age of criticism," as it has been called. Most of Balzac's novels would be included. They were naturally branded as immoral; "we advise no woman to read this volume," said a reviewer of *Le Père Goriot* in 1835. The second charge was usually that of "brutal realism" and "materialism." The third was exaggeration of the characters, "lack of moderation and of method," as the critic of the *Constitutionnel* declared repeatedly. Professors usually added an indictment of Balzac's style, the defects of which were to destroy all claims to survival for his novels, since "works of imagination lived by style alone" (*La Revue des Deux Mondes*, December 15, 1856). Finally and more unexpectedly, many contemporary judges belittled Balzac because "he was no creator." There was no invention whatever in his novels, asserted the *Chronique de Paris* on April 12, 1835. The most characteristic comment was a long article by Eugène Poitou which the *Revue des Deux Mondes* published on December 15, 1856, six years after the novelist's death. With no excuse of haste, with a perspective of ten to twenty years on Balzac's chief works, after a thorough estimate of all his merits and faults, the critic concluded: "Little imagination is shown in invention, in the creation of character and plot, or in the delineation of passion. . . . M. de Balzac's place in French literature will be neither considerable nor high." To Balzac's masterpieces, the most eminent of contemporary critics preferred what now seem utterly worthless productions.[7] Sainte-Beuve himself hesitated, or pretended to hesitate, between Balzac, George Sand, and Eugène Sue (*Portraits contemporains*, III, 89, and *Causeries du lundi*, II, 460), and saw little difference between one of the greatest novelists of all

[7] In *La Quotidienne*, April 11, 1835, a critic called Muret openly prefers to *Le Père Goriot* an obscure comedy, *Les deux Gendres*, by an obscure M. Étienne.

time and the forgotten Charles de Bernard, "the Americ [*sic*]
Vespuce of the land whose Christopher Columbus is M. de
Balzac."

Madame Bovary was received in much the same way in 1857;
and one wonders whether such contemporary insults do not con-
stitute the infallible test of greatness in literature. Naturally the
main charge, brandished by the prosecutor in the public trial,
echoed by many a critic, was that of immorality and materialism.
Flaubert felt that his honor as a man and as a writer was permanently hurt by such an accusation. His Norman compatriot and
fellow novelist, Barbey d'Aurevilly, and a score of well-known
arbiters of taste declared the "impure" novel to be mere "excita-
tion of the senses." Armand de Pontmartin, who enjoyed a respectable authority as a conservative critic, termed the book:
"sickly exaltation of the senses and imagination in restless democracy" (*Le Correspondant*, June 1857). Sainte-Beuve's article was
neither very courageous nor very lucid.[8] Always ready to protect the delicacy and virtue of the weaker sex against the brutali-
ties of contemporary novelists, the old bachelor wrote to a
friend, Mme du Gravier, on August 6, 1857: "I do not advise you
to read that novel. It is too raw for the majority of women, and it
would offend your feelings."

Worse still, Flaubert's masterpiece was condemned on purely
literary grounds. The *Revue des Deux Mondes,* whose blunders
in criticism over a century would make a most entertaining
anthology, opened fire on May 1, 1857. Charles de Mazade exposed the lack of truth and the lack of originality in the novel,
and accused Flaubert of imitating Balzac. Duranty, a "realistic"
novelist himself from whom more understanding might have
been expected, bluntly stated: "There is neither emotion nor
feeling nor life in this novel." Some censured its excessive length.
Sainte-Beuve, among others, found the lack of selection weari-

[8] Miss Margaret Gilman has contrasted it with that of Baudelaire, a greater
critic, in our eyes, but infortunately not influential with his contemporaries.
See her interesting article in the *French Review*, December 1941, pp.
138–146.

some and deplored "the method which consists in describing everything and in insisting on all that one comes across. . . . After all a book is not and cannot be reality itself." How often will the same sentence recur to damn the Russian novelists, Zola, Proust, Joyce, Sinclair Lewis, and others yet unborn!

But to Flaubert, the impeccable and patient polisher of sentences, the most vexing and by far the most surprising criticism must have been that of his style. The novel was badly written, in affected language, declared the *Journal des Débats;* it abounds in incorrect French ("fautes de français"), said the *Revue des Deux Mondes;* and the *Figaro* was more categorical: "M. Flaubert n'est pas un écrivain." Much later, Edmond de Goncourt in an address on Flaubert delivered November 9, 1888, recalled that it had been common for the literary newspapers of the Second Empire to assert that Flaubert's style was "epileptic" and that his prose was a dishonor to the reign of Napoleon III.

Twelve years later, Flaubert published *L'Éducation sentimentale.* The new volume could hardly be branded as brutal or cruelly objective like *Madame Bovary,* or overloaded with exotic color and pedantic archeology like *Salammbô.* Many modern readers consider it Flaubert's masterpiece. Yet few contemporaries seem to have perceived the originality of the theme or to have been touched by the tender delicacy of the delineation of Mme Arnoux. "Flaubert soils the brook in which he washes," exclaimed Paul de Saint-Victor, one of the most eminent critics of the times, who was not devoid of artistic sense. The celebrated Barbey d'Aurevilly erred even more outrageously. "Flaubert's is a purely superficial intelligence; he has no feeling, no passion, no enthusiasm, no ideal, no original views, no reflection, no depth; his talent is almost physical, like that of the embosser or of the wholesale designer, or of a cheap painter coloring geographical maps." His recent novel is characterized by one feature: "vulgarity, vulgarity drawn from the gutter, where it is to be found, under the feet of all of us." Five years later, the same critic was to hail in Flaubert's *La Tentation de saint Antoine* "the final suicide" of a novelist who had never done anything but "patch up a few miserable scraps in an old curiosity-shop." In spite of these gross errors, admirers of Barbey d'Aurevilly in proclaiming him the most inspired novelist of the last century add that "the critic in him often equals the novelist." [9]

The obtuseness of criticism toward Baudelaire was even more general. It reached such a climax of blindness and levity that the whole subsequent development of French criticism was permanently affected by it. If twentieth-century critics have often proved too lenient toward eccentric hoaxes, if they have been afraid to discriminate among innovations and to respect truly original works by rejecting fads and sham originality, it is to a large extent because they were paralyzed by the colossal mistakes which Schérer, Sainte-Beuve, Brunetière, Faguet, and scores of others among their predecessors committed in judging *Les Fleurs du Mal*.

And yet, in the years 1855–1865, Baudelaire was far from appearing as an unheralded comet in the literary skies. He had several friends among the Parisian men of letters, and respectable ones (Théophile Gautier, Banville, Babou, Asselineau, Nadar, for example); he had almost sedulously displayed high regard for influential elders (Victor Hugo, Alfred de Vigny, Sainte-Beuve) who might have been his literary godfathers. Moreover, he was neither a dreaded revolutionary with subversive political views (like the painter Courbet or the philosopher Proudhon) nor an innovator choosing unheard-of poetical themes or treating them with a surprising technique. The Baudelairian features which appear most irritating even to the poet's admirers (a few boyish blasphemies, a morbid attraction to decay and death, some Byronic dandyism) had been made fashionable by Gautier and the minor romantics. An unprejudiced reader should have been struck by the austere character of Baudelaire's love poetry. The "femmes damnées" were doomed, with a Dantesque gravity, to an eternal Inferno; an occasional and very slight touch of sadistic

---

[9] Léon Daudet, *Le stupide dix-neuvième Siècle* (Nouvelle librairie nationale, 1922), p. 139.

inspiration disappeared under the numerous hymns in which woman was worshipped with purity or transfigured into a mystic spirit.

Sa chair spirituelle a le parfum des anges.

The reception of *Les Fleurs du Mal* by contemporary criticism has been carefully explored.[10] A very few readers or reviewers soon perceived the originality of the poems; but they were either not influential enough or too vacillating to carry any large portion of the public with them. Unfortunately these rare flashes of clear-sightedness were dimmed by the pronouncements of the great majority of eminent critics. The age-old story of self-complacent stupidity in official and conservative opinion was once again rehearsed.

Several years before the publication of *Les Fleurs du Mal* (1857), a few forgotten and uninfluential critics had perceived Baudelaire's originality first as an art critic (Vitu compared him to Diderot in 1845), then as a trenchant prose writer (Marc Fournier saw the affinity between him and Stendhal in 1846); Nadar even singled him out as the most promising talent of his generation (unfortunately in a very obscure sheet, *Le Journal pour rire* of April 9, 1852).

Alas! official criticism hardly followed suit. Sainte-Beuve remained obstinately deaf to Baudelaire's flattery and to his request for a *Lundi* devoted to his works, which might have opened the royal road to fame, saved Baudelaire from financial distress, and perhaps given more poetical jewels to posterity. In 1860, he agreed to mention Baudelaire, along with Soulary and Bouilhet

[10] An excellent small volume by W. T. Bandy, *Baudelaire Judged by His Contemporaries* (New York: Columbia University, Institute of French Studies, 1933), contains an exhaustive mass of early critical reviews. Since 1917, Baudelaire, of all the French poets, has been the most often reprinted and the most diligently studied. The notes to the editions by Crépet and Le Dantec are a wealth of information. There is still room, however, for some desirable monographs on the early Baudelairians (Nadar, Babou, Asselineau, Privat d'Anglemont) and for some precise information on the actual and spiritual relations between Baudelaire and Chateaubriand, Baudelaire and Stendhal, Baudelaire and Champfleury, Banville, and the rest.

(an insulting grouping indeed!) among those "who adorn the decline and the sunset of the romantic Pleiad." In January 1862, commenting on "the coming elections at the Academy," he described

a quaint and mysterious kiosk, in which one reads Edgar A. Poe, recites exquisite sonnets, becomes intoxicated with hashish in order to reason about it later. . . . To that peculiar kiosk in marquetry, elaborately and intricately original, which has for some time attracted our eyes at the extreme point of the romantic Kamchatka, I would give the name of "la folie Baudelaire." [11]

A few contemporaries, more sensitive to true poetry or more eager for justice, protested: Hippolyte Babou condemned Sainte-Beuve's lack of acumen and courage; Glatigny, writing in a small sheet devoid of any authority, *L'Orphéon* (June 1, 1860), defined Baudelaire's originality in striking terms. Lescure, in the *Gazette de France* (July 17, 1860), initiated the now familiar naming of Baudelaire with Dante. Verlaine (in *L'Art*, November-December 1865), Barbey d'Aurevilly, lucid for once, Banville, in an article published after Baudelaire's lamentable death and obscure funeral (in *L'Étendard*, September 4, 1867), set forth, unheeded by the public and official criticism, Baudelaire's claims to greatness. The finest eulogies came, as usual, after the poet's death, and from obscure pens, those of Nadar in *Le Figaro* (September 10, 1867) and of Vitu in *L'Étendard* (September 3, 1867).

The other critics, those whom the public read, were not even able to explain why they did not like *Les Fleurs du Mal*. They resorted to grandiloquent attacks, producing torrents of abuse. Their self-righteous moral indignation was equalled only by the astounding absence of any poetical perception. It would be need-

[11] Sainte-Beuve's allusions are to be found in *Causeries du lundi*, XV, 352, and in *Nouveaux Lundis*, I, 401. In the case of Baudelaire, Sainte-Beuve, alas! was not inspired by jealousy or maliciousness, or even by a temperamental divergence. He was sincere but obtuse. As late as 1866, on receiving Verlaine's early volume of verse, *Poèmes saturniens*, Sainte-Beuve charitably warned him in a private letter against imitating such an unimportant predecessor: "Let us not take that good, old, and poor Baudelaire as a starting-point."

less and tedious to quote from their articles at length. But the main counts of their indictment may be briefly recalled for the enlightenment of future criticism.

A constant charge, though not the most serious, is that of immorality. Immoral the poems in *Les Fleurs du Mal* seldom or never are. The adjectives "decadent" and "unhealthy" were used along with immoral. Renan, if he had read *Les Fleurs du Mal*, would have pronounced them unhealthy. Taine, who knew Baudelaire and was surprised to find his *Poèmes en prose* "perfectly healthy in style" (letter to Paul Bourget, November 24, 1881), hardly relished his poems in verse, which are, of course, far superior. Taine, at any rate, did not express a public opinion on Baudelaire. Other critics had to, and did.

Pontmartin, in March 1866, branded *Les Fleurs du Mal* as "the perverse curiosities of a blasé age" and recalled the decadence of the Byzantine Empire, to which Nisard, thirty years earlier, had already compared the romantics. After the French defeat of 1871, he accused Baudelaire and Balzac of having a share of responsibility in the disaster (*Samedis*, VIII); to those evil teachers, he opposed the truly French poets, "our comforters" as he called them: Ernest Legouvé and Alexandre Piédagnel. Schérer, in his *Études sur la littérature contemporaine* (IV and VIII, July 1869 and September 1882), rebuked Baudelaire on the same grounds and thought it witty to parody one of the most pregnant lines of the Baudelairian "Danse macabre" into

Les charmes du fumier n'enivrent que les porcs.

The poet had been dead for twenty-five years when Brunetière, in the *Revue des Deux Mondes* of September 1, 1892, asserted that he "had introduced into French poetry a constant preoccupation with ignominy." Then, miraculously, the definition of ignominy or of obscenity must somehow have been altered. After 1920, Baudelaire became required reading in French universities, and more academic theses and scholarly estimates were written on him than on any other French poet.

A second charge, uttered even more forcibly and more dogmatically, was that of total lack of originality in subject matter. I refrain here from quoting freakish or ill-tempered opponents of Baudelaire, such as Louis Ménard or Jules Vallès. But the most serious and responsible arbiters of public taste asserted that Baudelaire was a mere borrower or plunderer. "This is neither poetry nor painting: it is mosaic," said Armand de Pontmartin (*Samedis*, VII, 46). The respectable Schérer improved upon that: Baudelaire's reputation was "what they call, in the slang of artists' studios, a practical joke [*une fumisterie*]" (*Études sur la littérature contemporaine*, VIII, 86). He added that that pseudo-poet did not even deserve the honor of an article by him (*ibid.*, IV, 291). He picked one of the most moving poems, "Les Petites Vieilles," and termed it "pretentious silliness." Continuing in this strain he wrote that a proof of Baudelaire's utter worthlessness was to be found in his prose, not one page of which "is worth quoting." It is easy to understand why; in prose, one must have something to say. But Baudelaire lacked intellectual substance. No wonder he had all the faults of a person who speaks without having any ideas (*ibid.*, IV, 289). Yet to any impartial reader of 1967, Baudelaire's prose, especially in his esthetic and critical articles, is perhaps more packed with original thought than any other of the nineteenth century!

Lacking ideas! there is the magical phrase resorted to by so many ponderous critics. Faguet, who boasted of a new idea every day and wrote a new book almost every month, attempted to judge nineteenth-century poetry according to its "wealth of ideas." He ruled out as secondary in that respect Victor Hugo and Baudelaire. And he naïvely added: "After Vigny, one must wait until Sully-Prudhomme to discover new ideas among French poets." [12] His method was simple: he summed up the theme of

[12] Émile Faguet, in an article on Baudelaire which is a masterpiece of lack of understanding, *La Revue des Revues*, September 1, 1910. André Gide replied to that unbelievably blind article with a brilliant defence of Baudelaire reprinted in *Nouveaux Prétextes*. Curiously, other critics, such as Théodore de Wyzeva (in the *Revue Indépendante* of July 1887), a contemporary and a friend of the Symbolists, experienced much difficulty in mustering any enthusiasm for *Les Fleurs du Mal* and blamed Baudelaire for at-

Baudelaire's poems ("La Beauté," "Les Phares," "Confession") in one or two lines and triumphantly proved that, reduced to an essential idea, those poems were mere empty commonplaces!

The third charge brought by most critics of Baudelaire from 1857 to 1917 concerned his style. They found it prosaic, incorrect, awkward, halting. Schérer could praise only one poem, "sculptured like a cameo": naturally he chose one of the worst poems in the volume, "Don Juan aux enfers." The same youthful poem is singled out for praise by Faguet, along with "L'Homme et la mer," which is hardly more original. Not one of the poems quoted by Faguet to support his criticism is among the truly beautiful *Fleurs du Mal*. Alas! it was not bad faith nor subtle treachery that led the critic to such an erratic selection. Faguet was an honest soul, but deaf to the music of Baudelaire.

Faguet's most famous rival was Brunetière, long the revered high priest of French literary judgment. Quoting too extensively from his comments on Baudelaire would hardly be charitable. In an article published in 1887 (thirty years after *Les Fleurs du Mal*) and reprinted in *Questions de critique*, he gave his interpretation of the poet: an inveterate liar. "He was born a liar; all his life long, he lied and mystified." "His poetry oozes midnight oil. That man was endowed with the very genius for weak and incorrect phrasing. . . . The poor devil had nothing or almost nothing of a poet, except the maniacal desire of becoming one." [13]

---

tempting to put ideas into his poetry. "His is the conscientious and sterile effort of an artist to express in poetry things which are unsuitable to it." Faguet's obtuse judgment quoted in the text is paralleled by another just as obtuse: replying to questions in *La Grande Revue* on the influence of Bergson, then already at the summit of his fame, he declared that, having repeatedly opened Bergson's volumes, he had failed to understand a single line in them. A good many outstanding French philosophers (Victor Delbos and the historian Thibaudet being exceptions) were then similarly unable or unwilling to understand Bergson.

[13] Scores of other critics or contemporaries of Baudelaire likewise remained, for sixty years or so, closed to the enjoyment of one of the least revolutionary, the most "classical" of French poets: for example, Alphonse Daudet, if we may trust the report given in the *Journal* of Goncourt (VIII, 235–236, April 30, 1891).

All these eminent critics appended the same conclusion to their severe remarks; for each of them maintained, according to the rule of the game, that he was criticizing Baudelaire from the point of view of posterity and not just expressing his own times or his private preference. Their prophecy was unambiguous: Baudelaire's fame cannot last. Schérer has not the slightest doubt. "There is no reputation more artificially inflated than that of Baudelaire," he wrote in 1882. Jules Vallès had asserted: "He will not remain famous for ten years." Brunetière, who showed some lenient kindness to the young Symbolists, implored them not to mix with Baudelaire's imitators, "who make themselves even more incomprehensible and pretentious than he was." Faguet was more naïvely touching. Writing in 1910, he rejoiced that all the posthumous works and the letters of Baudelaire were at last published (in this he was mistaken), all the anecdotes told, so that "we shall not again hear about that illustrious mystifier, whose sole excuse is that he is taken in by his own hoaxes. . . . I reread Baudelaire; and I am surprised that he imposed upon us for a whole generation: I find him, as I did formerly, a good second-rate poet, not a negligible one, to be sure, but essentially a second-rate one."

Never was criticism more flourishing than in the years 1870–1940 in France. Literary reviews were countless; weekly and daily papers opened their columns to accounts of new books. Some critics maintained the tradition of dogmatic criticism, guiding the public with a ponderous whip (Sarcey, Brunetière, Souday); others, with more wit or nonchalant grace, were no less obediently followed (Faguet, Lemaître, Anatole France, Remy de Gourmont, Thibaudet). The greatest writers of the age left volumes of criticism (Gide, Proust, Claudel, Valéry). Few novelists or poets resisted the itch of expressing a judgment on the works of their friends or rivals. The freest opinions could count on finding a review where they could be published in the freest terms. Moreover, the fashion was all for new movements, revolutionary groups, and "la jeunesse." One might imagine that no important work in the last seventy years was allowed to pass unnoticed.

Yet never have so many great books been obliged to struggle painfully against lack of attention or of comprehension. Seldom were the mistakes of critics more enormous. Some reputations were usurped so successfully that, even after thirty or forty years, many readers still accept as masterpieces *Cyrano de Bergerac, Le Lys rouge, Madame Chrysanthème, Le Jardin de Bérénice, Jean-Christophe,* or *Le Disciple.* Others, in perfect good faith, repeat that Mme de Noailles was a poet of genius, that Henri de Régnier was the chief of the French Symbolists, that Moréas' *Stances* or Maurras' *Anthinea* are perfect works, merely because critics have lured them into such superstitions. On the other hand, most of the truly powerful and original works have been scoffed at or ignored, especially in poetry, the richest branch of modern French literature, at a time when French poetry had become the most significant in Europe.

Some day, the critical statements inspired by the French Symbolists will make one of the most entertaining and disappointing episodes in the history of criticism. There were, it seems to me, three generations or waves of symbolist poets. The first is destined to remain the greatest. It included (if we leave out the forerunner Baudelaire) three inspired singers, Rimbaud, Verlaine, and Mallarmé, and two bitter and "cursed poets," Lautréamont and Tristan Corbière, all writing around 1870. A sixth secondary but at times delightful talent, Charles Cros, might be added to them. None of these six precursors was acclaimed or understood by contemporary critics. Remy de Gourmont himself, a friend of the Symbolists, did not truly feel the original genius of Rimbaud or the strange talent of Lautréamont. Brunetière, who devoted eloquent lectures to the "evolution" of nineteenth-century lyrical poetry, never dreamt of including Rimbaud among "the fittest" destined to survive. In 1887, in his article on Baudelaire, he mentioned Rimbaud as an empty mystifier, whom the shrewd common sense of criticism had happily deflated, and seemed to rejoice that the incomprehensible and corrupt poetical apprentice was probably selling flannel and muslin in some distant land.

In the same years, Mallarmé's obscurity and even his alleged obscenity were a standing joke for Parisian journalists and reviewers. Even granting that many of Mallarmé's poems are difficult, they could have been deciphered with a little good will. At least his contemporary Verlaine must be proclaimed one of the clearest poets ever writing in French, truly classical in the simplicity of his sensations and feelings, directly and deeply moving through his themes and his music. Few were the critics who then realized it. In 1875, the reader for the publisher Lemerre rejected his contribution to the third series of *Le Parnasse contemporain* with the remark: "The man is disreputable [*indigne*] and his poems are among the worst ever seen." That reader, who had been a poet himself, was none other than Anatole France. Later, much later, however, he depicted Verlaine as the poor and genial Choulette in *Le Lys rouge,* and he hailed him as "a poet one meets but once in a century" (*La Vie littéraire,* III, 317). Jules Lemaître, who then passed as the subtlest critic of his age and made a specialty of discussing "les Contemporains," sketched in August 1879 the "poetical movement in France." Generously granting six pages to Sully-Prudhomme, three to Coppée, he completely omitted both Verlaine and Rimbaud, and merely hinted that the case of Mallarmé hardly belonged to literary criticism. In the fourth volume of his *Contemporains,* Lemaître gathered all his audacity and devoted a whole article to Verlaine and his symbolist and decadent friends. Cautiously, diffidently, he apologized for writing about such sickly poets. Verlaine's poetry attracted him and he could not help finding it "adorable" here and there, but obscure and unhealthy, "the stammering of a neuropath," "the stuttering of insanity, of black night."

The second generation of Symbolists, writing between 1880 and 1890 (Henri de Régnier, Vielé-Griffin, Moréas, Samain, Verhaeren, for example), did not rise to the same flights of transcendent genius as their predecessors. They popularized the themes and the technique of Symbolism, sprinkled their verse with fluid images and ingenious riddles, experimented with rhythm, evolved theories and published manifestoes with dangerous facility. At any rate, there was nothing brutal or revolutionary about them which might have kept timid critics at a distance. They were, if anything, too intellectual and far too much in the French tradition of delicate and graceful "préciosité."

Nevertheless, the strangest misconceptions seem to have been aroused in the public, and in the critics who should have led the public, by their rather innocuous innovations. A clever journalist, Jules Huret, undertook in 1891 to question the leading literary personalities of France on "literary evolution." The answers of those eminent "chers maîtres" arouse our laughter today; they should rather make us pause and think that the same lack of understanding and mental laziness were opposed, at approximately the same time, to the Impressionists in painting and to the music of Debussy, and later on, to the Cubists and the Surrealists. Will our successors remember our flagrant injustice and do better?

The attitude of several of the critics who answered Jules Huret was one of placid disregard of contemporary literature; serious minds are traditionally afraid of being taken in by the eccentricities of a new school of poetry or art. "Symbolists are babies sucking their own thumbs," said Renan, who had not bothered to read them. Renan was a student of the past. But critics whose business it was to keep the public informed about the present were just as contemptuous. Jules Lemaître, with his clear common sense from Touraine, bluntly declared:

The Symbolists! . . . They are of no account. . . . They do not know themselves what they are and what they want; . . . I am sure there are not twenty among them who understand each other. No, you see, they are all "fumistes," with some degree of sincerity, I grant, but "fumistes."

Others saw in those poets, who were to revolutionize European poetry, nothing but ambitious and pushing upstarts, envious of their elders, skillful at self-advertising. Others still called them maniacs or savages, unacquainted with French grammar, mishandling the language, having no ear for the music of poetry. When interviewed by Huret, Jules Bois summed up the reactions of those critics: "Incoherent gestures, a stammering outcry, . . . the cacophony of savages who might have turned the pages of an English grammar or of a glossary of forgotten words."

A third group of poets, heirs of the symbolist movement, who were born around 1870, began writing at the end of the century. It included several of the great names of modern French literature: Gide, Claudel, Proust, Valéry; two lesser ones, Jammes and Fort, and a writer hardly touched by Symbolism, Péguy. Certainly none of them deserved to be eyed with suspicion as a decadent, a savage, a lunatic, or a barbarian, bent upon defacing the clear French language. Yet the last of those charges was brandished against every one of these men; and they were all in turn called obscure, unhealthy, and dangerous for the youth of the time.

Worse still, those writers, all of whom long were the respected patriarchs of French letters, remained practically unknown to the public until the end of the First World War. As late as 1920, critics proved deplorably blind or hostile to them. In 1914, Péguy met a heroic death on the battlefield, wearied and embittered by years of hard struggle against official France, unrecognized except by a small group of friends. Valéry had published several detached poems and some splendid and prophetic essays in prose in the late Nineties, but was known, even by name, to only a very few admirers. In 1917, when he offered the classical perfection of "La Jeune Parque" to his anxious and war-ridden country, literary circles were too busy lauding Barbusse, Géraldy, and Pierre Benoît; critics did not even notice the poetical masterpiece.

As to Claudel, neither the strange flashes of genius in *Tête d'or* (1890), nor the stately grandeur of *Cinq grandes odes, L'Échange,* or *L'Annonce faite à Marie,* towering masterpieces of the French drama, succeeded in disarming hostile criticism before the war of 1914, or in exciting the interest of critics. To quote a typical one, and not among the least eminent, Pierre Lasserre, in his *Chapelles littéraires* (1920), recalled his dismay on first opening Claudel's plays:

I was reading words and phrases in our language. . . . Yet I could understand nothing of what I read. . . . Never, even in the most abstruse Germanic thinkers or half-thinkers, in Fichte, Schelling, or Hegel, had I come upon a way of linking ideas so utterly alien to my own. I could not make head or tail of it.

Poor Lasserre was nevertheless neither jealous of a younger man (Claudel was precisely his contemporary) nor devoid of all critical flair. He often reasoned with solid common sense and wrote with sensitiveness and humor. He was not blinded by the official or conventional prejudices of university critics, for he was a declared enemy of the Sorbonne. Soon after his stolid mistakes on Claudel and Péguy, he was to publish the most subtle and the wisest volume on the most subtle of nineteenth-century writers (*Renan et nous*). But he simply could not and would not understand writers who challenged his conventional habits of thought, and unfortunately he boasted of his inability to understand.

It is even more surprising to find that in 1897, in a literary atmosphere which should have been highly favorable to such a volume (poetical wonder at the beauty of the world, sublimated sensuality, Nietzschean gospel of amorality, symbolist poetry), *Les Nourritures terrestres* found no echo whatever. Yet André Gide had already published some prose-jewels like the *Traité du Narcisse*. He was a master of pure and clear style. Just a few dozen copies of the book were sold. Critics ignored it unanimously, except for one very young man, Edmond Jaloux, who, discovering the volume in Marseilles, divined its originality and its future. A quarter of a century later, Gide's hymns to joy and his appeals to adventure and "fervor" found their public and shook a whole generation of young men.

The most typical of these cases, that of Proust, who was not recognized until 1919, deserves closer attention and may furnish a useful lesson.[14] Proust was neither young nor obscure when, on November 23, 1913, he published *Du Côté de chez Swann*. He was already the author of two ingenious volumes and of an interesting introduction to selections from Ruskin which he had translated. As early as 1896, he had been presented to the French public by no less a sponsor than Anatole France as a precocious talent combining "a depraved Bernardin de Saint-Pierre and an ingenuous Petronius." Maurras had devoted an article to him that same year. He numbered many zealous friends in the Parisian salons and on the staffs of several newspapers (*Le Figaro* and *Le Gaulois*, for instance).

But Proust's friends were the very first to be misled about him. They failed to perceive how original his first novel was. "Subtle," "refined," "delicate," "witty," were the epithets they used. Proust the man was, no doubt, all that, and those qualities (or faults) are not lacking in his great work. But the unprejudiced reader who opens today "Un Amour de Swann," that most probing and tragic analysis of love, exclaims at once: "original," "moving," "profound," "true," "great." None of the early reviewers apparently discerned those qualities. In fact, Proust's diligent friends harmed his reputation by annoying many a serious critic who steered clear of a new writer sponsored by fashionable snobs and esthetes.

Careful research has shown that Proust was not altogether unrecognized in 1913 and 1914. Three or four articles drew attention to his novel with words of praise in 1913: Élie-J. Bois in the *Temps* (November 12), Maurice Rostand in *Comoedia* (December 26), Lucien Daudet in the *Figaro* (November 27). None of

14 The critical reception of Proust's work has been diligently traced in several studies. The most valuable is that of Douglas Alden, *Marcel Proust and His Critics* (Los Angeles: Lymanhouse, 1940). Léon Pierre-Quint published Proust's letters to René Blum between 1913 and 1921 under the subtitle "Comment parut *Du Côté de chez Swann*" (Kra, 1930). Paul Souday, who felt very proud of his early articles on Proust, collected them in a small volume (Kra, 1927). See also *Marcel Proust: Reviews and Estimates in English*, compiled by Gladys Dudley Lindner (Stanford: Stanford University Press, 1943).

these, however, commanded a wide audience. Among the more influential reviews, only a very few, while multiplying reservations and criticizing much, perceived the originality of the Proustian novel. They were Paul Souday in the *Temps* of December 10, 1913, Lucien Maury in the *Revue bleue* of December 27, and Henri Ghéon in the *Nouvelle Revue française* of January 1914. As is often the case, provincial critics proved in France more independent and more lucid than their Parisian colleagues, but with little effect, since French literary reputations can be made only in Paris. A critic writing in a Belgian review, *L'Art moderne*, on April 19, 1914, and a professor from Lille in *L'Écho du Nord* of June 4, 1914, Henri Potez, even dared praise Proust's style—and the style of a new and original writer is in France the main stumblingblock to recognition, and, for several years, an easy mark for ridicule.

With these very few and relatively inconsequential exceptions, the critics who opened *Du Côté de chez Swann* failed to discern any worth in it. For six years, silence and obscurity shrouded the writer. The terrible war which France was then waging in no way explains such a silence, for many books were being published and a vast reading public went to literature for escape. Even in 1919, it took a vigorous campaign by a few ardent supporters of Proust to impose his second novel on the public and have the coveted Goncourt prize awarded to *À l'Ombre des jeunes filles en fleur*. Obstinate resistance had to be overcome. As frequently happens with literary reputations, a very small group of enthusiasts succeeded in winning famous critics and the general public to their faith. Henri Ghéon converted Rivière, who convinced Gide. Charles Du Bos went over to their views. These last three soon wrote some of the most penetrating pages—not since equalled by later critics—on Proust's greatness. In another literary circle, Léon Daudet successfully overcame the resistance of the Goncourt Academy. Without these men, it is not unreasonable to suppose that Proust might long have been left in obscurity; he might have died unrecognized and his bulky posthumous work would perhaps have remained unpublished to this very day.

Some of the early charges brought against Proust by highly esteemed contemporaries are typical of the mental confusion into which critics are thrown by an original work. First—and the indictment is particularly grave in France, a nation of grammarians—Proust was censured for not knowing how to write correct French. "Obviously, the younger generation does not know French any more; . . . the national language is turning into a shapeless *patois* and slipping into barbarity." Thus wrote Paul Souday, the critic of the *Temps*, who was by no means a determined adversary of Proust. Little did he pause to think that the same charge had been brought earlier against the Symbolists, Goncourt, Balzac, the romantics, in a word against all young writers ever since their elders displayed a fondness for reprimanding them. Others added that the style was involved, clumsy, purposely baffling to the reader. "It is like drinking a sleeping draught," declared Rachilde. And the lack of discrimination on the part of the novelist, his inability to organize, his obscurity were abundantly censured. None of the customary reactions to a new and important book was lacking in the press, not even the assertion that *Du Côté de chez Swann* was unworthy of French literature, since it lacked all the so-called Latin qualities of order, clarity, and balance.[15] It is not rash to prophesy that future ages (and informed opinion has already proclaimed it) will rank the stylist, the poet in prose, and the master of clear and harmonious language in Proust above the psychologist, the philosopher, or even the novelist.

Other contemporary critics did not fail to add that, although the new work displayed some laudable qualities, it certainly should not be called a novel. How many times has a similar and

[15] One is surprised to find that André Gide, one of the acutest critical minds of our time, was at first confused by the newness of the Proustian manner. He condemned it in a fragment paradoxically entitled "An Unprejudiced Mind" published in *Divers*. Later on, however, in *Incidences*, Gide wrote a rapturous eulogy of Proust's style, and in January 1914 he confessed as "the most smarting remorse of his life" his early misjudgment of Proust and the consequent refusal of *Du Côté de chez Swann* by the publishing house of the Nouvelle Revue française.

dangerously impressive statement confronted an innovator! "This is not a novel," "This is not a drama," or "It is anything but music." All the revolutionary creations which renovated the novel, the drama, poetry, musical composition, and painting were thus banished at the start. As might be expected, the most completely misunderstood part of the new work was the long episode "Un Amour de Swann," perhaps the most tragic and the deepest love story in the whole range of French literature. Paul Souday commented: "This enormous episode . . . is not positively boring, but rather commonplace." Maury saw in it a feeble imitation of *Les Liaisons dangereuses* and of the worst features of Bourget. Nowhere was the essential newness of Proust's novel perceived and praised by critics. Strangely enough, not the subject matter of Proust (which touches at times, especially in the later volumes, on the abnormal), but his manner was objected to. Yet what then appeared eccentric, decadent, obscure seems to naïve readers, twenty years after, perfectly normal, classical in the French sense, and crystal clear.

In the meanwhile, in France and all over the world, the opinion of critics and that of millions of readers were deceived on the true values of French literature. Anatole France and Pierre Loti, Paul Bourget and Romain Rolland, Émile Verhaeren and Mme de Noailles, Paul Hervieu and Brieux were hailed as the geniuses of the first years of the twentieth century. The unjustified glory to which they were thus raised made the next generation all the more eager today to deflate their once overpraised talents. Disparagement has been driven to excess, especially in the case of the first two. A new scale of values is gradually being substituted for the one which blind contemporaries forced upon themselves. The great poets of the pre-war era in France were Guillaume Apollinaire, Claudel, Valéry (who refrained from publishing his verse until 1917 and 1922), and to a lesser degree St. John Perse, whose first volume of verse appeared in 1911. The truly great prose writers were Proust, Gide, Péguy, and Colette, and in the field of the essay Élie Faure and André Suarès. Roger Martin du Gard probably never equalled his *Jean Barois* (1913). Jules Romains may have multiplied the volumes of his *Hommes de bonne volonté* and have scored an occasional success on the stage; but we doubt whether he will not survive in literature rather as the author of *Mort de quelqu'un* (1911) and *Cromedeyre le vieil* (acted in 1920). Alain Fournier's *Le grand Meaulnes* is one of the few fine novels of the pre-war years. Mauriac, Duhamel, Giraudoux, Larbaud, Durtain, Vildrac all made their literary début around 1910–1913; all remained unnoticed by the majority of critics.

Indeed, not only in France, but in Britain, in Germany, and most of all in Austria, not only in literature but in painting, music, the ballet, philosophy and psychology, the four or five years preceding World War I witnessed a miraculous and convergent series of creative moves unmatched since in Europe. Some of those who then forged ahead realized what they were trying to achieve: Kandinsky, Ezra Pound, Copeau, Apollinaire, Webern, Braque, Diaghilev. The critics, in their vast majority, remained unperturbed and failed to serve the creators and their potential public. To the lover of literature and to the historian of letters, few things are more disturbing than the welter of uncertainty in which the most cultured part of the reading public is content to remain in regard to the true talents of its age. Audiences who flock to lectures, students and professors in graduate schools, collectors of books and docile buyers of the season's best seller are equally unaware of the immense difference which will one day, and which presumably does today, separate a few great writers (or painters or musicians or statesmen) from the third-rate talents and even from the popular but tenth-rate ones. Critics, when questioned by indiscreet readers, take refuge in evasive answers or delight in enumerating dozens of names, like gamblers at the races who would stake an equal sum of money on all the horses so as to be sure not to miss the winner.

Thus it is that the best informed of us live amidst contemporary literature without even suspecting that great books are published today which will be revered forty years from now, that poems are being written which will be learned by heart by

our grandchildren, that philosophers or political thinkers are proposing to a listless public doctrines which will perhaps change the
course of history as much as Descartes, Marx, Gobineau, and
Nietzsche have done in the past. How many connoisseurs and
students of French literature assert daily that the present age is
the age of the novel, that French poetry is dead or dormant, that
there are no new talents to succeed the great generation of
Proust, Gide, Valéry, Claudel, Péguy! Yet in my opinion
Mauriac, Malraux, Green, Bernanos are the few novelists of the
first order who have appeared in France since Proust. Almost all
the novels which have been acclaimed recently will be forgotten.
On the contrary, poets are very numerous if sometimes esoteric
and blissfully ignored by the general public just as Baudelaire,
Mallarmé, and Claudel were in their day: several of them
(Supervielle, St. John Perse, and at times Fargue, Reverdy,
Éluard, Aragon, Michaux) will be read many years hence, as
perhaps will Pierre Emmanuel, La Tour du Pin, Jaccottet, and
Dupin. Their originality and sincerity make the present era one
of the richest in poetical blossoming that France has ever known.
Finally, among the prose writers who succeeded Giono, Malraux,
Montherlant, André Breton, Sartre, and Camus, the few genuine
talents (Butor, Simon) are placed every day in the same rank as
such mediocre manufacturers of hasty novels or pleasing short
stories as Marcel Aymé, Raymond Queneau, Marguerite Duras.

At the risk of appearing guilty of obstinate partisanship in my
insistence on the shortcomings of criticism, I think it necessary to
add one more series of enumerations and to glance at the list—a
long and glorious one—of French critics since 1820. That list
includes many of the most acute minds that France has produced.
To their intellectual gifts, a few of them added the sensitiveness
and the emotional or even sensuous perception of beauty without which there can be no complete critic. Yet their mistakes
have been numerous and sometimes unbelievably gross. Must we
accept them placidly and repeat them complacently, as an un-
avoidable sin due to man's fallible nature? Or can we serve criticism by being in the future more severe toward all the appren-

tices who style themselves book reviewers and critics without
having the necessary training and, more important still, without
the innate talent and qualifications for that art, the most perilous
of all because the most indiscriminately invaded by mediocre
pretentiousness? Can we ever hope that others will forsake their
obstinate fondness for far-fetched subtleties and for elaborate
systems borrowed from psychoanalysis, semantics, linguistics,
philosophy, or esthetics, and learn how to be modest and simple
in the presence of a work of art?

That fallibility is not the privilege of critics alone. Great novelists and poets have been just as blind, as has been already recalled,
although perhaps with better reason. One of the most acute
French minds in the first half of the last century was that of
Stendhal, for instance. And Stendhal's literary pronouncements
are not a little surprising. He worshipped Alfieri as an authentic
genius, he was deaf to most of the French romantic poetry, but
he found Crébillon a great novelist and declared, in his *Journal,*
that the greatest genius in eighteenth-century literature was—
Fabre d'Églantine. Victor Hugo, whose critical intuitions and
esthetic pronouncements are sometimes preposterous and sometimes extraordinarily penetrating, is, next to Baudelaire and to
Paul Valéry, the keenest critic among the French poets.[16] Yet in
his youth he fell into raptures over Soumet's worthless pseudo-
classical tragedies (letters of January 17, 1822, and September 6,
1823, to Jules de Rességuier).

But Stendhal and Hugo, like most creative writers, were rich in
esthetic ideas which helped to change French letters in their time.
The same can hardly be said of the critics who were famous and
influential during the romantic period. Planche, Janin, Nettement, Cuvillier-Fleury, Michiels, Nisard, Villemain, Chaudesai-

---

[16] His famous and felicitous phrases on Baudelaire's "frisson nouveau" and
on Rimbaud, whom he called "Shakespeare enfant," are remarkable instances of recognition of the genius of younger poets. He shrewdly called
Mallarmé, forty years his junior, "my dear impressionist poet." Verlaine relates in his *Souvenirs et promenades* how, as early as August 1868, Hugo,
meeting him in Brussels, recited to him several lines from the young and
unknown poet's *Poèmes saturniens.*

gues. They are mere names today for most of us; exposing their innumerable blunders might appear too easy and futile a pastime. Yet they were men of wide culture, deeply versed in the classical tradition (Nisard, Nettement) or conversant with foreign literatures (Villemain and Michiels particularly). They often wrote with brilliance (Janin and Planche). They could and should have led the public to the acceptance of the great French romantics, while they might thus have kept those romantic rebels from some of the excesses and boisterous revolt to which isolation from a hostile public drove them. The critics preferred to censure their contemporaries systematically. They naturally found them obscure, foreign, dangerous. They delighted in pointing out unmistakable signs of decadence in their works.[17] Gustave Planche, who (Sainte-Beuve excepted) was probably among all those prolific critics of the first half of the century the most sensitive to literary values, cannot today be reread without a smile or occasional bursts of laughter. In a clever essay on "Les Royautés littéraires" in 1838, he defined the critic's task as one of comparison of the present with the past and of divination of the future. But in 1836 he himself condemned Chateaubriand to oblivion (*Portraits littéraires* [3d ed.; II, 182]), ridiculed Lamartine for his *Voyage en Orient* (*Nouveaux Portraits littéraires*), perceived sure signs of Hugo's decline in *Les Voix intérieures* (1837), lavished inconsiderate praise on a poor declamatory poem by Auguste Barbier, *Il Pianto,* and found a bad English novel by Bulwer, *Eugene Aram,* worthy of Euripides and Shakespeare! As late as 1852, when the rumors of literary battle had long died down, he sketched a summary of the achievement of French letters ("La Poésie et la critique en 1852," *Nouveaux Portraits littéraires*). The drama had filled none of its promises of 1827. The novel had become a heavy industry, with not a single artist

---

[17] Cuvillier-Fleury, the influential critic of the *Journal des Débats,* branded Lamartine and Musset as decadent (article on Musset, February 24, 1850) and read, in those individual cases of disintegration, "the details of the public decadence of our country and of our age." But, two years later, he gave warm praise to the noble spirituality of such poets as Autran and Laprade.

worth mentioning. Criticism was mediocre. Lyrical poetry counted three names, Lamartine, Hugo, and Béranger, of whom the last-named alone, "limpid and accomplished," deserved to remain as a model.

One figure towers above all others in French criticism of 1820–1870: that of Sainte-Beuve. It long was customary to praise his subtlety and acumen as the highest ever possessed by any practitioner of the art of criticism. Most of his French successors have vaunted his biographical and psychological method as the most suitable for the study of literature. University professors traditionally quote him on Montaigne, Pascal, Racine, Molière. His *Port-Royal* is found in most respectable private libraries, although seldom actually perused to the end and all the more invariably revered for not being read. His English and American admirers have been prone to rapturous enthusiasm, from Matthew Arnold to Irving Babbitt, Lewis F. Mott, and William Giese.[18] His *Lundis* and his earlier and fresher *Portraits littéraires* contain, indeed, many essays in which the relation between a man's life and his work has been explored and traced as searchingly as is humanly possible.

But do we owe our present view of French literature to Sainte-Beuve? Has he played a considerable part in molding our opinion of the writers of the past? Remy de Gourmont has celebrated Sainte-Beuve as a "creator of values" and asserted that "the main idea that we form on Romanticism was framed by Sainte-Beuve" (*Promenades philosophiques*, I, 37). Such a statement seems to us contrary to all the evidence provided by texts. Sainte-Beuve is an eminent writer (although often an involved and pretentious stylist) and one of the most solid and scholarly literary historians

[18] Nietzsche had proved more severe in a few harsh but lucid lines of his *Will to Power* and in the paragraph on "Skirmishes in a War with the Age" of his *Twilight of Idols*. In France, some of the wisest reservations were formulated in an 1895 essay by Gustave Lanson, reprinted in his *Essais de Méthode, de Critique et d'Histoire littéraire* (Hachette, 1965). Proust's posthumous pages in *Contre Sainte-Beuve* (Gallimard, 1954) use the critic's notorious mistakes as a theme for Proustian variations.

that ever lived. His reading was unequalled in range and his flair for discovery of documents, extraordinary. No great critic, however, has ever been so often and so utterly mistaken about his contemporaries as Sainte-Beuve. A whole volume of extracts from his bulky work might be compiled under the title: "Les Erreurs de Sainte-Beuve." It would startle all his devotees and would serve as a wholesome warning to all practitioners of criticism.

His gravest shortcoming has often been mentioned: a strange inability to appreciate what is truly great. Even where he is at his best, in his criticism of the ancients or of the French sixteenth and seventeenth centuries, he falls short of our expectations in that respect: he can evaluate and dissect Theocritus, the Greek Anthology, or Virgil, but not Homer, Aeschylus, Plato, or Lucretius. On Ronsard and even, in my opinion, on Montaigne and on Pascal, he is disappointing. Even in Racine, whom he tenderly admired, he saw a lyrical and elegiac poet (*Portraits littéraires*, I, 94–95) and missed the supreme master of dramatic construction. The violent outbursts of passion of *Phèdre* and even of *Bérénice* apparently struck Sainte-Beuve much less than the superficial veil of soft tenderness and the outward orderly harmony. Our contemporary view of Racine, as Giraudoux, Péguy, and Mauriac have delineated it, has little in common with Sainte-Beuve's tender, sentimental picture of the tragic poet.

But Sainte-Beuve's shortcomings are especially conspicuous when he deals with the literature of his own century. It would hardly be an exaggeration to say that he has been truly fair only to three or four of his contemporaries: to Lamartine and Musset as poets, and to two writers, twenty years his junior, Renan and Taine (although his three articles on Taine's *Histoire de la littérature anglaise* in the third volume of the *Nouveaux Lundis* fail to do justice to the originality of that ambitious undertaking). The list of writers whom Sainte-Beuve overpraised would include Villemain, Guizot, Thiers, Mignet, Fontanes, Daunou, Chênedollé, Charles de Bernard, Vinet, and occasionally even more insignificant poets such as Jules Lefèvre, Polonius, Denne-

Baron, Mme Flora Tristan, Mme Tastu. On Feydeau's mediocre
novel, *Fanny*, he squandered more unrestrained praise than on
Flaubert's masterpieces; he compared the cheap psychological
analysis attempted in that book to *Adolphe* (*Causeries du lundi*,
XIV) and, even in his private notebooks, only reluctantly
recanted (*Mes Poisons*, p. 30). One of his major mistakes in
perspective, on Ponsard's *Lucrèce*, occurred in critical notes
which Sainte-Beuve sent anonymously to a Swiss friend in 1843
(since reprinted as *Chroniques parisiennes*). He had thus no reason to flatter the young author; he was, it is true, anxious to cry
up the poor and insipid drama in order perfidiously to depreciate
Hugo's romantic plays. It is hard, however, for the very few
antiquarians who may read *Lucrèce* today to trust the taste of a
critic who found the part of Brutus "very great" and "full of
soul." Most surprising of all are Sainte-Beuve's repeated eulogies
of Béranger. They would deserve a small monograph, or a niche
in the history of Béranger's extraordinary fame.[19] In 1834, the
critic compared Béranger to Rabelais, Molière, and La Fontaine.
In 1841 (*Portraits contemporains*, III, 179), he praised the "condensed perfection of his style." On July 6, 1845, attempting to
express his sincere opinion in writing to his Swiss friend, he maintained that Béranger's talent deserved to be called "sublime."
The same month, he expressed for "Le Délire bachique," a drinking song by Désaugiers, a more unreserved admiration than he
had granted to most of the great romantic poets (*Portraits contemporains*, V, 42). Again in 1850, the critic prophesied that
Béranger was "one of the poets of whom a great deal will survive" (*Causeries du lundi*, I, 298) and the same year, while
adding a few restrictions to his enthusiasm, he boldly asserted
that Béranger equalled the most eminent men of his time,
Chateaubriand, Lamennais, Lamartine, and surpassed them
through "his insinuative subtlety and gift for detail."
    It is hard to find valid excuse for so much misjudgment of bad

[19] See two old studies, Paul Boiteau, *Erreur des critiques de Béranger* (n.
pub., 1858), and Arthur Arnould, *Béranger, ses amis, ses ennemis, ses critiques* (Cherbuliez, 1864). The latter takes Sainte-Beuve to task.

or mediocre writers, through whom a critic of such acumen should have been able to see more penetratingly. It has been alleged that Saint-Beuve ceased to sympathize with the romantic movement around 1835, partly out of personal spite, since he had failed as a poet and as a novelist, partly out of fastidious taste and sincere classical conviction. But if so, he lost touch with all that was creative and alive in the literature of his time, and all his studies of the nineteenth century are vitiated by lack of sympathy and stubborn refusal to understand. Moreover, his disappointing inability to perceive and acknowledge originality included writers like Stendhal and Mérimée, Tocqueville, and even Leconte de Lisle and Baudelaire, in whom he could have discovered many a classical virtue and abundant distrust of romanticism.

The truth is, alas, simpler. Sainte-Beuve, like many other critics much less brilliantly gifted than he, proved incapable of assessing the true values of the literature of his time. Whenever he attempted a general synthesis, he failed lamentably, often through omission.[20] Several times, with an almost cruel enjoyment, he drew up the balance sheet of the romantic movement in France. Its assets were limited to two: the short lyrical poem, and a prose style which expressed emotion more adequately than before (*Portraits contemporains*, III, 321 ff.). On the novel, the short story, political thought, history, which Romanticism renovated, on the powerful impulse given by the romantic movement to metaphysical curiosity, to psychology, and to criticism, Sainte-Beuve said not a word. On the art of his time, he was hardly more lucid, extravagantly praising Gavarni, for instance; in art criticism, Charles Blanc and Théophile Gautier seemed to him to have reached the pinnacle (*Nouveaux Lundis*, VI, 315 ff.); yet he ignored Baudelaire and Thoré-Burger, the only two great art critics of the last century in France.

[20] For example in *Portraits contemporains*, III, 321 (January 15, 1842), when he aligns the writers of his time in three rows, apparently omitting Vigny, Balzac, and Michelet, but including Béranger among the three poets of the first rank.

With the three exceptions mentioned above, the men whom Sainte-Beuve underrated include the great writers of his time. Even when he studied them carefully and wrote very detailed monographs, like that on Chateaubriand, Sainte-Beuve displayed doubtful discrimination. Of all Chateaubriand's autobiographical works, he declared in 1850 (*Causeries du lundi*, I, 452) that only one reached perfection: *René*. We, on the contrary, should probably rank *René* lowest today, and certainly far below his masterpiece, *Mémoires d'outre-tombe*, which was dismissed by the critic as a failure (*Chateaubriand*, II, 434). It was mentioned earlier that, in Sainte-Beuve's eyes, Stendhal was merely a witty and clever man, of little consequence as a writer; Balzac repelled him. Walter Scott was a far purer novelist and "George Sand," wrote the critic, "need we recall it? is a greater, firmer, and more faultless writer," while "Eugène Sue is perhaps Balzac's equal in inventiveness and creative facility" (*Causeries du lundi*, II, 461, article of 1850).[21] Mérimée should have been more to Sainte-Beuve's taste. Yet, in his secret and venomous notebooks, the critic wrote that there was neither great art nor true naturalness in his masterpiece, *Carmen*. Again Sainte-Beuve, who seems to many of us to have had the gifts of a historian more than those of a critic, failed to appreciate Michelet, the greatest historian then alive. He gave him little or no place in his *Lundis*, while he devoted pages to nonentities, and his notebooks mince no words when he vents his unjust rage. He was almost equally unfair and certainly more than cold to Tocqueville (*Nouveaux Lundis*, X, 280).

Finally, on the poets of his time, Sainte-Beuve, a poet himself, began by being both well-disposed and uncommonly subtle in his appreciation (in his early articles on Hugo, for instance, of January 1827, *Premiers Lundis*, I). A personal estrangement separated the two men, which may be a sufficient excuse for the critic's later obtuseness. Nothing, however, should have prevented him

---

[21] Yet an American admirer of Sainte-Beuve, William Giese, dauntlessly asserted that, for some modern judges, "nothing sounder and juster has been written on Balzac than Sainte-Beuve's article of 1850"!

from understanding Vigny, with whom Sainte-Beuve's own poetic vein had something in common. But when the most beautiful philosophical poems of Vigny appeared in the *Revue des Deux Mondes* in 1843 and 1844, Sainte-Beuve was little impressed. He certainly did nothing to attract the public to those masterpieces and merely sent a few scathing and unfair remarks on "La Maison du berger" to his Swiss correspondent (*Chroniques parisiennes*). When, in 1864, *Les Destinées* were published posthumously, Sainte-Beuve, in one of his most unbelievable critical blunders, called them "a decline, though a well-sustained decline" in Vigny's inspiration, inferior to the poet's earlier achievement.

Although he praised Musset's verse, he did not feel or foresee the value of his plays (*Causeries du lundi*, I, 309). He was unable to discriminate between Leconte de Lisle, or Sully-Prudhomme, and several fourth-rate poetasters. His attitude toward Baudelaire was revolting. His letters treated him like a conceited child who should have reformed and given a few more "pretty prose poems or alluring sonnets" (September 4, 1865). His public estimate of Baudelaire's poetry was calculated to remain as uncompromising and disdainfully patronizing as possible. Yet, in the same years, the feared and respected critic could write of a worthless volume of verse by a certain Mme Blanchecotte: "Poetry is not dead. . . . At once, I recognized there a poet and a soul, a soul sorrowful in its harmony."

In short, no major critic was ever so consistently in the wrong in appraising his contemporaries as Sainte-Beuve. Literature and the public suffered alike from his blindness. Yet Sainte-Beuve was not one of those scholarly historians of letters who disclaim all competence when treating modern literature or refuse to open the new publications. Early in his career, in 1831, he had proclaimed the task of true criticism: not content with following great artists and taking stock of their creations, criticism must, he thought, proudly proclaim its heroes, blaze a trail for contemporary audiences, "make room for geniuses like a herald-at-arms, go in front of their chariot like an outrider." Again, in the final chapter of his *Chateaubriand,* he defined the difficult task of the critic:

He must, with clarity and decision, without wavering, distinguish what is good and will survive; say whether true originality redeems the faults of a new work? what sort of book it is? to what rank does the author belong? . . . The true critic anticipates the public, guides and directs it. . . . "To praise only with moderation is the sure sign of a small mind" (Vauvenargues). . . . "The true touchstone of a mind is the way it approaches a new writer" (Mlle de Gournay).

That Sainte-Beuve fell far short of his ideal should be acknowledged more openly than has been done by the admirers of his wide and penetrating intelligence, which erred in being too exclusively intellectual, deaf to greatness. A precise analysis of the reasons for Sainte-Beuve's failure will serve future critics better than the pious shrouding of his faults.[22]

The second half of the nineteenth century gave rise to a brilliant flowering of critical speculation in France. New methods were proposed and practiced. New attempts were made to discover an objective basis for critical judgment; deterministic and genetic explanations of artistic originality were suggested, which proved tempting in an age of science. Analogies were borrowed from evolutionist biology, physiology, and psychology. The keenest as well as the most powerfully creative minds were attracted by criticism and practiced that universal genre with varied success: some of the most original and prophetic statements on contemporary writers came, not from professional critics like Taine, Sarcey, Brunetière, or even Remy de Gourmont, but from poets and novelists: Verlaine, Zola, Bourget, Gide.[23]

22 In France, the shortcomings of Sainte-Beuve's method have been exposed more severely. In fact, the influence of Sainte-Beuve on French criticism has been very slight and seldom beneficent. Zola, in the volume of his complete works entitled *Documents littéraires,* and Proust in *Pastiches et mélanges* have scored Sainte-Beuve's blindness to the literature of his age.

23 Zola's pseudo-scientific esthetics of the novel deserves the ridicule which has been heaped upon it; but his critical essays on the drama, on Balzac and other novelists, and many of his articles written for a Russian periodical are illuminating.

The gravest fault of so many excellent interpreters of literature was once more their strange inability to believe that their contemporaries could produce works of genius, and their melancholy conviction that an irresistible wave of decadence was engulfing their country and the world. At the same time, while distrusting creative energy and innovation in art, they reserved their most enthusiastic appreciation for insipid books which had only superficial charm.

Montégut was among the broadest and most cultured of those critics. His knowledge of foreign literatures and his thorough familiarity with English writers gave him a huge advantage over several other essayists then in vogue. He was a prose writer of no mean ability, often less tortuous and flowery than Sainte-Beuve. Yet Montégut, one of the most attractive among the *minores* of the last century, did not understand the new poetry of Baudelaire and Leconte de Lisle. When he wrote on the French novel of the years 1860–1875, he fell into every stale complaint which critics have always uttered and presumably always will: imaginative literature is dying; no main tendency or coherent group of writers is perceptible in letters today. France is still waiting for a worthy rival to Fielding and Richardson (of course, Balzac, Stendhal, and Flaubert are not even mentioned). George Sand is the only great French novelist and, next to her, Octave Feuillet and Victor Cherbuliez are the finest portrayers of the age. The latter even recalls Shakespeare and Sophocles! [24]

Barbey d'Aurevilly's savage attacks on Hugo have been already mentioned. More examples of his failure to understand his contemporaries—Flaubert, Renan, Goethe, Zola—could be picked almost at random in Barbey's numerous volumes of criticism; inversely the ardent Catholic poured out his blessing on writers whose names are almost unknown today, and deservedly so: Roger de Beauvoir, Amédée Pommier, Siméon Pécontal (author of "several masterpieces"), Hégésippe Moreau, "the solitary Villon of our impious age" (*Les Oeuvres et les hommes,* volumes on *Le Roman contemporain* and on *Les Poètes*).

[24] Émile Montégut, *Dramaturges et romanciers* (Hachette, 1890), particularly pp. 29, 206, 227, 272.

Schérer's volumes of essays are so mediocre in their insensitiveness to art and beauty that it would be almost unfair to point out the blindness of their author. Pontmartin, whose *Nouveaux Samedis* attempted to rival Sainte-Beuve's *Lundis,* had an axe to grind: he appointed himself the defender of tradition in religion, ethics, and literature. Hence his intense dislike of all the poets whom he suspected of unbelief, pessimism, or lack of orthodoxy: even Lamartine was pitied as unfaithful to his youthful promise; Vigny was criticized as obscure; Hugo, as a madman producing literature in the same way that a factory turns out machines. Laprade alone deserved admiration. But why write poetry in our age? And, in an article on "Poetry and Poets in 1872," the critic quoted with approval the famous dictum of Fontanes in 1810: "All worth-while poetry has already been written." Luck turns against those prophets of despair: the dates of 1810 and 1872 were soon followed by the two most magnificent outbursts of poetry that France has ever had (Armand de Pontmartin, *Nouveaux Samedis,* IX, and for the other articles here alluded to, I, VII, X).

Taine, one of the most powerful minds that ever attempted literary criticism, proved equally incapable of sympathy with the younger generation, either in French or in English literature. He understood neither Flaubert nor Zola, although the latter, a dangerous disciple to be sure, loudly proclaimed his debt to Taine. Realism repelled him, in Goncourt and Daudet, as did the new poetry of Baudelaire and Verlaine. He was much more favorable to—Hector Malot! He strongly advised his daughter not to read the "decadent" writers (Verlaine, Rossetti, Swinburne, Daudet, Bourget). But he ranked Macaulay's *Speeches* "above all that I have read since Pascal" and *Aurora Leigh* above all the poetry written in the English nineteenth century except that of Byron.[25] Taine, however, never publicly criticized the writers of whom he confessed himself unable to approve. His earlier articles on Balzac, Stendhal, and the literature of the previous centuries rank, at times, among the decisive achievements of criticism.

[25] Hippolyte Taine, *Vie et correspondance* (Hachette, n.d.), IV, 28, 34, 137, 285, 327.

The last twenty years of the nineteenth century proved just as disappointing in their immoderate praise of mediocre writers and willful neglect of great ones. Coppée and Sully-Prudhomme (the latter was the first French writer to receive the Nobel Prize) thus long enjoyed an unjustified fame. Jules Lemaître raved about the charm of Sully-Prudhomme's prosaic philosophical epics, and one of the most influential moralists of his generation, Paul Desjardins, went even farther in enraptured admiration (in his *Esquisses et impressions,* 1889). Barrès, whose judgment on men and things was seldom worthy of his colorful prose, confessed to Jules Huret in 1891 that Symbolism had produced only one book worthy of attention: *Le Pèlerin passionné* by Moréas. At the same time there lived a dramatic critic, Sarcey, whose *feuilleton* could either kill a play or establish it securely on the stage. A perusal of his reviews of the drama of the last century arouses irresistible laughter today, and makes us ponder with anxiety the value of our own dramatic criticism: he affirmed in 1878 that the drama of his time could boast of five supermen: Augier, Labiche, Meilhac, Ennery, Sardou. But he could be only contemptuous of newcomers such as Curel, Porto-Riche, or Maeterlinck, and confessed his total inability to understand Strindberg, Hauptmann, and Ibsen's dramas, which he thought both obscure and insane.[26]

As director of the staid *Revue des Deux Mondes,* Brunetière enjoyed the authority of an arbiter of taste in literature equal to that of Sarcey as a dramatic critic. His blind hostility to Baudelaire, to the novelists of his generation, even to Renan is notorious. The only redeeming feature for so much ponderous disapproval is Brunetière's comparative leniency to the Symbolists. Without really understanding their effort, he welcomed them as a beneficent antidote to Naturalism and naïvely reasoned that, Symbolism being defined as the concrete presentation of an abstract idea, at least those young poets realized the importance of having ideas. To a grave professorial critic, nothing can justify poetry more convincingly than an intellectual content.

[26] The hostility of European critics toward Ibsen for ten or fifteen years is one of the strangest aberrations in the history of criticism. He was called mad, decadent, perverted, revolutionary, devilish, but not once recognized as primarily a skillful dramatist.

Brunetière's contemporary and rival in the Nineties was Jules Lemaître. His manner was as light and humorous as Brunetière's was pompously heavy. He had been a graceful poet in his youth, a carver of artistic tales, and a clever playwright. His influence as a critic was wider than that of any of his contemporaries; he demolished many a reputation with subtle irony. And yet, how disappointing is his series of articles on *Les Contemporains,* read at a perspective of forty years! Lemaître was not, like Brunetière and Faguet, primarily a literary historian bent upon classifying and revaluing past literature. Contemporary works were his main concern. But the picture of French letters between 1880 and 1914 extracted from his score of volumes would be fragmentary and false. Victor Hugo's poetry is condemned as lacking in ideas. Baudelaire does not count. Mallarmé "probably does not belong to literary criticism" (*Les Contemporains,* VIII, 40) and can be tolerated only by foreign readers, who do not have to forget habits of clarity and preciseness before approaching his poems (*ibid.,* V, 43–48). Verlaine and other Symbolists are equal torturers of "the very genius of the French tongue" and fall into unintelligibility (*ibid.,* IV, 66). The truly great and truly French poets are Sully-Prudhomme, Heredia, and Coppée. To Grenier, Rabusson, Mérat, Des Essarts, Silvestre, all prosaic nonentities, Lemaître gives an honorable mention. The truly important poets of the symbolist generation are thus all ignored.

Anatole France, who collected four volumes of essays on contemporary literature and published many more articles in the *Temps,* proved slightly more sympathetic to Baudelaire, although hardly penetrating. He contradicted himself on Verlaine and, after having distrusted him, secretly felt attracted by his Bohemian capriciousness. But he never liked Mallarmé and was repelled by Rimbaud, or perhaps reluctant to read him. Like many French critics his obsession with clarity and purity of style made him prefer the shallow and conventional poets (Sully-Prudhomme, Coppée, Plessis in *La Vie littéraire,* I, Catulle Mendès, Judith Gautier, Vacquerie, Vicaire, and others whose frail charm has long vanished). He tried to respect Balzac's power but wrote nothing valid on him; he cleverly mocked Zola's coarseness without suspecting his epic imagination. Sandeau, Édouard Rod, and Feuillet appealed to him more warmly, as being more "classical." The critic's tastes, in this case, are an involuntary and dangerous indication of the rank to which Anatole France as a poet and novelist may be assigned some day, after having enchanted the whole world by his suave and shallow banality.

Since 1910, no critic has enjoyed undisputed pre-eminence. The number of gifted and subtle appraisers of literature has increased tenfold with the multiplication of reviews and weeklies. Anatole France's prophecy that criticism would soon invade and devour the whole of literature has seemed to be near fulfillment. Luckily, the great variety of critical temperaments also brought endless contradictions in critical opinions of any one book. The most excessive terms of praise were profusely bandied about by critics who were also novelists or dramatists, and expected reciprocity: [27] those who tried to be severe and judged from rigid standards often failed to perceive originality or to like what did not conform to their prejudiced views (Souday, Lasserre, Massis). Those who insisted on remaining versatile were also undiscriminating and either avoided judging recent literature (Thibaudet) or welcomed every minor and superficial work and thus lost the public's confidence (Jaloux). The best critical pronouncements of the first half of this century will doubtless prove to be those of Gide, Rivière, and Du Bos, men who wrote only a few, carefully meditated critical articles, but did not set out to be the regular guides to the public through the vast literary output of their day. They seldom spoke against a book which they may have thought contemptible; they did not attempt to restrain the fame usurped by worthless volumes and thus correct the public taste, misled by publicity, superficiality, or a passing vogue; they did not even try to lead the younger writers to a

[27] Jules Romains' series, *Hommes de bonne volonté*, was very seriously and favorably compared to Balzac's *Comédie humaine* by André Thérive. The same critic, in *Galerie de ce temps*, insisted that Colette's *Chéri* is an incomparable masterpiece, "one of the most beautiful ever written in French." Countless other examples might be added.

clearer consciousness of the forces at play in contemporary letters and of the main currents of thought and sensibility molding
them.

No conclusions—not even provisional ones—need be appended
to this long enumeration of representative errors of taste, vision,
and judgment. I believe this accumulation of evidence to have
been necessary to a fair statement of the critical dilemma which
the following chapters will try to analyze in a more positive
spirit.

PART TWO

THE PROSPECTS FOR A BETTER CRITICISM

CHAPTER IV
Some Critical Platitudes

TO collect with diligence the mistakes of others and to smile at them from our none-too-secure vantage point of a century of progress can only be entertaining to a few cynical spirits and for a brief interlude. I have in the preceding pages laboriously tried to illustrate some self-evident propositions: That a critic, as distinguished from a literary historian, must sooner or later venture to judge the recent works of literature, painting, music, and in so doing show that his long familiarity with past masterpieces has not altogether blunted his ability to recognize new greatness. That the bold and lucid appraisal of his contemporaries is indeed the most treacherous task facing a critic, but by far the most challenging and momentous one; for by discharging it with honesty and courage, he can influence literature in the making, and mold timid and hesitant opinion. That, weighed by those exacting standards, great critics who were able to estimate the new as well as revalue the old have been very rare indeed, far rarer than great poets, great painters, great philosophers. It may be that no masterpiece remained unknown for more than thirty or forty years; it is certain that almost all great works were first slighted or condemned by the most responsible observers, and much laudatory ink was squandered by critics, and many valuable hours lost by readers, on nonentities.

The case that has been argued thus far had no need to be strained unfairly. Instances of gross critical blunders and neglected masterpieces could easily have been multiplied. I have not concealed that in most of the examples quoted, though not in all, there was usually a very small minority of contemporary reviewers who from the first displayed some insight. In cases like those of Shelley or Keats, Rimbaud or Cézanne, César Franck and

Rodin, that minority was, however, almost infinitesimal. These rare exceptions do not vitiate the argument.

For if a few judges, often obscure men with no superior gift of discernment or prophecy, were able to perceive the originality of Stendhal or Baudelaire, is not this a proof that it required no superhuman foresight to do so? Other reviewers, official and more influential, could have done it if they had been less prejudiced or more alert. Future critics may try to be more openminded. Today, after months of patient excavation in the basements of big libraries, scholars may delight in unearthing periodicals in which an unknown reviewer had discerned the genius of Baudelaire, Wagner, or Debussy before anyone else had suspected it. Such obscure prophets should not indeed go without honor, but for all practical purposes they hardly counted in history and they do not atone for the general sin of criticism. No one read them or took them seriously when they wrote. For the average reader and buyer of books does not, like the exhaustive scholar, patiently scan fifteen or twenty reviews of a new book. He glances at one or two, signed by some fashionable critic, and seeks no further.

Official, or influential, criticism, as practiced in the leading periodicals, must then be reformed, if criticism is ever to become fair and lucid. If, instead of Leigh Hunt, who was not taken very seriously, and a few obscure gazetteers, an authoritative critic had discovered the genius of Shelley and Keats in their odes, the history of their reputation in England might have been greatly altered. In 1840 Stendhal was lauded with almost rapturous enthusiasm by Balzac for his recent *Chartreuse de Parme,* and his death, two years later, was the occasion of two penetrating articles in *La Revue des Deux Mondes* and *Le Courrier français.* He was thus not totally ignored. But Balzac as a critic enjoyed small credit and the other two reviewers apparently even less. Stendhal's finest novel remained utterly unrecognized and was practically lost for over ten years. It happened then that an obscure professor of literature who had rediscovered it by chance converted to his enthusiasm a group of young men at the École

Normale in Paris; he thus initiated the new cult called in France "le Beylisme." But the public was no more ready to admire Stendhal-Beyle in 1850 than in 1840. It was no better prepared to acclaim Shelley in the Victorian era than it had been in 1820; it did so because a few bold spirits had led the way and imposed their taste. The shrewd and powerful critic who could have done the launching earlier simply was not there, or (like Sainte-Beuve and Mérimée with Stendhal) did not deign to display his shrewdness.

Enough facts have been ascertained in the previous chapters. I am now at liberty to adopt one of several attitudes toward this problem of the failure of contemporaries to recognize genius. The first and most spontaneous course might be to pour out our indignation against so much accumulated injustice. Without delay we might then brush aside all the errors of criticism and seek an infallible basis for our future critical judgments in psychology, semantics, linguistics, or some other so-called "exact" discipline. Such a Utopian venture would soon lead to new disappointments. The world would become an insipid paradise if there were an infallible remedy for every evil and a prompt solution to every difficulty.

Leaving indignation to youthful apostles of perfect justice, an older and more sophisticated observer might go to the other extreme. If he has the training of an historian, he may also have acquired the historian's skepticism: he may look upon man's record as an endless succession of failures, now tragic, now amusing; he may boast of having become "realistic." "The only thing we learn from history," Hegel wrote, "is that we never learn anything from history." Genius will always be unrecognized, says the literary historian, for the very reason that it is genius and hence rises far above its contemporaries. Critics are human and fallible. Moreover, is it not excellent training for promising artists to wrestle with hostility and misery? Let us leave an insoluble problem alone, and find a secure haven in compiling a bibliography of Milton or an index to Shakespeare's images. Let us even, like Browning's grammarian, explore for the thousand-and-first time the tortuous mystery of some Greek preposition. We may even, if hard pressed for thesis subjects for our disciples, encourage them to expose the shameless stupidity of the contemporaries of Beethoven, Wordsworth, Kleist, Baudelaire, or Cézanne who knew no better than to insult or ignore the genius of those great men while they lived and struggled. In the meanwhile, let us banish from our seminars, as controversial and somewhat vulgar topics, any consideration of those who are writing in our midst, starving perhaps or reduced to silence by the bitterness of ironical journalists and contemptuous academic critics. The minds of scholars seem professionally or congenitally incapable of believing in any genius living in their own time. They refuse to admit that genius can remain neglected for a number of years. "Like murder, talent will out," they comfortably say.[1] "God's in His heaven, all's right with the scholar."

Between these two extremes there should be room for a middle road, a third attitude which might be termed neither idealistic (the adjective is sadly in need of rehabilitation) nor realistic (a magic word for the disillusioned and naïve generation between wars), but realistic-idealistic. It may be acknowledged that the problem of recognizing genius is hedged round with difficulties, for genius can be clothed in many a varied and misleading garb, and greatness in a work of art, as in wine, is a slow and growing process. Let it be confessed that I have no infallible recipe for critics, no magic touchstone which will instantly tell authentic genius from imitators. Finally, we cannot cherish the illusion that, where great minds like Goethe, Sainte-Beuve, Matthew Arnold have failed, critics of the future are going to succeed at once. The very difficulty of the task, however, acts as a stimulus. Can we not try and go part of the way toward a better, nay, an ideal, criticism? Can we not at least chart on our map the blind

---

[1] It would be interesting, but perhaps demoralizing, to compile statistics of murderers who were never caught, and of crimes which remained unpunished after twenty or thirty years; it is said that the proportion in America would be four out of five.

alleys and the dangerous roads in which our predecessors went astray, and perhaps avoid them when threading our way through the *terra incognita* of contemporary literature?

Let it not be said that such an ambition reveals an overweening arrogance, and that academic writers had better keep away from contemporary literature since they have always fumbled notoriously in judging it. Institutions of learning have multiplied in the last hundred years; they have renovated every field of human knowledge—except, probably, literature, philosophy, and the arts. Their attempts at teaching students to write a play, a novel, or a poem have not, let it be owned, increased the number of geniuses alive in 1967, nor even raised the general level of short stories, plays, and poems now being produced. At any rate, they could more profitably teach a wider public to discriminate values in the creations of their century and encourage the young people in their curiosity about the bold works of their own age. They might even induce them to apply close and sympathetic attention, time-honored methods of analysis, comparison, and personal interpretation to Kafka and Claudel and O'Neill, and not merely to writers like Henry James, Edwin A. Robinson, and T. S. Eliot, professors' ideals, redolent of the past and rich in subtle allusions for the learned few.

There is no more convenient cloak for human laziness than the cheap optimism which asserts, with a shrug of the shoulders, that everything will be all right in the end, and that no one can mention a single "inglorious Milton" to whom criticism and posterity have long been cruel. The truth is that each of us could quote a good many names, in every field of artistic creation, that deserve to be ranked with the finest; but we find it very hard to impose them upon a critical public which hates nothing more than having its serenity disturbed.[2] Dictionaries (even those which are entitled "biographical and critical") and histories of literature, painting, and music, the least revolutionary of all human enterprises, are, in more than one sense, self-perpetuating. A few new names may be inserted after a safely prolonged so-

[2] For such examples see Chapter VI.

journ in Purgatory; a few old ones may be dislodged from the eminence they once usurped, when generations of schoolboys will have stared vacantly at Cicero, Ben Jonson, Burton, Jeremy Taylor, Bunyan, La Bruyère, Manzoni, Macaulay, Lessing, and finally damped the respectful enthusiasm of their elders for those glorious names. It is easier to amend a political constitution—even in the United States of America—or our own moral behavior than to alter our established perspective on the literary master-pieces of the past.

Yet the endeavor is more than worth while. We shall never know what future talents were nipped in the bud by hostile criticism or neglect, since the men thus attacked ceased to devel-op their talent or to direct it into the channel of artistic and literary creation. We shall not even know whether, romantic as it may sound, some of them were not actually driven to suicide or madness or misery through lack of public encouragement. Only a self-righteous Pharisee would retort that they deserved their fate, if strength of character was thus lacking in them. Poets and musi-cians are afflicted with more sensitiveness and less practical shrewdness than an army general, an industrialist, or a college president. We do know, however, of many authors and artists for whom life was a merciless struggle—not against their ideal vision, or their medium, or artistic obstacles—but against a listless public and hostile criticism. Time, energy, and masterpieces were thus irretrievably lost.

I admire the placidity of those critics who remain unmoved by the pleas of writers for justice and recognition, or by their bitter outbursts of anger at being consistently maligned and misunder-stood. Keats was not killed by a few venomous reviews; but is it unreasonable to suppose that a little more recognition would have encouraged him to write more poetry in the last year of his life? It would probably have led vain and worldly Fanny Brawne to esteem him more highly than she did and to return his love with less coquettish calculation. Even if the poet's life had not been lengthened somewhat by success, he might have composed a few more masterpieces like the splendid "Fragment of an Ode to Maia" or the perfect sonnet "Bright star! would I were steadfast as thou art," perhaps the most beautiful single sonnet in the English language. With a little more understanding from critics and from the public would not Baudelaire have composed more *Fleurs du Mal* between 1857 and 1867, and perhaps more of his amazingly penetrating articles? But those ten years were spent imploring that recognition like a beggar, lecturing to a scornful public in Belgium, planning translations, novels, and plays in the vain hope of paying off his accumulated debts. Berlioz might have created more works like his *Symphonie funèbre et triomphale* if he had not been forced to fight against jealousy and inertia in the musical world. The reception of his compositions by contemporary critics sadly justified the bitter irony with which, when success, too late, crowned him, he remarked in his memoirs: "My musical career would no doubt at last become quite charming, if only I could live one hundred and forty years." Cézanne, who burst into tears when a friend one day condescended to admire his paintings, then universally derided, would have been less tortured by bitterness and harrowing doubt about his own merit. César Franck might have composed more music if scores of critics had not pronounced his works, to the very end of his life, to be "the affirmation of incompetence pushed to dogmatic lengths." Success came to him, at last, in his sixty-ninth year, at a concert given exactly seven months before he died. Hugo Wolf, if less worn by his desperate efforts to have his music played, might not perhaps have fallen into madness and premature death. It is not inconceivable that Rimbaud might have continued writing, if more fellow poets and critics had understood his "verbal alchemy." Mallarmé and Claudel, if less deeply wounded by the gibes of journalists and the blindness of critics, might have refrained from cultivating esoteric obscurity or strangeness; and their art, as well as the public, would have gained. Thomas Hardy would probably not have given up novel-writing if *Jude the Obscure* had not been obtusely and perversely misrepresented.

He noted in his *Journal:* "A man must be a fool to deliberately stand up to be shot at." [3] How regrettably embittered Stravinsky may have become since it has been the fashion among critics to belittle his later works, how regrettably overconfident Sibelius and Shostakovitch may have grown through excessive praise which uncritical music commentators have heaped on their work, time alone will tell. Only the staunchest determinist may contend that the history of literature and the arts could not have been other than it was. If our fond speculations on what might have been cannot alter the past, can they help us alter our own selves in the future?

Flaubert, who had a passion for truth and justice and who scourged in more than one of his letters the most blatant faults of criticism, spent his spare moments in compiling a "Dictionary of Accepted Opinions." It was to include the platitudes, the trite statements, and silly inanities which we all hear, and probably utter, every day. Flaubert dreamt that, after having gone through that "sottisier," self-respecting individuals would be cured by ridicule and would rid literature and conversation of the worst of those conventional ideas and phrases.

Flaubert's "Dictionary" was never completed. It is doubtful whether it would have triumphed over mankind's worst sin, mental inertia. Society women with bank accounts richer than their vocabularies would doubtless get brain-fag and fill all the hospitals in the country, if they were forbidden to use more than five times a day the convenient phrases, "the play is perfectly lovely," "a marvellous lecturer," "he's simply grand," or "he gives us food for thought." For a hundred years teachers have been trying, with scant success, to eliminate from the critical style of their

---

[3] On Thomas Hardy's bitter disappointment at the onslaught on *Jude the Obscure,* see Florence Emily Hardy, *The Later Years of Thomas Hardy* (New York: Macmillan, 1930), pp. 38–43. Wordsworth was equally disappointed at the hostile reception given his *Excursion.* He wrote to Henry Crabb Robinson on August 2, 1816: "As to publishing, I shall give it up, as nobody will buy what I send forth; nor can I expect it, seeing what stuff the public appetite is set upon."

students such stock phrases as: "the book is interesting," "the style is simple and clear," "the best novel I have ever read," "stimulating," "uplifting," and the like. In men's colleges, critical impressions are dissected with reluctance and rendered, with a concise vigor worthy of young admirers of Ernest Hemingway, by two or, at most, four adjectives: "swell" or "lousy," "snappy" or "stinking."

We shall always err, and few of us, even among would-be literary critics, will ever be eager to strain our imagination for new formulas when the line of least resistance offers such ready temptation. May we not, however, appeal to that desire for orig- inality which marks the modern intelligentsia in art and letters, and ask them to shun the beaten track? It would be a rewarding task to collect a list of the most conventional banalities uttered by our predecessors when judging the poetry and music of their age. Critics familiar with such a catalogue of preposterous fallacies, or "idols," as Bacon might have called them, would perhaps think twice before venturing a sweeping assertion; they would muster all their power of attention and examine themselves with humil- ity before condemning an author with a strange imagination and a new style. I dare not envisage a golden age in the future when criticism will be infallible. It would be most ungenerous of critics to utter the definitive truth on a contemporary work and thus leave nothing to be redressed by their successors, and deprive scholars yet unborn of the pleasure of some day contradicting them. Luckily for us, critics will always sin. At least let them do so in a newer and more ingenious way, through the avoidance of platitudes already ten centuries old. They may thus more surely win the mercy of their Maker, who, supreme Artifex that he is, must long ago have lost patience with our monotonous rehashing of age-old errors and our unimaginative, unoriginal sins.

A) Some causes of the most common mistakes of critics may be dismissed fairly summarily. Critics are men, hence fallible; occasionally they are women, and frailty is their name. The first pitfall in which they often flounder lies at the feet of all. Behind much inability or unwillingness to recognize a new talent there is often personal prejudice—all the more dangerous for being, in many cases, unconscious and disturbingly naïve.

Critics are often jealous or afraid of writers, especially of the rebels and nonconformists among them. In Europe, if not in America, a successful critic is a man of importance. He may be the editor of an influential review, the Librarian of the House of Lords, or, in a musty "National Reading Room" of Paris, the formidable bearded gentleman who casts a withering look, from behind his desk, at the young man impudent enough to ask for a volume not mentioned in the unfinished catalogue. He is sought after in fashionable drawing rooms, respectfully questioned on the literary trends of the day, and he wears several decorations at his buttonhole. More often still he is a professor, hence (in many continental countries) a state official, accustomed to hierarchy and entitled to respect. In France, since 1830, very few were the critics who had not been trained for the teaching profession (even Taine, Lemaître, Souday, Sartre, Thibaudet had been) or did not, at some time in their career, become professors. Sainte-Beuve himself taught for a short time. Remy de Gourmont, Jacques Rivière, and a versatile writer like André Gide are the few shining exceptions. It is a natural weakness in professors to become easily patronizing to new and obscure writers. Do not scholars embody the whole classical tradition and the long series of past geniuses whom they annotate, edit, and own?

Such critics live, moreover, in a world of stable values. They are accustomed to regular meals, fragrant cigars, respectability in their homes, docile audiences laughing every year at the same jokes. It is natural for them to be repelled by artists and creators. To them, Verlaine is an incurable drunkard and, through his shameful life, a corrupter of youth. Little do they think that, twenty years hence, they will lecture on him and call him a classic. For the present, the scoundrel deserves to starve. As Paul Claudel wrote in a bitter poem celebrating the Bohemian Verlaine,

Chacun lui donne de bons conseils; s'il meurt de faim, c'est sa
faute. . . .
L'argent, on n'en a pas trop pour Messieurs les Professeurs,
Qui plus tard feront des cours sur lui et qui sont tous décorés
de la Légion d'Honneur.

Wagner may boast of his unrecognized genius; to grave critics he
is above all characterized by his incurably ill breeding. Balzac is a
conceited upstart, Zola a dogmatic reasoner on the novel and a
"specialist of the abdomen." Baudelaire is a shabby, half-starved
poet, who lives in a miserable lodging with a woman of bad
repute, a colored woman at that. César Franck is a timid, shrivel-
ling piano teacher who, of course, will never be admitted to the
Institute. Cézanne is a queer, ill-tempered eccentric, a coarse
southerner who never learned how to draw. Gobineau is a third-
rate diplomat who has taken it into his head to write books.
Mallarmé is a failure as a teacher of English in a French lycée
and the occasional writer of sonnets which journalists laughed at
as pornographic, since they could make no sense out of them at
first sight. Karl Marx, Pareto, Lenin are miserable exiles, reading
books all day long. D. H. Lawrence is an abnormal sex-maniac,
surrounded by adoring hysterical women.

Conversely, musicians like Reynaldo Hahn and painters like
Van Dongen are extolled to the skies because they dress with
distinction and know how to pay a compliment to a lady. Anatole
France and George Bernard Shaw may scoff at the public to their
heart's content; their irony is suavely sugar-coated and delights
their readers, who feel as clever as they. The most skillful strate-
gist of letters will not fail to be gently and harmlessly iconoclas-
tic, in the best manner of Lytton Strachey and Aldous Huxley: it
is the surest way to win the snobs. One may commonly hear
Boston ladies praise Mr. N. for his latest novel with the words:
"Extracts of his book have been given in the last *Reader's Digest*.
Besides, you know, he comes from one of our oldest New England families!" M. Maurois is regularly quoted at cocktail parties
by persons who want to display their familiarity with the latest

stars of French literature. "And, my dear, he is such an inspiring lecturer!" In some countries, it is an asset for an author to have been born with a high-sounding title: Countess de Noailles, Princess Bibesco, or, since lords are few and far between in English literature, the Honorable (for as a writer he is little more) Maurice Baring.

It may happen that the critic is an elderly person, and perhaps a former "creative writer" himself, who tried his hand with moderate success at novel or drama. Age and disillusion have made him a wiser man. Can he foolishly apply the word "genius" to a young upstart who was a newborn infant when he was already famous and respected? Even more difficult than to discover genius among young men forty years our junior is, however, the recognition of greatness among our classmates. The most entertaining and probably the worst of all volumes of criticism would be a compilation of what their former schoolfellows wrote, if they wrote at all, about Shakespeare, Balzac, Beethoven, Tolstoi, Mahler, Hemingway, Tennessee Williams.

Finally, and still more frequently, the critic cannot divorce literature from politics, art from religion. If he is a staunch conservative, he smells revolutionary tendencies in a new writer; if he is a radical, he flings the accusation of "fascist" with unstinted generosity; if he is a Stalinist, he is quick to discern Trotskyism. In this way politics invaded literary estimates in England during the Revolutionary and Napoleonic wars, when to be a devotee of Rousseau or a disciple of Godwin put a writer under suspicion. Since the eighteenth century it has hardly ceased to color critical judgments in France. In our own century French critics have been either for or against romanticism, for or against foreign influences, for or against democracy. A great many names have been literally imposed upon the public through a conspiracy of partisans, often recruited among fanatical admirers of a master addicted to dogmatic statements. Such a master was Maurras. Moréas and Toulet, charming but inconsequential poets, were raised by disciples of Maurras to the stature of giants; but, the day after Mallarmé died, in 1898, Maurras scoffed at his sonnets as replete with erotic allusions. Historians have not yet exploded the myth that a group called "École Romane" played a part in "overthrowing" Symbolism. Even the most independent French critics and the leftist reviewers were intimidated or hypnotized by the obstinate repetition of a few statements: for example, that Maurras was a great prose writer, Jacques Bainville an infallible political prophet, Hugo a swaggering rhetorician, and romanticism a monstrous disease.

B) The mistakes due to perverse political partisanship are, however, less serious than those which are prompted by unconscious though apparently reasonable and detached mental habits. A well-trained student of literature who does not mistake passive and pseudo-scientific objectivity for impartial criticism soon learns to discount the organized hostility of a clique of reviewers (be they American Neo-Humanists, French reactionaries, German anti-Semites, or orthodox Communists). He stands on his guard and warns the public against partiality.

A more dangerous prejudice, to be met among radicals and reactionaries alike, among religious fanatics and fierce unbelievers, independent of all party lines, is a distrust of all that is new in art, literature, and thought. Misoneism is the learned name for it, and conservatism a less formidable one if we divest the word of its common political connotation.[4] Moralists have traditionally blamed the worship of the new for most of the evils of fashion, political turbulence, or licentious behavior. The fear of newness, or, as D. H. Lawrence puts it, the dread of "a new experience, because it displaces so many old experiences," is equally widespread, and equally detrimental to statesmanship, morality, and

---

[4] For it has been remarked that people who hold what the French call "advanced views" in politics (liberal, progressive, radical, or socialist) often balance their own audacity by a narrow conservatism in literature and art. Voltaire, Mérimée, Stendhal, Paul-Louis Courier in France are typical examples of such a dual attitude. Alfred de Vigny noted in his *Journal d'un Poète* in 1830 that liberals bent upon breaking the old shackles were the staunchest supporters of literary rules (record of a conversation with Benjamin Constant).

literature. Good old Pope condemned it, with little lasting result, in one of his most platitudinous paraphrases from Horace ("Epistle to Augustus," II, 1, 49):

> I lose my patience, and I own it too,
> When works are censur'd, not as bad, but new.

All men are tempted, as they grow in years and wisdom, to go on liking what they liked in the first radiant bloom of their youth. In what is doubtless a silent and ineffectual gesture of protest against the opposite behavior of their wives, they insist upon wearing the same kind of tie, the same type of hat or cut of clothes, upon smoking the same brand of cigar, reading the same newspaper, and having their dwindling hair trimmed in the same way as when they were twenty. Modern habits of cleanliness are hard enough, which force us, as an old German professor once complained, to part with our shirt and send it to the laundry just when we were beginning to get used to its comfort. Forty seems to be the perilous age for men, as well as traditionally the critical one for women in French novels ("le Démon de Midi," said Paul Bourget after Psalm 91). "It is shameful to live beyond forty," exclaimed Dostoevski—who himself lived to be sixty. At that age we draw our car away from the train and allow our younger fellow passengers to go on at full speed to the abyss of the future: we are content to rest on a comfortable sidetrack and prophesy dire catastrophes. As Anatole France used to put it, it is an indefinable relief for us when we grow mellow or slightly overripe to whisper in our own ear that there have been no pretty girls since our courting days, no faithful wives since we married, no good books since ours were printed. Once, making a strenuous effort, we managed to accept the French Realists; we forced ourselves again to like Walter Pater, George Moore, Oscar Wilde. Then Shaw, Galsworthy, H. G. Wells, and other social prophets came, and that was too much. Or, if in our teens we delighted in Hardy and Conrad, we perhaps accepted Virginia Woolf and Somerset Maugham, even *Sons and Lovers* and *The Portrait of the Artist as a Young Man;* but to Lawrence's later excesses and Joyce's pornographic [*sic*] and philological tricks, we are determined to say *No*. Or else, having succeeded in our youth in accepting the vision of the French Impressionists, we strained our eyes and tortured our brain to keep up with the Post-Impressionists. But no further. We balked stubbornly at Cubism or Surrealism, Rouault and Picasso. Of course, early detractors of Brahms and Van Gogh, of Stravinsky in his *Rites of Spring*, and Cézanne were ignorant fools; we, luckily, knew better and forced those great men on our age. But we must now rest content. Hindemith, surely, is mere modern cacophony, Boulez and Stockhausen are even more revolting, Stravinsky's late works are necessarily inferior to his earlier ones, since they require a new adaptation from us; Picasso should have stuck to his charming blue and pink period; Joyce and Lawrence had to turn crazy after a certain age, as most Englishmen (even born in Ireland) do from boredom, repression, and, if they stay at home, excess of tea and vegetable marrow.

We even invent convincing theories to support our present dislikes. Somewhere in the evolution of literature and art we draw an imaginary line to divide the healthy innovations (those of our own generation) from the morbid and insincere attempts of youth. We explain with the most plausible logic that art can only go astray when it refuses to select, or when it becomes incommunicable. And we explain in perfect sincerity that all that is new has already been said; all has been tried, then probably rejected as unworkable or sterile. We may, if we are entrusted with the training of the younger generation, admit Henry James or Edith Wharton or Edwin Arlington Robinson as a subject for a scholarly essay. We shall even welcome Robert Frost in our seminars: he fits in comfortably with the English tradition, and a man who loves and idealizes New England and writes poetry so near to everyday prose cannot mislead us. But there firmly we stop. "God wrote one book, and that is enough," said a clergy-man who once turned his daughter out of the door because she insisted upon writing poetry. Experience, refined taste, mature wisdom are on our side while we thus justify our conservatism and our fear of taking risks. It is strange that those virtues have never failed to impress the public, even after a whole century of lip service paid to the worship of youth, and distressing havoc wrought by obstinate and venerable old statesmen to their countries and to the world.

> Do not let me hear
> Of the wisdom of old men, but rather of their folly,[5]

was the warning of a poet-critic who lived long enough to give us, with *The Elder Statesman,* one of the most disappointing dramas of our age. The history of criticism is thus studded with naïve decrees, long impressive in their curt finality, which echoed La Bruyère's famous "Tout est dit." Jeffrey's "The age of original genius is over," Fontanes' declaration in 1805 that "Tous les vers sont faits," Macaulay's assertion that no poetry worth reading had appeared in England since his *Lays of Ancient Rome,* have been recounted already. The more we believe in progress as an ascending curve the more prone we are to imagine that our present age is very near the zenith. If we paused for a moment to consider the extreme youth of the modern novel, to dream of the immense strides which will soon be taken in criticism, psychology, and sociology, to picture the deserved contempt in which physicists and physiologists of the year 2400 will hold our so-called new physics, our belief in bacteria and vitamins, our twentieth-century surgery, we should either smile cynically at our ludicrously modest achievements or take pity upon ourselves.

The formula invariably resorted to by the conservatives, a dangerous one because it is perfectly plausible and occasionally justified, is the familiar assertion: "There are limits to artistic innovations, and some rules cannot be broken, because they are based upon human nature itself." Here again a glance at our predecessors who stubbornly held a similar conviction and were proved mistaken is most conducive to humility, though not, I hope, to timidity.

For the same formula was used by the most competent con-

[5] T. S. Eliot, *East Coker.*

noisseurs of music before Monteverdi's revolution which practically created modern music. As late as the seventeenth century, everyone in Europe burst out laughing when the phrase "German music" was uttered. The existence of any gift for musical composition among the "Tedeschi" was readily taken to be impossible. Suddenly Telemann, J. S. Bach, and P. E. Bach, Gluck and Handel heralded the unequalled glory of German instrumental music. A little later, Beethoven's compositions were gravely condemned by many a competent critic. Some things had not been done before him; they were banned as impossible and as preposterous innovations. For instance the notes F and B were not to be put in succession, but Beethoven broke the practice in his most celebrated overture and, after a struggle, his example became finally accepted. In the third decade of the nineteenth century (it may be remembered that Beethoven was born in 1770), the two English musical papers were still assuring their public that the German innovator was a fraud. One, *The Harmonicon*, termed his later sonatas and quartets "obscure," "eccentric," and "unmelodious"; while the *Quarterly Review and Magazine* explained that Beethoven could not be a great musician since he had not written fugues, as all great musicians should. It added that he had "mistaken noise for grandeur, extravagance for originality" and was "deficient in grace and clearness." [6] A few years earlier, an eminent critic, discussing the first performance of the *Eroica Symphony*, voiced the common verdict that the work had only "a certain undesirable originality, . . . due to the unusual and fantastic, not to the beautiful and sublime." He added that, in the opinion of several hearers, Beethoven was making himself "unendurable to the music-lover."

Mr. Deems Taylor, from whom we borrow the above quotation, adds a few others just as devastating: on Mozart, whom a contemporary, Sarti, after hearing part of his *D Minor Quartet*, called "a barbarian," "only a piano player with a depraved ear";

[6] See W. H. Hadow, *Studies in Modern Music* (London: Seeley, 1896), I, 58 ff. For the reference in the following paragraph, see Deems Taylor, *Of Men and Music* (New York: Simon and Schuster, 1937), p. 111.

on Brahms, whom Tchaikovsky cursed as putting the final seal to the decline of German music. We might cull many such pronouncements from any history of music. A French critic whose power was, in his time, formidable, Fétis, said of Wagner's *Tannhäuser*, "There is not a single spark of melody in the whole production." The London *Athenaeum* termed it: "A recitative as uncouth and tasteless as it is ambitious." Robert Schumann, a compatriot of Wagner, was just as severe; but Schumann's music had, in its turn, been defined by the English as "a display of unattractive cacophony." Wagner himself brutally slighted and dismissed young Hugo Wolf. Rimsky-Korsakov confessed, of Debussy: "Better not listen to him; one runs the risk of getting accustomed to him and might end by liking him." Debussy's *L'Après-Midi d'un Faune*, indeed, was denounced, to Mallarmé's dismay, as "lacerating the ear"; and when *Pelléas et Mélisande* was given, the more competent critics—the Germans especially, including Richard Strauss—insisted that Charpentier's *Louise*, and certainly not Debussy's opera, was the masterpiece of recent French music.

Fear of the new is indeed a more prevalent evil in music (among critics and concert-goers alike) than in literature. But nowhere is the disease so virulent as in the pictorial arts: perhaps because painting and sculpture affect our senses even more directly than music and certainly more than the written word perceived by the eye and transmitted first to the intellect. Examples of fierce hostility to great painters are numberless in the history of art since Delacroix and Ingres. A few typical ones may be added from an era which is not yet remote.

In 1913 an exhibition of modern French paintings in New York drew comments from the most respectable art critics of America, from which we shall extract a few representative quotations.

Kenyon Cox, in *Harper's Weekly*, March 15, 1913, openly rejoiced at the show of "modern" art, for if a drastic emetic is thus swallowed once for all, the evil may be cured forever. He then went to the exhibition, ready to distrust his own conservatism and trying to laugh. Alas!

The thing is not amusing; it is heartrending and sickening. . . . The real meaning of this Cubist movement is nothing else than the total destruction of the art of painting. . . . Now all discipline has disappeared, all training is proclaimed useless, and individualism has reached the pitch of sheer insanity or triumphant charlatanism. . . . Cézanne seems to me absolutely without talent and cut off from tradition. . . . Gauguin is a decorator tainted with insanity. . . . As to Matisse, it is not madness that stares at you from his canvases, but leering effrontery.

In *The Century Magazine* (April 1913) Mr. Royal Cortissoz, was hardly less vehement.[7]

From the incomplete, halting methods of Cézanne, there has flowed out of Paris into Germany, Russia and England, and to some slight extent the United States, a gospel of stupid license and self-assertion which would have been swept into rubbish were it not for the timidity of our mental habit. . . . The farce will end as soon as we look at those paintings.

Of Rodin, Kenyon Cox had declared in 1913: "pathological . . . hideous. . . . That row of Rodin drawings at the Metropolitan Museum is a calamity." And, in an amusing volume, Mr. Walter Pach, who championed modern painting against the official verdict of American respectable criticism, told how, for many years, the name of Manet was followed in the Catalogue of the Metropolitan Museum by the words: "Pupil of Couture. . . . An eccentric realist of disputed merit. . . . His pictures were several times rejected at the Salon."

The European public had been only slightly less conservative than that of the New World. Cézanne's reception in Paris and his rejection by the official museums are a well-known and lamentable story. Readers of Virginia Woolf's vivid biography of Roger Fry have been amused, or perhaps grieved, by the account of the fearless undertaking of that conscientious Quaker. Having discovered the Post-Impressionists, he decided to become their

[7] This article, and the one previously quoted by Kenyon Cox, were reprinted in *Three Papers on Modern Art* (New York: American Academy of Arts and Letters, 1924).

stalwart champion and organized an exhibition in London, in November 1910, prudently entitled "Manet and the Post-Impressionists" (Cézanne, Gauguin, Van Gogh, Picasso, Derain). The reactions of the public may be classified under six different formulas: a joke, a swindle, a childish affair, anarchistic art, a display of madness, an insult to the British public. The London *Times* was grave and haughty. "It begins all over again, and stops where a child would stop." And it appealed, with irresistible self-assurance, to the verdict of Time, "le seul classificateur impeccable"—which, of course, could only confirm the negative judgment of the *Times*. Several physicians proved conclusively that there were signs of insanity in the pictures. Wilfrid Blunt, a bold revolutionary in his day and a gifted writer, vented his rage in unambiguous words:

Nothing but that gross puerility which scrawls indecencies on the walls of a privy. . . . The method is that of a schoolboy who wipes his fingers on a slate after spitting on them. . . . Apart from the frames, the whole collection should not be worth £5, and then only for the pleasure of making a bonfire of them. . . . They are the works of idleness and impotent stupidity, a pornographic show.

Poor Roger Fry, one of the most honest men that ever devoted his virtues to the cause of art, made relentless enemies for having introduced Gauguin, Matisse, and Picasso to London. When he died, almost thirty years later, Professor Tonks declared that it was for English art "as if a Mussolini, a Hitler, or a Stalin had passed away." [8]
The strange irony which almost invariably accompanies such vituperation against newness in art is that critics seem unable to analyze the new into its component elements and to link the alleged "revolutionary" artists with their predecessors. After a span of ten, twenty, or thirty years, they suddenly recover their critical faculty and acknowledge that those rebels of art were indeed "classics." Very often they even appear to have been mere

---

[8] See Virginia Woolf, *Roger Fry, a Biography* (London: Hogarth Press, 1940).

imitators; we then regard them as modest links in a long chain, an end and not a beginning *ex nihilo*. The very artists who were most violently attacked for breaking with the past then seem the most closely connected with august, time-honored traditions. Brahms, after long years of protest from concert-goers, gradually finds himself linked with Beethoven; Cézanne immediately calls to mind Poussin; Rouault, the painters of stained glass in the Middle Ages; Cubism, nay, Surrealism itself were already (in 1940) presented as symptoms of a classical and Cartesian reaction in art;[9] Manet reminds us instantly of Goya; any visitor to an exhibition of Renoir will spontaneously exclaim: "Here is an eighteenth-century master." But no one, in the Eighties and Nineties, apparently noticed the obvious connection with Boucher and Fragonard. Scholars, who were first puzzled by Proust's newness, now neatly "decompose" Proustian originality into elements which they trace back to Saint-Simon, Balzac, and Goncourt. Giraudoux appears less original after forty years, and is classified as an inheritor of Mme de Sévigné and Jules Renard. D. H. Lawrence is obviously a scion of Rousseau; and professors delight in their own subtlety when elucidating Joyce's esoteric allusions to Adam and Ulysses, to Swift's Stella, and Victor Bérard's Homeric lore.

C) While pursuing this review of hackneyed banalities which too few critics have been original enough to eschew, I shall briefly list some familiar fallacies which prevent new art from being encouraged and recognized. Few quotations will be necessary, for those platitudes are the very ones that we hear and utter every day.

a) Other ages were all fortunate in being governed by great currents or important artistic movements. Authors radiated round a central focus; artists grouped themselves comfortably together behind a master or a manifesto so that contemporaries could distinguish a few clear vistas in the works of their time.

[9] See an excellent work by René Huyghe, *La Peinture française, les contemporains* (Tisné, 1940).

Today, however, confusion reigns supreme. No "elite" imposes its views on the public; the field is surrendered to young upstarts and false talents. Of that confusion Sainte-Beuve complained repeatedly.[10] After the romantics, lamented the critics, all groups have disappeared; years later they discovered that Realism had been an important movement, but that a similar void had succeeded it. Symbolism came, followed by a score of other "isms" in literature or painting. Still the critics complained that their own age alone was one of confusion, while their predecessors had been fortunate in being able to study a beautifully ordered literature. "There are no more 'schools,' no more traditions, there is no more discipline," observed the arch-skeptic Anatole France (*La Vie littéraire*, II, 199). Similar complaints have been uttered by hundreds of critics since.

b) The same critics likewise remark that the present era is full of interest, brilliantly gifted, rich in intelligent attempts, but devoid of geniuses. Talents galore, the critic repeats; too many of them, but all secondary; not one great composer like Brahms or Wagner, not one great painter leading the minor ones as Cézanne or Delacroix—allegedly—had done; no Tennyson, no Hugo, no Balzac, no Goethe, no Johnson to give their name to the age. Needless to add, no other period in the past, not even that of Beethoven, Molière, or Shakespeare, ever acknowledged the undisputed authority of those masters; no critic ever admitted that his own time enjoyed more than secondary talents.

c) A far more attractive excuse for the unproductiveness of their age, or for their own inability to discern its great men, the critics find in the magical word: transition. Eureka! It dawns on them that they live in an unfortunate era of transition. The time is out of joint; the world is blindly but surely groping toward a new light. A new social order is evolving; old beliefs, traditional manners have crumbled down. How can art and literature flourish when the social state is chaotic and mankind, haunted by

[10] See especially his article on Joubert in *Portraits contemporains*, II, 309, written in December 1838. The same charge, and those which are examined in the following pages, will also be found in a typical volume of conservative French criticism, *Les Jeunes*, by René Doumic (Perrin, 1896).

unheard-of problems, is suddenly forced to choose between the past and the future?

We do indeed live in a period of transition. In the Twenties, a periodical adopted the word as its battle cry; in 1926 Edwin Muir wrote a volume entitled *Transition;* the Second World War was an age of transition, like the pre-war years, and the post-war years in their turn, and the decade before the First World War. But the late nineteenth century ("fin de siècle") was equally certain that it witnessed a transitional crisis of all its values; so were the contemporaries of Marx and Darwin, and Arnold,

> Wandering between two worlds, one dead,
> The other powerless to be born.

So were the romantics, as Musset's celebrated opening of the *Confession d'un Enfant du siècle* recalls; so was the eighteenth a transitional century if ever there was one; so was the period of Locke, Bayle, and La Bruyère, and that of Donne and Malherbe, and the Renaissance, and the barbarian invasions, and the collapse of paganism. One might go back *ad infinitum.* Men have always stood on the ruins of a lamented past and on the threshold of an ominous future. Why indeed should times of changing social conditions, crumbling beliefs, wars, and revolutions be less conducive to philosophical speculation or artistic creation than "static" or lethargic eras? All the evidence that we can muster points, if anything, in the opposite direction. The number of geniuses and talents certainly did not increase in Spain, Italy, Holland, Sweden during their quiet era of static and contented happiness. Renan thought he could pay no greater compliment to his native country than to link it with the Greek and Jewish peoples, as living in a perpetual state of transition or intellectual turbulence. Wars, invasions, revolutions, unstable governments, mental ferment afflict the Jewish soul, the Athenian and Parisian minds; but monotony and sterility never weighed down upon the history of such peoples.[11]

[11] Harping on the transition theme has become especially prevalent since the spread of the new fashion of regarding literature as a mirror to social trends. It saturates some of the most valuable attempts at criticism of our age, such as David Daiches' *The Novel and the Modern World* (Chicago:

d) Other charges, and often contradictory ones, are brought by critics against the literature of their time. The young writers do not know how to write; the young painters cannot draw; the young musicians have not learned the elements of musical composition. They merely spare themselves the trouble of learning the rules of their trade or the technique of their art, hoping that their laziness and ignorance will be taken for originality and genius.

Or again, the innovators repudiate the principle of selection. They do not know how to choose, and merely accumulate a mass or disorderly material. They delight in chaos, glaring patches of color, or ear-lacerating dissonances. What was being said lately of the Surrealists was said lately of Proust and Joyce, earlier still of Debussy, Van Gogh, and Dostoevski, a hundred years ago of the Realists, before that of Balzac, Victor Hugo, and Delacroix. It is an easy excuse for the indolent critic who refuses to train his eyes, his ears, or his brain to an unconventional selection from vast reality.[12]

If the critic is even bolder, he will jump to the offensive and justify his distrust of younger authors and artists by asserting that they are merely a group of pushing upstarts. Being aware of their artificiality or of their emptiness, they have decided to get together and make a vociferous group. They have conspired with their friends and, like gangsters, have thus succeeded in stealing some of the public interest. Earlier, the French Classicists were

---

University of Chicago Press, 1939) in which the technical experiments of Joyce and Virginia Woolf are explained—if one may use that verb—by the period of transition in which those writers lived.

[12] Occasionally, a critic is courageous enough to blame himself, and not the younger writers, and to confess his own laziness candidly. Desmond MacCarthy does so in his volume *Criticism* (London: Putnam, 1932), apropos of Rimbaud and the younger French writers who strain his attention. He begins an essay on D. H. Lawrence with the admission: "It is certainly the duty and it should be the delight of a critic to examine his contemporaries. This is the most difficult part of his work. Critics are most at home with old books. . . . I was aware of Lawrence for fifteen years, also that to understand contemporary thought, I must tackle him. Yet I put it off and off. . . . Why did I shirk it so long? Chiefly laziness."

accused of logrolling, and the sixteenth-century Pléiade before them. In the eighteenth century, it was the turn of the Philosophes and the "coterie holbachique." Then the Romantics, the Parnassians, the Symbolists, or the Bloomsbury group in England. Mr. Van Wyck Brooks once revived the old and worn-out accusation and vituperated against the fashionable writers of today, Proust, Joyce, Eliot, as mere "coterie literature."

e) If the critic is pressed for less trite and more precise reasons to justify his distrust of contemporary attempts, he resorts to an argument which he deems unanswerable. "In any case, I much prefer classical music"; or "Say what you like, none of the modern painters gives me as much pleasure as Raphael or Titian or Rembrandt"; or "Racine gives me all you find in Proust, and much besides."

It may very well be that there is nothing in modern music to equal Mozart, that recent poetry has not had its Keats or its Dante, that the whole French novel of the last thirty years can boast of no Balzac or Flaubert. But is such a comparison fair?

No one exploded the fallacy of thus crushing modern literature under the weight of the vaguely defined "past" better than Wordsworth. In 1809, long before he became "the lost leader" and a conservative contemner of his younger contemporaries, he explained, in a letter to *The Friend*, that persons who declare the present age inferior to those which have preceded it are guilty of two errors:

One lies in forgetting, in the excellence of what remains, the large overbalance of worthlessness that has been swept away. . . . The second is not considering that the present is in our estimation not more than a period of thirty years, or half a century at most, and that the past is a mighty accumulation of such periods, perhaps the whole of recorded time. . . . What can be more inconsiderate or unjust than to compare a few existing writers with the whole succession of their progenitors?

Wordsworth's reasoning seems to us fully convincing. All those who distrust the whole of modern art and literature because it does not "equal the best of the past" should keep in mind: (1)

That we should only compare the last quarter of a century to any other period of twenty-five years, and then recognize that, if a few such periods were richer than ours in music, painting, philosophy, and poetry, many were far poorer indeed. (2) That, even in the richest quarter of a century in the history of English poetry, German music, or French prose, there was much extravagance, obscurity, artificiality, and superficiality which is today forgotten, and that we cannot dismiss the bad or mediocre productions of our age quite so easily and agree on the true values. (3) That one third or perhaps one half of the best works of the last twenty-five years, those which may well comprise our chief claim to the attention of posterity, are not even known to us: they may consist of unpublished letters (like those of Mme de Sévigné or Diderot), unpublished memoirs (like those of Pepys, Saint-Simon, Casanova), unpublished or neglected poetry (like that of Traherne, Blake, Rimbaud, or Gerard Manley Hopkins), or simply of works like the paintings of Cézanne and Sisley, the novels of Stendhal, or the poems of Shelley and Claudel, which few contemporaries are discerning enough to admire as the masterpieces of their age, equal to the best of the past.

D) But the worst, because at the same time the most disloyal and the most effective, attacks launched against most of recent literature and art should be grouped under another heading in our imaginary dictionary of trite ineptitudes. They come from men whose motives, doubtless sincere though often misapplied, are patriotic, moral, and religious. Their tone is one of self-righteous indignation or outraged defence of public sanity.

It is a sorry sight to survey the history of past and present criticism and discover how often critics of no mean repute have fallen back upon careless accusations and cheap slander. Alfred Noyes, the English poet—fortunately not one of the greatest— declared, after the French military defeat of 1940, that such a collapse was no surprise to a reader of Proust's corrupt novel depicting a corrupt society. Soon afterwards the London *Times Literary Supplement* (of December 21, 1940) defined Proust as "the faithful chronicler of the final period of bourgeois decadence which culminated in the present war." (As if Zola and Balzac had not already described the bourgeois decadence of their time! As if we could believe that the long-promised collapse of the bourgeoisie was really at hand!) Young American critics, always lured by sociological interpretations of literature which unleash their love of impressively long words and lend ponderous gravity to esthetic studies otherwise thought unworthy of a scientific age, naturally followed suit and wrote on Proust as a prophet of the French collapse. Mr. Van Wyck Brooks discovered that not only Proust and Valéry, but most English and American writers of our time were negative or, as he called them, secondary, and that our generation stood in dire need of "primary" writers—writers with a comforting message.[13] In an age which considers the epithet "two-dimensional" the worst insult for a painting, a novel, a symphony, or a woman, Oliver Allston (Mr. Van Wyck Brooks's mouthpiece) proposed an original criterion for greatness in literature: it must consist of three dimensions, breadth, depth, and elevation. And elevation he found sadly lacking in Dreiser, O'Neill, Hemingway, and other contemporary Americans, while Longfellow, Whittier, and Harriet Beecher Stowe had, no doubt, monopolized that third dimension some generations ago. For a very brief while, under Marshal Pétain's masochist influence, the French thought in 1940 that they should burn all they had adored, and blame Proust, Valéry, Surrealism, and Cubism for their faulty strategy and lack of tanks and airplanes. Fortunately Mauriac and Gide soon reminded them that they had lost enough of their national heritage as it was, and might at least retain the best achievements of the previous twenty years, which were in the field of arts and letters. A glance at past criticism should be enough to make those modern seekers for purity and sanity recover their senses. Ever since nationalism invaded literature, that is to say since the French Revolution,

[13] Van Wyck Brooks, *On Literature Today* (New York: Dutton, 1941). On Proust, see for example Edwin B. Burgum, "Proust's Account of the Fall of French Civilization," in *Accent*, I (Summer 1941).

almost all the great writers of France have, at one time or another, been called "un-French" (Rousseau, Hugo, Stendhal, Vigny, Nerval, Rimbaud, Zola, Claudel); the Germans had similarly decreed that Heine was non-German; American imitators of Mr. Van Wyck Brooks may one day appoint a congressional committee to brand two thirds of their writers non-American. In all this, literature suffers less than criticism and the public. Meanwhile, some works will be extolled to the skies because they are "national": *Cyrano de Bergerac,* or a play—now forgotten, but which threw the public and critics into raving enthusiasm and took its author straight to the French Academy—*La Fille de Roland* by Henri de Bornier, or Lavedan's *Servir:* the last two, needless to add, are but worthless if "elevated" platitudes. Kipling and Masefield in England, the author of *John Brown's Body* in America, whose genuine talent deserved a much better fate, were similarly in danger of being underestimated by posterity as a punishment for an early and excessive fame, evoked by the patriotic and national quality of their writing, not by its esthetic merit.

The charge of not being patriotic or "uplifting" or "elevated" enough is often accompanied by two others which may be dealt with summarily, though they can, when wielded by renowned critics, plant grave suspicions in the minds of the public. One consists in accusing younger writers and artists of being slaves to foreign influences. Any trained and self-respecting historian of literature and the arts will answer that writers most widely influenced by foreign cultures are usually the most original and the most national: Ronsard, Molière, Rousseau, and Gide in France, Chaucer and Milton in England, Goethe and Rilke in German literature. Many Russians consider Pushkin as the most Russian of their poets, Glinka as the most Russian of their musicians; both were permeated by foreign influences. Manuel de Falla is none the less Spanish for having welcomed the influence of several schools of European music. Dryden and Pope were English to the core at the very moment when they imitated French models; Shelley and D. H. Lawrence were never more English than when they lived away from their native land as voluntary exiles and denounced the hypocrisy of their countrymen. Joyce could hardly have been more Irish if he had lived the last twenty years of his life in Dublin, and not in Italy, France, or Switzerland.

The insistence of critics and journalists upon the treatment of native subjects by their native writers often has a baneful effect upon the literature of new countries. This has been conspicuous in modern America. Henry James was not at his best when laying his refined plots in the American scene. Willa Cather has been better inspired by the story of an American boy abroad (*One of Ours*) or by French Canada (*Shadows on the Rocks*) than by "American" subjects. The same is true of Hemingway. Dos Passos was perhaps more moving in *1919* than he has been in his ambitious and ponderous kaleidoscopes of Chicago and Manhattan. Nothing could be more harmful to American fiction than the convention that a novel, to be truly "American," must depict a boy born in Denver or Kansas City, going to school in Wisconsin or Texas, discovering love in New York, drinking in Chicago, observing nature in California or human degradation in Detroit or Atlanta, getting a divorce in Nevada, committing a crime in Mississippi, or joining the Salvation Army in Brooklyn. Too many cumbersome all-embracing epics of American life, too many rapturous hymns to America on the pattern of Walt Whitman, Vachel Lindsay, and Carl Sandburg should remind poets and novelists that big subjects do not always make great books, and that the most American of writers will not necessarily be the one who treats of the American scene in an American way, but the one who is the greatest artist and perhaps the most modest genius.

At periodic intervals and especially in moments of crisis, critics also accuse the literature of their contemporaries of not being universal. Only universal art, they say, appealing to all readers with a minimum of culture, is destined to survive and is worthy of our democratic era. And they decide that Raphael and Rembrandt, Bach, Milton, and Dickens are universal, but that Manet, Cézanne, Rodin, Debussy, Baudelaire, Proust, Joyce are not.

Any comparison between geniuses of unequal value is of course unfair and misleading. How universal is Dante's appeal today, or Milton's, or Shakespeare's in *Measure for Measure* and

The Winter's Tale, or Dickens' in *The Pickwick Papers?*—that is a more than debatable question. Conversely, he is a bold prophet who can assert that Stravinsky, Picasso, Joyce, and Proust will not some day be universal. Tolstoi, in *What Is Art?*, one of the least intelligent books ever written, is the worst offender in charging lack of universality to the art of his time. The French Realists as well as the Symbolists, Baudelaire, the painters of what is called today Impressionism and Post-Impressionism appeared to Tolstoi as extremely special artists, trapped in a blind alley, expressing nothing but the most egotistical minutiae of their own nature. Seventy years have elapsed. Generations of readers, not French alone, but German, Russian, English, American, Asiatic, have suddenly recognized themselves in Baudelaire, since 1920 the most widely read and translated of all the nineteenth-century poets in any language. Cézanne, Gauguin, Van Gogh, Rodin, if one may judge from museums and exhibitions the world over, have also acquired universality. Indeed, Mallarmé, whom Tolstoi branded as the most narrow and incomprehensible of poets, enjoys a fame, inside of France and out, second only to that of Baudelaire. Proust, who was also accused in 1925 of being "a coterie writer" and who certainly made few concessions to "universality" (being interested neither in labor nor democracy, offering no moral, patriotic, or religious message, making his novel one of the bulkiest ever written and one which cannot easily be retailed in convenient slices to the public), is probably today the most universal novelist of our century. During World War II an English journalist noted with some surprise that the translation in two close volumes of *Remembrance of Things Past* enjoyed a real popularity among British prisoners of war. Some years ago, it was announced that the success in the Soviet Republics of a translation of Proust was such that the Russian government feared the influence of such "petit bourgeois corruption" on proletarian readers and considered banning the book.

E) From the charges of insufficient national spirit and lack of universality to the even more common charge of immorality, the transition is easy. It would certainly be hard to discover the great books that were not first branded as immoral, at any rate in the last two or three centuries, for the moral obsession really came into the West with the Puritans and the Methodists in England, in France with the bourgeois nineteenth century. Before resorting to the charge of immorality when we want to damn, to ban, or merely to avoid reading certain books, we should do well to think twice, and picture to ourselves how ludicrous our indignation may appear fifty, nay, fifteen years hence. Unless it be that of obscurity, no article in an imaginary "Dictionary of Accepted Ideas" would be as amply illustrated as that of the immorality of new works.

For once, I shall avoid quoting examples from French literature, from George Sand and Balzac to Proust, Céline, and Montherlant. The French have long passed as the masters of naughtiness and eroticism—others would say of sanity and candid acceptance of life as an indivisible whole. Tolstoi, himself not a model husband, but long steeped in French literature, denounced it later for debauchery, lust, and profligacy. That reputation, if it were ever justified, is no longer the sole privilege of French literature. The Anglo-Saxons have gone it one better. The library of virtuous French *jeunes filles* used to consist of a few translations of novels by Walter Scott, Dickens, George Eliot, Cooper, and Jack London. But then, when the knowledge of English spread among the younger generation, daughters not infrequently brought home the latest novels in English, Faulkner's *Sanctuary*, Caldwell's *Tobacco Road*, Steinbeck's *Grapes of Wrath*, O'Neill's dramas of murder and incest, or even *Lady Chatterley's Lover* and *Tropic of Cancer*. Nothing can equal the dismay of bewildered French mothers brought up on *Uncle Tom's Cabin* and *Silas Marner!*

A few examples, whose eloquence needs no comment, will show how some of the most famous works of literature in English were judged by irate contemporaries.

Of Leigh Hunt's *Story of Rimini, Blackwood's Magazine* has this to say in May 1818: "No woman who has not either lost her chastity or is not desirous of losing it, ever read the *Story of Rimini* without the flushings of shame and self-reproach." Thirty years later, a novel which is today a classic (perhaps, in spite of its melodramatic and old-maidish hysteria, the most "classical" of the English novels of the last century, that is to say one of the least disorderly and leisurely), *Wuthering Heights*, was described thus by the *Quarterly Review:* [14]

The spectacle of those . . . animals in their native state [Catherine and Heathfield] is too odiously and abominably pagan to be palatable even to the most vitiated class of English readers. With all the unscrupulousness of the French school of novels it combines that repulsive vulgarity in the choice of its vice which supplies its own antidote.

With *Jane Eyre*, the same critic was hardly more lenient: she denounced in Charlotte Brontë's story "a coarseness of language and laxity of tone which have no excuse in our time; . . . sheer rudeness and vulgarity" and concluded that it was "pre-eminently an anti-Christian composition."

I have recalled in a previous chapter the outburst of indignation which first greeted *Richard Feverel*, another classic of English fiction. Even George Eliot's novels, which the modern reader blames above all for the intrusion of that moralistic preaching from which its free-thinking and independent author could not refrain, were censured as licentious. Ruskin called *The Mill on the Floss* "a study of cutaneous disease" and, in the same essay, "Fiction, Fair and Foul," described George Eliot's characters as being "like the sweepings of a Pentonville omnibus."

America, which had no Queen Victoria or Prince Albert, was then just as Victorian in her prudishness. The treatment meted out to Poe and Whitman has been recalled earlier. Hawthorne's *Scarlet Letter*, today a school classic, acceptable even to the

---

[14] December 1848. The author of the review was Miss Elizabeth Rigby (later Lady Eastlake). It is quite natural that *Wuthering Heights* should have appeared bold to contemporaries: for the first time an English novel depicted a real woman physically and unreservedly possessed by love. Many contemporaries were roused. But was it true, and did it seem immoral because it was true and new? Such are the questions they should have asked.

movies, the most carefully supervised industry for morality, was denounced in the following terms by A. C. Coxe, in *The Church Review* (January 1851):

Let this brokerage of lust be put down at the very beginning. Already, among the million, we have imitations enough of George Sand and Eugène Sue; and if as yet there be no reputable name involved in the manufacture of a Brothel Library, we congratulate the country that we are yet in time to save such a reputation as that of Hawthorne.

Why choose such a repulsive subject? asked the indignant moralist. And he answered his own question rhetorically, bringing in, as usual, the corrupting influence of the French:

Is it because a running undercurrent of filth has become as requisite to a romance, as death in the fifth act to a tragedy? Is the French era actually begun in our literature? And is the flesh, as well as the world and the devil, to be henceforth dished up in fashionable novels, and discussed at parties by spinsters and their beaux, with as unconcealed a relish as they give to the vanilla in their ice-cream?

Poetry was, of course, not immune from such attacks. Rossetti was accused by Ruskin and others of being a "sensuous" poet, which he doubtless was, but interpreting and appraising his poetry might have been a worthier task.[15] On August 4, 1866, a ferocious article appeared in the *Saturday Review* which lacerated Swinburne's recent *Poems and Ballads:*.

Libidinous song: . . . a mind all aflame with the feverish casuality of a schoolboy over the dirtiest passages of Lemprière . . . tuning his lyre in a stye. . . . No language is too strong to condemn the mixed vileness and childishness of depicting the spurious passion of a putrescent imagination, the unnamed lusts of sated wantons, as if they were the crown of character and their enjoyment the great glory of human life. . . . A volume crammed with pieces which many a professional vendor of filthy prints might blush to sell if he only knew what they were.

[15] Robert Buchanan attacked Rossetti's poems with violence in "The Fleshly School of Poetry" in the *Contemporary Review*, October 1871. In 1881 he apologized for his attacks. Why had he not resisted his prejudice ten years earlier and judged the poetry as poetry?

The article, which appeared anonymously, was in fact by John Morley, who never acknowledged it and later regretted it when he had become a friend of Swinburne's; the latter, amusingly enough, was aware all along but never told Morley that he knew who had thus pilloried him and won for his volume a *succès de scandale*.

So widespread indeed is the charge of immorality against all innovators that it has been brandished repeatedly by critics in fields where it was almost a contradiction in terms: architecture, music, and painting, where not the subject but the manner was stigmatized. In such cases it is usually linked with the parallel charge of decadence. All the great musicians of the last century were accused of writing "music of decadence and death." Debussy's music, for instance, was described in the most serious French reviews as "pernicious, invertebrate, nihilistic, dissolving because it is in a state of dissolution."

When reread fifty years after, the criticism of painting is the most entertaining of all. I have purposely refrained from borrowing examples from pictorial criticism: they are so numerous and as a rule display such extremes of preposterous absurdity toward contemporary art that it would be almost unfair to rest any conclusions on what is perhaps the most futile province of man's accomplishment: art criticism. Let it be recalled that, all through the nineteenth century and in the twentieth the adjectives "immoral," "morbid," "crazy," and "ugly" have been practically interchangeable. After an interval of thirty or forty years, opinion has crystallized anew around some of the artists thus vilified, and the epithets "sane," "robust," "beautiful" have been then in order.

If there were ever sane, robust, and normal painters in the last century, they were Delacroix, Courbet, Monet, Renoir, Cézanne. Yet Delacroix's long struggle against contemporary opinion and taste is legendary. No invective was too harsh for his "Dante et Virgile aux Enfers" (1822) and for most of his paintings until his death. "Extravagant delirium," said Delécluze; "murder of painting," exclaimed Gros. His "Justice de Trajan" was described by

Alphonse Karr as "a butcher-boy daubed all over with glaring vermilion." Gavarni was even more insulting—almost unquotable. As late as 1859, Maxime du Camp advised Delacroix, then sixty-one years old, to give up painting and turn to music and literature, his real vocation; he cruelly analyzed "the artist's premature death, which paralyzes his hand, closes his eyes, and deprives the mind of any notion of truth." Manet was called "putrefying," striving after "a chaotic disparity of colors, of impossible forms, to arrest our gaze and stupefy us." "Filthy," "ignoble," "disgusting," and a whole gamut of damning adjectives were used to define Courbet. His *Baigneuses* were openly accused of distorting and misrepresenting the beauty of Parisian women, and thus injuring the tourist trade of France. Monet was characterized, in 1874, as a painter "who will not condescend to turn his stammering into articulate words." Degas, according to the more polite among the critics, "feigned madness." All were called "Communards," which, three years after the Commune, was far from being a harmless insult. Indeed, several connoisseurs seriously suggested a firing squad for all the Impressionists.[16] Concerning Cézanne, who was born in 1839, who first exhibited in 1866, and who died in 1906, Ambroise Vollard collected a number of typical estimates printed between 1904 and 1907.[17] A few of the most typical may be reproduced here:

The procedure somewhat recalls the designs that schoolchildren make by squeezing the heads of flies between the folds of a sheet of paper. [*Le Petit Parisien.*]

This exhibition will put an end to the quarrel by demonstrating in a most peremptory fashion that Cézanne is nothing but a lamentable failure. [*La Lanterne.*]

A kind of art that might have been produced by a Zulu islander. [*Le Monde illustré.*]

Let us leave it to others to admire the monkeys *à la Cézanne*, painted with mud, not to say worse. [*La République française.*]

[16] See Gustave Geffroy, *La Vie artistique*, Vol. III: *Histoire de l'Impressionnisme* (Dentu, 1894); Th. Duret, *Histoire des Peintres impressionnistes* (new ed.; Floury, 1919).

[17] Ambroise Vollard, *Cézanne* (New York: Crown Publishers, 1923).

"A madman," "a drunken scavenger," "an ingenuous bricklayer," "a fake," and "a swindler" were phrases which recurred everywhere. At the same time, the Louvre rejected his paintings, the Minister of Fine Arts (himself an art critic named Roujon) refused his friends a decoration for him. In 1899 the German Emperor, Wilhelm II, positively forbade Tschudi, the Director of the Berlin National Museum, to exhibit Cézanne's paintings.

Cézanne, fortunately, was well-off, and a stubborn man besides. He could wait. Others (Renoir, Pissarro, Gauguin, after he gave up his prosperous business as a stockbroker, Sisley, after his family lost their fortune in 1870) had to vegetate in abject poverty. Still others were discouraged and driven to humble drudgery in which their promise was stifled. When they were safely dead and buried, art dealers, shrewdly realizing that these painters could no longer "swamp the market" with new work, began speculating on their unknown masterpieces. Every gallery in the Old and the New Worlds competed for a Manet or a Cézanne. Meanwhile it was the turn of Modigliani, Picasso, and Rouault [18] to be cursed as ugly, distorted, morbid, immoral, unChristian, and to suffer humiliation and poverty.

Again the public was the real loser. If the best men in the country, the most competent (as their titles, decorations, and books testified) refused to be polluted by looking at a Cézanne or a Degas, how could the timid general public have done better, and the rich men have squandered a few francs on their crazy paintings? The most difficult thing in the world is for the majority of mankind (especially those who have gone through school and college, read the newspapers and reviews, and dutifully listened to the broadcasts of "eminent authorities") to have an opinion of their own on life and politics, books and paintings. The result of the invectives flung at Cézanne and Van Gogh was to impoverish the public (spiritually) and to enrich (materially)

---

[18] Rouault, the greatest religious artist of our times, was, as is usual, most bitterly attacked by orthodox and even mystical Catholics: Léon Bloy, whom Rouault revered as his master, poured invectives upon his paintings (Lionello Venturi, *Rouault* [New York: Weyhe, 1940], p. 16).

a dozen dealers. Likewise, by overwhelming D. H. Lawrence, Proust, and Joyce with charges of obscenity, critics, probably disinterested, vitiate the public taste or keep it from becoming enlightened and promote the success and the sale of a much lower kind of literature.[19]

F) The last of our honored platitudes has been already touched upon, since it is closely allied to immorality: for the last hundred and fifty years, persons discontented with their age and some of its intellectual manifestations have delighted in calling their contemporaries "abnormal," "insane," "degenerate." A history of the notion of decadence should some day be written, and the myth exploded once for all. It should not take, in the meanwhile, a great array of examples to make critics refrain from such hackneyed charges and to warn the public to be on its guard whenever a narrow-minded and low-souled critic resorts to them.

The notion of decadence is one of the least scientific in the range of critical ideas, and the term one of the loosest. The word apparently came into use from analogy with the history of the Roman Empire, interpreted by Montesquieu and Gibbon as a decline and fall. Yet even in history, nothing is more perilous than misleading analogies drawn from the ancient world. The modern world has witnessed the decadence of some cultures, or some countries, soon followed by the emergence or the resurgence of others. Speculations on the decline of the West, of the British Empire, or of the white race had better be left once for all to pompous philosophers and overwearied journalists. The analogy is even more groundless in literature. There was an alteration which may be called a decline in the ancient languages;

[19] Edmund Wilson has related in *The Triple Thinkers* (New York: Harcourt, Brace, 1938) a touching visit paid to Paul Elmer More on a Sunday afternoon at Princeton. Three of the ablest minds of America happened to be gathered there: More, Gauss, and Frank J. Mather. They unanimously outlawed, without having ever opened it, "the greatest literature then alive" (*Ulysses*). More characterized *Manhattan Transfer* as "an explosion in a cesspool"; his effort at explaining Proust is pathetic. In the same years, his friend Irving Babbitt, of Harvard, damned the whole of imaginative literature since the archvillain, Rousseau, as "crawling on all fours."

the "silver age" of Latin literature was certainly inferior in creativeness and power to the age of Virgil and Lucretius; and an
archaic or formative period in Greek art and in Latin verse preceded the so-called Golden Age. But which is the golden age in
English letters? and was the golden age of France the thirteenth,
the seventeenth, the nineteenth, or the twentieth century, which
gives thus far excellent promise of rivalling the others?

The charge of decadence began to be a favorite one with
critics around 1820–1850, when they resorted to words of moral
opprobrium to damn the writings which, for literary or partisan
reasons, they did not like. In France, all the great romantics
(Lamartine, Hugo, Musset, Balzac, for example) were called
decadent, separately and collectively. Nisard, a powerful critic in
his day, fired a big blast at the romantics in a volume on the *Latin
Poets of the Decadent Era* (1834), which implied throughout
that Hugo and his friends stood to Boileau and Racine in the same
relation as Ausonius and Rutilius Numatianus had stood to Virgil
and Lucretius. Sainte-Beuve, one must regretfully acknowledge,
took up the cudgels after 1840, and many of his articles then
denounced

a refinement of immorality and depravity, which is becoming a more
and more daily occurrence [*sic*], a ghastly wound spreading every
morning. There is a dose of sadism, concealed but not beyond recognition in the inspiration of our two or three most renowned novelists.[20]

Hernani, Les Orientales, Musset's *Nuits,* Balzac's novels were
thus termed decadent. Soon, however, Flaubert and many a
minor realist outdid Balzac; Leconte de Lisle seemed decadent to
Pontmartin, apparently because he was not a good Christian and
worshipped formal beauty to excess. Then Baudelaire came, flout-
ing *Les Fleurs du Mal* in the face of the bourgeois; he boasted of
his dandyism, of being doomed, as an artist, to the venomous
curses of contemptible Philistines; he pretended to abhor nature

---

[20] Sainte-Beuve, "Quelques vérités sur la situation en littérature," July
1, 1843 (*Portraits contemporains,* 1st ed., II, 327).

and to praise make-up in women and artificiality in art. Verlaine soon followed, exclaiming in a celebrated sonnet:

Je suis l'Empire à la fin de la décadence.

Young men gathered around the shade of Baudelaire or Verlaine's café table and called themselves: the Decadents. Nothing more was needed to gull official critics. Baudelaire, Verlaine, Rimbaud, and Mallarmé went down in histories of literature as "the Decadents." The fashion spread abroad: to England, where, in truth, it soon proved affected and sterile, to Italy, Germany, Russia. It was the "Fin de Siècle" era, the twilight of a civilization. The supreme flowers of European literature had blossomed. No one could ever go farther on the road to refined intellectuality, perverted sensation, crepuscular grace. Literature and the arts were dying.

Seventy more years have elapsed, and our perspective is altered. Now critics, forgetting the naïvety of their elders, are busily declaiming against the shameless decadence of Céline or Dubuffet. As their predecessors had said, "after *Madame Bovary*, what?," they now repeat: "after *Ulysses, Lady Chatterley's Lover, Le Voyage au bout de la nuit*, what and whither?" Let us not prophesy. Let us not cry up these books if we do not think them truly great. But let us remember that mankind has always marched on, in spite of the Maginot Lines of criticism. The worst fools seem to be those who were so easily duped by the childish hoaxes of a few artists and therefore did not read their works or look at their paintings with an open mind. Tolstoi, alas! was one of them, in his distressing comments on Baudelaire.[21] Worse still, at that very moment, physicians and psychophysiologists invaded

[21] As late as December 1916, a New York magazine, the *Art World*, editorially attacked Baudelaire as "an alcoholic, drug and sex-pervert" and blamed him for much of the "abnormality" of modern art. Fortunately, France was fighting a war. That would revive her. "France, again clear-eyed and star-searching, will, under the creative pressure of a sublime regenerative national emotion, once more produce a crop of such masterpieces that the world will know that Gaul still lives." Like Leopardi gazing at the broom-covered slopes of Vesuvius and at man's stubborn foolishness, one would like to comment: *Non so se il riso o la pietà prevale.*

literary criticism. Max Nordau, an Austrian doctor, undertook to elucidate modern letters in a thunderous volume, *Degeneration*, which was at once translated into all languages and lavishly quoted as a definitive scientific diagnosis of the modern evil. Zola, Nietzsche, Wagner, nay, Tolstoi himself were assailed. The French Symbolists were illuminatingly dissected! Verlaine "has all the marks of a degenerate." Mallarmé refuses to explain his poems—obviously because he cannot understand them himself. Baudelaire, their ancestor, wrote verse which is mere "infantile amusement." Some of his poems "circulate only in manuscript because they are too infamous to bear the full publicity of a marketable book." All these younger French poets are mere "filibusters of fame" and make a noise in the world for their own gain. (Which one of them died rich, Dr. Nordau forbears to say.) The Viennese physician supported his diatribe with evidence drawn from the French critics (Brunetière, Faguet, Lemaître) who had all censured the obscurity and decadence of their compatriots;[22] he added gravely that these Symbolists were clearly abnormal, since they suffered from "the group-forming tendency which is a peculiarity of degenerates, . . . the victory of the gang over the individual."

It is hardly necessary to add that most of the writers and artists thus singled out as decadent stand now among the most creative and the healthiest of the nineteenth century. Far from closing an era of weariness and experimenting with disease, Baudelaire, Rimbaud, Mallarmé have proved the "heroic founders of a new line." The whole of modern poetry flows from them, just as the whole of modern painting flows from the Impressionists and the Post-Impressionists. Not the French alone, but foreign critics[23] now

22 The French nationalist critics, who are usually the most ardent railers against immorality, decadence, insanity in their countrymen, probably do not suspect how seriously they are taken by foreign readers, who instead of understanding them prefer to believe that all is rotten in modern French literature. The fulminations on French decadence (by Lasserre, Carrière, Maurras) have been read or translated uncritically abroad.

23 John Middleton Murry, *Countries of the Mind* (New York: Oxford University Press, 1931), I, 116. T. S. Eliot, *Selected Essays* (New York: Harcourt, Brace, 1932), pp. 336–338.

invariably call Baudelaire a classic, one of the truest in the last hundred years, a healthy, masculine genius. So, they now say, was Cézanne. Ill-guided critics abused the word "decadence" to such an extent that the charge is in danger of becoming the most glorious term of praise bestowed on a modern writer. Laura Riding, a writer who has, in English poetry, tried to open up a few new directions, wrote some years ago:

In France, there is always decadence, it is the great national genius and source of life. The French have, indeed, a natural aptitude for decadence; it is in them a sign of health.[24]

If critics and journalists would stop labelling as decadent the works they do not like or do not try to understand, and calling morbid or crazy a disease which merely happens to be different from their own, it would be a great step forward in the difficult problem of maintaining relations between the public and contemporary artists. The whole debate about decadence in art could be stated, it seems to us, in a few words with common sense and modest wisdom.

To begin with, it is obviously true that great creators have sometimes been insane [25] (though the proportion of such cases to normal or sane men has never been accurately estimated): Tasso, Nerval, Hölderlin, Lenau, Schumann, Nietzsche, Hugo Wolf are well-known examples. Others have been afflicted with some disease, unspecified like Pascal's, epileptic like Flaubert's or Dostoevski's, tubercular in many other cases. Several were syphilitic, or drug addicts. Some sexual difficulty may have been at the root of other talents (Rousseau, Gogol, Kleist, Tchaikovsky, perhaps D. H. Lawrence). A preoccupation with homosexuality has characterized many more writers, and can hardly be said to be more prevalent now than at other periods of history (the Greeks with Socrates, Plato, Sophocles, and countless examples;

[24] Laura Riding, *Contemporaries and Snobs* (London: Jonathan Cape, 1928), p. 92.
[25] "Great wits are sure to madness near allied,
And thin partitions do their bounds divide."
Dryden (*Absalom and Achitophel*, I, 163-164)

Catullus, Virgil's *Eclogues*, Michelangelo's *Sonnets*, Leonardo, Shakespeare's *Sonnets*, Winckelmann, Platen, Wilde, Verlaine, Rimbaud, Stefan George, Walt Whitman, Proust, Gide, Hart Crane, several contemporary American dramatists.

The moralist may rightly deplore it. But no one has ever succeeded in establishing a precise relation between genius and insanity, or between genius and homosexuality. Creators in art and letters are usually men who, as children, were "frustrated." They discovered in themselves problems and conflicts, projected their inner torments into imaginary creations, and solved them, or merely expressed them, in works of art. If they had been perfectly normal, happy, and adapted to their environment, they might never have indulged or experienced the creative urge. The history of mankind would then be a dreary desert of barren normalcy.

But are Dostoevski's novels or Proust's, Lenau's poems or Whitman's made less significant by the abnormality of their author? Are they less true to life and human nature for it? Every schoolboy today knows how to stick imposing labels on the writers he is made to read at school: Psychopathic, paranoiac, schizophrenic are quick and convenient explanations. They explain little. The truly scientific, that is the modest and empirical attitude, should be: "In reading Lucretius today, does it occur to me that, as many Christians believed, he might have killed himself in a fit of insanity? Does it bear on his poem in any way? Do I discover in *The Birth of Tragedy* or *The Genealogy of Morals* germs of Nietzsche's threatening madness? Do I ever surmise that all was not well with Flaubert's nervous system? We all happen to know that Van Gogh went mad, because the interest taken in private life has been excessive; can we guess it from most of his paintings? Do we guess it in the case of Méryon, of whom we know much less? Rimbaud's biography is such a thrilling adventure-novel that we are all familiar with it: if we read and studied his works, should we even be embarrassed by allusions to his passion for Verlaine? An excessive emphasis on the private lives of great men, whom we call great only because they composed works that we fail to read, has marked the true degeneration of criticism in the last forty years.

Is it true, however, that modern books often treat of more "morbid" themes than most of the masterpieces which we have been taught to admire? Probably, though by no means certainly. Yet one may doubt whether even the Surrealists of today have been more attracted by monstrosities than the pornographic painters and sculptors of antiquity still visible in Naples and Pompeii, than the painters of many "Ledas," than Bosch, Breughel—not to go back to the Egyptian statues of Akhenaton or to the monsters of archaic art. Their strangeness seems to us only more childish and more voluntary, but not essentially different. What we call progress in literature consists of refinements in technique (Joyce, Proust, and Tolstoi may make Fielding, Smollett, and Walter Scott look like primitives). Such progress is often questionable and entails losses of which we are well aware. A more real progress has consisted in discovering new realms, first in the exterior world (nature, exotic scenery), then in man's behavior and consciousness. *La Princesse de Clèves* (1678) introduced into the novel the new theme of love after marriage and the character of the husband; *Madame Bovary* caused a scandal in 1857 because it treated adultery openly; Proust made a similar innovation when he chose homosexuality as one of the main subjects of his long novel. Others, in poetry and painting, have, as it were, opened some of the secret drawers in which man conceals or involuntarily shuts some of his deepest (and to the conventional moralist, most shameful) motives. Should they be censured for annexing new provinces to literature and enlarging man's knowledge of man?

There is only one type of decadence which is dangerous in art and literature, and unfortunately critics seldom scourge it as it deserves: it consists in being conventional and imitative, in tritely expressing cheap and superficial emotions. It may please the public for a few years; the critics praise it, because they do not think the public deserves better. Gradually, however, readers will listen to other creators who will convince them that life in art is better than death, boldness superior to convention, true emotion to sentimentality. Who knows which among our modern writers will go down in history as healthy and which as decadent? Proust or Maurois, Lawrence or Wodehouse, Hart Crane or Edna St. Vincent Millay, O'Neill or Saroyan?

A morbid fear of disease and an unhealthy insistence on sanity are signs of a secretly morbid constitution. Only the weak and the old tremble at every germ they may inhale, at every bacterium lurking in their food, and at every draft that blows. America, the youngest of the world's nations and the most open-minded audience for art, had been warped by an unwholesome obsession with health, robustness, "ebullient vitality," normalcy. Conventionality, timid sentimentality, a pale idealization of life, childhood, motherhood have thus far prevented a great country from delivering its full message in sculpture, painting, and even, though to a less extent, in literature. Many of the worst traditional platitudes of European criticism have been repeated and magnified in the New World.

Tradition is but an empty word unless one has recaptured the spirit of adventure which created the tradition and imposed it.

CHAPTER V

Obscurity and Obscurism in Literature

ANY reflection on the worst failures of past critics soon leads to the central problem of criteria for a better judgment on literature and art. By what standards are we to examine a new work? Can we discern in it the lasting values which posterity will continue to praise long after the more transitory qualities have faded away?

I have already confessed our inability to provide criticism with revolutionary standards which would enable it to appraise with infallible lucidity the Protean virtue called greatness. Criticism must always remain an adventure or an act of faith. No recipes are valid in an art in which technique and method count much less than the personality of the one who practices it. But progress, in a modest sense, is possible even in the field of art; and I have tried thus far to point out some blind alleys in which our predecessors have been caught. We have posted a few signs to warn our successors away from the worst pitfalls of past criticism. Too much attention given to the man, his private life, and his idiosyncrasies has diverted critics from independent appraisal of his works; political and religious partisanship has obscured the lucidity of their judgment. Platitudes have been endlessly accumulated, and every observer has blamed the confusion, the transitional character, or the decadence of his age instead of sharpening his own vision and helping his readers thread their way through the maze of a vast literary output. The facile and unfair charge of immorality has been resorted to whenever conventional prejudices were shaken. Prophets of despair have been even more numerous in literature and the arts than in philosophy and history, unaware in their wrath that nothing resembles the decaying end of a movement more than the sturdy beginning of a new one, and that "a corn of wheat brings forth much fruit" only after it has been laid to rot and perish.

The worst possible response to these modest conclusions would be that hasty inference which might be drawn by fanatics of standards, eager to reach a short cut to safe literary judgment: a new book is immoral, unconventionally bold, scatological; therefore it is great. Modern writers like Joyce, Céline, or the American author of *Tropic of Cancer* have charted a new land (not unknown to Rabelais and his contemporaries) in describing the bodily functions of their heroes: they are to be hailed as pioneers. Or else, one will say, let us rush to exploit the new mine of literary discoveries: homosexuality. Proust has reached the depths of human tragedy while exploring that theme. We shall reach even more tragic depths by surpassing his boldness.

More ridiculous than those appraisers of new works who fall into conventional banalities worn threadbare by centuries of repetition are the snobs who think they play safer by running counter to all the current fashions. We should not be unduly severe toward snobs. They can be as valuable to the cause of good literature as they are occasionally harmful. They have helped spread the fame of Proust, Valéry, Cézanne, T. S. Eliot; they alone can convince people who want to be "up-to-date" that they must read to the end such monuments of dullness as Thomas Mann's *Joseph and His Brothers* or Jules Romains' *Hommes de bonne volonté*. Then they buy *Finnegans Wake* even if they do not read it, applaud Surrealism and Neo-Thomism. Their co-operation is, however, a half-hearted and perilous one: they desert new fashions just as quickly as they adopt them. One morning, Aldous Huxley or W. H. Auden or Shostakovitch may suddenly discover that his enthusiasts have melted away; St. Thomas Aquinas is unanimously decried by those who extolled him yesterday; semantics joins technocracy or the economic interpretation of history in the limbo of outworn fads. Snobs, and critics who fail to direct their servile fickleness to higher ends, are largely responsible for what has been called the worst disease of the modern world and especially of the New World: the mania for accelerated obsolescence.

Another tentative conclusion drawn from the preceding pages

may be summed up in the French saying, attributed to Catulle Mendès: "Le succès ne prouve rien, pas même contre." Success in literature is a sociological phenomenon, due to the mood of the public even more than to the work temporarily acclaimed and bought. It expresses a correspondence between the new book or play and the intellectual fashions of the time; or else it fulfills a secret expectation in the public and unleashes latent emotions and reactions in readers suddenly revealed to themselves. Famous examples are the liberating shock of Goethe's *Werther* or Lytton Strachey's ironical portrait of a queen too long and complacently idealized. Success also rewards the leader of a group, when that group (the French classical school, the romantics, the German Expressionists, the younger English poets of 1930–1940) has succeeded in storming the bastions held by an older generation. A crowd often acclaims itself in celebrating the leader—political or intellectual—who voices its mute aspirations: it matters little whether the leader was carried by a tidal wave or by a mere ripple momentarily mistaken for one.

The prudent critic is justified in being diffident before the universal and sudden popularity of a new work. That work may be important, as *Andromaque, Les Précieuses ridicules, La Nouvelle Héloïse,* and *Les Misérables* were. But more often than not that popularity may go, not to an entirely worthless writer, but to a second-rate talent mistaken for a great one: Cowley, Byron (in his early tales), Galsworthy, Mary Webb, even Katherine Mansfield (in her short stories), Virginia Woolf, Charles Morgan; or in French, Delavigne, Béranger, Alexandre Dumas *fils,* Octave Feuillet, Albert Samain, Anatole France, Jules Romains, Robbe-Grillet, Ionesco.

Such success, usually accompanied by exaggerated praise of a skillful but minor talent which dazzles critics for a while, loses its brightness after the death of the author—at times, even before, as the melancholy examples of Paul Bourget, Romain Rolland, Maeterlinck, George Bernard Shaw, and H. G. Wells, painfully surviving their former fame, may recall. The public is apt to prove all the harder on writers who had impressed it for a while, as if revenging itself upon an innocent author for its own gullibility. Georges Ohnet is a famous instance in French literature of a sudden rise to fame followed by an even more sudden decline. The most surprising literary boom in England was probably that of Martin Tupper; it cannot be explained by publicity campaigns, like many similar booms in the present century, for Tupper lived in the midst of the dignified Victorian era. His *Proverbial Philosophy*, a series of moral platitudes in what one cannot without flattery call verse, was for several years the most popular volume in Great Britain. Serious critics were as rapturous as the sentimental middle-class reader.

Martin Tupper [wrote the *Spectator*] has won for himself the vacant throne waiting for him amidst the immortals, and, after a long and glorious term of popularity among those who know when their hearts are touched, has been adopted by the suffrage of mankind and the final decree of publishers into the same rank with Wordsworth and Tennyson and Browning.

The *Court Journal* celebrated the volume of insipid moralizing as "in its wisdom worthy of the disciple of Solomon, in its genius the child of Milton." Desmond MacCarthy, from whom the above quotations are borrowed,[1] relates how Martin Tupper, in a country where men of letters are seldom thus honored, was received at the Mansion House, and invited to Buckingham Palace by the Prince Consort. He was on the verge of being made a peer; "with prudent foresight he had coronets painted on his dinner service." All of a sudden, his glory collapsed. The *Proverbial Philosophy* was derided, then forgotten. To the new generation Martin Tupper was not even a name.

The history of letters is full of similar examples. A sociologist may write an elaborate monograph to explain why, to take only American examples, the easy charm of *Gone with the Wind*, or the skillful artistry of *The Bridge of San Luis Rey*, or the sheer mediocrity of *Anthony Adverse*, enjoyed such enormous success in the last scores of years. We believe it more honest to admit

[1] Desmond MacCarthy, "Literary Booms," in *Criticism* (London: Putnam, 1932), p. 126.

that there is simply no adequate explanation, and that literary success is just as irrational and fortuitous as the sudden vogue of a feminine hat, or of a popular song suddenly repeated by a million lips and not even distinguished by any unusual stupidity. In an age which has used determinist and materialist methods to discover the elusive causes of man's behavior—vainly, to be sure—it is fitting to remind the ambitious pseudo-scientists unleashed in the fields of sociology, history, and literature that our praise-worthy attempts to discover logical causes for the fundamental irrationality of all that concerns man often verge on the ridiculous. It is probably more modest, hence more scientific, to admit candidly that success is often due to the two most potent of all goddesses, Fortune and Imitation, whom perpetual altars should honor.

The function of the critic is all the more important as we refuse to conceive of his task as being that of a drugstore clerk filling a prescription or of a scientist applying infallible standards. Taste, the most variable attribute of man, is fickle and uncertain even in a critic. But any meditation on the countless mistakes of his predecessors should instil into the critic's mind a few precepts of elementary wisdom:

"If a work is too easy, too smoothly pleasing, too 'nice,' if it requires no vigorous adaptation from me," the critic should tell himself, "the chances are that it is not deeply and truly good. If it is tawdry, mawkish, sentimental, the odds are even more clearly against it: many critics have been deluded by facile emotion and superficial charm, from the admirers of Thomas Moore to those of Rupert Brooke, of Longfellow and Whittier to Robert Frost and Edna St. Vincent Millay.

"If a new work strikes me as ugly and revolting, it may be just that; but it may also have character, individuality, energy. It is unpleasant, and I am tempted to be horrified. Let me remember that El Greco in his day, later Delacroix, Cézanne, Picasso, Rouault struck their contemporaries in exactly the same way; that Sargent or Mary Cassatt, Marie Laurencin or Raoul Dufy, though far more pleasing, are likely to be remembered only for their rival claims to rank among the worst painters of our times. A shudder of horror felt before a new painting is often the sure sign of a secret or nascent admiration in the reluctant onlooker. Let me learn to be grateful to any shock which forces me to shake off my lethargy.

"If a new work of art or literature seems to whisper a secret message into my ears; if it brings me a joy hardly felt before and shared by few others around me, let me welcome the new friend with receptive trust. Most of my colleagues do not share my emotion or my enthusiasm. I respect their judgment and that of the public. Yet I also remember that the majority rule, even in the truest democracies, does not yet apply to esthetic and intellectual pursuits. The Gallup Poll may some day consult the public to determine the greatest book of the year or the finest picture in a museum; [2] luckily in these troubled times there is no dearth of political topics on which the mysterious being called 'the average citizen' may express an opinion. In the meanwhile, the reader who is neither a snob nor a cynic may retain the right to quote Anatole France's famous saying: 'There are always more fools in the majority than in the minority.'

"Finally, if I suspect the new work to be original, let me reinforce my impression or re-examine my opinion by an attentive reperusal; let me become conscious of the solid grounds on which first my instinctive judgment, then my reasoned appreciation are based. Instead of urging excitedly that I have discovered a masterpiece accessible only to the few, let me fulfill worthily my

[2] Psychologists have already spent untiring efforts in tabulating how long the average visitors to a gallery spend before each of five or six masterpieces belonging to different schools. Let us hope they draw conclusions concerning the taste of the public and not the value of the pictures. In an amusing volume, *Ananias or the False Artist* (New York: Harper, 1928), the American art critic Walter Pach denounced the fallacy that the duty of a museum curator is to attract as many visitors as possible to his gallery. Since good art alone will not always do the trick, a curator may organize an aviation meeting in the open air next to his Museum on a cold winter Sunday. The crowd, having shivered long enough, will rush through the gates and may thus catch a glimpse of a Rodin or a Titian!

duty to the public. The role of the critic is indeed to teach his readers to share in the new vision of an artist; to explain to them why Cézanne and Matisse, Proust and Joyce at first seem strange and difficult; to provide them with a thread or a skein of threads to help them through the maze of a difficult cyclic novel or of a symphony which differs sharply from the traditional."

Does it not happen, however, that readers try sincerely to understand a new literary or artistic production, and fail? If so many shrewd judges have been baffled by a novel or a poem which subsequently proved to be an epoch-making masterpiece, is it not through fear of being mystified? Not a few obdurate skeptics declare that some of the masterpieces accepted as such today are mere hoaxes practiced successfully on a grand scale (Lautréamont's long prose-poem, Joyce's *Ulysses*, Surrealist writings, the painting of the Cubists, those of Rousseau, le Douanier, or of Picasso. In any case they blame the writers or the artists, and not the critics, for the misunderstanding which has widened the breach between the two groups. For, in recent years, the writers have kept the public at a distance through voluntary obscurity. They have delighted in raising opaque screens between their vision and the dim eyes of the public, perhaps to conceal their own lack of depth, and to provoke ecstatic praise for transcending our understanding, though there was nothing in their deceptions to be understood. The problem is a fundamental one in any discussion of modern literature. The difficulty or the obscurity of that literature seems to many observers to have steadily increased in the last decades, and to have assumed the form of a conscious and voluntary system which we call Obscurism.

Critics may be said roughly to have fallen into two opposite camps when encountering obscurity. Some of them, inclined to side with the snobs or favorably disposed toward difficult innovations and ready to devote much time and energy to solving them, have revelled in what they did not understand. With naïve humility, they have revered Mallarmé, Stefan George, Joyce's later

works, some of the pranks of e. e. cummings [3] and of the Surrealists for the touching reason that they could not understand
them, or have succeeded in deciphering tortuous meanings from
them only after most arduous labor. Others, usually older men
imbued with a deeper sense of their own dignity and expecting
writers to bow to their mature common sense, have turned sternly against makers of difficult riddles. They have brought much
comfort to the general public by saying: "You do not understand Valéry or Proust or the younger English poets, my dear
reader, simply because there is nothing to understand; those writers do not even understand themselves." A few jokes about
Proust's involved sentences or Joyce's philological stunts or Gertrude Stein's pedestrian rigmarole were sure to arouse laughter by
relieving the secret qualms of middle-aged readers who thought
they had lost their wits since leaving college or fallen behind
their times.

Strangely enough, literary obscurity and the deliberate practice of Obscurism have, for the last half-century, become especially conspicuous in France, of all countries. In the land where
lucid intelligence had always been worshipped, the long-vaunted
French clarity seemed to have yielded to a passion for strangeness
and dizziness. After Mallarmé and the Symbolists, whose obscurity had been looked upon as the decadent exaggeration of a few
eccentrics; after Proust, who was long accused of being difficult,
the fame of Paul Valéry suddenly invaded even the most conservative circles of France. In the Twenties, every short article
signed by him was anxiously sought by book speculators; his
most insignificant autograph brought unheard-of prices; a copy
of his highly difficult *Charmes* was seen carelessly lying on
drawing-room tables at all the "five o'clocks"—as the French call
them—of society women, and shared the intimacy of actresses'
boudoirs with the then no less fashionable *Summa* of St. Thomas

---

[3] The most modest among modern artists refuse to use capital letters even
for their own names and initials, and have subdued the proud English
tongue by no longer capitalizing the pronoun which expresses the first person
singular.

Aquinas, a few lipsticks, and the entrancing French perfumes labelled "Ivresse d'amour" or "Aime-moi ce soir." In 1927, Valéry was even elected to the French Academy. The poet of hermetic obscurity succeeded Anatole France, who had been for three decades the high priest of limpid clarity. All friends of clarity cried out in protest. France had gone mad: without clarity, her prestige among nations was doomed.

Is obscurity a new phenomenon in the history of letters? Is it a disease of the modern age, caused by the greater complexity of the world around us and the inability of twentieth-century minds to make sense of an increasingly baffling world? Many people would answer affirmatively. They imagine obscurity and difficulty to be characteristic of contemporary works of art, and deplore the long evolution which has finally turned poems, paintings, and music into incomprehensible riddles. They are, of course, mistaken. Every age has always naïvely considered itself the apex of a long evolution, and either boasted of it or deplored it. The notion of evolution has been sadly abused and should be relegated to a very low place in the history of arts and letters. Every man of genius is a new beginning. Obscurity is no more than decadence or modernity a grace or a stigma of the present age alone. During many periods in the past, the charge of needless obscurity was advanced, with as much apparent justification as it is today.

The supreme charm of Greek literature lies probably in its youthful freshness; it is admirably and unconsciously original, it is a literature without any ancestors or models. It is nevertheless rich in very difficult works, in which the Greeks indulged their genius for playful subtlety and overornate ingenuity. The choruses of Aeschylus and Sophocles are obscure not only to modern readers, unfamiliar with highly stylized phrases and complex metrics; they were obscure to the Athenians of the fifth century. Few modern poems equal in deliberate and splendid difficulty Pindar's second and fourth Pythian odes: even to a reader versed in mythical allusions as a contemporary of the great Theban might be, the boldness of the images, the extreme concentration of the thought, the artificiality of the language, and the method of indirect expression (all devices resorted to by our modern obscurists) must have constituted insuperable obstacles to a ready understanding of the poet's meaning. Some of Plato's dialogues are as difficult as anything in modern philosophy; and many contemporaries of Aristotle must have been baffled by the obscurity of some passages of his *Nicomachean Ethics*. No historian ever equalled Thucydides for difficulty of style. As early as the first century B.C., the obscurity of the *Peloponnesian War* was condemned by Dionysius of Halicarnassus, who wrote: "You can almost count on your fingers the people who are capable of comprehending the whole of Thucydides" (*De Thucydide*, c. 51). Cicero joined in censuring the Greek historian's excessive search for brevity and ambiguity of syntax, declaring him "hardly intelligible" (*Brutus*, VII, 29 and XXVII, 66). At the beginning of the third century B.C., two Greeks wrote some of the most enigmatic poetry ever attempted: Aratus, the difficulty of whose *Phaenomena* is due in great measure to the astronomical subject, and Lycophron, nicknamed "the obscure," whose long relation of Cassandra's prophecies as repeated by the slave Alexandra to King Priam doubtless exemplifies all the types of obscurity (allusive, symbolic, apocalyptic) found in subsequent literature.

Obscurity was also rife in medieval works, and often in the greatest of them. The Norse *Eddas* are far from clear. Dante's *Vita Nuova* is certainly as difficult a poem as any. Later, Gongora's *Soledades*, in 1613, were both admired and censured for their voluntary obscurity: like James Joyce's prose epics, Gongora's model of "cultivated" poetry (as the Spaniards called that movement) was at once elucidated by subtle interpreters who unravelled the mysteries of hyperbolic metaphors, newly coined words, sibylline syntax, and extreme subtlety of thought. A great contemporary of Gongora, Shakespeare, at his best is often dazzlingly obscure. Both in the Elizabethans and the Metaphysical poets, overelaborate conceits, telescoped images, farfetched comparisons, a passion for strangeness or for excessive analytical subtlety provided inexhaustible sources of obscurity.

It would probably be difficult to discover a single great poet at whom the charge was not levelled. Donne was no exception. Chapman was long accused of being obscure; in the nineteenth century Swinburne had to defend him against that stricture. Dr. Johnson blamed Collins for "harshness and obscurity" and declared that he would like to like Gray's "Progress of Poesy," but could not discover the meaning of the first stanza. We have recalled in a previous chapter that many of Wordsworth's poems were found utterly obscure, as were Coleridge's "Ancient Mariner" and "Christabel," Shelley's "Alastor" and "Adonais." Browning was supposed to offer unheard-of difficulties to the understanding of the reader. Endless jokes were made on his obscure nonsense, like the story of a student who, after concentrating for hours on Browning's poems, realized that he had been pondering all along an index of first lines to Tennyson. Then came Meredith, who seemed to outstrip Browning in difficulty. Rossetti was gravely censured for being esoteric (Walter Pater had to refute the charge in a fine essay reprinted in *Appreciations*). "The Windhover" and other beautiful poems by Gerard Manley Hopkins are indeed obscure and can be interpreted plausibly in conflicting ways; so are several of Yeats's works, and some by the subsequent English poets (the Sitwells, T. S. Eliot, W. H. Auden, C. Day Lewis).

That obscurity has been a constant feature of the German mind is too well known to bear illustration here. A German writer would deem himself insulted if he were called clear or lucid: he prefers to worship the "Gott des Rausches," the God of intoxication, and to surrender to eddies of dizziness [4] which bring him into pantheistic communion with subterranean forces. The Second Part of *Faust*, Novalis's *Hymns*, Hölderlin's *Odes*, Stefan George's poems, and Rilke's *Elegies* are all undeniable German masterpieces, which repeated and attentive readings may not succeed in elucidating.

The recent French critics who have been dismayed by their

[4] "Dem Tamuel weih' ich mich," says Goethe's Faust. "No dizziness I vow myself."

compatriots' tricks of obscurism seemed to assume that before Mallarmé French literature had always been orderly and lucid. They were mistaken. The charge of obscurity is an old one, even in France. Ronsard was found farfetched, pedantic, incomprehensible in his Pindaric odes. The great Rhétoriqueurs before him practiced, more perversely, some of the feats of virtuosity of our contemporary versifiers. Maurice Scève was avowedly a seeker after mysterious meanings concealed behind subtle symbols or bold manipulation or traditional syntax. His contemporaries, such as Pasquier and Du Bellay, openly criticized the deliberate difficulty affected by a poet, "who, in his desire to avoid the commonplace, has fallen into an obscurity which is as difficult for the most learned to explain as for the most ignorant" (Du Bellay). All modern admirers of Joyce are familiar with the comparison between him and Rabelais, another great coiner of philological monsters. Some, though comparatively few, of Rabelais' chapters indeed defy comprehension. It seems that Montaigne himself was censured for his obscurity. His faithful disciple, Mlle de Gournay, answered the charge in her preface, written three years after the death of the essayist. The subject matter being new and deep, she argued, and for a few only, why should Montaigne have written for the many and their narrow souls? Again in 1613, a well-known churchman and novelist, Camus, regretted the obscurity of the *Essays*, "too difficult for ordinary readers, and even for skilled ones, demanding close attention and subtlety."

In the seventeenth century, which gave the French their classical period, difficult works were rare but by no means lacking. The novels of that age were mazes of involved plots and confusing psychological subtlety; Mme de La Fayette herself was criticized for obscurity in her style. Corneille boasted of the difficulty of some of his plays like *Clitandre* and *Héraclius*, which had to be seen twice to be understood. Clarity is not the chief virtue of other dramatists of the century, including Rotrou. Nor was it an innate virtue of the French during the Renaissance or under Louis XIII. They gradually and painfully acquired it, thanks to their teachers and to literary theorists permeated with

Latin and Greek culture, who taught them the merit of analyzing ideas into their component elements, of orderly composition, of a neat, "functional" style which is neither picturesque nor suggestive, but intellectual, straightforward, and clear.[5] It was only in the second half of the seventeenth century that the French became famous for thinking clearly and writing tersely and unambiguously. Ridicule, the surest weapon in France, was mercilessly levelled at obscurity, which the spirit of the age branded as a breach of politeness, a lack of respect for the audience, to which even difficult thoughts should be made "pleasing" and easily accessible.

During the literary reign of Voltaire, while French clarity radiated over the whole of Europe, conquering Germany herself, the French wearied of a virtue which tended to reduce literary pleasure to mere intellectual enjoyment. Poetry, the novel, even philosophy had become so obviously pellucid that they appeared superficial. Words had ceased to give emotional or sensuous joy to readers of poems on love and nature. Mystery seemed to have vanished from the soul of man or to have been reduced to a transparent veil, such as that nonchalantly thrown over the plump ladies painted by Boucher and Fragonard. Rousseau, followed by Chateaubriand and the romantics, restored a welcome share of obscurity to the French language, and to French ways of thinking and feeling.

From that time on, almost every great figure in French letters has been accused, at one time or another, of being obscure. Stendhal's first admirers, Sarcey and Taine, had to answer the charge before starting a Stendhal vogue. Yet his novels are today, if anything, too clear for our taste. Stendhal in his turn censured

[5] The late Daniel Mornet has studied in a methodical manner the slow process through which the French acquired the gift of clarity in the course of the seventeenth century. More than the climate, the soil of France, French wines, or some mysterious virtue in the French language, which have been diversely offered as explanations of "French clarity," education, as given first by the Jesuits, then by French lay teachers, molded the minds of French boys to organize ideas in a logical order, to think consistently, and to write clearly and concisely (Daniel Mornet, *Histoire de la clarté française* [Payot, 1929]).

Vigny's *Eloa* for its obscurity (in his articles in the *New Monthly Magazine* of 1823). Mme de Genlis had complained of Lamartine's obscurity in the *Premières Méditations*. A playwright named Dupaty, who was to be elected to the French Academy against Hugo in 1835, proved in *La Minerve littéraire* of 1821 that "Le Lac" was incomprehensible. Planche condemned Sainte-Beuve's volume of poetry, *Pensées d'Août*, as impossible to decipher. Victor Hugo appeared even more difficult to his early critics; strangely enough, they quoted as convincing illustrations poems which we naïvely find almost too limpid today.[6] Leconte de Lisle was long ridiculed for being obscure. A senator, who did not approve of the poet's being Librarian of the Senate, used to say scornfully to his friends: "I pity you if you understand what our Parnassian librarian writes."

All poets of all schools have thus been accused of insulting their audiences with obscurity—the Symbolists and the Moderns only a little more than the others. A contemporary critic who finds fault with the "new school" of poets naturally begs them to return to true models of French clarity, Baudelaire or Verlaine for instance. Yet in his time the same Baudelaire was found utterly incomprehensible by many of the most famous critics: Brunetière among others. Tolstoi, who wrote the most abusive tirade against obscurity in *What Is Art?*, singled out Baudelaire for special censure. He asserted that *Les Fleurs du Mal* contained "not one poem which is plain and can be understood without a

[6] A certain Chatelet, who directed scathing sarcasm at his *Orientales* in 1829, said of the poem "Le Feu du ciel": "That is Hebrew to me." He found the fourth part, on Egypt, especially "undecipherable." He quoted lines from "Les Têtes du sérail" which he could not understand, and declared of "Le Voile" that its author was "mentally delirious. . . . He understands himself just as little as he makes others understand him." A little later, another critic, L. V. Raoul, confessed he was baffled by the first poem in *Les Feuilles d'automne*, "Ce Siècle avait deux ans." A third named Courtat undertook to rewrite one of Hugo's most celebrated poems, which every French child now knows by heart, "Les Pauvres Gens." Out of 256 lines he found 158 obscure or faulty. Paul Valéry was amused by a certain French colonel, Godchot, who sent him "le cimetière marin" rewritten in clearer French verses, of twelve instead of ten lines.

certain effort." Baudelaire's *Poèmes en prose* (in our opinion far inferior to his verse because somewhat too obvious) seemed to Tolstoi even worse in that respect. "Their meaning has to be guessed like a rebus, and remains for the most part undiscovered." Verlaine's musical jewel "C'est l'extase langoureuse" was dismissed as obscure by the Russian writer, who added as the dullest of Philistines might: "What it all means remains altogether unintelligible to me." After quoting other examples of "absolutely incomprehensible literature" (*Là-bas* by Huysmans, Kipling's short stories), Tolstoi sweepingly condemned all those moderns as obscure, because perverted by bad food, spirits, and tobacco, and begged them to write like those admirably clear and universally understood artists . . . Goethe and Hugo.

Tolstoi's erratic criticism (it ranks among the most mistaken ever made by a man of genius) drew abundant ammunition from Brunetière, Lemaître, Anatole France, Doumic, and other French critics who had been the first to vituperate Verlaine and Mallarmé for not writing clearly. Mallarmé certainly was difficult, and has remained so; but he can be elucidated once his vocabularly and his syntax have been carefully studied. Critics balked at such an effort, and preferred dismissing him as "obscure" or as a poet who could only be understood in German or English translation. Indeed, according to the pompous precept, "all that is not clear is not French," the practice soon spread among critics to label "foreigner" or "traitor" any French writer who could not be understood at first sight. Lasserre termed both Rimbaud and Claudel "anti-French." The sin of the modern obscurists was blamed on the baneful influence of Nordic writers, lost in their eternal mists. Ibsen's *Ghosts,* for instance, as obviously didactic as any drama ever written, seemed "difficult" to Sarcey, and *The Wild Duck* was called "Le Préau de Charenton," "the courtyard of Bedlam." In the present century, the charge of obscurity should have died in ridicule, if platitudes of criticism ever could be killed. It has been thrown indiscriminately at poets who are actually very difficult (Mallarmé, Valéry, St. John Perse) and at others whom a slight effort enables one to understand. Among the latter should be grouped most of the Symbolists (like Henri de Régnier, Moréas, Vielé-Griffin) whose works will probably not survive because they are too clear (i.e., without depth or secrets), and the great majority of modern prose writers and poets. Claudel, in my opinion, is seldom obscure.[7] Péguy never is; on the contrary, his endless repetitions and illustrations of the obvious are the gravest flaw in his writings. Proust never is, or almost never; he proclaimed himself an enemy of systematic obscurity.[8]

A few provisional conclusions seem to be warranted by the preceding enumeration:

Far from being a mere search for provoking originality or a sure sign of decadence, obscurity often goes hand in hand with depth and greatness. Racine, La Fontaine, Voltaire, Flaubert are not obscure; Descartes and Bergson are not; Keats is not. One may wish however that Pope were a little more obscure, and Addison, and Goldsmith, and Landor; or among more recent poets Thomas Hardy and A. E. Housman. We should be more assured of their survival as truly great poets if they were. Several Frenchmen who were neither traitors to their cultural heritage nor incapable of lucidity themselves have deplored the traditional emphasis of the French on clarity.[9] Analytical clarity and the

[7] In his ode "La Maison fermée," Claudel has ridiculed the charge of obscurity with humorous satire; he imagines the poet's family bitterly accusing him of having wasted the good money spent on his education, which should have taught him the first duty of a sensible man: not to increase the number of things that the common man cannot understand.

[8] Marcel Proust, "Contre l'obscurité," *Revue Blanche*, II (1896), 69–72, reprinted in *Chroniques* (Gallimard, 1927), pp. 137–144.

[9] The passion for clarity, said Barbey d'Aurevilly, should not go to the extent of liking empty glasses. Remy de Gourmont, in *La Culture des idées* (Mercure, 1900), p. 131, regretted the scarcity of obscure writers in French. Clear minds, he added, perhaps unfairly, are those which see only one thing at a time; as soon as ideas and sensations bubble in a brain, it is confused by turbid eddies. Paul Valéry, who was stung to the quick by the reiterated charges of incomprehensibility (he is not uniformly obscure as a poet and ranks among the most exquisitely lucid of prose writers), wrote epigrammatically: "L'esprit clair fait comprendre ce qu'il ne comprend pas."

lack of any demands on the reader's attention almost succeeded in killing French poetry in the eighteenth century.

Much of the obscurity in great works of the past has now worn off. It may be that we have learned to adopt the artist's vision, to speak his quicker language, to perceive the emotions suggested by his images. In several cases, the obscurity was not real; contemporaries merely termed obscure what they would not try to understand. Shelley's "Adonais," Wordsworth's ode on immortality, Browning's "A Grammarian's Funeral" or "By the Fireside" are tolerably clear to us today and would have been to contemporaries of those poets, if they had not preferred calling the authors names to overcoming their own mental inertia.

Some obscurity has persisted, increased at times by the evolution of language and syntax; but we never dream of holding it a sin in Dante or Gongora or Shakespeare or Corneille, though we expend our facile indignation on new works by moderns to whom we begrudge our attention. Any sincere devotee of Shakespeare should confess that an accurate understanding of the most celebrated tragedies or sonnets requires as much effort (perhaps more amply repaid) as a careful reading of any modern poet. The passing of time and a thousand reiterated quotations have made us accept as sublime famous lines which we recite by heart and which should provoke, if not abide, our question.[10] The method of "explication de textes," practiced since 1900 in French universities and adapted by I. A. Richards and his disciples to the modern demand for pompous logic, has brought those who practice it to a clear realization of the very considerable, and often unfathomable, obscurity which persists in most great works of the past.

Several valid reasons explain why in this democratic age, when

---

[10] The famous passage in *Macbeth*, V, v, which has provided novels with countless titles and begins "She should have died hereafter" is probably not understood in all its details by three fourths of the people who quote it, beginning with the conditional "She should," which many readers take to mean "She ought to." Or the sense of "wasted" in the famous line "When in the chronicle of wasted time." Or the one or two hundred quotations from *Hamlet* familiar to all semiliterate persons.

literary works are written by common men for an unlimited
public of supposedly common men, obscurity, instead of decreas-
ing, has become much more marked in the great books of the last
hundred years. With the opening of the nineteenth century,
writers and artists were suddenly faced with greatly expanded
audiences. The connoisseurs and patrons who had supported
them had been dispersed in the critical years of the French Revolution and the Napoleonic wars. A new elite was needed, and
eventually appeared. But the former communion between artists
and a small, refined public was never recaptured. Poets and painters felt reduced to bitter isolation in a democratic society where
money was the primary value and quantity had the better of
quality. Novelists took great pains to describe the society in
which they had to live; but, from Balzac to Aldous Huxley and
John Dos Passos, they openly scorned or satirized their environment of leisurely worldlings or avid, ruthless money-makers.
When they were not inclined to lecture their public or to
vituperate it, they shocked its moral conventions or its pedestrian
and restricted intelligence.

After 1800 that public consisted of middle-class readers among
whom women often predominated. Mischievous artists and Bohemian writers soon discovered that the respectable persons who
made up their audiences secretly delighted in being satirized or
insulted. Advanced painters specialized in ladies' portraits which
the models only grew to resemble after thirty years. Novelists
and moralists like Céline and Bernanos opened their books with
violent tirades against the stupid bourgeois and the avaricious
Philistines who had buried all ideals—and the bourgeois rushed to
buy the volume. In France where novels are sold uncut and
fastened with a band bearing an alluring invitation, publishers
would print a few magical words: "Women, you will read here
how perfidious and impure you can be. Here you will find a
faithful picture of the tortures you impose upon men." The next
morning the novel would be found in the drawing room of every
fashionable Parisian lady.

Behind many of those childish pranks it is easy to read a

desperate call for sympathy on the part of the tormented artist, a protest against a society where he had no natural place and lived only on the charity of an indifferent public. Ever since a writer has had to depend for a living on sales and royalties, he has been haunted by the fear of starvation; the loss of public favor, even a temporary neglect by unpredictable fashion, meant poverty to him. To remain in the eye of the book-buying public which he secretly scorned, he had either to lose his self-respect and write cheaply or to indulge in endless repetition of the same theme. Desperate anxiety and a bitter resentment at their forced sub-servience to the public mark most of the writers and artists of the last hundred years.

An utter lack of confidence in the critics caused many writers to disregard the public's demand for clear and "uplifting" litera-ture. They were no longer inspired by any fear or respect for the men who had so often unjustly accused them of immorality or obscurity. Creators ceased trying to win over the intermediaries who had repeatedly insulted them instead of interpreting them, and determined in the future to assert their own originality, re-gardless of consequences.

Finally, around the middle of the last century, a conviction spread among many thoughtful minds that the new idol, modern science, had failed the fanatics who had placed an excessive trust in it. That conviction has grown ever since. Determinism and materialism based upon an early enthusiasm for science disap-pointed those who felt that there were "more things in Heaven and earth." Lessons were drawn from history, and they proved disappointing. The "science" of education was to improve the modern man, and it failed signally. Economists and social scien-tists ventured prophecies founded on an array of facts and figures and compelling logic; they failed even more lamentably. Philo-sophical systems which had attempted to account for the world and man's mind turned out to be mere heaps of majestic ruins, admirable only for the bold poetical imagination spent in creating them. As photography, the movies, and the radio made possible the accurate rendering of the outside world or the recording of the human voice, painting, music, and poetry boldly spurned such low achievement and undertook to escape into a private refuge, ignoring the prosaic outer world, or to change the world instead of depicting it minutely or analyzing it logically.

In a famous sentence of his eleventh thesis on Feuerbach, Karl Marx proclaimed a revolutionary creed which has been adopted by many literary and artistic creators: "Philosophers have long enough tried to give different interpretations of the world; the real task is to transform it." Rimbaud, the inspirer of so much modern poetry, had made a desperate attempt to discover "the secrets for changing human life." [11] First in poetry and painting, then in other branches of literature and art, the most original innovators among the Moderns decided that, intelligence having failed miserably in its claim to understand this world, imagination should henceforth bend it energies to the creation of another world, where a superior and disconnecting logic would prevail. Cézanne, in one of his few but pregnant artistic declarations, said one day to Joachim Gasquet: "Art is a harmony parallel to nature." Cubism, Surrealism, nonobjective painting, recent poetry have all stressed the higher validity of the artist's own vision as opposed to any realistic description or interpretation of the world. That such private vision or creation of an independent universe would lead to strangeness and obscurity was only to be expected.

The dividing line between the past and the modern age should not be drawn at the beginning of the romantic era or of the Industrial Revolution, as is done in traditional histories of literature. In France, where the whole modernistic movement in poetry and painting originated, 1860–1870 will probably appear as the critical decade. Then suddenly, painters who first exhibited at the "Salon des Refusés" in 1863 and a few poets (Rimbaud, Mallarmé, Lautréamont) turned their backs on the accurate and pseudo-scientific explanation of the world and undertook to develop a new and difficult technique to express their boundless

[11] "Il a peut-être des secrets pour changer la vie" (*Une Saison en Enfer,* "Délires I"), he has Verlaine say of him.

metaphysical ambition: the recreation of a surreality defying all the rational conventions of man's knowledge.

Both the growing isolation of the artist in the modern world and his inordinate ambition to create a world *ex nihilo* and to sever all links between his dreams and the deceptive pursuits of science have thus greatly increased the difficulty of the best poetry, painting, or music of the last hundred years. Critics have accordingly adopted one of two opposite attitudes: they have rejected as perversely obscure the most representative works of modern artists, or they have submissively acclaimed them as undeniably profound and original *because* they were obscure. The former bowed servilely to a lazy public which was flattered by being told that it was superior to infantile or mystifying artists. The latter were at times genuinely modest and implied that a new work must be great since it was beyond their understanding. More often, however, they were mere slaves of snobbish vogue, and seemed to say: "This difficult book is undoubtedly sublime, since I am among the few capable of admiring it." But they refrained from analyzing either the book or their own view of it to a public which hardly deserved to be initiated.

Once again, some further elucidation of the notion concerned may not be amiss. Behind the convenient label "obscurity," one may indeed perceive a variety of complex elements among which it should have been the critic's duty to discriminate.

A) A new work may be obscure because it actually has no meaning whatever.

a) This may be due to sheer mystification on the part of the author. Ever since Alcibiades played his pranks upon the gaping idlers of Athens, there have been practical jokers among snobs as well as artists. Their mannerisms vary little: meaningless repetition, absence of capital letters and of punctuation, breaking up of words or of letters in words (as others had broken up rhythm in poetry, the limbs of a woman in a painting, or the atom in the laboratory). Such difficulty is innocuous, and the critics should be grateful to writers who exercise their sense of humor. Gertrude Stein delightfully disrupts our somnolent acquiescence to ordinary prose in order to lull us far more securely to sleep. e. e. cummings experiments with verse in the best traditions of the most harmless of innovators: the academic revolutionaries. At the time of Dadaism, Louis Aragon wrote "Sérénade," one of the most "universal" of poems, and easily accessible to all persons literate in the Latin alphabet. It read:

a b c d e f
g h i j k l
m n o p q r
s t u v w
x y z

A few years before the First World War, some French artists, whose great predecessors had been repeatedly accused of playing jokes upon the public, decided to test the public's gullibility by having a painting done in the most original way: a brush dipped into several pots of paint was tied to a donkey's tail. The animal fretted for a few minutes near a white canvas, on which his tail left strange thick patches of color. A notary public witnessed the whole proceeding. When the painting was completed, it received an impressive title "Sunset over the Adriatic" and was exhibited at one of the Paris Salons. Its mass effects, unusual color scheme, and tactile values were duly discussed by admiring or hostile observers; but no one suspected the originality of its asinine authorship.

I take it as a sign of health that pompous critics and insincere snobs should occasionally be fooled by such jokes. "Arbiters of taste," as estheticians and professional commentators on art sometimes call themselves, can only be grateful to those who occasionally recall them to their proper humility. An easily discernible mystification is less misleading than many a grave remark cryptically uttered by a composer or painter upon his work. "I wrote this in a state of trance, driven by a superhuman force" or, as some modern painters hardly thirty years old complacently reveal today in the remarks which they append to their master-pieces, "This picture was painted when I was outgrowing my surrealist phase and was entering my classical period." Grave spectacled ladies led by a voluble spinsterish commentator are then duly shown how massive harmony in the coloring, symmetry among the three legs, two noses, five apples, and one guitar cleverly disposed on the canvas, spatial values, and effects of depth are premonitory signs of Mr. So-and-So's classicism.

Behind some of the hoaxes of recent art one may discover, not the skillful imposture of Chatterton or Macpherson, but a bitter thirst for more sincerity in art and truer discrimination in the public. Dadaism and Surrealism have been fertile attempts to return to nothing, in order that a new accumulation of material and a new choice among richer and newer materials (which included automatic writing, subconscious and often erotic layers in the mind, a strange vocabulary, and an unconventional syntax) might replace the endless repetition of old motives and the conventional fidelity to the impoverished choice made by our ancestors during the Romantic era or the Renaissance.

b) This obscurity which comes from meaninglessness may also be a revolt against logic. Love of nonsense brings with it valuable gains: disconcerting humor, striking surprise, exuberant childish vitality. The limerick has enjoyed an extraordinary vogue in recent years, along with comic strips and detective novels: an austere observer would read in that vogue one of the surest signs of intellectual decline in our so-called ruling classes. Walt Disney has taught millions to laugh at his farcical pursuit of the absurd, while critics have asked us to marvel at his profound "philosophy." In 1939, the oldest seat of learning in Great Britain, Oxford University, conferred its noblest title, an honorary Doctorate of Laws, on P. G. Wodehouse. The most dignified Anglo-Saxon considers it a discreet display of the most precious gift of his race—that of retaining a child's freshness through the serious occupations of his mature years—to quote from *Alice in Wonderland* at least once a week and thus disarm with a smile of ecstatic pleasure hostile audiences, depressed partners, and busi-

ness rivals. Youth and even childhood were reverently worshipped in the Old and the New Worlds during the period between the two World Wars. It is hardly surprising that such a
public should applaud nonsense in verse. Poets had small difficulty in pandering to our infantilism. Already in 1912 Marinetti
had offered to "set words at liberty," to replace question marks
by x's, repetition of words by signs $+ x$ reiterated, and to express in the futuristic manner both the vast and profound sound
of bells and the impressions of those who hear their peal or their
knell by the metallic words: "Ding dong bells amplitude of sound
4,000 meters." Even the stale Tennysonian hymn "Ring out, wild
bells, to the wild sky . . ." takes on new beauty after such attempts. Edith Sitwell similarly discovers new names for the worn-
out stars: "He looked at the sky and saw the prunes" is her
original rendering. Max Jacob, Jean Cocteau, and scores of
French Surrealists had already used and abused such devices. It is
clear that much meaningless obscurity of recent literature is due
to an element of childish and rather harmless clowning, which
critics might have taken with an amused and polite irony.

    c) Finally, some of the meaninglessness of modern art is due to
the effort of certain artists and writers to avoid the trite expression of ideas and to lead their art back to its essentials. Critics
have erred notoriously in demanding "ideas" from a painting or a
sonnet, and in condemning as empty all that could not be reduced
to an idea or a theme. Since Cubism, the tendency toward meaninglessness has been a wholesome one in painting. Even the excesses of geometric design and the squares of glaring color which
painters have borrowed directly from oriental rugs may be
deemed "purer painting," and less ambitious in their offense to
the bourgeois than the literary and far too meaningful canvases of
Gustave Moreau or Salvador Dali. Modern poetry, as is well
known, has similarly striven toward pure music: alliteration,
onomatopoeia have reached back to the incantatory value of
words. Between 1925 and 1930, endless debates took place in
France on the purity of poetry; the music of poetry was analyzed
more closely than it had been in centuries. The most musical

poetry, however, was written in ages which had not consciously endeavored to banish sense in order to retain pure sound: by Shakespeare and Shelley, Ronsard, Racine and Verlaine, Goethe and Heine. That modern theories of poetry erred in trying to divorce sound from sense seems clear beyond proof. The suggestive value of words counts more than ideas in poetry; but a good many human beings find an intellectual pleasure in poetry and music, as well as a more mysterious and probably more moving sensuous pleasure. Meaning, and even some clear and orderly though not too obvious pattern, may add to the evocative value of sounds and increase the artist's chances of awakening a lasting response in his reader or hearer.

B) The total absence of meaning is an infrequent exception in significant literary works, and hasty critics have generalized unduly when deploring the absurdity and incomprehensibility of contemporary works. In many cases where readers complain of obscurity, there is a meaning, though it is not easily discernible.

a) It may happen that the meaning is extremely profound or subtle, and can only be elucidated with prolonged attention and an adequate culture. Such is the case with some of the more abstruse philosophical writing, often though not necessarily the greatest: Plato in the *Timaeus*, Plotinus, Hegel, Schelling. But this intellectual profundity is not ordinarily to be found in the novel, in drama, or in poetry, where it would be out of place. The finest philosophical poetry was seldom inspired by deep philosophical systems: it expressed the vision of an intense imagination fired by a harmonious, often a mystical explanation of the world (Lucretius, Dante, Shelley, Lamartine, Hugo, Claudel, Rilke).

b) Obscurity in poetry is usually due much less to thought too deep for communication than to the way poetical imagination moves. Consistency, "the hobgoblin of little minds," in Emerson's famous phrase, is not necessarily a virtue in anything that pertains to imagination or sensibility. Continuity in the succession of ideas or images was never a feature of lyrical poetry: from the Hebrew prophets and Pindar to Rimbaud and Hopkins, the great lyricists have leapt like antelopes over the intermediary links of thought, leaving the plodding gait of the elephant to pedestrian prose. Their logic is not unreason, but a speedier and superior logic; similarly, intuition is not antithetic to intelligence, but is rather a higher and purer form of intelligence, free from the dross which normally weighs down our mental efforts. To the reader accustomed to newspapers, magazines, and textbooks, even to advertisements in which the different reasons for buying a certain toothpaste or silk stocking are duly set forth, numbered from one to ten, poems like "Kubla Khan," Rimbaud's "Illuminations" or Yeats's lyrics come as a confusing kaleidoscope of bright images and strange sounds.

c) The paradox of our modern age is that the greater difficulty of poetry (and a good deal of artistic prose, since some of the finest poetry of our day is not written in verse form) has come at a time when the education of the ordinary child aims at requiring the least possible effort on his part. Instead of the intensive practice of translating Thucydides, Virgil, Dante, or Pascal, by which our ancestors were trained, we have undertaken to make study in school as concrete and entertaining as progressive devices allow it to be. If a child is asked to concentrate for thirty minutes upon a problem which he cannot easily solve or a passage in a foreign tongue which he cannot readily construe, the modern teacher-psychologist fears for his mental health, begs him to relax, lest the poor dear should fall prey to the most feared disease of our time—frustration.

Or, if the child is given any training in unravelling difficult thoughts, it is almost exclusively of a logical and strictly intellectual kind. He is encouraged to see problems everywhere, even in a poem by Robert Herrick or a song of innocence by William Blake. His approach to literature will be through "understanding poetry." He spends long hours trying to decipher the sequence of "thought" and master the jargon of Mr. I. A. Richards or Mr. Kenneth Burke. His logical and logomachic powers are thus highly developed; but the training of imagination and sensitive perception of beauty is quite neglected. However illogical it may be, this evil has afflicted even more important fields than the enjoyment of beauty, in art and poetry; recent years, both in peace and war, have revealed in our educated classes and in our leaders an imagination, stifled or left purposely undeveloped by scientific, legal, critical, and business training.

At the very moment when the prophets of an age of science (seldom true scientists themselves) were announcing the doom of poetry because it refused to worship scientific logic,[12] poetry was flourishing more radiantly than it had done since the Renaissance. Ever since the romantic period and the Industrial Revolution, it has stood in the vanguard of man's spiritual activity; its achievement in France, Germany, England, America has surpassed that of any other branch of literature, or of philosophical and tentative social speculation. This great advance of modern poetry has not been accomplished by imitating the methods of science, and even less of applied science, or by writing for the million. The modern poet has revolted against the worst vulgarizing of poetry attempted by the romantic bards: Tennyson's *Idylls of the King* or *Enoch Arden,* Schiller's cheaper lyrics, "The Diver," "The Glove," "The Bell," Hugo's epic moralizing in *La Légende des siècles.* He has insisted upon the reader's meeting him halfway, instead of allowing him to wait somnolently for the man of genius to spoon-feed him. His meaning has been refined with subtlety, caressed with tenderness, and invested with a chaste sensuousness which has turned the form into a vesture of flesh vibrating under every shudder of an acute sensibility. An unusual syntax, setting forth familiar words through skillful placement in the line, proceeding with bold ellipses, has recovered a fresh strangeness for a poetry which seems to add to the most conscious technique the spontaneous potency of magic incantations. Critics may have thought it their duty to the public to condemn such esoteric poets and to fight for clarity. A glance at the ruins of poetic reputations reveals that of those who were cried up for a while the deadest were also the clearest: like army

[12] See Max Eastman, *The Literary Mind: Its Place in an Age of Science* (New York: Scribner, 1931).

generals or thinly veiled women whose first line of defence covered no unravished secret or inner bastion, they soon lost their once lauded clarity of meaning to become effete and literally meaningless. Lovers of poetry have decided otherwise. After thirty years they reread Mallarmé and Rimbaud, St. John Perse and Paul Valéry, Gerard Manley Hopkins and Yeats, Stefan George and Rilke. There was a voluntary element in their poetry, at times even an excessive refinement of elusiveness. But their "heavenly alchemy" succeeded in recovering the secret of the greatest poetry: it loaded its words with a powerful electrical charge which, having long accumulated in the poet's inner experience, could suddenly strike the responsive reader as with a flash of lightning and vibrate in him with prolonged echoes. "A poem is a mystery, the key of which must be sought by the reader," the great and most conscious master of voluntary obscurity, Mallarmé, declared to Edmond de Goncourt in 1893; and he added sadly to one of his mocking critics: "Besides, what is writing but covering a white surface with black?" [13]

It is obvious that such calculated obscurity was driven to excess by imitators of the better poets. The critic's task is to discriminate between what is genuine and profound though obscure and the obscurism which, merely following a fashion, conceals an inner emptiness. As early as 1861 Sainte-Beuve complained of "the snobbishness of difficulty" in literature, and called it a disease of his age (*omnia semper eadem!*) that fashionable readers "who never thought of what they sincerely liked, but of what they should like in order to impress their circle of friends most worthily" (*Causeries du lundi*, XV, 287). Some of the voluntary obscurity of recent poetry is due, not to a profound and complex experience which the poet is trying to re-create in his readers without weakening or cheapening it, but to an utter disregard of both his public and his inner experience. Because Lautréamont

[13] The French phrase used by Mallarmé was: "D'ailleurs, écrire, n'est-ce pas mettre du noir sur du blanc?" In the Parisian lycée where he taught he would gaze with gentle irony at one of his pupils, a negro, whom he delighted in sending to the blackboard where he would write with clarity—with white chalk on a black surface.

and Rimbaud in the 1860's wrote, not for their fellow beings, but to express their own world or their vision of the world, hundreds of French poetasters who had only a very paltry universe to communicate have followed suit. Others resorted to allusions which no reader could possibly understand or enjoy without lengthy footnotes explaining that they wrote a certain line when they were in love with a girl in a red hat or on a morning when they sat in a botanical garden. A pedantic craze seized some of the most gifted writers of our time. Ezra Pound demands that we be familiar with French, Provençal, Italian, Catalan literature in order even to guess what he is aiming at. T. S. Eliot presupposes in his readers the cultural level of a Harvard Ph.D., steeped in Jessie L. Weston, J. G. Frazer, Dante, Jules Laforgue, Tristan Corbière, St. John of the Cross, etc. James Joyce's amazing gift of word creation finally made him a writer for a small band of two or three hundred philologists, trained in ten ancient and modern languages, or the few music lovers who are content to be intoxicated by sound without sense.

Such private associations lavishly used by recent poets have not unjustly brought warnings from true lovers of poetry. The finest poetry of the past often drew for its evocative power upon a rich fund of mythological or biblical lore which readers possessed in common with the poet:

And ride in triumph through Persepolis [Marlowe];

While smooth Adonis from his native rock
Ran purple to the sea [Milton];

Mother of Hermes and still youthful Maia [Keats];

La fille de Minos et de Pasiphaé [Racine];

Mais les bijoux perdus de l'antique Palmyre [Baudelaire];

Bewundert viel und viel gescholten, Helena,
Vom Strande komm' ich [Goethe].

Recent upheavals in education may soon cut younger generations from this past heritage, leaving their poets and artists without any fund of allusions and symbols to draw from and therefore unable any longer to appeal to readers whom the excesses of a purely elective or vocational education have deprived of the best means of communication—a language rich in allusions or in suggestive force. Modern poets who prefer alluding to some unexplained event of their private life or some mysterious complex of their subconscious self make use of a gratuitous obscurity: they limit the zone of vibration in their reader instead of extending it as the great "obscurists" in the past have done.

One may deplore that tendency. Already in recent years philosophers, sociologists, psychologists, economists, art critics, literary analysts have delighted in adopting a pedantic terminology which has shut them off from straightforward persons who insist upon enjoying art or literature without speaking of "tactile values" or of an "objective correlative," who refuse to replace the traditional commonplace statement "I have fallen in love" with "I have responded to stimuli" or "I feel a strong visceral tension." The influence of this "science of poetry" upon the general public is growing less and less; the few experts who practice it find themselves isolated from other men through their hidebound and barbarous language. By following in their path poets can only lose. In France, England, and America poetry, in spite of its splendid achievements in the last few years, reaches far too small a portion of the public which is ready to welcome it. The novel and the sophisticated drama are also in danger of stressing the difficulty of their content and of becoming vanguard literature. Let the true artists remember that at other times difficult art and obscure literature were best felt and understood by the people. They are today in Russia, according to some reports. Let the critics perform their duty, not to a small audience of tired middle-class readers, accustomed by radio and magazines to being spared personal effort to understand, but to a wider public which can respond with good will when made to understand that true obscurity in art is a genuine homage paid by the creator to his audience.

C) Voluntary obscurity has become especially conspicuous in literature since followers of Poe, Baudelaire, and Mallarmé attempted to isolate the chemical essence of poetry in all its purity. It is only one aspect of a general modern phenomenon: poetry taking a clearer cognizance of its own purpose and method, and every poet being at the same time a critic of poetry. Where John Donne or Maurice Scève or Gongora would not have dreamed of reasoning and justifying his practice as poet, Paul Valéry, Stefan George, and even Yeats analyze the reasons which impel them to demand from their public more than is accorded the ordinary literary vulgarizer. "Take our verse at its price or leave it," they seem to reply to readers who charge them with obscurity. Mallarmé, who was beautifully clear in his early sonnets and in the first version of "L'Après-midi d'un Faune" (1866), suddenly discarded his early manner and from 1867 on composed very difficult sonnets and poems ("Ses purs ongles" and "L'Hérodiade," for example). Difficult poets ever since have seized and retained the initiative. When, through the irony of fate, the "obscurist" Paul Valéry was called upon to pronounce the eulogy of the all too lucid Anatole France in the august sanctity of the French Academy, the poet mocked with suave irony the commercial habits of the public which imagines itself cheated unless it understands gratuitously the book it has bought:

What could be more precious than that delightful illusion of clarity which inspires in us the feeling that we are growing richer without effort, are savoring pleasure gratuitously, are comprehending despite our inattention, are enjoying the spectacle without having paid for it?

But modern literature is not solely a skillful combination of riddles, a game for sophisticated wits. Mallarmé and Valéry notwithstanding, it counts many imaginative creators who are victims, or worshippers, of blind inspiration. Romanticism is far from dead, even though rash prophets, every five years for half a century, have announced that we are entering an era of classical synthesis. Much of the obscurity of recent literature is mere continuation of the difficulty which was found in the poetry of the Renaissance or of romanticism: some of our poets are still "bards," and not alchemists patiently melting their pure gold. They are more imaginative than voluntary, more gushing than consciously restrained: they compose their works hastily, their brain and eyes "in a fine frenzy rolling." In French literature, along with the obscurism of Mallarmé, Valéry, Éluard, there has flowed another current of obscurity which originated with Rimbaud, and found its chief masters in Claudel, St. John Perse, Aragon, Audiberti.[14] Their obscurity is not one of content, or of grammatical ambiguity. They project disconnected images, scorning to polish them. They recover the magnificent strangeness of the more primitive bards, and their inspiration springs forth with an ebullience of resourceful strength. When such a poet strikes a vein of great inspiration he is comparable to the authors of the Vedic Hymns, to the Old Testament prophets, to Shelley and Hugo: Claudel is not unworthy of those great names. But at times the inspiration flags, the phrasing is rough, the metaphors vague, the words tumultuous and thundering; and we are reminded of the image, dear to Claudel, of the painful travail of childbirth.

This poetry can be symbolic and symbolist, like Mallarmé's and Valéry's. But the Symbolism of Rimbaud, Claudel, and their successors is less calculated: it does not envelop a subtle meaning in allusive metaphors. Rather it expresses three or four meanings simultaneously. Each reader, according to his power of attention or his imaginative response, is free to select one or another as the meaning which, to him, seems true. One, for the artist eager to seize the outer world and to relish concrete joys, may be purely sensuous. Another may appeal to philosophers in quest of intellectual profundity. Another may awake in the reader dreams and visions which re-create the imaginative experience of the author. True symbolism is thus the fusion in a harmonious whole of

---

[14] Stephen Spender and Dylan Thomas in England, sometimes Robinson Jeffers in America could be grouped with these. D. H. Lawrence could be added, had he had a more poetical gift.

several elements (sound, color, and sense) or of several layers of meaning, of which the clearest and most easily perceived by the intellect is also the most superficial. The sacrifice of the Mass has also different meanings, all equally valid to the theologian, the scholar trained in the history of ritual, the artistic temperament whose sense of beauty is gratified, and the humble servant-girl who kneels devoutly in a corner of the cathedral. The myth of Aphrodite rising from the waves likewise offered a variety of interpretations to the Attic peasant, to the superstitious slave, to the cynic, to Socrates discoursing with Alcibiades, and to the sculptor Praxiteles. Modern poetry, like the true poetry of all ages, is often marked by its obscurity or its multiplicity of alternative meanings. One or two of them may have been consciously perceived by the author; others remained obscure or unknown to him. Shakespeare probably never guessed the depth and the variety of meanings which he placed within a speech of Hamlet or Macbeth. André Gide, in a subtle preface to his pleasantly cryptic volume, *Paludes*, declared:

Before I explain my book, I want to wait for others to explain it to me. To elucidate it too soon would be restricting its meaning too soon. For, if we know what we intended to say, we never know whether we said *that alone*. One always says *more than that*.[15]

Several of the poets least inclined to the mystification of their public have likewise confessed their inability to elucidate, and even to understand fully, their own poetry. Gérard de Nerval, who, long considered as one of the *minores* among French poets, has only lately come into his own as a very great poet, wrote three of the most beautiful sonnets in French: "Je suis le ténébreux," "La connais-tu, Dafné," "La treizième revient"; yet they are also among the most enigmatic ever composed. Hundreds of poetry lovers who know them by heart and are entranced by their charm could not explain their meaning rationally. Nerval

[15] See similar statements by Paul Valéry in *Rhumbs* (Le Divan, 1926), p. 93, *Choses tues* (Gallimard, 1932), p. 29, and *Littérature* (Gallimard, 1930), p. 85.

himself, when urged to elucidate them, declined. In a letter to Alexandre Dumas he wrote: "They are hardly more obscure than Hegel's metaphysics or Swedenborg's *Memorabilia*, and they would lose some of their charm if they were explained, supposing the thing were possible." Gerard Manley Hopkins, one of the most earnest of English poets, replied in a similar vein to his friend Robert Bridges, who had found "The Wreck of the Deutschland" obscure: "I was not over-desirous that the meaning . . . should be quite clear, at least unmistakeable. . . . Why, sometimes, one enjoys and admires the very lines one cannot understand." In a brief and pregnant essay on "Poetry and Verse," [16] Hopkins proposed one of the finest definitions of poetry:

Poetry is speech framed for contemplation of the mind by the way of hearing or speech framed to be heard for its own sake and interest over and above its interest of meaning. Some matter and meaning is essential but only as an element necessary to support and employ the shape which is contemplated for its own sake.

To his friend Bridges and to his future readers he gave this advice: "Take breath and read it with the ears, as I always wish to be read, and my verse becomes all right."

Such statements—and many more could be quoted aptly [17] seem to me to present the problem in its true light. Too many critics, because they lacked humility and applied a logical and intellectual standard to works which had first to be heard and felt, have failed to recognize the talent or genius of contemporary poets. There are, as I have tried to show, many reasons why modern poetry should be difficult. Instead of chafing at its apparent lack of logic, and rejecting the shell without looking for the

16 *The Note-books and Papers of G. M. Hopkins* (New York: Oxford University Press, 1937), pp. 249–251.

17 For example, Paul Valéry and T. S. Eliot. See, by the latter, a brief discussion of obscurity in his preface to *Anabase*, by St. John Perse, and this sentence in his essay on "The Use of Poetry and the Use of Criticism": "I know that some of the poetry to which I am most devoted is poetry which I did not understand at first reading; some is poetry which I am not sure I understand yet, for instance Shakespeare's."

pearl, a true critic should fulfill his task: that of an especially active reader who can win the public to the enjoyment of a new type of beauty, though it may be only dimly perceived. The best elucidation of a poem one can make for oneself is to learn it by heart: it is the only homage worthy of a sonnet or an ode that we have felt to be beautiful, though strange and mysterious. Much has been lost in modern education and by modern readers when the practice of learning passages by heart yielded to easier and more superficial exercises: reading at a glance and guessing in the flash of thirty seconds which of five statements is right.

Obscurity in literature is not necessarily a mark of depth. But it is well to bear in mind that it has often accompanied great works, and that poems or symphonies at first held obscure have outlived superficial clarity. Beauty in literature and the arts is often found to reside most lastingly in works which offer different generations ever-renewed secrets and a multiplicity of parallel interpretations, among which each age will choose its own.

CHAPTER VI

The Search for Standards and the Myth of Posterity

ANY discussion of criticism sooner or later encounters the word "standards." The notion designated by that word has replaced in modern times the concept of rules. Our predecessors, especially in the French seventeenth century, had been eager to discover a set of formulas, supposedly derived from Aristotle and Horace, according to which the critic was to judge and the author to compose.

> The rules, a nation born to serve obeys,
> And Boileau still in right of Horace sways.

Thus said Pope, not without a grain of salt.

Much was written against those rules in the romantic period, and much is being written in their favor in the present century. André Gide and Paul Valéry among the French, T. S. Eliot and Lytton Strachey among the English, have appeared as the champions of the same rules that were reviled a hundred and twenty years before by Victor Hugo and the English and German romantics. Those rules certainly did not prevent a great and free literature from being written; they contributed to the emergence of a drama which has not been equalled since Racine's death; they did not render the criticism of the Classical Age much worse, if at all, than the personal invectives, the hackneyed inanities and the meretricious book reviewing which pass today for criticism in the press of civilized countries. The slogan "Freedom in art!" rallied the French romantics to battle under the banner of Victor Hugo. A century of freedom has imbued us with diffidence toward the unrestrained lawlessness of some modern artists and the formlessness of too many plays and novels. In artists, the voluntary acceptance of limits, and even of hurdles over which to practice their bouncing feats, is a sign of ebullient youth, and not of submissive decrepitude. Moreover, is there any keener joy for a writer rigorously trained in artistic discipline, or for a borderline Protestant like Gide or Eliot, than becoming reverently conscious of strict rules which he may some day delight in breaking? After a long century of individualism, many of our contemporaries seem to be overweighed by their absolute artistic freedom which has rendered any revolt insipid. They might say with the proverbial Scotsman: "I do not like the French Sabbath; it is impossible to break it."

The old rules of criticism as well as of tragedy and epic poetry are dead and gone. Not all the nostalgic regret of recent prophets of the past will ever revive them. Can they be replaced by standards, that is to say by criteria, according to which we could infallibly distinguish a great work from a good one and a good one from a poor one? It is a tempting dream. Since Taine and Brunetière, many critics have been jealous of the achievement of science. Many of them have bent their energies to one aim: the imitation of one or another of the methods practiced by science (enumeration and classification, search for "causes" or sources, objective analysis of content, philological dissection of words, determination of the dependence of an artist upon his environment, study of his psychology or psychophysiology).

But sciences have, or in some cases they think they have, their objective and universal standards. Can philosophical and literary disciplines also evolve a safe method for discovering the truth or for reaching beauty? Or, if none can be devised, can we at least trust Time, the one infallible judge? Historians are fond of appealing to that supreme arbiter. Time, they say, has decided between President Wilson and Senator Lodge, between isolationism and collective security, high tariffs and free trade. (Has it indeed, one would be tempted to ask, or have we not decided for Time, and lent our ephemeral answers to the eldest of the gods?) Similarly they rely upon Time to decide one day between the romantics and the classicists, the admirers and the detractors of Cubism, of Joyce, Thomas Mann, Picasso, and atonal music.

The word "standards" applied to literature and the arts, or to the art of criticism, arouses a prompt suspicion in many of us. It has been a favorite term either with scientists who condescended to offer some of their accurate recipes to critics or with advocates of a new humanism. The latter performed a valuable task in urging the American public to prove more discriminating in acclaiming books which gave them pleasure. They distrusted extreme Impressionism, which presupposes a refined and personal taste in the reader, who erects his own impressions into laws; they fought against the democratic fallacy which claims that anyone's taste is as valid as anyone else's; they put us on our guard against the temptation, carried over from trade and advertising, to believe that the latest work of art is also the most original, and the new convention necessarily superior to the old. The positive part of their message was, however, more disappointing than their criticism of present-day evils. Their own formulation of standards remained timid.[1] Their advocacy of the Emersonian "inner check" often proved pitifully desiccating. They regularly opposed all that was strong and important in the works of their times, and took refuge in the comparatively easy reassessment of Buddhist wisdom, of Plato, and Emerson. Because vitality, the most precious of American qualities, is often accompanied by vulgarity, they distrusted vitality, and lost contact with the living productions of their country—a grave loss indeed and a regrettable detachment for a professor or critic. One renders very doubtful service to one's times and one's country by regularly opposing all of one's contemporaries and compatriots—even if one is right in thus standing alone. An indulgence in pedantic

[1] See W. C. Brownell, *Standards* (New York: Scribner, 1917), and his earlier volume on *Criticism* (New York: Scribner, 1914); Norman Foerster, *Towards Standards* (New York: Farrar & Rinehart, 1930). Irving Babbitt stood on safer ground when he defined his educational and humanistic ideal (especially in *Literature and the American College* [Boston: Houghton Mifflin, 1908]) than when he criticized modern literature as Rousseauistic and addicted to irrational disorder.

terminology and an affectation of genteel superiority have too often accompanied their advocacy of standards. Even the most versatile and most lovable personality among the Neo-Humanists, Paul Elmer More, failed to help contemporary American literature discover its own type of greatness, and remained blind to achievements in other modern literatures from which their intellectual and spiritual crusade might have drawn reinforcement.[2]

Scientists are more dangerous still when they venture to deal with literature. The havoc wrought by distinguished physicians, for instance, when they retrospectively diagnosed the diseases of Rousseau, Baudelaire, and Dostoevski or offered all-too-clear elucidations of the physiological sources of Blake's or Poe's genius, of Leopardi's or Schopenhauer's pessimism, is all the more deplorable as the medical profession is often the most deeply cultured of all and could bring invaluable help to the humane and discriminating enjoyment of literature that criticism seeks to foster. Other and more exact scientists are even more perversely prone to proselytizing. They have only recently formulated their own methods, which range from statistics and questionnaires to laboratory techniques. They take pity upon their colleagues who cannot even agree that a certain work of art is good or who expend their efforts upon a philosophical problem which they have agreed is insoluble. The most generous among them have suggested to critics and professors of literature that they borrow the fixed methods and quantitative criteria of science. Too many scholars and teachers of the humanities have lent a willing ear to those prophets of an age of science. The result has been disastrous. The student of literature can never proceed like the chemist, applying fixed standards in order to test the value of a reaction or, like the clerk in a drugstore, mechanically filling pre-

---

[2] Paul Elmer More, for instance, failed to discern the constructive purpose and the intellectual ambition of much of the seemingly revolutionary French poetry of the present century. In an article of June 1935, reprinted in the third series of the *New Shelburne Essays*, "On Being Human," he made a sweeping condemnation of those poets as repudiating the thinking faculty for a trancelike state. This might have been true of a few followers of Rimbaud, but even there the statement needs qualification.

scriptions. True artists and scholars unbiased by passing scientific fads feel no envy for the scientist who has found his fixed standards. They even reciprocate his condescending pity; for, in criticism as in the pursuit of truth, happiness, and beauty, the important thing is, not to succeed, but to try, not to find, but to search. Standards are laudable, not when they have been reached and applied, but when they are pursued; that very pursuit is the mark of a genuine critical gift. Adventure will never disappear from criticism; and where risk and fallibility are highest—in the candid discrimination of values in the works of our contemporaries—successful criticism is also most worthy of praise.

Even those who have appeared as the staunchest advocates of Standards with a capital *S* have been shy of defining them. Imagination is apparently not a common quality with critics, and the startling innovations of modern literature have not been followed by a corresponding renewal of the content of criticism. There are few new standards of criticism today; and the most modern works of literature and painting are liked for very old reasons. Any attempt at scientific accuracy in defining the standards of beauty seems doomed to failure, if we may judge from the clumsy endeavors of the superscientists of our day: the social scientists and the structuralists.

One of them, John B. Watson, who enjoyed some fame among professional psychologists some fifty years ago as the founder of behaviorism, offered an easy means of judging the value of writers: their sales receipts. If at forty a novelist does not sell his stories at a higher price than he did at thirty, the chances are that he has not developed as a writer. Popularity, measured in terms of financial profit or prestige, would thus become the test of a writer's importance, as the astronomical monthly salaries of movie actors determine the degree of reverence in which they are held by the public. It is hardly necessary to point out that such a standard of literary value is as unscientific as could be, and does not deserve a serious refutation. Many of the most influential books in philosophy and political thought as well as in literature have been unnoticed by contemporary buyers. Even the readers who, carried away by the behavior of their neighbors, rushed to purchase *Anthony Adverse, The Robe,* or *The Song of Bernadette* entertained no illusions as to the validity of their taste or the quality of those best sellers. Harold Bell Wright or Georges Simenon, who sell by the hundreds of thousands, must be aware of the modesty of their claims to greatness or to survival. Indeed, the successful writer whose tenth novel sells at fifty times the price of his first manuscript often looks inwardly with regret toward the youthful years when he had not yet learned to repeat himself, and wisely reflects that there must be something wrong with his books if they are so readily understood by a wide and not too discriminating public.

Another of those modest scientists who prefer discovering an objective and mechanical standard of literary value to relying on their own taste was a specialist of pathological physiology named Frederick Lyman Wells. He wrote in a scientific journal, *Archives of Psychology,* a serious article entitled "A Statistical Study of Literary Merit." [3] Mr. Wells gathered ten graduate students or scholars at the English Graduate Club of Columbia University. He asked them to grade ten American writers (Bryant, Cooper, Emerson, Hawthorne, Holmes, Irving, Longfellow, Lowell, Poe, Thoreau) for ten different qualities: charm, clearness, euphony, finish, force, imagination, originality, proportion, sympathy, wholesomeness. The psychologist then skilfully combined varied curves ranking each of the American classics according to his grades in each of the ten deadly virtues. The final rank assigned placed Hawthorne first, Poe second, Emerson third; Thoreau only reached the eighth place, after Lowell, Longfellow, Irving, and Bryant; Cooper, who is a greater man for Europeans than for Columbia graduates, was at the bottom of the list, where he probably belongs. One wonders, incidentally, why

---

[3] No. 7 (August 1907). We are indebted for this reference to Henry Hazlitt's witty volume, *The Anatomy of Criticism: A Trialogue* (New York: Simon and Schuster, 1933). Mr. Hazlitt's chapter on "Standards" contains some of the most pertinent reflections ever made on that subject.

Melville, Whitman, Mark Twain, and Emily Dickinson were
omitted from the list. But nothing could be more arbitrary than
such a selection of ten writers, unless it be the selection of ten
"qualities." How can a serious-minded scientist imagine he is thus
contributing valuable statistical and objective material to the determination of literary "merit"? The standardless critic who remains modest enough not to ape the paraphernalia of exact science can only feel baffled.[4]

Any sophomore doubtless realizes after his first course in English literature that the five or ten greatest geniuses in his language
are great for very different reasons and that no one standard can
ever comprehend their diversity of achievement. Every philo-
sophically minded critic in every age deludes himself into proposing some new standard of taste or some new formulation of a
very old one. A few of them will be briefly discussed here.

According to those contemporary critics who are hypnotized
by our democratic ideals, the merit of the individual talent is
scant in any great work of art; the artist is simply the mouthpiece
of the age and country and way of life which have produced
him. The century of the common man in which we live, those
critics contend, is no longer interested in Mr. So-and-So's response to nature or to love or to the workings of his own subconscious mind. The lyrical poet who delights in singing his raptures
or his sorrows was tolerable in individualistic ages. Today, we
can only accept a writer, and he can only claim survival in men's
memories, if he interprets his times and civilization in a national
or humanitarian epic, celebrates factories, bridges, and our democratic achievements; or, better still, if he embraces and describes
the whole of his surroundings in a vast synthetic fresco. Balzac
and Zola had done it for their age; Tolstoi is praised for *War and
Peace* far more warmly than for *Anna Karenina*, probably a superior work of art, or for *The Cossacks*, in many respects his

[4] The psychologist here mentioned appears, from his bibliography, to be a
specialist in "fatigue" and "mental adjustments." Let us hope he since kept
in his own province.

masterpiece. Galsworthy, the author of *Buddenbrooks*, Dos Passos, Thomas Wolfe, Jules Romains have enjoyed a fame higher than their merits justified, for had they not painted an all-embracing fresco of their civilization? The time we spent with them was not wasted and our pleasure in reading them was not the selfish escapist enjoyment of forgetting a world which made constant demands upon us; they taught us, they informed us. Thanks to them, we were enabled to understand pre-war Germany, Edwardian England, and Republican France. Proust himself, imprisoned in his abnormal memory, was only saved in the eyes of those critics because his long novel provided a sociological document on the decline of the aristocracy, or on the place of the Jew in society, or on the military caste in recent French history.

Thus spread one of the most fallacious heresies of our times: the consideration of literature as a document on an age, as a mirror to the manners of a people. Great works are read, in our own language or in translation, to illustrate "the way of life" of our ancestors or of foreigners. Literature is a modest handmaid to the history of civilization. Homer enlightens us on the ethnic values entertained by the Greeks of the eighth century B.C., Dante on medieval conceptions of this world and the next, Racine on the formal manners of the court of Louis XIV; Tolstoi, surprisingly enough, on the qualities of the Russian people which made it possible for them to push the Germans back from the Volga in 1942. According to that view of literature an artist, with a few strange exceptions which some psychological complex or physiological abnormality will soon explain away, is always the product of his environment. The most valuable artist is the one who left the most faithful or illuminating picture of the society which molded him. He is judged, not for his imaginative power but for the degree of accuracy of his novels on the Stock Exchange, the Chicago slums, or the unemployed miners. Scholars will some day write painstaking monographs on "Social Life in the South from the Novels of William Faulkner," "The California Farmer According to the Poems of Robinson Jeffers," or "Twentieth-Century English Sex Life According to D. H. Lawrence."

The weakness of such a deterministic view of literature as a physiological secretion of society or as a faithful expression of a country and an age is too obvious to need discussion here. The greatness of art lies, in some cases, in its relative independence of the surrounding public. The architect or the dramatist cannot well do without a public; often the novelist and the sculptor have received no encouragement from their contemporaries; the painter, the lyrical poet, and the musician can occasionally forget their environment altogether and create their works for a future age or to please themselves alone. Yet, even in the drama, the most "social" of all literary genres, the faithful mirror to the manners of an age is to be found in the worst or the mediocre and commonplace plays, not in Racine or Ibsen, in Shakespeare or Shaw. The greatest geniuses of an age do not even enlighten us on the taste of their public, since, as I hope has been amply demonstrated, they often passed unnoticed among their contemporaries, or were violently repudiated as untrue, strange, incomprehensible. We may today hail the insight and accuracy with which Balzac depicted French society under the Bourbon restoration; his contemporaries, however, thought differently. The public found little that was true to life in *Madame Bovary* (today required reading in courses in French history, where it is treated as if it had been written purposely to inform foreigners on provincial life in France). Most of Zola's contemporaries were convinced that he gave an utterly distorted or fanciful picture of French society. The fact is that the French public of 1820–1880 recognized itself in Alexandre Dumas, Eugène Sue, Cherbuliez, and other novelists already forgotten, but not in the great masters praised today as the mirrors of their age. Dickens may similarly provide modern historians with useful documents on early Victorian England, and Hawthorne on the Puritans in New England. But none of them ever set out to give objective historical value to his imaginative creations. They avoided the wealth of detail on furniture, dress, schools, trade, church, factories which weigh down modern novels deliberately based on factual information.

I may probably concur with the general opinion which sees in great writers and artists the truest expression of their age, but with a few important reservations: only the mediocre talents actually depicted their age as it was, or as it wanted to appear in its own eyes; only the mediocre talents are the product of their environment and seem well adapted to their surroundings. If history were bent upon seeing past ages as they really were, it should unearth and patiently scan hundreds of unreadable novels or plays, cheap operas, and bad paintings. The great artists always transcended their own times; their originality clashed with the taste of their contemporaries; their imagination transfigured the environment in which they lived. Balzac, Flaubert, Dickens, and Hawthorne appear as the true expression of their age, not because they faithfully rendered it as it was, but because, through sheer genius or talent, they have imposed upon posterity their own vision of their age. In the same manner, Hogarth has forced upon us his interpretation of old England, Ruysdael, Teniers, and Breughel their view of the Low Countries. Oscar Wilde's famous and easy paradox is at bottom truer than he himself suspected: literature seldom imitates life with serious profit, but life imitates literature. We see today with the eyes of Gauguin and Cézanne; we love like Proust's heroes (only a little more normally); we swear and drink like Hemingway's characters; and some of us perhaps eat like the heroes of Thomas Wolfe. But let us not cherish the illusion that an artist is great because he imitates or expresses his own times, and thus adds sociological value to his idle imaginative creations: nonconformity, or even bitter revolt against their age and environment, has been a far more common characteristic of great artists than acceptance or sympathy. The epithet "timeless," which cheap book-reviewing is now casting into disrepute through excessive use, remains the best one to define the work of the truly important writers. From the particular and transitory elements which surround them, they extract the universal and lasting beauty which is truth.

Other criteria have been recently proposed, with greater though still partial success. Where psychologists and determinists have conspicuously failed, philosophers have for centuries tried to define the nature of beauty. One is bound to admit that their aesthetics is seldom the most valuable part of their system and appears too often as a stopgap, appended to their metaphysics, because a metaphysician was supposed to offer a total explanation of the universe and had to include man's artistic activity in this system. Neither Kant nor Hegel nor Schopenhauer (the last perhaps the most keenly aware of the problems which confront an artist and a critic) has brought much help to the literary critic. In this century, after Bergson, who most regrettably never fully stated his views on esthetics, the omniscient Croce is doubtless the most important philosopher that has systematically examined the problem of beauty.[5] He has applied his theoretical views in many volumes of critical essays embracing three or four literatures and in his austere review, *La Critica*, which for many years published the most unbiased and most pregnant critiques in Europe.

Like all philosophical temperaments, Croce was naturally dissatisfied with extreme critical relativism, which reduces taste to a personal reaction, the validity of which cannot even be questioned. Poe once called the Latin proverb "De gustibus non est disputandum" an "insane adage," and Howells, who was no worshipper of traditional rules, condemned the cheap answer of a stubborn ignoramus, "I know what I like," as "that pernicious

[5] George Santayana has written with greater charm than any other philosopher on individual literary artists, and some of his views on art are among the most subtle ever proposed in the English language, and by far the most sensitively and felicitously expressed (*The Sense of Beauty, Reason in Art,* and some chapters of *Obiter Scripta*). But their merit lies in the attractiveness of detached passages, not in any coherent doctrine which might help literary criticism. He did not attempt to pass judgment on his contemporaries.

maxim of those who do not know what they ought to like." He might even have added: of those who do not know why they like what they like and who are more often than not the victims of convention or imitation. Because dogmatism in philosophy as well as in esthetics has always been and will always be partly unsuccessful, it does not follow that all individual judgments are equally justified and that every age and group should cultivate its own standards. I may prefer George Bernard Shaw to Shakespeare and Jacques Prévert to Keats, but in that case I do not know what I ought to like and deprive myself of deeper joy for the sake of titillating satisfaction.

Croce, who did much to tear criticism away from the narrow minutiae of philological exegesis, repudiated both the old rules of the pseudo-classical ages and the extreme impressionism which ranks works of art according to the fleeting pleasure one may receive from them. He rejected likewise the consideration of technique as divorced from content and all the exterior theories which attempted to assign determining causes (the artist's biography, race, environment) to a masterpiece. The dogmatic judge, the skeptical relativist, and the scholar intent on analyzing words and rhymes all remain alien to the essence of the artistic work. Croce's ideal critic should be at the same time historical and esthetic. He reproduces in himself the intuitions of the artist. He is, in his own way, a creator who becomes the thing he contemplates and judges it from the inside.

Such "creative criticism," as J. E. Spingarn, Croce's chief interpreter in English-speaking countries, called it, would loom so formidably that it would instantly kill the critical ambitions of nine tenths of the present writers of reviews, essays, and monographs. It would be equally fatal to any adverse judgment of an important but faulty work. If only those who can faithfully repeat in themselves Balzac's or Carlyle's creative impulse were entitled to judge Balzac and Carlyle, how could we ever reach the fair balance between the shortcomings of those writers and their merits which is indispensable to any appraisal of their importance in letters?

Croce tried to provide his ideal critic with a standard of taste. All exterior criteria (dogmatic, philosophical, or moral) being banished, a work should be valued according to "the degree of harmony between the poet's vision and his handiwork," or between the intuition and the expression of the artist. A good novel or poem would be characterized by its inner harmony; a bad one would strike us as dissonant. While such a criterion is often valid, and has the great merit of judging each writer by his own standards and not by some exterior and rigid yardstick, it fails to provide different critics with any common standard. Some of the examples enumerated in the first part of the present work have made it clear that what is dissonant to me may be exquisitely harmonious to my successor or even to my neighbor. According to earlier judges, Donne deserved to be hanged for his wrenching of accent, yet his music comes to us fraught with poignant loveliness. Browning seemed to some of his contemporaries to have reached the apex of discordance, but today "Love among the Ruins" sounds almost too sweetly musical to our ears. The same may be true before long of Gerard Manley Hopkins or even of W. H. Auden's jingle in his *New Year's Letter*. Beethoven and Debussy in turn lacerated the ears of our ancestors. Cézanne's paintings struck obtuse but apparently candid observers as the shocking combination of distorted vision and inadequate craftsmanship. Forty years later, his flowers, jugs, and apples are ranked by millions among the most "classical" and harmonious works of modern art.

Croce's esthetic standard thus fails to answer the two most tantalizing riddles of criticism: First, are there not degrees in beauty or in greatness? There may be more perfect agreement between the feeling and the expression in a love song by Herrick or Campion than in a sonnet by Shakespeare or an ode by Shelley; yet we *know* Shakespeare and Shelley to be the greater poets. Too exquisite a balance between content and form may have more charm and prettiness than actual power. A song of Verlaine or of Yeats, while more instantaneously and more fully satisfying to our ears and to our senses, will not haunt us with the same pathetic intensity as a sonnet of Baudelaire or a lament by Shelley on the tragedy of life.

The second difficulty of the Crocean test is obvious as soon as one deals with innovators and rebels in art. An artist with a keen sense of the past, who starts where some of his predecessors left off and uses a medium already perfected by a long process of evolution (Racine, Milton, Leopardi, Keats in literature; Titian or Raphael in painting; Mozart in music) easily reaches that ideal correspondence between his vision and his expression which constitutes one of the chief marks of greatness in art. But new ideas, new moods, and novel themes appear with the evolution of history, social changes, or scientific discoveries. Old molds become conventional, old forms appear stale, the harmony of yesterday becomes monotonous to ears which are too well attuned to it. Revolutionary artists then extend man's concept of beauty: strangeness has a more vivid appeal than regularity and serenity. The imaginative Elizabethans and the romantics delight in luxuriance, proclaim with Keats that "poetry should surprise by a fine excess." Others follow who reveal an even stranger beauty in discontinuity and in discord. Jerky rhythm, roughness of syntax, ludicrous contrast are the devices commonly resorted to by innovators, whether Donne, Hopkins or Eliot, Hugo or Rimbaud, or their peers in other arts: Goya, Degas, Gauguin, Schönberg, or Stravinsky. Through them, a new beauty is revealed to our timid sensibilities; for boldness and character, as well as inner balance and serenity, can be attributes of the beautiful. The Crocean standard, while having the signal advantage of judging the work of art from the inside and on its own merits, suffers from the weakness of all standards: it is valid for the masterpieces of the past and doubtless enlightens us on some of their secrets, but it assists us little if at all in understanding a radically new type of beauty.

Another standard of taste, which has lately enjoyed great vogue, must, for lack of a more felicitous name, be called the functional notion of beauty. From interior decoration and architecture, it has spread to judgment on the style and even the content of a literary work. A writer is to be commended if he has done adequately what he set out to do. If he intended to write a realistic novel, let him be appraised as a realistic novelist. If the poet attempted an epic, let the critic judge his work solely as an epic, and refrain from reproaching the epic with not being dramatic or lyrical. A student of *Paradise Lost*, the late Clive S. Lewis, began his exegesis of the poem by the assertion that the only fair procedure for a critic is to examine how successful Milton's poem is as an epic and to consider his purpose, which was clearly defined. In the same manner, said Mr. Lewis, a corkscrew was made to open a bottle, and it would be unfair to complain that the corkscrew is useless for digging a hole in the ground. Most of the critical questions would thus be reduced to two, which thousands of critics had already asked long before functionalism was heard of: "What has the author tried to do? How has he done it?"

The origins of this test of usefulness as a standard of beauty are indeed less recent than some of our students of modern architecture imagine. They probably should be traced back to the very original development of esthetic ideas which took place in the eighteenth century: many of those who then meditated on Greek art discovered that the secret of the Greeks was to have made utility the basis of beauty.[6] Stendhal was permeated by these views; he invested them with his incisive style, and transmitted them in his turn to the poet and esthetician whose definition of the beautiful has exercised the deepest influence on modern art: Baudelaire.

This functional standard, like the Crocean one, represented a great advance over the old dogmatic rules of beauty, for it

[6] Diderot, in his "Essay on Painting," ch. 6, wrote: "beauty, the foundation of which is always utility." Mengs asserted that "the thing which is the fittest for the purpose for which it was meant is the most perfect of its kind," and added that "ugliness is sometimes beautiful if it fills a useful purpose." Stendhal, who owes much to eighteenth-century philosophical and esthetic ideas, popularized that definition of beauty as "la saillie de l'utile" in his *Histoire de la Peinture en Italie*, Part V, ch. 83, and Part VI, ch. III.

judged a work of art from the inside and not on its conformity with scholastic rules borrowed from some grammarian. It undoubtedly should remain one of the valid points of view from which a critic should look upon artistic and literary works. It is especially useful in any study of style, considered as the faithful garb of the writer's personality and not as an exterior attire thrown over the writer's meaning, like a cloak chosen at random for its conspicuousness. I have quoted elsewhere [7] the concise formula of a British art historian, Sir Walter Armstrong, "Beauty is fitness expressed," as the best definition of the French classical ideal. The best Attic prose—that of Lysias or Thucydides; the best French prose—that of Pascal and Voltaire, of Stendhal and Mérimée; in English that of Swift, of Hazlitt at times, and of Hemingway when he does not fall into mannerism, are indeed excellently adapted to the subject matter or to the mood of the author, and produce their fullest effect without wasting superfluous ornaments.

But these "functional" prose writers are not necessarily the greatest, or the only ones to be great. Bossuet, Rousseau, Renan, and Camus add more ornamental beauty to their prose than can be justified by strict utility. Even in English, where the danger of overwriting has proved much graver than in Romance languages, one cannot altogether dismiss the sonorous pomp of Sir Thomas Browne and De Quincey or the imaginative luxuriance of Ruskin, Pater, and Moore. Only brief fragments or polished jewels can be called functional in poetry: but Virgil and Shakespeare, Keats and Goethe are not altogether free from graceful intricacies. Functionalism may, even in architecture, be conducive to a simplified style for bathrooms, kitchens, school buildings, but it does not necessarily build the most beautiful type of museum, palace, or cathedral. It is, in my opinion, a misguided manifestation of a Puritan spirit applied to arts and letters. Purity, sobriety, streamlined simplicity are esthetic virtues; but so are charm, refinement, complexity, and strangeness. Much that is beautiful has had no particular aim and remains useless in its loveliness. The Greeks

[7] *Qu'est-ce que le Classicisme?* (Nizet, 1965).

could be the masters of pure functional architecture, but they could also delight in the grace of the Erechtheum or the Temple of the Wingless Victory. Their most beautiful myths, Pindar's metaphors, Plato's dialogues, certainly did not despise leisurely superfluity and that wealth of intricate detail which delights our intellect as well as our roaming fancy.

Moreover, a mechanical application of the standard "How has the author done what he tried to do?" would not infrequently condemn as failures some of the most moving masterpieces. For genius is not always conscious of its aims; a potter or an architect may know exactly what will emerge from his wheel or his blueprints, a poet and a painter must make allowance for the share of God, or demon, in artistic creation.[8] When he composed *Hamlet*, Shakespeare may have intended to write a play on the revenge motive, along the lines of Kyd's *Spanish Tragedy;* but the varied meanings of depth and beauty which have been read into his drama were doubtless not consciously present in his mind in 1602. Molière dashed off his *Don Juan* to make use of a popular theme and rival a successful play translated from the Italian. Both *Hamlet* and *Don Juan* would be shorn of some of their most moving scenes if strictly "utilitarian" and functional criteria were applied. Victor Hugo undertook to supersede the classical tragedy with *Hernani:* as a drama, his play may be a failure; but it lives as lyrical poetry. Goethe in the Second Part of *Faust*, Shelley in *Prometheus Unbound*, Keats in "Hyperion" certainly did not fulfill their original intentions, but they reached depths of meaning and heights of poetic flight which immortalize these ambitious and nonfunctional masterpieces. Balzac thought he was writing novels for the general public, and they turned out to be epics of philosophical mysticism. Zola was convinced that he would live as the originator of a new scientific and realistic novel, and is admired today chiefly for his visionary and imaginative

[8] Goethe, one of the most lucid and serene of writers, was not blind to the role of the unconscious in artistic creation. He wrote to Schiller on April 6, 1801, that "all that genius creates is done unconsciously," and elsewhere that most great works were not deliberately planned by their authors, but were "works of circumstance."

power. Others who intended their stories as children's literature live through the ages for their symbolism, while *Gulliver's Travels* with its mordant satire on humanity is a perennial favorite in the nursery. A mere caricaturist like Daumier retrospectively appears as a profoundly tragic painter. The history of art and letters is full of such instances of discrepancy between a creator's intention and his achievement, his vision and his technique. Both the Crocean and the functional standards tend to overestimate the importance of inner harmony and exact balance between intuition and expression in an artistic work. The logical application of such tests would lead to the ranking above all others of virtuosos and voluntary creators who, like Henry James or Jules Romains, succeed in doing far too completely and consciously what they intended to do. The stamp of genius is often better recognized in a failure than in perfect agreement between conception and achievement. The artists who move us longest are those who never ceased to be at war with themselves: [9] Goethe, who, suffering from the pangs of love at seventy-four, wrote his heart-rending "Marienbad Elegy"; Rodin, Tolstoi, Baudelaire, Rembrandt, nay Racine himself, and, as far as is known, the authors of *King Lear* and *The Divine Comedy*. As soon as he has reached the perilous and frail equilibrium of a technique corresponding to his inner vision, the true creator becomes conscious of his demon's call urging him on to new attempts:

> And every attempt
> Is a wholly new start, and a different kind of failure.[10]

[9] The following sentence by one of the leading American poets of our age, Robinson Jeffers, seems very apt here: "The war between a poet and his genius is one of the most interesting of human shows. It is a war of collaboration, and it ought to be a war without victory; for whether the man triumphs after a while, as in Wordsworth's work, or the bright spirit, as in Blake's, the collaboration ends, and the work ceases to be significant." This sentence occurs in his review of Mark Van Doren's poems and is quoted in Sydney S. Albert's *Bibliography of the Works of Robinson Jeffers* (New York: Random House, 1933), p. 147.

[10] T. S. Eliot, *East Coker*, Part V. It is also obvious that an artist who aims low, and tries to write a drinking song, a detective novel, or an effete short story can easily be functional and do exactly what he intended; not so with

Among the standards of artistic merit which have enjoyed keen
favor in the last two centuries, two words stand out as the most
popular in modern criticism: personality and sincerity. Historians
of ideas should undertake to write a history of those words and
of the notions they represent. I have attempted it in *Literature
and Sincerity*, in 1963. It is doubtful whether, before the eighteenth century, a book was ever praised as expressing the personality of its author. In fact, under Louis XIV, one of the most
personal books ever written, Montaigne's *Essais*, was currently
blamed as being "foolish" ("un sot projet," as Pascal called it),
superficial, filled with irrelevant details, disorderly and affected in
its nonchalance (criticisms of Vigneul-Marville, Nicéron, Male-
branche). Suddenly, a new chapter in the history of taste opened,
with Shaftesbury, several French and Italian critics, Diderot, and
Rousseau: it then became common to assert that a work was
great in proportion as it expressed the artist's personality. The
Romantics followed, and they actually *lived* their books: their
biography became part and parcel of their genius, and often the
only tragic or deep element in them. Long before Oscar Wilde
sadly coined the phrase which fits him so well, they "put all their
genius in their lives and only their talent in their works." Goethe
himself, who did not live the romantic life of Casanova, Chateaubriand, or Byron, but whose biography is perhaps the finest masterpiece of all, called personality "the highest joy on this earth"
(in *The Divan of East and West*) and shortly before his death
(on February 13, 1831), he remarked to Eckermann: "In art and
poetry, personality is everything."

It would be vain to bewail the power which the new notion
was soon to hold over creators and critics alike. Lyrical poetry,
the essay, memoirs, even the novel and the drama gained much
from the emphasis upon personality. Many of the classical masterpieces published before the nineteenth century strike us as
slightly cold and remote, with all their restrained sobriety, compared with the more ardent cries of passion of Shelley, Musset,

---

the creator of *Hamlet* or of *The Human Comedy* (unless the latter be that
of William Saroyan!).

and Lenau, the confessions which Heine, Browning, and Baude-laire whispered into our ears. Modern audiences are moved more intensely if they are made to feel the presence of a personality more powerful than their own behind a tragedy or a symphony. The intellectual connoisseurs are fewer among them than they were among the listeners to Racine's and Sophocles' tragedies, and the persons who seek an emotional catharsis in art are probably far more numerous.

It does not follow, however, that personality is the secret of greatness and that an artist has a surer chance of survival if he displays his personality in his works and, as the phrase goes, pours his soul into his writings or his music. Neither Racine nor Velasquez nor Raphael can be said to be great because of his personality. Critics may delight in discovering psychoanalytical secrets in Molière and Shakespeare, but the greatness of those geniuses lies elsewhere: often in the magnificent impersonality which Flaubert never wearied of praising in Homer and Shakespeare and a few other supreme artists, "no more apparent in their creation than God in nature, everywhere present, nowhere visible." If the expression of personality were the sole criterion, Cervantes, Velasquez, Goethe, Mozart, and Tolstoi would run the danger of being ranked very low in the hierarchy of great men. On the other hand, many poets, musicians, and painters who were too directly personal (Byron and Musset, countless romantic painters and musicians) suffer in our estimate: they did not realize that the more powerful the personality, the more discreet and indirect should be its means of communication with the public. An "objective" novel by Tolstoi teaches one more about Tolstoi than his diary; Berlioz's music more than his memoirs, Proust's descriptions of society and nature far more than his letters.

This "personal heresy," as it has been called, has reached ridiculous excesses in contemporary criticism. It has led many moderns to believe that the greatest works are always the most original. Beauty has been taken to consist in difference, or even in sharp contrast. The favorite pleasure to be derived from a book, a painting, or a lecture was that of stimulation, provocation, or, worse still, "a thrill." Artists were thus tempted to strain their originality, to cultivate it through tricks, paradoxes, and perverted idiosyncrasies. From their most tender years, children have been taught to develop "self-expression" and to assert their personality before they even have one. Hence the lamentable weakness, in this century, of so much of the literature published in college literary magazines and in self-styled vanguard reviews. Some of the works which we now agree to find great were startling innovations in their time; but how many other innovations have been swept away as abject failures! Many were not revolutionary at all: Shakespeare, Racine, Milton, Mozart, Pushkin, Keats, Valéry seemed at first to differ little from their contemporaries or their predecessors. They hardly dreamt of being original: they just happened to be, even when they imitated or borrowed. As the French saying puts it, "La vraie originalité est celle qu'on a malgré soi."

Closely connected with this superstition of personality as the sole basis for greatness in art is the pervading faith in sincerity. The critic, who looks back upon works of the past which once enjoyed extravagant fame and are today discarded, is tempted to explain their failure to survive by their lack of "genuineness." John Lyly, Abraham Cowley, Southey, De Quincey, Poe, Swinburne were not sincere enough; the painters Le Brun in the seventeenth century, Meissonier or Burne-Jones in the nineteenth were not; nor were the musicians Liszt and Weber: hence their gradual decline into obscurity.

Art would be easy indeed if sincerity were the basis of merit. Alas! unless sincerity be defined as perfect harmony between a splendid form and a powerful emotion, hence as equivalent to greatness (which would merely be begging the question), one is bound to admit that many of the worst wrecks in the history of letters were once produced, with a sob in the voice and a bleeding heart, by desperately sincere artists; on the contrary, some artists of supreme genius were hardly more sincere than great actors who have carefully rehearsed every one of their tears and their passionate embraces. The worst of the romantic and Pre-

Raphaelite painters were the most sincere; so are the composers of sentimental songs and of well-meaning Sunday-school stories. But was Homer sincere in the twenty-fourth canto of the *Iliad,* Virgil in the *Georgics,* Petrarch in his *Canzone,* Sir Philip Sidney in the most graceful sonnet of his *Arcadia* ("Look up, fair lids, the treasure of my heart"), Shakespeare in that most magnificent opening of one of his sonnets, "Full many a glorious morning have I seen . . ."? Ronsard has been praised for three centuries for the pathetic sincerity of his *Amours de Marie;* a scholar suddenly discovers that these heart-rending lines are borrowed from a Neo-Latin poet, Marullus. Du Bellay never sounded more sincere than in that *Défense et illustration* in which he championed an original method of enriching the French language; another scholar comes and reveals that he merely pillaged an Italian predecessor. In truth, with many of the greatest masterpieces, the question of sincerity is absolutely meaningless. It matters in no wise whether Titian, Rembrandt, Racine, Mozart, Pushkin were sincere or not. In what sense is a novelist like Jane Austen, Gogol, or Flaubert sincere?

Few notions have been as harmful to criticism as well as to writers as that mystical concept of sincerity put forward as a test of human and artistic greatness. Montaigne and Pepys did not boast of the superior value of their indiscreet revelations. Rousseau was the first to grant himself a certificate of unequalled "goodness" for having confessed with unflinching courage all his sins (even, perhaps, a few imaginary ones) and those of his friends. Volumes of confessions and memoirs have since multiplied a hundredfold. Some of the most restrained writers of the last century arranged to have their autobiographies echo like a voice "from beyond the grave," and by postponing the full publication of their indiscreet disclosures until half a century after their death, skilfully acquired a longer lease of fame than their works justified. No one reads the novels by the Goncourt brothers, but their *Journal* and the Academy and the literary prize they founded have made their name immortal. Others, from Goethe to Anatole France, aimed at no minute accuracy in the record of their youth. They knew that "an event of our life is important, not because it is real, but because it means something," as Goethe put it, explaining to Eckermann his choice of the two words "Dichtung" and "Wahrheit" as a title for his reminiscences. But other romantics, like Musset or Hazlitt in his *Liber Amoris*, had been more daring, or less modest, and their followers today are legion. A modern writer is convinced that he will be sincere, hence great, if he confesses every minute detail of his private life: André Gide conceals little of his rapturous experiences in North Africa; Montherlant disguises under a transparent veil his series of feminine conquests, real or imaginary; Maurois represses his usual sense of humor to relate how he courted his first and then his second wife. Few writers can resist publishing their diaries or their memoirs even before they have entered the nostalgic period of middle age: Julien Green confided to the public at thirty-seven, Roy Campbell, the flamboyant South African poet, at thirty-two, Louis MacNeice at thirty-one, Jean Prévost at twenty-eight. Salvador Dali exultantly triumphs over Rousseau in "sincerity" (and in melodramatic pose) by beginning the series of his prodigious feats with the embryonic stage of his "secret life." Others relate and, let us hope, invent thefts, murders, Oedipus complexes, even an occasional incest in order to add flavor to their otherwise tame autobiographies.

Nothing is more difficult than to be truly sincere; nothing requires more zeal and more art. If sincerity is sometimes the mark of greatness, it is also the mark of the worst failures in literature: nine tenths of feminine poetry, for instance, which oscillates between sincere sentimentality and immodest cries of passion or desire; and more than nine tenths of the writings of very young men. At the very age when they believe themselves to be most directly sincere, young writers cannot help feeling, acting, thinking—when they do think—and expressing themselves like other young men, and like their favorite masters. The worst literature produced in the world is doubtless also the most passionately sincere: love letters. Critics who boast of recognizing true art through its sincerity should be condemned to the

most discouraging of wartime jobs: that of censoring, hence presumably of reading, all the love letters written by soldiers to their
sweethearts. Even the letters of lovers who threaten to commit
suicide, and in a few cases probably do so, contain the most
naïvely false writing: newspaper records of such cases amply
prove it, and in literature, the letters of dying Werther or Jacopo
Ortis.

There is often, indeed, far more sincerity in objective literature than in autobiographical analysis. An author can confess
himself much more freely if he lends his own motives, vices, and
dreams to an imaginary character (Balzac's Rastignac, Flaubert's
Madame Bovary, Dostoevski's Myshkin) than by relating them in
his own name. The dangerous facility of memoirs, diaries, personal effusions in poetry makes them the most difficult of all. A
young man, in order to be sincere, has to mature, shake off influences, avoid melodrama and declamation, weed out all that is not
deeply himself. Some exceptional geniuses, Rimbaud and Keats,
have succeeded in that task before the age of twenty or twenty-
five. The majority of men and women have to struggle for years
before they become themselves. At forty, when looking at their
adolescent years in retrospect, they discover how untrue to
themselves they were in their early confessions or lyrics. The
most helpful advice that critics could give to young artists is the
old Greek motto which Nietzsche made his own: "Become what
you are." [11]

Philosophers and critics may continue for centuries proposing
standards of artistic excellence, and their contributions will be
valuable if they express changing trends in taste or bring to our
attention qualities we had failed to discover in the old masters.
But it seems clear to me that any effort to test greatness by one
standard alone, however comprehensive, is an idle pastime. Man

[11] The old Greek sentence was Γένοἰ οἶος ἐσσί. Nietzsche translated it:
"Werde wer du bist," and the meaning obviously is: Become the one who,
secretly, you are. See the volume on *Literature and Sincerity* mentioned
above.

strives to bring as much reason as possible to this irrational world; but the most reasonable form of wisdom is that which acknowledges its own limitations. In the realm of beauty as in the realm of feeling, neither analysis nor methodical consistency can ever reach the ultimate secrets of elusive reality. Oscar Wilde's witty remark is more than ever worth quoting in the present era of scientific, psychological, and linguistic ascendancy over mere enjoyment of beauty: "There are two ways of disliking art; one is to dislike it, the other is to like it rationally."

A skeptic might easily draw up a long list of works which fulfill all the criteria of excellence discussed above: they may be sincere and personal, they may do exactly what they attempted to do, and their form may be neatly adapted to their content, yet they are all distinguished failures. On the contrary, these tests may be found to be insolently violated in a book which we nevertheless feel and know to be a masterpiece. As every teacher of literature is well aware, analysis succeeds best with second-rate writers; the first-rate artist defies it precisely where he is great; indeed, that transcendence which forces us to be content with experiencing an artist's greatness with humility is often the surest proof of his genius. Disconcertingly enough, such greatness is often made up of faults as well as of qualities; and the true critic is he who accepts, while fully discerning them, the limitations of a superior talent as conditions for a higher good. The Second Part of Goethe's *Faust* is obviously deficient in unity, harmony, clearness, continuous progression, yet it is superior to most of his other works and to most of German literature. *King Lear, Antony and Cleopatra,* nay, even those favorite dramas with English teachers, *Julius Caesar* and *Henry IV, Part I,* could easily be damned on the grounds of confusion, exuberance, weak characterization of secondary figures, loose plot, inconsistencies: their greatness is hardly impaired by such faults, if faults they be. As is often the case with a work of art, the whole is not the sum of the parts. If different readers were asked to give the reasons for their admiration of the same masterpiece, be it *Hamlet,* Beethoven's *Ninth Symphony* or Rembrandt's "Pilgrims at Emmaus," they would probably fail to agree: but each of them might bring out part of the complex truth.

David Hume, whose essay "Of the Standard of Taste" reaches disappointingly vague conclusions, relied empirically on "the uniform consent and experience of nations and ages" as the best criterion of artistic value. He quoted the amusing passage in *Don Quixote* in which Sancho illustrated for the Squire with the long nose the diversity of men's humors and abilities in matters of taste:

Two of my kinsmen were once called to give their opinion of a hogshead, which was supposed to be excellent, being old and of good vintage. One of them tastes it, considers it; and after mature reflection pronounces the wine to be good, were it not for a small taste of leather, which he perceived in it. The other, after using the same precautions, gives also his verdict in favor of the wine; but with the reserve of a taste of iron, which he could easily distinguish. You cannot imagine how much they were both ridiculed for their judgment. But who laughed in the end? On emptying the hogshead, there was found at the bottom an old key with a leathern thong tied to it.

I cannot readily agree with Hume that the uniform consent of men on any given writer is a sure sign of his greatness; I would, however, repeat the conclusion of a previous chapter that permanent greatness is seldom all of one piece. Variety, either in breadth or in depth, and an element of mystery which future ages may explore with renewed delight, give a book or a painting the most valid promises of a continued appeal, and hence of universal agreement as to its goodness. Our inability to explain clearly the reasons of our admiration is due to the limitations of our nature in the presence of genius, as well as to the inadequacy of our critical vocabulary. Though we have progressed far since the determined critical effort started by the eighteenth century, we are still the slaves of imitation and laziness when we express a judgment on a work of art. A history of words of praise used in the past or around us would be one of the most useful contributions to the understanding—if not to the establishment—of standards. Boileau and Addison were content with discreet and vague epithets: "just," "elegant," "wonderful," "the finest in the world." Classically minded critics today look for virtues which they call: unity, composition, simplicity, lucidity, serenity, sanity, truth. The more precious eras of taste are more sensitive to qualities of delicacy, subtlety, ingenious refinement, brilliance. With the romantics, other substantives came into fashion, which denoted a deep change in esthetic sensibility: swiftness, richness, strangeness, surprise, vision, suggestiveness. The standards of our contemporaries are revealed by their favorite words of praise: powerful, vital, challenging, stupendous. Students on the undergraduate level require of a book or a lecture that it have "punch" or "guts," that it be "snappy"; graduate students prefer what is solid, well organized, consistent. Girls in college are content with the adjective "fascinating"; or, if they have been lucky enough to invite their favorite author for a lecture, reward him with the enraptured compliments: "Isn't he magnificent?" or "Isn't he attractive?" or bestow on him the most adulatory epithet that used to be reserved for their new hats, "Isn't he divine?" Elderly ladies who, having first looked for their stimulant in their husband, then in their cocktail, resort at last to a fashionable writer or lecturer, declare him to be "stimulating" or "exciting." Even more elderly ladies reward him with the most pathetic of all compliments: "You have given me an inspiration."

Such words or phrases, which betray the implicit standards of an age, do not enlighten us much on the true merits of a writer or an orator. They do, however, bring out the variety of the demands we make on a work of art, according to the fashions of our times and to our own individual temperament. Behind that endless variety, two very general groups of esthetic qualities can probably be differentiated, each of which should be judged on its own standards. Nietzsche would have designated them as "Apollonian" and "Dionysian." The adjectives "classical" and "romantic" would be the most apt had they not been emptied of their content by so much abuse. The first group of writers or artists aims at purity and harmony; their works appear serene, even somewhat detached, and fill us with the rare pleasure of repose and perfection. No country, no age has had a monopoly of those virtues, not even the Greeks, whose ideal of beauty succeeded more than any other in being characterless and seemed to tell posterity in the words of Keats's Oceanus: "Receive the Truth, and let it be your balm." Sophocles, Virgil, Raphael, Velasquez, Poussin, Racine, Mozart, Wordsworth, Keats, Goethe are the most conspicuous examples of that type of greatness. Their qualities are not easy for contemporaries to discern; for other writers who are far from their equals also seem to be endowed with them—Landor, Arnold, Housman, Leconte de Lisle, Pascoli, Schiller, Platen, and the American poet H. D. As a rule, it is only after much uncertainty that critics agree that what is academic coldness in one is living perfection in another. Few critics dare acknowledge that those qualities of classic purity and harmonious serenity can be found in any of their contemporaries.

The other type of greatness can be recognized more easily: it has those salient features which add character to beauty. It startles or provokes the public, often falls into excess, or resorts to strangeness, but occasionally rises to summits where one experiences the emotions of the sublime. It is easy for carping critics to count the obvious faults of such geniuses and to oppose their fervor with common sense and good taste; most often, however, their greatness first revolts, then enraptures their contemporaries. The examples of such greatness which is combined with newness and originality are many: Aeschylus, Lucretius, Shakespeare, El Greco, Rembrandt, Goya, Beethoven, Hugo, Balzac, Wagner, Dostoevski.

With each of these two very general groups of artists, the critic's task should be primarily to accept the vision of the creator and to ask himself: Has the creator succeeded in imposing his own vision upon me? Has he been true to the world which he created, whether it be one of apparent serenity and exquisite finiteness (like Racine's or Jane Austen's or Flaubert's or Tolstoi's) or one of excess and unreal but haunting vigor (like that of Shakespeare's tragedies, of Dante, Dickens, and Balzac)?

If, as has been repeatedly asserted, the critic should search for standards but never believe that he has found the one infallible golden key, he should nevertheless learn from the mistakes of his predecessors what have been the chief causes of error in the misunderstanding of greatness. In most cases where bad works have been mistaken for great by their contemporaries,[12] critics and readers were deceived by facile charm, cheap elegance, sentimentality, and blinded to diffuseness and wordiness in expression, to want of reality, and above all to want of imagination. Such faults are found in the writings of most women, from Felicia Hemans to some of the most popular contemporary poets whom gallantry forbids us to name, and from George Sand to Mme de Noailles: hence the ruthless ravages of time on the works of art produced by women. Men have not been immune from the same faults: most of the writers who were at first or are now, in our judgment, ranked too high by contemporary opinion [13] lacked neither sincerity, technique, nor refinement; they depicted their own times faithfully, with well-meant sympathy; they appealed first to a fondness of readers and critics for conventionality and optimism, and, lulling the critical faculties, made them share the superficial vision of timid artists.

Many of the critics' mistakes could be avoided if, instead of accepting what is superficially pleasing, they would force themselves to look for the one quality in a creator which is most likely to disconcert them and most likely to assure his survival. Rather than sincerity, personality, or even profundity of ideas (which is

---

[12] It would be worth while to examine systematically a dozen or so cases of swollen reputations that suddenly collapsed, and analyze the elements which, after having imposed upon contemporary judgment, could be said to characterize bad literature. An example of such a study will be found in an article by Edith Sichel, "Some Suggestions about Bad Poetry," *Essays and Studies by Members of the English Association*, I (London: Oxford University Press, 1910), I, 136–167.

[13] Many examples have been quoted in Part I of the present work: among French novelists, those of Charles de Bernard, Octave Feuillet, Eugène Fromentin, Édouard Rod, Erckmann-Chatrian, and among the later ones, Giraudoux, Morand, Lacretelle, Larbaud, Camus, Saint-Exupéry, Nathalie Sarraute.

out of place in poetry, fiction, comedy, sculpture), we would call this quality intensity. The criterion is not new: Longinus praised it in Homer and called it τόνος, the Latin rhetoricians translated it variously by *vis, robur, vigor*. Modern critics have too often lost sight of it and been tempted to find more value in intellectual subtlety, originality of subject, breadth, and scope. Yet progress in art lies not in the conquest of new realms or in perfecting older techniques, but in feeling more intensely a few baffling mysteries. Poets, philosophers (and critics, too) are content with composing endless variations on a few commonplace themes; but if those age-old emotions or ideas have been intensely felt, they are endowed with a dynamic force of radiation which will long vibrate in other hearts and other minds.

Energy and intensity, however, are not unmistakable standards: melodrama and hysterical art may seem to possess them and deceive us; vulgarity may come from an excess as well as a lack of vitality; powerful writers like Faulkner, Hemingway, and Jeffers in America, D. H. Lawrence in England, Mauriac, Céline, Malraux in France, occasionally dissipate their intensity or strain it to a point where it becomes cheap and rhetorical excess. Others mistake a brutal for an intense experience and insist on depicting nothing but violent scenes of love or war, sadistic bullfights, drunkenness, murders, rapes, and other such idyllic events: they forget that if great artists usually live more intensely than ordinary mortals and load their creations with a heightened life which exalts their readers, their intensity lies not in the subject, but in an imaginative experience of moods and emotions. The test of validity for a novelist or a poet should be not only: "Has he felt passionately what he has expressed?" but "Has he felt or imagined intensely, and does his inner fire burn through his words?"

When that fiery energy, that gift of creating and imparting life, are found in contemporary artists, one may safely declare them to have some elements of greatness. Faults are abundant and obvious enough in O'Neill, Jeffers, Faulkner, Hart Crane, in Lawrence and Joyce, in Proust, Mauriac, Claudel, Giono, Sartre, in the greatest Spaniard of our century, García Lorca, or in the painter Rouault; yet I cannot believe that we err in ranking them far above their contemporaries. On the contrary, one may discover much charm and intellectual pleasure in Virginia Woolf, Margaret Kennedy, or Rosamund Lehmann, in Thomas Wolfe and Sinclair Lewis, in Duhamel, Gide, Thomas Mann, and in Gauguin or Matisse; [14] but our sense of values should warn us that they will not rank with creators who compel us to live with their vision and to be haunted by their characters or their magic of words. The leading note of every age is struck, not by the pleasing and effete writers who are most celebrated by reviewers, but by those creators who are most robust and intense. Our own era will, in my opinion, certainly not survive as a period of social discussion or political thought, even less as the age of the short story or the novel: it may be called by our successors "The Age of Proust" or "The Age of Joyce" or "The Age of Sartre"; it may be defined above all as an age of poetry. When more ephemeral productions are buried in oblivion, only a few masterpieces may emerge, marked by the intense energy imparted to them by their imaginative creators. Guillaume Apollinaire, a charming and delicate poet, but a robust critic, who interpreted Cubism to our generation and practically created Surrealism, declared, one year before the First World War in which he was to meet his end: "All the artistic works of an age mold themselves, in the end, on the most energetic, the most expressive, the most typical creations of that age." [15]

[14] It may seem one day unbelievable that for ten years or more critics should have sung the praises of a charming talent like Virginia Woolf's, as if she had really given her characters life, and not just a blurred halo of fleeting gleams of consciousness. It may seem even more unbelievable that masters of colorful decoration like R. Dufy, Matisse, and Gauguin himself should have been celebrated for thirty years as the equals of authentic geniuses.

[15] This sentence occurs in a splendid little volume of art criticism published by Apollinaire in 1913, *Les Peintres cubistes* (Figuère, 1913), p. 20. In a manifesto which appeared a few weeks after his death in *Le Mercure de France* (December 1, 1918), "L'esprit nouveau et les poètes," Apollinaire charted some of the new vistas open to modern art and poetry: we have only begun to explore a few of them.

Such a search for standards may appear too negative. But though I can hardly find an infallible rule for critics, I can perhaps urge them to more courage in their task. Some readers may in the meanwhile be tempted to say: "There can be but one sure test of the greatness of an artist: his approval or rejection by posterity. Why rack our brains to assess the true rank of Stravinsky and Hindemith, Picasso and Derain, Joyce and Proust? Time will do it for us some day, and there is no appeal from the august tribunal. Let us in the meanwhile reread safely classified masterpieces, those of Horace and Molière, Dr. Johnson and Jane Austen, Goethe and Emerson, which provide us with the added pleasures of delightful familiarity and of comforting security."

Such a belief is flattering to our soft complacency. But it is as conducive to laziness as the blind faith in progress which passively awaits an ultimate and inevitable improvement through the continuous advance of science; it is as demoralizing as the worship of youth which has characterized our century, proclaiming naïvely: "The young people are far more wonderful than we were; they will solve the problems of the world; let us put our faith in them and, in the meanwhile, dress like the young, drink, smoke, dance, and forget." The belief in posterity likewise asserts that contemporaries should not try to solve insoluble enigmas. Others will do the task, automatically, after a few years or a few decades. No true talent ever remained buried. "Let us listen rapturously for the hundredth time to Schubert's *Unfinished Symphony*, to Bizet's *Carmen* or Ravel's 'Bolero,'" say those concert-goers who profess to love classical music exclusively. "Why should crazy conductors force us to listen to a new composition which will necessarily disrupt our soothing reverie and strain our attention? We then have to formulate our opinions among our friends; we may say the wrong thing, never having heard of the author before, and thus display our ignorance, and lose our reputation as enlightened music-lovers."

If our widespread faith in posterity's ability to redress wrongs or to pronounce judgments in our place is tempting, is it justified? Surprisingly enough, this convenient reliance upon the infallibility of Time has seldom been questioned.[16] Critics have usually found it very comfortable to abdicate their dangerous prerogative in favor of their grandsons, or have taken pride in enjoying, with the hindsight of posterity, the works of masters unacknowledged by their contemporaries: Vermeer, Bach, Kleist, Stendhal, Baudelaire. Naïvely, they call those masters "modern" and praise them for having possessed, in their remote times, qualities almost like our own.

The notion of posterity, however, deserves closer scrutiny.

A) It rests on the assumption that our successors, fifty or eighty years from now, will judge the works produced, say, between 1920 and 1970, more impartially and more competently than we are in a position to do ourselves. There are, to be sure, several good reasons why they should. In fifty years, critics and journalists will not be much impressed by the social prestige enjoyed by a writer who is also a member of an academy, a university professor, or an influential and feared critic. Judgments will then be formulated with more independence. What is more, the ephemeral fashions of today will be forgotten or only remembered to make our grandsons smile.[17] Besides, all the works of any given writer (Lawrence, Joyce, Rilke) will then be available, including their memoirs or letters. Critics will thus be enabled to envisage the whole of an author's production as a comprehensive pattern; they will delight in discovering the evolution of his

[16] Sainte-Beuve, however, was repeatedly obsessed by the problem and wondered if the contemporaries of a great man were not in a position to pronounce a truer judgment than his successors. Anatole France has a few destructive remarks on our blind faith in "Time" in *La Vie littéraire*, I, 111–116, and *Le Jardin d'Épicure*, pp. 219–221. On this subject as well as on other aspects of criticism, the keenest views have been expressed by Henry Hazlitt in *The Anatomy of Criticism: A Trialogue* (New York: Simon and Schuster, 1933), pp. 128–153.

[17] But a new fashion, just as illogical and ludicrous, will prevail in 1990 or 2020 to warp the judgment of "posterity." Walter Raleigh, who perceived some of the inconsistencies of current literary criticism, wrote in a volume published posthumously: "A great part of literary criticism might be typified by a picture of a lady in a hobble-skirt laughing at a lady in a crinoline" (*On Writing and Writers* [London: Edwin Arnold, 1926], p. 225).

talent and rendering it by a magical curve or a harmonious division into periods of growth, achievement, and decline.

Above all, and this point is especially dear to professors and literary historians, much supplementary information, which a student of contemporary literature sadly misses, can be supplied about dead writers. The biographer of Balzac or Goethe knows exactly the antecedents of those writers, the racial stock from which they have sprung, the family atmosphere in which they grew up, the kind of elementary and secondary studies to which they were submitted. We are even told specifically, a hundred years after, about the disease Rousseau suffered from, the women Byron and Musset loved, the bed in which Stendhal slept, the bills, paid or unpaid, that Baudelaire owed his tailor. Our keenest joy lies in discovering the list of books that Voltaire or Hugo had in his library and undertaking learned studies of sources and influences: scholars flatteringly assume that any man, and especially a novelist or a poet, has necessarily read all the books he owns and owns all the books which are dear to him.

Granting that such supplementary knowledge acquired by the patient efforts of scholarship is invaluable to help us *understand* the genesis, and even the content, of "Tintern Abbey" or the "Ode on a Grecian Urn," one must proceed to ask: does it enable us to *feel* those poems more intensely? Is it essential that a critic should avail himself of all that precise information before he can be moved by those poems and pronounce them beautiful or great? If such were the case, any direct enjoyment of contemporary art would be forever banished, and knowledge about a thing of beauty would gradually replace immediate experience of the beautiful. Even German scholarship at its worst would be reluctant to accept such a consequence.

Moreover, the numerous scholars and critics who refuse to evaluate recent works because they lack the detailed knowledge which posterity alone can acquire forget that contemporaries enjoy other means of information, at least as important as the bookish sources on which future judgment may rely too heavily. It is my belief that modern scholarship could do very useful work in documenting recent literary works, collecting material about living writers (even material as irrelevant at first sight as interviews, idle talk by friends of the writer, hostile or favorable criticism which may influence him, details about his reading, his behavior, his method of work). Taine gathered some information of that kind on Flaubert; the Goncourt brothers noted down more about their literary friends, adding not a little gossip of their own; the French psychologist Binet made interesting reports on how artists imagined and composed.[18] The interviews of the *Paris Review*, the rambling avowals of *Faulkner on Faulkner* will be of service to our successors. Sainte-Beuve was haunted all his life by the problem of the respective values of the contemporary criticism of living writers and the verdict of posterity; he occasionally contradicted himself and, twice at least in the boundless range of his critical writings, envied the clearer perspective which remoteness in place (i.e., judging French literature from Switzerland) or time affords a critic.[19] For the most part, however, Sainte-Beuve realized that a courageous critic could not abdicate in favor of posterity. While in my opinion he failed to assess his contemporaries with any degree of justice or insight, he considered it his duty to try. "Why should one hesitate to hail greatness as soon as one comes across it? . . . Must we wait until we are far from a building in order to admire it?" Thus wrote the critic in the early Thirties (*Portraits contemporains*, I) after a reading of extracts

18 Professor William York Tindall has advocated more scholarly research in the field of contemporary literature by professors of English in "Scholarship and Contemporary Literature," *The English Institute Annual, 1940* (New York: Columbia University Press, 1941), pp. 42–60. His own practice, as exemplified in a volume entitled *D. H. Lawrence and Susan His Cow* (New York: Columbia University Press, 1939), was somewhat too ponderous to illustrate his views happily. Professor Fernand Baldensperger applied to Aldous Huxley a subtle method of the discovery of bookish sources in an article published among *Essays in Honor of Albert Feuillerat* (New Haven: Yale University Press, 1943).

19 Sainte-Beuve, *Portraits contemporains*, Vol. III (rev. new ed.; M. Lévy, 1876), apropos of the Swiss critic Vinet, and *Nouveaux Lundis*, X, 24-25 (article on A. Lefèvre). The allusion in our text to a passage of Sainte-Beuve in 1833 is to an article on Loève-Veimars, June 24, 1833, reprinted in *Premiers Lundis*, II, 199–200.

from Chateaubriand's *Mémoires*. He asserted in 1833 that contemporaries were not mistaken in being struck by the confusion of living literature, and that the oversimplified perspective of posterity, which would discern avenues and currents, was often misleading. Again and again, the impeccably diligent scholar combined with the subtle critic in Sainte-Beuve repeated that documents and works could never reveal to posterity the secret of a work of art, or even render the personality of the author faithfully. He preferred contemporary reports, in which the whole truth about a writer was implicitly present, to the distorted view of posthumous research, which exaggerated the significance of a few unpublished documents or separated the work from the man and exalted the former unduly, as he thought had been done in the case of Stendhal and Balzac.[20]

B) The extraordinary faith of many critical experts in the goddess posterity seems to rest on a false analogy. If we are too near a picture or a mountain, we cannot see it in the right perspective. We cannot see the forest for the trees. In the same way, we must draw back to a safe distance from a contemporary work and place it serenely in its true relation to what came before and after.

Much is to be said for such a common-sense view. The influence which radiates from *Ulysses* or Proust's novel or Baudelaire's poems gives us valuable enlightenment on the depth or "fecundity" of those works. Imitators of a great painter or musician gradually reveal his latent weaknesses. A retrospect of twenty-five years shows "posterity" that Thomas Hardy's novels suffer from grave flaws, that Wagner's operas and Monet's paintings are not as timeless as we had imagined. Ravel's "Bolero" and

[20] Sainte-Beuve's most characteristic passages in which he questions the verdict of posterity occur in: *Portraits contemporains*, V, 210 (article of July 1, 1844, on Pascal); *Portraits littéraires*, III, 383 (article of May 1, 1846, on Ch. Labitte); *ibid.*, III, 311 (article of January 5, 1856, on Voiture); *Nouveaux Lundis* X, 24-25 (article of March 27, 1865, on A. Lefèvre); *Port-Royal*, Book IV, ch. 7 on Nicole and the footnote on the last page of same, Book IV.

Shostakovitch's *Fifth Symphony* wear thin after the tenth hearing, and make us believe that our enthusiasm in discovering them came from rather superficial qualities.

But the scores of years which have elapsed since Proust and Joyce published their novels, even the hundred years since Baudelaire, Wagner, Melville, Browning, make but a few links in the endless chain of time called posterity. Will not our judgment on *Les Fleurs du Mal and Moby Dick* be modified tomorrow by a new generation, as signs seem already to promise? Our estimate of Browning and Wagner has been subtly revised downward in the last four decades. Which is the "infallible" verdict of Time, that of 1940 or that of 1960?

On closer analysis the very notion of posterity sinks in a welter of uncertainty. Unless, by that august term, posterity, we mean ourselves as supreme arbiters on Dante, Shakespeare, Beethoven, or Cézanne, the appeal to posterity is an appeal to an opinion almost as fluid and fickle as that of contemporaries. One of the very few accepted rules governing literary reputations is that when a writer has enjoyed a very great fame in his lifetime and reigned in his old age crowned with official honor, his death is followed by a period of disparagement or neglect. That stay in Purgatory usually lasts for twenty or thirty years, after which a rank is assigned to him: with what justice, no one will presume to tell who has not discovered the magical touchstone of greatness. Goethe, Victor Hugo, Renan, Anatole France, Pierre Loti, Rodin, Tennyson, Swinburne, Kipling, Hardy, Galsworthy are recent and memorable examples.

Conversely, if fame came slowly to an artist, it is likely to last for some twenty or thirty years after his death (Wagner, Debussy, Brahms, Gauguin, Cézanne, Vigny, Flaubert, Browning, Meredith, Kafka, Rilke) and the sojourn in Purgatory will be postponed for that period. Consequently, the judgment of posterity should not normally be expected before the pendulum has swung back and forth at least once, say for half a century after the death of a creator. If a great man's contemporaries and successors had to wait all that time to recognize his talent, the loss to themselves and to arts and letters would be incalculable.

But a safe judgment is not even reached at the end of half a century. Indeed, the posterity of a writer may differ widely if one considers at it intervals of fifty, one hundred, or two hundred years after his death. Which is the true posterity of Ronsard, who died in 1585? He was neglected and forgotten in 1685, revived and acclaimed in 1825, again half neglected in 1860, celebrated in 1925. The fame of Du Bartas was glorious in England and Germany for two centuries; Goethe admired him almost above all others. Then he fell into oblivion. He may some day be revived, as Maurice Scève, another sixteenth-century poet long ignored, has been recently. Victor Hugo, who died in 1885, has already been disparaged by posterity, then exalted for the very poems which were least admired by his contemporaries. Which is the posterity of Donne and Gongora? that of 1730 or that of 1930? and the posterity of George Herbert? that of Pope, reviled by the romantics, celebrated in this century? that of Shelley, loved as the poets' poet forty years after his death, more recently attacked by other poets as a sentimental fabricator of "sound without sense"? [21] Brahms, whom his contemporaries rejected as difficult and harsh, has long ago displaced Tchaikovsky, once the public favorite, from orchestra programs. May not Brahms be displaced in his turn by another composer?

The greatest of all writers would probably provide the most conclusive example of posterity's endless variations. Fifty, a hundred, and even a hundred and fifty years after Shakespeare's death, posterity ranked him far lower than has been done since 1780. But is our present estimate likely to endure? Or if this question seems sacrilegious to some, let us glance at the contradictory utterances of "posterity" on individual plays like *Measure for Measure, Troilus and Cressida, Antony and Cleopatra.* T. S. Eliot gravely pronounced *Hamlet* "most certainly an artis-

---

[21] The phrase is T. S. Eliot's, in *For Lancelot Andrewes* (London: Faber, 1929), pp. 120–123.

tic failure," and the unequalled prestige of that play since the romantics may indeed be due to other than artistic or intrinsic merits. Another play, *Coriolanus*, is declared by George Bernard Shaw "the greatest of Shakespeare's *comedies*," and by Lytton Strachey "a remarkable, perhaps an intolerable, play," in which rhetoric "is the beginning and the middle and the end." Fortunately, the agreement of posterity on Shakespeare and Milton, Racine and Rousseau will never be universal. They are discussed because they are still alive. "Dante will always be admired," Voltaire once said, "because no one ever reads him." Such passive agreement is the worst fate that can befall a great book.

C) It is a disconcerting experience to witness the difficulty to which believers in posterity have been put to justify their faith: they have alternately displayed naïve boastfulness and skillful sophistry.

The most prevalent explanation is that genius was ahead of its times, but that posterity has now caught up with Donne, Bach, Keats, Baudelaire, Wagner. There were only fifty persons able to understand Shelley and Keats in 1820, only fifty peers of Wagner at the time of *The Flying Dutchman* (1845); a few hundred at the most could rise to the height of Melville, Renoir, Rodin, Debussy, when those artists began to create. But now, any cultivated person is naturally the equal of those giants of the past. In fact, he is slightly superior to them since he has learned how to discard a certain number of their works as "minor" and retains only the very best as worthy of his fastidious attention.

Only staunch partisans of the doctrine of continuous progress can accept such a preposterous claim. In a few cases only, great artists have been revolutionary innovators who had to convert their audience to a new technique (Monteverdi, the Impressionists, the poets and novelists of the subconscious). As a rule, progress in art depends upon technical improvements only to a very small degree; and that progress can never be represented by a rigid line indefinitely ascending; many a zigzag, many a blind alley branching off from the main highway, break the ideal line which symbolizes the development of a literature or an art. Genius was no more ahead of its own times than of ours; it is ahead of all times. We are no cleverer than Stendhal's or Beethoven's contemporaries because we recognize without effort their greatness.

Schopenhauer, who bitterly resented the obscurity in which his philosophy was allowed to languish, reflected on the misunderstanding between "great men" [22] and their contemporary critics. He attacked the fallacy which excuses the blindness of contemporaries on the pretext that a genius is ahead of his age; genius is ahead of the whole of humanity, but men are glad to lay the burden of their pathetic shortcomings upon their predecessors of a single epoch. In his view, only a few men in each generation can understand genius: the fifty or a hundred "peers" of Keats and Baudelaire mentioned above. Those happy few accumulate with each generation, and gradually silence opposition or triumph over the neglect which first shrouded original works.

The explanation is rash in its optimism, coming from the arch-pessimist! It is true enough that a small band of admirers of Wagner and Brahms, Monet and Cézanne, Shelley and Rimbaud have gradually converted a wider public. "Posterity" still includes just as many fools and snobs as the contemporary public which had branded those men as decadent barbarians and immoral lunatics. But not being very sure of their own taste, they follow a few bold leaders. If the leaders had arisen among contemporary critics of *Tannhäuser*, *Prometheus Unbound* and Impressionist paintings, the "vulgum pecus" would have followed just the same and much sooner.

We naturally hear of all the cases in which "posterity" has redressed the wrongs of earlier opinion and lavished posthumous glory on geniuses once neglected. We fondly quiet our qualms of

[22] Schopenhauer had little hesitation about his own rank among German philosophers and subscribed unhesitatingly to Goethe's proud saying: "Nur die Lumpen sind bescheiden" ["Only knaves are modest"]. See Schopenhauer's essay "On Reputation," usually published with the other and very keen essays "On Style" and "On Criticism."

conscience by telling ourselves that eventually *all* wrongs are thus righted. Are they, indeed? Our inertia makes us resent any drastic revision of literary reputations. Ranks have been established once for all: great men on one side, second-rate talents neatly divided from them, nonentities forever forgotten. Scholars and critics regard any attempt at reclassification as a hoax or as a personal insult. Decency apparently requires that all men agree on a scale of literary and artistic values, just as they agree on a common code of honor or politeness. It is a breach of manners, among professors of English, to hint that Ford, in *'Tis Pity She's a Whore,* Tourneur in *The Revenger's Tragedy,* Middleton in *The Changeling* are the equals (to say the least) of Shakespeare in at least one third of his plays; that Dryden is commonly ranked much too high, while poets like Drayton and Campion, even Herrick and Marvell do not enjoy the full fame which they deserve. Burke, Jane Austen, Newman are still surrounded with excessive praise, while John Clare and Beddoes are forever relegated to an inferior rank. It is equally difficult to break the artificial boundaries which, in French literature, separate the so-called great writers from the second-rate ones. Rabelais, in my opinion, is much overrated, while D'Aubigné, at the end of the sixteenth century, is entitled to rank among true poets. A great part of early seventeenth-century poetry (by Jean de Lingendes, J. B. Chassignet), tragedies by Montchrestien and Du Ryer unjustly eclipsed by Corneille, even comedies by Desmarets deserve to be restored to a far higher rank than "posterity" has granted them. La Rochefoucauld and La Bruyère are overestimated, while their equals, Chamfort and Vauvenargues, are not usually included among the "classics" of France. Diderot's fame should at the very least rival Voltaire's; it has taken half a century of effort on the part of Diderot enthusiasts to establish his claims. Yet many readers of Voltaire, if they were not prejudiced by established reputation, would really be disappointed and bored. Similarly it may be hard to convince "posterity" that Gérard de Nerval and Maurice de Guérin are superior, as poets, to Musset and Vigny. It is my conviction that Scarron, as a comic writer, and Rotrou, as a tragic poet, deserve a higher rank than they have regularly been granted; but our worship of traditional glory will not allow Molière's and Racine's supremacy to be thus challenged. It is also my conviction that André Chénier occupies an inexplicably high rank in histories of French poetry, and that his contemporary, often his equal, Parny, is unduly neglected; but the accepted scale of values is as reassuring to educators as the Maginot line was to generals in 1939. Petrarch enjoys one of the most universally overrated reputations in literature, but how many of us read him with fresh eyes or dare confess their disappointment if they do? Finally, to take one musical illustration which has already been discussed by a competent authority, Romain Rolland,[23] posterity, in its eagerness to compensate Johann Sebastian Bach for the relative indifference in which he was held by his contemporaries, has completely sacrificed Handel and Telemann to him. Yet Handel is not very far below Bach; Johann Sebastian himself admired Telemann and transcribed his music in his own hand. Once more, a difference of degree between two artists has become, in the verdict of historians and critics, an unbridged gulf.

D) The infallibility of posterity appears, on closer scrutiny, one of the most potent myths holding sway over critics' minds. It takes an uncommonly robust faith in the pre-established harmony of the universe to assert that "Time, which takes survey of all the world," must always be right. Any scholar who conscientiously goes through a file of periodicals one or two centuries old must have stumbled upon some poems or essays of arresting beauty: yet they were signed by obscure names and practically lost to posterity. Every historian should remember that undeniable masterpieces were sometimes created only through a stroke of luck, because an editor or stage director needed a work at the last minute and elicited it from a writer hitherto unknown, even to himself. Similarly, one or two critics are responsible for the fame of Lautréamont, Gerard Manley Hopkins, the Douanier Rous-

[23] Romain Rolland, *Voyage musical aux pays du passé* (Édouard-Joseph, 1919).

seau, Franz Kafka, Italo Svevo: without their discernment posterity might still be unaware of the very existence of those important writers or artists. Like all his contemporaries, we might still consider Daumier as "a mere caricaturist," if one or two critics gifted with rare insight had not shown to us that he was also one of the great painters of the last century. Many such discoveries await the bold and open minds who are willing to re-examine the traditional hierarchy attributed to Time.

For Time, as Mazarin used to say, "è galant 'uomo," and the most prolific father of illegitimate children conceivable. In the implicit opinion of the many, he alone makes masterpieces. We see nothing but diverse talents among our contemporaries, and especially among our literary friends. But Time will turn some of them into geniuses.[24] Time will decide once for all that two or three books of Conrad or Lawrence are worth reading, one or two by Hardy, Gide, Mauriac, Thomas Mann; that two or three plays of O'Neill are worthy of posterity, one or two poems by Eliot and Rilke, one or two compositions by Stravinsky. But which? Apparently few of us are willing to venture an opinion on issues which will be plain to any adolescent fifty years hence.

Yet, what is that august tribunal of posterity before which every critic bows? Anatole France answered the question when commenting in *La Vie littéraire* (I, 111–116) on an Academician who refused to judge contemporary works so that posterity might be free to utter its "infallible and final conclusions":

I doubt that posterity is infallible in its conclusions. And my reason for feeling so is that posterity means you, me, other men. We are posterity for a long series of works of which we know little. . . . Far from being infallible, posterity runs every risk of being mistaken. It is ignorant and indifferent. Just now, on the Quai Malaquais, I am watching the posterity of Corneille and Voltaire. It walks leisurely under a cheerful April sun, a veil over its nose or a cigar on its lips, and I assure you it cares very little about Voltaire and Corneille. Hunger and love keep it busy enough as it is.

24 See in Goncourt's *Journal* (II, 214) the following entry: "A book never *is* a masterpiece, it *becomes* one. Genius is the talent of a dead man."

Let us grant that not all criticism is worthless and that our successors may discern the true merits of Joyce and Claudel when half a dozen superior critics have had time to illumine them. Let us also grant that some qualities of a new book (its solidity and above all its fecundity) can only be judged with years. Let us add that only with time can an original artist gradually accustom the public to his new vision; [25] and that familiarity, or, as Proust called it, memory, makes the fourth hearing of a new symphony or a new play both more pleasant and more discerning than the first.[26] Whoever loves poetry, that is, learns it by heart when possible, discovers, in reciting it for the hundredth time, subtle beauties that had escaped him time and again.

But there are other elements of artistic beauty which should have been perceptible to—nay, should have blinded—contemporaries. The "Ode to the West Wind," the "Ode on a Grecian Urn," Baudelaire's "Le Balcon," Rimbaud's "Le Bateau ivre," or Bach's fugues, Beethoven's sonatas, César Franck's symphony, or Cézanne's landscapes are characterized by the most traditional and obvious virtues: harmony, composition, balance, profundity, truth, intensity, power, perfection of form. Surely, those qualities were present in those works when they first appeared, and

[25] There is some truth in Wordsworth's sharp pronouncement: "Every author, as far as he is great and at the same time original, has had the task of creating the taste by which he is to be enjoyed." Wordsworth was there quoting or paraphrasing a remark made to him by Coleridge. The *Essay, Supplementary to the Preface* of the 1815 edition of his poems, from which these lines are quoted, is devoted to an indictment of critics who failed to understand their contemporaries.

[26] Proust, who had to accustom his public to his vision and to his style, is among the "creators" who gave constant thought to the misunderstanding between original artists and their contemporaries. The chief passages, all marked by keen insight into the problem, occur in: the preface to Paul Morand's *Tendres Stocks*, in which Sainte-Beuve's "stupidity" toward Baudelaire is arraigned; the preface to his translation of Ruskin's *La Bible d'Amiens*, which contains a striking definition of the critic's function; *Du Côté de chez Swann*, I, 145; *Jeunes Filles en Fleur* I, 95-97, on the role of memory; *ibid.*, I, 115, on newness in art, and again I, 169, and II, 22-23; *Du Côté de Guermantes*, I, 44-45, and II, 19-20, on Bergotte and Renoir; *La Prisonnière*, I, 44 and 218. See also, on Sainte-Beuve's deficiencies, a letter to Paul Souday, in *Correspondance générale* (Plon, 1932), p. 68.

were not begotten by Time or lent by our generous memory. Yet
no one—in many of these cases literally no one—perceived them.
The contemporaries of those masterpieces cannot have tried very
intelligently or very patiently to understand them. They were
the slaves of fashion. Are we not also when we profess our un-
bounded admiration for Bach, Keats, Baudelaire, Cézanne? The
true test of critical lucidity, or sincerity with works of art of the
past is easy to practice. But it is too embarrassing to our superstitions and lazy optimism, and those who should lead and train the
public taste have seldom resorted to it: it consists simply in training students and readers to feel and judge a page of prose or verse
without being told the author's name; in withdrawing catalogues
and titles from an exhibition of paintings; in discontinuing the use
of programs in concerts and in withholding the composer's
name.[27]

In conclusion, if there enters an unpredictable element of

[27] I. A. Richards has experimented with this method of "practical criticism," and some teachers use it in their classes, although they resent being
put to the same test themselves with contemporary literature. Tolstoi, being
already famous, once forgot to sign a story which he sent to a literary review; the story was rejected, but immediately and apologetically accepted
when the identity of the author was later revealed. Anatole France relates
in *Le Jardin d'Épicure* how, in a military examination, candidates are
given an unsigned passage, which the press ridiculed the next day as illus-
trating the poor taste of some old captain: the passage was actually one of
the finest from Michelet's *Tableau de la France*. In the memoirs of Sophie
Augustine Leo, published in the *Musical Quarterly*, XVII (1917), 391, one
may read how a concert was once given in Paris, in which first a Beethoven
trio was played, then one by Pixis. The audience consisted of cultivated and
musical people. The composers' names had been inadvertently interchanged
on the printed programs. "Beethoven, taken for Pixis, was heard in quiet
indifference; Pixis, taken for Beethoven, was noisily applauded." Berlioz
laughed long at the public's bewilderment when the mistake was revealed.
Liszt, who gave that concert (it occurred on February 11, 1837), commented amusingly on it in the *Gazette musicale* for July 16, 1837: "When
the Beethoven trio was played in the place originally assigned to Pixis, it
was found so uninspired, mediocre and tedious that there were some who
left the hall, declaring that the presumption of M. Pixis in presenting his
work before an audience that had just listened to one of Beethoven's
masterpieces was downright impertinent." He added that the work by Pixis
was not only mediocre, but very different from Beethoven in style.

chance in the survival of some names at the expense of some others, the verdicts of posterity are man-made. The phrase of Terentianus Maurus, *habent sua fata libelli,* is an everlastingly apt quotation; but no implacable fate controls the history of fame. Posterity is not an enigmatic goddess whose capricious decrees must be instantly obeyed by her suitors, the critics. A great part of her unchallenged prestige is due to imitation and passivity. Children at school, students in colleges, and adults in later life are taught by the whole weight of tradition and official authority: that Xenophon is an easier writer than Plato; that Livy should be read before Tacitus; that Corneille wrote four masterpieces and a score of second-rate plays; that *Henry IV* should be read at school, in preference to *Richard II; The Merchant of Venice* in preference to *Cymbeline;* that *Eugénie Grandet* is Balzac's masterpiece and *Les Premières Méditations* Lamartine's best poems; that the romantics were less perfect artists than the Augustans or than the French Classicists, and so on. Young men who disregard all warnings of their elders against gambling, marrying too soon, enlisting in the Air Force, and other youthful temptations accept with extraordinary docility the lessons of their masters: they become almost convinced that to have read *The Pilgrim's Progress, Rasselas,* and Carlyle's *French Revolution* is a requisite for a literary education; that Trollope is one of the important novelists of England; that professors' poets (Wordsworth, Arnold, E. A. Robinson, Frost; Vigny, Leconte de Lisle in French; Schiller in German) should be their favorite ones. When they have become fully adult, they are engrossed by their professional activities and no longer care enough about literature and art to find out what they really feel and think about masterpieces and pseudo-masterpieces. Or they go through the mill and emerge as professors with a vested interest in the acceptance and perpetuation of traditional opinions.

Strangely enough, posterity, to which we bow as we do to every majority, as the consent of the many, owes little to numbers. The history of the gradual or sudden rise to fame of some authors and artists, as was sketched in the earlier chapters of the present work, should be written fully.[28] Yet its conclusions can be foretold. The "verdict of time" is in fact the judgment of a very few enthusiasts. Arnold Bennett, who did not always write for the few, had the merit to proclaim it in a little book alluringly entitled *Literary Taste and How to Form It:*

Why does the great and universal fame of classical authors continue? The answer is that the fame of classical authors is entirely independent of the majority. . . . It is made and maintained by a passionate few. . . . It is by the passionate few that the renown of genius is kept alive from one generation to another. . . . The majority can make a reputation, but it is too careless to maintain it. . . . The few conquer by their obstinacy alone, by their eternal repetition of the same statements.

The ancients were aware of this and dismissed the *profanum vulgus;* Voltaire, whom some moderns revere as the ancestor of democracy, wrote to the chief of police Hérault in 1734 that he should only listen to the opinion of a few chosen minds on his books, "because the vulgar is always and everywhere led by a small number of exceptional men, in literature and in politics." [29]

After the passionate few, sometimes among them and with them, come the professors. They adopt one volume by a writer

[28] The revival of Donne between 1920 and 1940 or of the English religious poets of the seventeenth century would be cases in point; the early reputation of Shelley, Keats, Browning, Meredith was also established by a very few enthusiasts. It would be equally revealing to trace the obscure beginnings of the Stendhal, Rimbaud, and Mallarmé cults, or of the recent ascension to the zenith of posterity's starry skies of Maurice Scève, Gérard de Nerval, Gerard Manley Hopkins, Rilke. The Impressionist "movement" in painting began in obscurity and ridicule. Manet, in 1863, was hated and abused. Gradually he won to his vision Berthe Morisot, Pissarro, Monet; Monet in his turn won Sisley, Renoir, and Bazille; Cézanne and Guillaumin joined the group in 1874 for their first group exhibition. The public remained bitterly hostile until 1887: it accepted Renoir only in 1892, Cézanne much later, and Sisley only when he died, in 1899. Four or five enthusiastic admirers of these painters (Duret, Durand-Ruel, Geffroy, Caillebotte, Vollard) succeeded in getting them accepted by a unanimously adverse public.

[29] Sainte-Beuve also confessed it, not without bitterness, in a letter to Ernest Feydeau on August 25, 1860.

(*Richard Feverel, Sons and Lovers, Eugénie Grandet, The Turn of the Screw*) for very questionable reasons, and that book soon eclipses all the writer's other works; or they decide, as French pedagogues did between La Harpe and Nisard (between 1770 and 1850), that seventeenth-century literature should be consecrated as "classical" and serve exclusively to educate the youth. They single out a few symphonies by Beethoven, a few overtures by Wagner, a few "Lieder" by Schumann or Fauré, to be heard forever. The passionate few, if they are successful, are soon joined by the snobs and the publishers or the art dealers; the professors are submissively followed by their former pupils and by the crowds who are only too glad to echo the decrees of the "experts." Thus it is that the vast majority of students and the public never express a sincere opinion on *Oedipus Rex, King Lear, Andromaque* or *War and Peace:* it is probably most fortunate that they do not, and some of us shudder at what they might otherwise have to hear and read! They form the gregarious troop which tyrannizes over timid souls under the name of posterity.

If critics and above all professors have such enormous power over the decrees of fame, they should fulfil their duty more courageously. We shall certainly not claim that they ought to discover in advance what the opinion of posterity will be and "get on the band wagon." On the contrary, conscious that they are molding amorphous judgment through their own criticisms, they should deliberately approach contemporary works with courage, lucidity, a lofty sense of values, and freedom from mercantilism, conventionality, and prejudice. The task of feeling and judging with insight is not an easy one; but it is even more difficult for untrained and hasty journalists and occasional readers, who will do it in any case, than for critics, scholars, and teachers, who should attempt it more confidently than they have done in the past.

CHAPTER VII

Toward a Reconciliation of Scholarship, Criticism, and Literature

A FITTING epigraph for this last chapter might be borrowed from a keen essay on literary fame written by Schopenhauer, one of the few philosophers who have devoted some attention to the misunderstanding studied in the present work:

> The right standard for judging the intellectual work of any generation is supplied, not by the great minds that make their appearance in it, but by the way in which contemporaries receive their work.[1]

Understanding and sympathy in the critics and consequently—though not necessarily to the same extent—in the public have seldom welcomed the most original writers of the last three centuries. The cynics complacently remark that great writers have nevertheless been just as plentiful as ever, and that struggle and suffering are a boon to them. Unacknowledged artists occasionally take pride in being slighted by a vulgar audience and pin their hopes on being acclaimed by future ages.[2] Revolt, isolation,

[1] Schopenhauer, "On Reputation," *Essays on the Art of Literature,* trans. T. Bailey Saunders (New York: Burt Co., n.d.). A recent reprint of those essays appeared as *The Art of Literature* (Ann Arbor: University of Michigan Press, 1960). Nietzsche may have remembered Schopenhauer's essay when, in his third lecture on "The Future of Educational Institutions," delivered at Basel on February 27, 1872, he said: "We well know that a just posterity judges the collective intellectual state of a time only by those few great and lonely figures of the period, and gives its decision in accordance with the manner in which they are recognized, encouraged, and honored, or, on the contrary, in which they are snubbed, elbowed aside, and kept down."

[2] Shelley is a well-known example. Keats, in a pathetic letter of June 9, 1819, to Miss Jeffrey, explained that England had great poets because she had persecuted them during their lives, and never treated them like the Raphaels of Italy. Two years later, Keats was lying in his obscure grave in

arduous fighting for recognition may have been good for a few. Modern educational theorists, who have apparently failed to discover secrets for the production of genius, may some day confess their dismay at finding that frustration and social maladjustment in a child are the surest promise of greatness. My contention is that an implicit agreement between the writers or artists of an age and at least a portion of the contemporary public has characterized the great periods in which genius has flowered: the ages of Pericles and of Augustus, the thirteenth and fourteenth centuries in French architecture, sculpture, and drama, the Italian Renaissance, the Elizabethan period, the "Siglo de oro" in Spain, the age of Louis XIV. I have not concealed the fact that numerous mistakes of judgment on the value of contemporary artists were made even in those favored eras. Critics, no more discerning then than they have proved since, were securely entrenched in their dogmatism, which may have been more favorable to creation than our own eclectic relativism.[3] But artists did not feel obliged to revolt against their public, their predecessors, and their teachers; they were not called upon to express an opinion on every social and political problem of the day. While most of the modern creators are convinced that they must first repudiate the influences and lessons of their elders and stand apart in order to discover their originality, artists of former ages were content to build on foundations already laid by their predecessors; less time and energy were spent by each artist in making a fresh start, and more in raising the structure a few stories higher. The Greek and the Elizabethan dramatists, the medieval sculptors and the Italian and Dutch painters, the lyric poets of the Elizabethan age, the dramatists and the prose writers of the French seventeenth century, though in no way less personal or more humble than their

---

Rome. Stendhal's prophecy, made in 1840 in a letter to Balzac, is famous: "I shall be read in 1880." Baudelaire wrote, in the bitterness of his heart, in his posthumously published notebooks ("My heart laid bare," XIV): "Les nations n'ont de grands hommes que malgré elles."

[3] The point has been made by no less subtle and undogmatic a modern than André Gide, in an interesting lecture given at Weimar on April 5, 1903, "De l'importance du public," *Oeuvres complètes*, IV, 188.

modern descendants, readily accepted the traditions, even the
themes and the technical devices bequeathed by their elders.
Their individualism found enrichment in coöperation both with
other artists and with their public.

Social conditions have changed irretrievably since the democratic revolution, the Industrial Revolution, and the emergence
of the fourth estate, the press. The spread of nominal literacy
among the millions has increased immensely the amount of jour-
nalism and periodical writing, if not the number of good books or
great authors.[4] So much of the modern production is necessarily
mediocre, to say the least, that a gifted author may be forgiven
for striving to separate himself from it. Moreover, the advocacy
of traditions has too often become a reactionary attitude on the
part of pompous academicians and a pretext for distrusting adventure and newness. Yet a felicitous and stimulating correspondence between creators and their public is not impossible today;
it is certainly to be desired. The intermediaries between writer
and reader are more numerous and better trained than ever before: they are the critics, the book reviewers, and the scholars.
Can they play their part more worthily in endeavoring to bridge
the ever-widening gulf?

The program for a better criticism which was proposed in the
previous chapters, though negative in part, was yet constructive,
like all that brushes aside old prejudices. It was certainly not an
excessive demand that the lucid and courageous critic (we never
even wished him to be the perfect or the ideal critic; the notion
of perfection seems to be as incompatible with the art of criticism
as with the novel or essay) should be at all times cognizant of
some of the most conventional errors committed by his predecessors; to beware of easy success, of superficial charm; to refrain from damning new works as immoral, morbid, or obscure

[4] In spite of our chronic lamentations on overproduction by modern
artists, no dramatist of the last three centuries produced as many plays as
Lope de Vega, or even as Aeschylus, Sophocles, and Aristophanes. Few philosophers have written as much as Plato and Aristotle, few painters painted
as much as Titian and Rubens.

when they perhaps require a mere readjustment of our comfortable prejudices; above all to look for depth, energy, and imaginative intensity. What should the critic be if he is to perceive and encourage those qualities beneath which the secret of greatness most often lurks?

Knowledge of the past is obviously the prerequisite for high standards in criticism. Such knowledge is not without its dangers: long familiarity with older masterpieces has repeatedly blunted the scholar's curiosity for the new and convinced him that Shakespeare, Milton, and Beethoven can never again be equalled, certainly not in our own age—a view which scholars contemporary with those great men held just as stubbornly as we do today. Familiarity with foreign literatures and with the world around him is equally indispensable and tends to correct some of the worst vices of criticism: provincialism and complacent contentment with one's narrow intellectual habits. Only broad culture can endow the critic with a fair sense of proportion, which helps him assign a place to a new work, without hailing it hastily as "epoch-making" or dismissing it with contempt because it upsets his traditional routine.

Few important critics, however, have been found among the very learned men; Sainte-Beuve was the outstanding exception. Unreserved enthusiasm for the past is likely to arouse diffidence about the present, which cannot be explored indiscreetly like the past. Erudition is tempted to concentrate on the qualities in a new work which are reminiscent of the past and to weigh influences, imitations, and parallels without mercy; it inters a recent book in a niche neatly carved in the scholar's walls, where it will rest forever in dusty death. Goethe, after having tried with rich Hellenic lore to write an epic on the theme of the Achilleid, confessed with discouragement: "Only faulty knowledge is creative." It is true that poets and artists who knew most about antiquity seldom recaptured its spirit. It is equally perilous for critics to know and to remember too much. Those who have spent long years evolving an original philosophy of criticism or tracing the genesis of old masterpieces have often refused to lend a willing ear to new works. They have been reluctant to accept the world of a new novelist, the vision of a new painter, the experience or the music of a new poet.

When all is said, enjoyment of beauty should precede understanding, analysis, and interpretation. If, next to religion and politics, literature and the arts have repeatedly been the objects of men's most passionate quarrels, it is obviously because they pertain to the senses and the feelings of men more than to their intellects. Other things being equal, the most satisfactory critic is he who possesses and retains a capacity to feel a thrill in the presence of beauty and originality, and to submit to that shock with sensuous—the adjective being in this case equivalent to wise—passiveness. Analysis, evaluation, and objective judgment of the work which first provided sensations "felt in the blood, and felt along the heart" must follow in due time; and, to still use Wordsworthian terminology, our emotion once "recollected in tranquillity" may have been enriched through intimate association with our inner life; it may on the contrary prove to have been a short-lived and unjustified emotion. We have all been overpowered in our teens by sentimental novels which we judge in retrospect as disgustingly mawkish. Even in our so-called mature years, some of the most enthralling raptures we have experienced may have come more from our own passing moods (patriotic fervor, nostalgic desire for romance, longing for escape) than from the intrinsic merits of the work which moved us. The raptures into which the first performance of *Cyrano de Bergerac* threw the most sedate Parisian critics, in 1897, are famous: Maeterlinck was similarly hailed as a rival of Shakespeare. Enthusiasts of Rostand and Maeterlinck were not wrong in giving free rein to their admiration for dramatists who heralded a new fashion; they erred in refraining from analyzing and purifying their first impression. Far from being afraid of contradicting himself or of being ridiculed, the critic of a new work should first candidly convey his "shock," but reserve his definitive and more objective estimate for some months later. The book reviewer is unfortunate and necessarily only half reliable if he can never reread and re-examine his first impression. If he is lucky enough to live in a country where monthly or quarterly reviews discuss new literature or where critical essays are reprinted in book form, he may undertake his periodical self-examination several times in a year. The crucial question which should then occur to him is this: "Has that powerful shock given me by Rostand or D'Annunzio or Kipling or Thomas Wolfe or Norman Mailer proved lasting? or was it due to my particular mood when the book came out, or to vigorous but vulgar and superficial qualities in it? Have those lines haunted me since I first read them? Have I seen the sky and the sea and the trees with the eyes of that painter whose landscape enraptured me six months ago? Has a true symbiosis taken place between those characters in a novel or drama and the fancies or the dreams of my brain? Do Mr. Bloom and M. de Charlus and Joseph K. actually coexist with me?"

The best definitions of criticism are in our opinion those which allow for the shock which our senses, emotions, and intellect must experience before a thing of beauty. Better than all logomachic circumlocutions of past and present philosophers of criticism, better than definitions which stress intellectual examination and stern judgment,[5] is Hazlitt's straightforward pronouncement: "I have endeavored to feel what was good and to give a reason for the faith that was in me, when necessary and when in my power." Taken all in all, Hazlitt, in his best moments, is the least unsatisfactory of all English critics, and the best antidote to the modern scientific explanations of literature which find "gusto" and "zest" praiseworthy, at most, in a wine-taster.[6] And the second truest critic in English, by some standards, is Walter

---

[5] Far better, certainly, than Arnold's high-sounding formula on Sophocles, applied by his disciples to criticism, on "seeing life steadily and seeing it whole" or his "seeing the object as it really is." As to Arnold's much-vaunted explanation of poetry as "a criticism of life," even the most Arnoldian critic of our times, T. S. Eliot, had to reject it as "frigid" in his preface to *The Sacred Wood* (2d ed.; London: Methuen, 1920).

[6] Virginia Woolf, in a fine essay in *The Common Reader* (2d ser.), defines Hazlitt's attitude as "loving and taking the liberties of a lover." With all his emphasis on fervor and gusto, Hazlitt is no mean psychologist; and he could write.

Pater, who rightly knew that the primary task of a critic is to feel the world of shapes and colors and sounds, not to reason about it abstractly. The preface to *The Renaissance*, even more than its celebrated conclusion, proposed, in Pater's too-languid prose, one of the most vigorous critical programs ever suggested to criticism: to feel the virtue of a writer, to disengage it, to set it forth. With the French, for whom artistic enjoyment has never been far from the great national art of gastronomy and occasionally from a refined eroticism, it is rare to find a definition of criticism which does not emphasize the words "please" or "pleasure." La Fontaine, Molière, Racine, Boileau used to formulate their aim, as "to please." A modern churchman like Abbé Bremond readily called the critic "a professor of pleasure"; Baudelaire used an even more un-English substantive in the grave and prophetic letter in which he divined and explained Wagner's originality after Tannhäuser: "My *volupté* had been so strong and so terrible, . . . I resolved to inquire into its causes, and to transform my *volupté* into knowledge."

But the critic cannot remain imprisoned within the walls of his ego. Truly enough, his capacity for artistic pleasure must be greater than that of other men, and he must first submit to the suggestions intended by the artist so as to re-experience them inwardly. A critic with a one-sided personality is not likely to be an impartial judge of the work of men who differ from him; if he is content with expressing his views only on authors with whom he feels a deep affinity, he may well turn out to be (as several poet-critics have) the most profound of interpreters. If the reviewer is professionally obliged to comment on a great variety of new productions, his public will want him to be a chameleon-critic, as Keats wanted the poet to be "the most unpoetical of anything in existence, a chameleon-poet." Many of the book reviews written today in countries like Germany, where "Sachlichkeit" is the supreme virtue, or in America, where a false conception of objectivity leads to ranking all opinions on the same plane, and printing several conflicting or repetitious accounts of the same work and letting the reader decide (as if he could!), are but feeble and colorless examples of criticism. Any eighteen-year-old beginner could turn off the kind of dramatic, musical or screen criticism printed in our daily press. Lack of personality is certainly more dangerous for a critic than passionate partiality.

"It is only by intensifying his own personality that the critic can interpret the personality and work of others." Thus wrote Oscar Wilde, reflecting the charming paradoxes of his contemporaries, the French impressionist critics. He was wise to use the verb "interpret." For, after submitting to the shock of the work of art, the artist's second duty is to *interpret* and *communicate*. Mere prolonged delight in one's artistic enjoyment makes a pleasant but narrow dilettante; it hardly suffices to make a critic. Anatole France's famous paradox, limiting criticism to "relating the adventures of one's soul among masterpieces," can be easily disposed of as begging the question. For masterpieces are taken to be works already approved by tradition or by the passive and anonymous judgment of posterity. French impressionist critics (as Lemaître and France called themselves) have been the least adventurous of all in the presence of new works (by Zola, Rimbaud, Mallarmé). For newness had, for them, something brutal and provoking which was hardly conducive to nonchalant reveries; and they were unwilling to risk a value-judgment, which alone could declare which among the new works were "masterpieces." In fact, even about Racine and Renan—writers whom he acknowledged unquestioningly as great, and plundered freely and charmingly—Anatole France had little to relate which was original or penetrating.

Pure impressionism is, in truth, hardly tenable as a critical attitude, and its results have been disappointing. It may give rise to urbane essays like those of Anatole France and Jules Lemaître, to the boyish wickedness of candid "avowals" like those of George Moore, but it limits criticism to being, in Oscar Wilde's phrase, "the only civilized form of autobiography." It tells us little about the merits of the work which set the reveries of the critic roaming. What is worse, it seldom succeeds in converting us to the preferences of the egotist critic, since he has avowedly enjoyed a poem or a play for highly personal and often whimsical reasons which we cannot experience or recapture in our turn.

A truer critic is he who, having been powerfully moved by a literary work, devotes his gifts of sensibility and analytical interpretation to winning readers to the book and to his own vision of it. That critic may be gifted as an artist and able to re-create the work of art, to instil a new life into it after having dissected it. He may, on the contrary, be a mere analyst and display to his readers the secrets of the structure of the work, trace its sources and genesis, weigh its originality and power. In either case, his duty is to be the "uncommon" reader, better equipped than the casual reader to detect allusions and technical devices, and to reconstruct the inner workings of the author's imagination. In the interpreter as in the creator, energy or intensity is probably the gift to be prized most highly: for the energetic critic alone can draw from the artist his secret and perhaps unconscious intentions, remain aglow with the enthusiasm which he experienced at the first shock of beauty, and fire his own readers with admiration.

Then comes the third stage of a critic's activity and he should not shirk it, frightened though he may be by the long record of his predecessors' errors or by the new and distorted application of scientific principles. The critic has to feel, understand, and explain: he has also to *judge*.

Such an assertion requires more elucidation today than it used to for many of our predecessors. For centuries, dogmatism ruled supreme in criticism, and its absolute decrees, based on esthetic, moral, or social standards, too often failed to grasp the individual inner law of each work of art. At the end of the eighteenth and at the beginning of the nineteenth centuries, there took place in philosophical and literary disciplines perhaps the most revolutionary change in two thousand years: Renan defined it in *L'Avenir de la science* as the substitution of the category of the relative for the category of the absolute in all that pertains to the human mind. As a corollary, the idea of development taught contemporaries of Herder, Hegel, Lamarck, and Sainte-Beuve to study every phenomenon in its slow process of growth, instead of assuming its full-blown and "static" creation. The result was a more comprehensive understanding of every individual in himself and for his own sake, the realization of the complex influences which had molded him, but also a more passive acceptance of peculiarities and even monstrosities as justified since they obeyed, in their strange fashion, the law of their own nature.

Literary criticism, like all other intellectual disciplines, gained immensely by that revolution (often called the Romantic Revolution, since it was contemporaneous and in many respects identical with it). New relations were explored between the author and his surroundings, the idea and the atmosphere in which it appeared, the style and the prevailing fashion. Sheer dogmatism became discredited, or served as a mere screen for partisan prejudices and stubborn principles, usually religious or political in character. The ablest dogmatists did little more than display the utter inapplicability of their attitude to our times: they flourished in the land of Academies and official respectability, and their names were Brunetière, Maurras, Massis, Seillière, *et alii.*

But the necessity of formulating value-judgments was not removed when rigid dogmatism was dethroned. Let us judge with the constant proviso that our judgments are relative, but let us judge none the less. For the alternative to judging can only be an exhaustive bibliographical list accompanied, at the most, with a dry synopsis of the work's content. And our age is already suffering gravely from an epidemic of bibliographical mania. Any reviewer who mentions three out of twenty new books, any teacher who includes four volumes on his required reading list and four others on his list of suggested reading obviously judges, that is, eliminates, prefers, and selects. No summary of a novel or play, no description of a picture, no reduction of a poem to its subject matter can ever escape the personal factor of the mind which discriminates, analyzes, mirrors, and distorts. The most consciously objective critic is also the most misleading, since he is his own dupe. Better proclaim with Remy de Gourmont that "the great effort of a sincere man is to erect his personal impressions into laws."

It has often been said that the truly rational attitude is that which makes full allowance for the limitations of reason. The truly relative attitude in a critic, in my opinion, is to avoid making a fetish of relativism and to confess one's own preferences instead of concealing them with puritanical repression. Even the very able defence of extreme relativism attempted by one of the most brilliant American professors has failed to prove wholly convincing.[7] "The poetry of an age never goes wrong," since it expresses the sensibility of that age; it is our standards of measure which vary, according to Professor Pottle. A critic merely declares great what he likes, and evaluates nothing but his own sensibility. The poetry of Pope is neither better nor worse than that of Wordsworth. Pope "had as much capacity for feeling as Wordsworth, but his feelings were aroused (or expressed) by different things."

Such a placid acceptance of the way in which every age felt its emotions seems difficult for the "energetic critic" whom I pictured as the most desirable sort. First, because few critics are narrow-minded enough to let what they like and that alone be called great; any critic conscious of his duties to his public has said a hundred times: "I do not like Voltaire, or Zola, or El Greco, but I acknowledge that he is great"; or else, "Joyce repels me, and William Faulkner displeases me, and Miller and Malraux irritate me, but my very dissatisfaction puts me on my guard: there are elements of force, of originality, perhaps of greatness there." Moreover, the poetry of an age has often gone wrong: for example, in England between Chaucer and Spenser, at the time of Cowley and his imitators, and of Lord Lyttelton, Akenside, Whitehead in the eighteenth century, and of the Yellow

---

[7] *The Idiom of Poetry*, by Frederick A. Pottle (Ithaca: Cornell University Press, 1941, Messenger Lectures). See pp. 21, 34, and 16 for the quotations contained in the text.

Decade, and even the Edwardians and the dull post–World War II era. It has gone wrong in France with the so-called "great Rhétoriqueurs" who preceded the Pléiade; again in the eighteenth century, when French poets, more numerous and fecund than ever, proved also more mediocre. Many an age simply failed to find faithful expression in its poetry, or in its novel and drama. Finally, I doubt that Pope ever felt anything as *intensely* as Blake or Shelley did; and I doubt likewise that Dr. Johnson recited Pope's verse with the same rapture that generations of young men have since felt in declaiming Coleridge and Yeats. And we doubt that the power to communicate an imaginative experience with words and sounds was ever as intense in Pope and Dryden as in the chief Elizabethan and romantic poets, and even the best of the Metaphysicals. If the spirit of an age is rendered by third-rate poetry and painting, that age simply never comes to life in the artists who have mirrored it. A critic must be ready to understand as many different eras of taste as possible; but he must not avoid preferring some to others. Pseudo-objectivity in a critic kills enjoyment, passion, taste, and surely devitalizes his criticism.

Each critic must judge according to his personal preferences, first answering the primary questions: "How good or how bad is this new work? How am I affected by it? What does it move or provoke in me? What is the quality of my enjoyment?" The most honest critic will be neither the dogmatist appraising works of art according to their conformity with some abstract criterion, nor the pseudo-scientific critic repressing his instinctive tastes and distrusting his pleasure so as to become perfectly dehumanized. He will candidly confess his preferences, state his own standards without wishing to impose them, and enable the readers to deduce from his verdict, so to speak, the personal coefficient of the judge's fallible and partial personality.

But a work is not absolutely good or bad. "What's aught but as 'tis valued?" as Hector says in Shakespeare's strangest play.[8] One can damn every play produced on the American stage in the last ten years, for the excellent reason that none of them can compare

[8] *Troilus and Cressida*, II, ii, 52.

with Shakespeare, Ibsen, and Shaw. Anyone is free to discover one masterpiece a week among current novels, if he has retained a capacity to be easily delighted. It is therefore necessary for the critic to judge a work according to its purpose and to ask: "How does this book rank among books of its kind, and is that kind high or low?" This is a tolerably good first-class work, a critic might say of *Mourning Becomes Electra;* or, of *Murder in the Cathedral,* this is a rather disappointing work which strove to belong to the highest class, but still remains higher in the literary scale than the plays of Noel Coward or of William Saroyan. The most highbrow critic should not hesitate to state, for instance: "This is an excellent work of its kind, but its kind is a detective story, a sentimental poem, or another one of those diaries jotted down by some well-informed journalist for easily satisfied readers." Academic critics have been so ridiculed for their insistence on separate literary "genres" and their passion for ranking and bestowing prizes that they have been cowed into a timid reluctance to judge: they refrain from judging and classifying, and impartially rank everything on the same plane. They stifle their own sense of values, merely listing the book in its alphabetical order, with a few words as to its content. The Greek verb from which "critic" is derived, means, we should remember, "to separate," hence to judge. No worse injustice can be done to an important work than to place it, through a levelling-down process, in the same rank as the most insignificant productions. Such refusal to judge, on the pretence of misconceived objectivity, puts all the new works of an age on the same plane: the very lowest one. But some things in life and literature deserve contempt; they ought to receive it.

Finally, the judgment of the critic, while remaining sincere and candid, should express more than the narrow subjectivity of one personality. It often happens that the greatest critic may oppose the general trend of his age. But an ideal critic would be capable of guiding his contemporaries, for he would reveal to them their own better taste. Not content with relating his narrow impressions and the private associations they call up in his soul, he would attempt to answer two more questions: "Is this work good for me alone, or would it be equally appreciated by other men living in different surroundings, outside of my province or even of my country? Does it have a special interest for our age on account of contemporary circumstances, or do I discover in it that concentrated intensity, that universal human truth, that promise of ever-renewed significance, which are likely to go down to other ages?" A critic, in our opinion, should free himself from the obsession of posterity and cease calling upon the future to back his frail utterances. His duty is to judge for himself and his generation, while remaining detached enough from ephemeral prejudices to discriminate between temporary fashions and profound forces. In expressing his own carefully considered opinion and winning his readers to it through his enthusiasm, insight, and taste lies the safest chance of the critic's contributing to the collective and random accumulation of unchallenged evidence called the verdict of posterity.

To do so, however, the critic should satisfy another requirement in addition to all those which have been already listed: he should be able to write. All his scholarship and acumen will be wasted, unless he can impart the results of his cogitations in convincing language. The critic has often been likened to a "gourmet" delighting in his artistic enjoyment with refined expertness; but we insist that he should also be an interpreter and a judge, or, as Hazlitt defined his role, a taster for the public. If, convinced that he has grasped the truth about an author, he proves unable to communicate his conviction to others, he has failed in his primary function.

"Truth remains true, the fault's in the prover." [9]

He may boast of his kinship with the difficult writer (Mallarmé, Joyce, Rilke) whose secrets he has deciphered, and even fancy that he has become the equal of the mind that conceived them; but he will have lost his kinship with the public.

In recent years, critics seem to have perversely delighted in keeping aloof from their readers. They have been writing like

[9] Robert Browning, *Christmas Eve*, l. 229.

exclusive initiates or like the least literary of all men of science, the social scientists. Their findings are set down—one dares not say, written—in a style calculated to repel the friends they might have recruited among the public. They take with them a few undaunted disciples into the sanctum of their laboratory, where they experiment on the work of art, murder and dissect, and formulate their laws with a parade of pedantic terminology which reminds one of Molière's quack doctors. On the other side, journalistic book reviewers resort to a "snappy" style and a deluge of vulgarisms, playing down to the cheapest part of their audience, and reducing an article on literature, painting, or music to the level of the lowest political reporting. Between these two extremes, the gradual disappearance of the genteel tradition has left a gap which is among the few real inferiorities of American cultural life as compared to the British and the French. Edward Dowden, Leslie Stephen, Edmund Gosse, and even their successors T. S. Eliot, John Middleton Murry, Virginia Woolf, David Cecil, Frank Kermode, Alfred Alvarez, and, among the professorial critics, Herbert Grierson and Lascelles Abercrombie have all been fallible and, at times, timid interpreters of literature; but their style bears rereading after twenty or forty years and the charm of their best essays will outlive the value of their pronouncements. The masters of French criticism in the present century had, until Roland Barthes, Lucien Goldmann, Charles Mauron appeared, been gifted writers whose polished or urbane prose accompanied the most searching penetration; even the most scholarly and scientific among them insisted upon presenting their results with as little pedantic jargon as possible.[10] Since the generation of Woodberry and Paul Elmer More, American critics who wrote for the general cultured public with urbanity and charm have been far too rare: either they failed to reach the readers whom they meant to enlighten and became isolated figures (J. E. Spingarn, George Santayana, Prosser Hall Frye, Ed-

---

[10] The few exceptions would probably be among the dead, Ramon Fernandez. Élie Faure in his more apocalyptic passages, and Charles Du Bos in his later and too "Jamesian" essays.

mund Wilson, even Waldo Frank, although his style is more turgid than urbane) or they gradually came down to the level of a wider audience which had refused their early demands as too exacting for popular success (Stuart Sherman, William Lyon Phelps, Van Wyck Brooks); superficiality and haste marred their later writings. The younger generation of psychologists and semanticists has initiated a healthy reaction against the emptiness of much critical writing; their efforts should be encouraged, even if their success proves infinitesimal as compared with their claim to be the true heirs of Aristotle and Coleridge. But many of their readers of good will cannot help entertaining grave misgivings as to the validity of their attempts so long as they ignore two of the essential demands which we may reasonably make upon critics of all times and of all schools: they must share their superior knowledge with readers treated as friends to be enlightened; they must interpret literature and the arts through a style of beauty, and not in the jargon of scientific barbarians.

The program for criticism thus outlined is not a very ambitious or original one. Yet it has seldom been fulfilled, particularly in America. In the opinion of Americans themselves,[11] literary criticism remains to this day in their country "the most immature aspect of American literature," as Poe and Lowell had feared in their times. Literary historians labor unceasingly to perfect our knowledge of the past; psychologists laboriously dissect works already acknowledged as great; estheticians gather clouds about the purpose, meaning, and essence of art. But they all work in a vacuum, and have little contact with the literature which is painfully endeavoring to come to life in their own times. America has enjoyed a true critical renaissance in the last fifty years; no province of literature attracts today so many eager talents as criticism, not even poetry. Yet the twofold duty of the critic, as we define it, has been regularly shirked.

That duty is to the artist and to the audience. The critic cannot

[11] See Morton D. Zabel, in his introduction to *Literary Opinion in America* (New York: Harper, 1937).

be content with understanding works of art isolated from the living author who produced them. He must write and judge for the artist. He has long ceased to be a schoolmaster brandishing a rod to castigate the mischievous pranks of the creator's fancy. But he can still assist the writer through his very severity, reveal to him where and why he failed in his purpose, answer the suggestions latent in a mysterious text, discover what the artist meant, perhaps without realizing it, and what he said perhaps without meaning it. The critic is more attentive and better informed than the common reader; he is a reader with a library and a retentive memory; he can compare a new publication with the previous works by the same writer, trace the writer's development, warn him of the dangers of repetition and haste which beset a successful man of letters. He may even enlighten a creator on the influences he has undergone (the most profound are often the least conscious), compare his attempts with those of other writers in the same country or abroad, explain to him what other living writers are doing along similar lines. If the critic is wise, he will, while judging with a keen knowledge of the past and the fastidious taste which familiarity with masterpieces develops, respect the individuality of the newcomer. For the all-too-frequent demand we make upon a contemporary artist (asking him to resemble great artists of the past) is unjust; Proust does not have to be like Balzac, or Mauriac like Flaubert, or Lawrence like Galsworthy. The only relevant question is: do these new writers express with imaginative power and style a vision which is profoundly theirs? In other words, the critic's duty is not only to bring to the assistance of the artist a rich fund of knowledge and a cultivated taste, but also to hail the discovery of unexplored lands, to be an adventurer, at times a prophet.

Artists, however, will seldom listen patiently when reprimanded. The stronger their individual temperaments, the less docile they are likely to prove. The story of the doleful complaints made by writers against criticism is a long and pitiful one.[12] I have repeatedly deplored the tragic misunderstanding

[12] See the introductory chapter for a number of illustrations.

which separates geniuses from common men whom geniuses
might raise above their mediocrity. The gap has become wider at
the very moment when the number of professional interpreters
of genius (the critics) has increased tenfold. Since the Schlegels,
Coleridge, and Sainte-Beuve, criticism has become one of the important literary genres and has attracted some of our most gifted
minds and best stylists. Yet it has hardly fulfilled the expectations
demanded of it at the beginning of a democratic era and elo-
quently defined by Carlyle: "Criticism stands like an interpreter
between the inspired and the uninspired." Some may rashly declare that genius finds its audience sooner or later—posthumously, when it can no longer draw nourishment from the sympathy of discerning readers. We have contended that an immense
gain would be made if that audience could be assembled in the
artist's lifetime, by more lucid interpreters. "If there had been no
Liszt perhaps after *The Flying Dutchman* there would have been
no Wagner," wrote an American musical critic.[13] The same
doubts can be legitimately entertained for many a Wagner or
Baudelaire among our contemporaries. We have more universities
today, better schools of music, finer art exhibitions, more numerous commentators in the press and on the radio than our predecessors could ever have dreamt of. Yet we have improved neither
man's imagination nor his judgment, neither his sensitiveness to
beauty nor his taste. The "march of progress," in spite of our
fond illusions, proceeds less through improvement in the general
intellectual level than through that of a few exceptional individuals. The only serious hope for correcting man's infinite mistakes
is in enabling more men to catch up with the rare prophets who
appear among them. One of the most universally gifted among
those prophets, Leonardo da Vinci, is reported to have said:
"There are three classes of people, those who do not see, those
who see when they are shown, and those who see by themselves."
The men of the first group will always be content to read Hector
Malot, Harold Bell Wright, or Marie Corelli. The second group
waits for the men who see by themselves, to initiate them to the

[13] Deems Taylor in *The New York Times* of February 1, 1942.

vision of a new artist. The happy few of the third group, alas! are too often content to fall into raptures over Rimbaud, Rilke, or Picasso, but refrain from explaining the artist to his potential public.

Great creative eras have ordinarily been preceded or accompanied by fervent discussion of literature and the arts, if not by impeccable criticism. Even hostility to innovations is better than the callous indifference fostered by the exaggerated claims of commercial publishers, for whom every book in town is a masterpiece. In an age which, to sell books at all, has to sell them in department stores and drugstores, it is not surprising that the questions on the lips of potential purchasers of books should be: "Is there any value in it? Shall I get my money's worth?"

In past centuries, when the power of publicity and money was comparatively inconsequential, interest in literary matters was kept alive by poets and critics. Treatises like those of Sidney, Webbe, Campion, Daniel, Dryden in England, Du Bellay, Chapelain, D'Aubignac, Boileau in France, spread esthetic discussion on poetry and the drama and inaugurated periods of lively poetical and dramatic creation. The artist was far from independent financially; he humbled himself in dedications to patrons. But he often met some connoisseurs who helped him with the most valid assistance an artist can receive: loyal but exacting criticism, encouraging the creator to mature and to aim always higher.

The power of money has become formidable since the age of Balzac and Dickens. Publicity has succeeded in enlarging the audience of some writers, who are not necessarily the worst, although seldom the very best. The direst consequence is to throw the writer into a vicious circle: when publicity has helped make him famous, he needs more and more to keep in the limelight; he seeks it, and only utterances on the agricultural problems from an Ohio farm, on the integration questions from a Southern author, blueprints for world peace, reporting from Russia or China, biographies of Washington or Lincoln can maintain the link between a former novelist or poet and his public.

The result is pitiful. American literary critics have often lamented it, for it is probably the gravest issue facing literature and the arts in the United States: in their youth few writers are more brilliantly gifted than the Americans; few are more disappointing after the age of forty-five. Every American critic has commented on that strange inability to mature which seems to be the lot of the American man of letters: the finest generation of novelists writing in the English language in the present century has not escaped it (Dreiser, Lewis, Dos Passos, Caldwell, Farrell), and the promise of poets and dramatists who at twenty-five or thirty stood an excellent chance of ranking among the classics of American letters has been fulfilled only in part (Sandburg, Vachel Lindsay, Edgar Lee Masters, O'Neill, Jeffers, and among their successors, Hart Crane, Robert Lowell).

The problem is a familiar one to all those who since 1910 have watched with fervent hope the emergence of American literature to its place among the three or four leading literatures of the world. The solution is not simple; [14] but it lies above all in gathering and maintaining an enlightened audience for the American artist. The deplorable expatriation of the Twenties and Thirties, which sent T. S. Eliot to England, Ezra Pound and Santayana to Italy, kept Berenson in Italy, and sent scores of gifted authors to France, impoverished both authors and public. The independent Anglo-Saxon spirit is apparently reluctant, not without reason, to adopt any state organization of literature which today smacks of totalitarianism (academies, a national and federal theatre, a state opera, official salons for painting, sculpture, and decorative arts). Independence in intellectual and imaginative creation is undoubtedly a more precious advantage than any profit which organization could bring. Even privately conducted enterprises like the

[14] Ernest Hemingway relates in *The Green Hills of Africa* how he met a German who questioned him about America's great writers. "We do not have great writers," he replied; "something happens to our good writers at a certain age. I can explain but it is quite long and may bore you." He discards even Emerson, Hawthorne, Whittier, and company, "all our early classics who did not know that a new classic does not bear any resemblance to the classics that have preceded it." Among the reasons why America destroys her writers, he mentioned: money, and faulty critics.

great symphony orchestras of America, exhibitions of the Pennsylvania Academy or the New York Academy of Design, and the oratorical flights of Archibald MacLeish,

"Un poète mort jeune à qui l'homme survit," [15]

have not remained untainted by monotonous and pompous officialdom.

In literature as in industrial and economic life, however, freedom from any state control often comes to mean unlimited power left to financial interests. Conscientious publishers, producers, editors of magazines with meticulous care give the public exactly what it is supposed to like, and nothing better. A certain type of film, play, novel, or condensed magazine article has been the fashion this year. They will turn out more films, plays, novels, and magazine-consommés of the same brand, always assuming the public to be more sheepish, more vulgar, and more easily satisfied than it really is. Ten or twenty times more students go through the universities, ten or twenty times more boys and girls go through high schools than three generations ago; working hours have been shortened, mechanical facilities have increased, so that our leisure should be today more plentiful than it ever was. Yet there is no sorrier sight to watch than the vacant faces of those former high school and college students when, at thirty-five or fifty, all their mental alertness having vanished, the spark gone from their eyes, they dutifully chew their gum to keep from yawning, while absorbing the chewing gum for the eyes of the movies or the chewing gum for the ears of the radio. The same men who once read Joyce, Faulkner, Proust glance at the headlines of their tabloid papers, turn straight to the page of the funnies, to devour them with the same dutiful sense of boredom as they swallow their hamburger at lunchtime and their highball after dinner.

Statistics inform us that in normal times approximately 5,000,-000 students are enrolled in American colleges and universities. Many of them study and enjoy literature while there; some at

[15] The line is by A. de Musset, paraphrasing a prose sentence of Sainte-Beuve's.

least must want to continue reading good novels and poetry, and keep up with literary developments after they leave college. They realize that artistic and literary works do not merely provide a cowardly escape from life ("life" being identified with dictating from an office chair, looking at charts and figures, obeying computers, and answering the telephone); that literature and art are life multiplied, heightened, humanized, and made more concentrated and more alive than life itself. With the best will in the world, how can they keep abreast of developments in arts and letters? There are dozens of scholarly reviews in America, which are all forbidding to the layman, even if he is also a gentleman of culture; there are many poetry reviews, but too esoteric for his general interests; there are the leading monthly magazines, from which literature has been gradually crowded out. Now and then, nostalgic for the studies which he pursued at twenty at Harvard College or on the Princeton campus, the tired, or retired, businessman would like to read an article on the American theatre in the last five years, or on the significance of James Baldwin or Saul Bellow; he vaguely hears that Lowell is considered by some a great poet, Robert Penn Warren a considerable novelist, that since 1910 American poetry has been second to none in originality, that Surrealism expresses the modern temper in art, that Frank Lloyd Wright is respected throughout three continents. In vain does he open *Harper's Magazine* or even the *Yale Review* to look for good critical articles revaluating past and recent literature and evaluating the very new works. Either criticism is relinquished to hasty appraisals of a few new books or remains hopelessly timid and conservative. Review editors take it for granted that the public will welcome ten articles on economic problems, five monotonous presentations of age-old debates (fascism vs. communism, science vs. religion), four stories of travel in Alaska or Central Africa, but not one comprehensive study on Faulkner, O'Neill, new trends in American poetry, new directions in the American opera or cinema.[16]

[16] As to the hopelessly conventional character of the poetry published in the *Atlantic Monthly*, the *Yale Review*, and the rest, the less said the better.

Millions of dollars are spent on science, scholarship, education in this country. A few thousand dollars could probably found a review which would grant its proper place to literature without being exclusively literary. Such a review would not necessarily be, and probably should not be, attached to any university (although some inspiration might be drawn from the fine results achieved by the *Virginia Quarterly Review,* and occasionally by the literary articles and especially by the careful poetry reviews of Louis Martz in the *Yale Review*). It would be more humane and less strident in tone than the *Kenyon Review* has been in recent years, it would be more solid and more exacting than the *Saturday Review.* The revived *Southern Review* points the right direction. New York should obviously be the seat of the monthly publication of which we dream: it would draw upon American writers more than does the *New York Review of Books* and cover more works in briefer articles. Other reviews, on parallel or rival lines, would soon follow in other parts of the country. Political problems, both local and foreign, social, agricultural, military topics would be discussed in such a review, for literature cannot without loss be divorced from life, and the public for literature and criticism must be drawn largely from nonspecialists interested in all aspects of life. But one third of the space should be devoted to literary works or to critical studies on literature. Many countries of continental Europe had such reviews, and they were able to flourish. If it were broad in outlook, serious yet not technical in tone, and tolerably well written, a cultivated public would gradually gather round such a periodical. Young men would respect its authority because it would not systematically oppose innovations; older and more staid readers would accept its views on political events or on modern literature more willingly than they trust the supposedly "radical" *Nation* and *New Republic* or the occasionally brilliant criticism of *Commentary.* There is probably no greater gap in American cultural life today than the absence of such a review—in fact, the absence

---

Many review editors are apparently convinced that the poetry of our age is represented by Marianne Moore and John Berryman.

of any tribune for criticism, of any meeting ground for writers and their potential public.

Has America the men to carry out this program? Let us, unreservedly, answer *Yes*. And she could easily find, or train, many more than she has. Any visitor to American colleges is struck by the amount of promising talent that flowers in the young men and women and by the quality of the younger members of the faculty. Their minds are alert, their spirits are bold; their imaginations are easily fired by the discovery that, contrary to the teachings of "crabbed age" and superannuated professors,

"Great spirits now on earth are sojourning."

They revere the living writers, have acclaimed Kafka, Camus, Teilhard de Chardin; and the realization that the age of greatness had not passed irretrievably with Milton, Wordsworth and Browning inspires them with the eager desire to follow and rival the geniuses now alive. The more care their elders take to ignore or disparage contemporary works, the more surely will young men be attracted by a literature which they imagine more novel than it probably is. They leave college with the keen desire to write. No literary groups exist which could welcome them after they have left college; they are soon discouraged by the commercial mold of the "snappy" articles or conventional book reviews which they are asked to turn out. They fall back upon the cheapest, that is to say, the best-paid kind of short-story writing. Solid, searching, and personal articles on literature, written with some perspective once a month or once a quarter, are nowhere in demand. Reviews of literature and art in *Harper's* and the *Atlantic Monthly* are relegated to the very last, unread pages. Some of the most promising interpreters of literature in our times have consequently been discouraged at twenty-five or thirty for lack of a suitable public; others, like Henry S. Canby and Joseph W. Krutch, have failed to give their full measure as critics; Waldo Frank, who might have been an excellent spokesman for American letters in Europe and South America, became a solitary figure in his own country, an apocalyptic prophet; Allen Tate and Yvor Winters seem even more isolated, since none of their pronouncements is likely to affect the sale of a book or the public taste. Even Edmund Wilson, years after he published one of the best volumes of literary essays for the layman, *Axel's Castle* (1931), had hardly increased his authority with the general public; in almost any other country his cosmopolitan culture, his discriminating taste, and his balanced judgment would have become a force, brought fully to bear on the literary opinion, and perhaps on the creation, of his times. Joseph Frank, one of our very best critical minds, addresses himself chiefly to specialists.

There is another and very important group of men, of whom much might have been expected: they are the scholars. They are impeccably trained in our graduate schools; they have breadth of knowledge, are fully acquainted with the historical perspective; they are not narrowly limited to either the present or to the American scene; what is more, they have, or should have, leisure, "high seriousness," and an "aurea mediocritas" which makes them neither anxious to acquire the torments wealth brings nor envious of authors whose books sell momentarily by thousands.

The scholars too have disappointed us. They seem, in many cases, to have lost contact with the living literature of their day. They have divorced themselves from criticism. They have seldom attracted the finest part of the youth whom they should have trained. They have often taken away from humane studies the very life and humanity they were supposed to foster. A great many charges have recently been levelled at them. We shall quote the most typical of those accusations. If they are not justified, scholars should answer them fearlessly; if they are, scholars are intelligent enough to admit and outgrow their faults.

Some are clearly so unjust that we may rank them with the large mass of satirical gibes which, from the time of the ancients, Montaigne, and Descartes, have been hurled at teachers and pedants. Strangely enough, they were often uttered by professors or former professors, either sincerely dissatisfied with the monotonous drudgery of a career upon which they had embarked with eager expectations or anxious to distinguish themselves from their colleagues by smiling at their ineffectual mediocrity. Academic men should perhaps rejoice at the merciless soul searching and mutual disparaging which is a feature of their scholarly gatherings: one seldom hears such qualms on the validity of their pursuit (and attempts to justify their existence) among Rotarians, salesmen, doctors, army officers, or war veterans at any of their periodical conventions. Lack of complacency is the first condition of progress. Pronouncements like the following by the late Stuart Sherman, who gave more promise as a critic and essayist than he ever could fulfill, may thus be taken with a grain of salt and welcomed as healthy severity:

The very best men do not enter upon graduate study at all; the next best drop out after a year's experiment; the mediocre men at the end of two years; the most unfit survive and become doctors of philosophy, who go forth and reproduce their kind.

Others, when the events of 1940 and 1941 made them suddenly aware of the fond delusions they had entertained for a decade of isolationist selfishness, blamed the teaching they had received and the teachers who had failed to be prophets. It is obviously and traditionally easier to abuse teachers and politicians than to speak sternly to the students and the alumni who often dictate what they want to be taught or to the voters who elect the politicians in their own image—if slightly disfigured. Archibald MacLeish denounced, in a fiery speech on "the Irresponsibles," [17] the divorce between the learned and the creative world, between scholars and writers. The two formerly blended in one: the man of letters.

He was a man of learning whose learning was employed, not for its own sake in a kind of academic narcissism, but for the sake of decent living in his time. He was a writer whose writing was used, not to mirror an abstract and unrelated present, but to illuminate that present by placing it in just relation to its past. . . .

The country of the man of letters has been divided between his

[17] Archibald MacLeish, *A Time to Speak* (Boston: Houghton Mifflin, 1941), pp. 113–118.

heirs. . . . Past is the scholar's country; present is the writer's. . . . The irresponsibility of the scholar is the irresponsibility of the scientist upon whose laboratory insulation he has patterned all his work. The scholar has made himself as indifferent to values, as careless of significance, as bored with meanings as the chemist. . . . The Ph.D. thesis is the perfect image of his world. It is work done for the sake of doing work—perfectly conscientious, perfectly laborious, perfectly irresponsible.

In the same year, 1941, Allen Tate branded the defeatism of the scholar on a purely literary plane: sociologists and specialists of education have taken the offensive against the humanist; they have convinced many school principals that "the least thing about man is his intelligence, if he have it at all; the greatest thing his adjustment to society (not to a good society)." [18] Scholars should have fought back and maintained the tradition of literature as a form of knowledge. Instead they have humbly taken refuge in the "social values" of literature, or praised it for being a mirror—a mirror to the decay of capitalism or to the anarchy of modern civilization. Or they have treated it as something severed from life which, according to the nefarious formula, should not mean, but be; that is, have no content and no relevance to our moral and spiritual life.

From the most varied quarters similar charges have been proffered against the scholar and the professor of literature. Norman Foerster was among the first to protest against the scholar who stubbornly refused to feel and judge as a human being.[19] Some of the most eminent professors of America and England have warned their colleagues against making their research a pretext for systematic neglect of the present and turning literary history into a discipline completely divorced from literary criticism. Indeed, some of the severest strictures on dried-up scholarship

18 Allen Tate, *Reason in Madness* (New York: Putnam, 1941) (essays on "The Present Function of Criticism" and "Understanding Modern Poetry").

19 In *The American Scholar* (Chapel Hill: University of North Carolina Press, 1929) and again in the first chapter of a volume by several collaborators, *Literary Scholarship, Its Aims and Methods* (Chapel Hill: University of North Carolina Press, 1941).

have been heard at the annual meetings of those august gatherings of academic brains, the Modern Humanities Research Association in England and the Modern Language Association of America. Their authors were scholars whom few will suspect of being "unsound" or addicted to fickle impressionism: Carleton Brown, E. K. Chambers, Ronald S. Crane, Ifor Evans, Albert Feuillerat, Howard Mumford Jones, Austin Warren.[20] It was a conspicuous honor for the Modern Language Association of America, whose publications have occasionally been forced to accept, for lack of more ambitious attempts, some uninspiring examples of inhuman or subhuman scholarship, to have listened on its fiftieth anniversary to words like these pronounced by Professor Livingston Lowes:

In fifty years an emphasis has gone far towards passing from scholarship for larger ends to scholarship for scholars. Are the humanities by any chance in danger at our hands of ceasing to be humane? . . . Humane scholarship moves and must move within two worlds at once—the world of scientific method and the world, in whatever degree, of creative art. The postulates of the two are radically different. And our exquisitely difficult task is to conform at once to the stipulations of each without infringing on those of the other. The path of least resistance is to follow one and let the other go. Research, which is the primary instrument of science, is felt to be the easier and it is also the more alluring. . . . Too many of the keenest youngsters in the universities are going into other fields. We are in some danger, if I mistake not, of attracting diligent coral-insects, rather than adventurous and constructive minds. . . . The ultimate end of our research is criticism, in the fullest sense of an often misused word.[21]

Ten years elapsed, and the same appeal was to have been heard in December 1942, at the association's fifty-ninth meeting, which was cancelled on account of the war. A critic who has done much, against severe odds, to improve and enlarge the audi-

[20] Precise references are given, under these names, in the Bibliographical Notes at the end of this volume.

[21] John Livingston Lowes, "The Modern Language Association and Humane Scholarship," *Publications of the Modern Language Association of America*, XLVIII (1933), 1399–1408.

ence of American men of letters, Henry S. Canby, had chosen as his theme the topic which, since Emerson treated it in his Harvard address of 1837, has never ceased to be timely. The independent American scholar, for whom Emerson fought, has won his battle. The output of American scholarship is quantitatively huge, qualitatively not unequal to that of France or Germany. Has not the battle been overwon? asked Henry Canby.

I submit that the extensive literary research of the last quarter-century has made teaching more accurate, has trained new researchers in better methodologies, and beyond that has almost completely failed to insure in the teaching of literature the growth, the fervor, the taste, the insight, the assimilation of what can only be assimilated and can never be directly taught. . . . I submit that this generation of young people has reason to say to the American scholar, I asked for bread, and you gave me a stone.

The young people are indeed dissatisfied with the teaching of literature dispensed to them in graduate schools and even, through progressive invasion by graduate school and seminar methods, in undergraduate courses. Due allowance must obviously be made for the natural tendency of youth to be discontented with the education it receives and with its elders; full account must be taken of the difficulties which stand in the way of a teacher of literature, who has to train not only memory, intelligence, critical power, but also taste, personality, intuition, and imagination. It remains true, however, that the divorce between academic teaching and creative writing is widening daily. An immense and in many ways successful endeavor has been achieved in American graduate schools since 1890. Our knowledge of the past has been increased. But have students learned to enjoy masterpieces of former centuries more intensely, or even to read them better? Have they been incited to write better themselves, and has contemporary literature markedly gained in recruiting its talents from, let us say, five hundred thousand young men and women graduated yearly from college, instead of ten thousand as formerly?

Two American reviews once published a symposium of ten articles entitled "Literature and the Professors." [22] A few charges recurred with disquieting insistence: (1) The teaching of English literature is marked by the pursuit of objective detachment which represses and often annihilates the personality of the teacher. Scholars too often lose all sense of values by having too long avoided value-judgments. (2) Scholars fail to teach their best students the primary condition of criticism: how to read.[23] (3) Literature, in their seminars, comes to mean "anything in print, if it has been in print long enough," but not contemporary works. It is taken for granted that no one can judge the present for lack of the "right perspective." The scholar fulfills dutifully his responsibility to the past, but shirks his responsibility to the present. In the words of a scholar, then not long out of college and ungratefully harsh toward his teachers, who has become a luminary of our profession and a great scholar-critic: [24]

Professors tend to develop a vested interest in the past and a morbid fear of the future. Like slaves of some deceased pharaoh, having duly attended to the details of interment, they remain in the tomb.

That mood of dissatisfaction with the teaching of literature has not been limited to a group of young men impatient at the exacting disciplines of scholarship and eager to free themselves from the shackles of scientific method. Some of the most thoughtful minds of our times have confessed their concern over the results of modern education and have sweepingly indicted our academic curricula for soullessness and lack of content. In a speech, still timely, delivered in December 1940 before the American Association for the Advancement of Science, Walter Lippmann boldly

[22] The *Southern Review*, VI, no. 2 (Autumn 1940), and the *Kenyon Review*, XII, no. 4 (Autumn 1940).

[23] See Joe Horrell and Wright Thomas in the *Southern Review*, VI, no. 2 (Autumn 1940). The same inability of students to read a text, attributed to faulty teaching, is deplored by Professor Ronald S. Crane in "History vs. Criticism in the Study of Literature," *English Journal*, XXIV (October 1935), 645–667.

[24] Harry Levin, in "Pseudodoxia academica," *Southern Review*, VI, no. 2 (Autumn 1940).

accused our prevailing education of destroying western civilization. He called for an urgent reconsideration by modern educators of their purposes and their underlying assumptions.

The plain fact is that the graduates of the modern schools are the actors in the catastrophe which has befallen our civilization. Those who are responsible for modern education—for its controlling philosophy—are answerable for the results. . . . They have had money, lots of it, fine buildings, big appropriations, great endowments, and the implicit faith of the people that the school was the foundation of democracy. If the results are bad, and indubitably they are, on what ground can any of us who are in any way responsible for education disclaim our responsibility? [25]

This eminent journalist, borrowing the ominous eloquence of an Old Testament prophet, lamented the lack of traditions and substance in modern education, its aimlessness, and its irrelevance to the profound needs of the modern world.

Modern education has renounced the idea that the pupil must learn to understand himself, his fellowmen and the world in which he is to live as bound together in an order which transcends his immediate needs and his present desires.

Teachers of literature are, we believe, no more guilty than teachers of engineering, history, or civics. It is by no means certain that economists have been keener in understanding the present than literary scholars have in interpreting contemporary literature. Indeed, the most pompous and ludicrous accounts of annual conventions held by the learned societies of America are those, not of literary scholars, but of anthropologists, sociologists, and psychologists. Since, however, it is the proud privilege of scholars to criticize their own species mercilessly, let us openly accept our full share of responsibility. This may at least prove that we are not diabolically confirmed in our errors. The practice of the scholar has been excellent so far as it has gone; but it has

[25] Walter Lippmann, "Education without Culture," published in *Commonweal*, January 17, 1941, and in the *American Scholar*, X (1941), 184–193.

not gone far enough. He has accomplished some comparatively simple tasks so efficiently that he has not dared even to look at the more difficult ones remaining beyond his exiguous fence. Lovingly, he built and polished a base for criticism to build on; but criticism seldom followed or, when it appeared, scorned the base and erected its structure in the air.

The scholar's seven deadly sins bear more pretentious names than Avarice or Lechery, but are more innocuous.

1) His favorite indulgence is bibliography. He compiles impressive catalogues of learned titles on which all his repressed sensuousness is expended. The most minute, often the most insignificant, studies written on Dryden or Whitman or Zola are duly enumerated. The silliest journalist who has expressed an opinion on Eliot or on Rilke is thus enshrined. The bibliographer could easily, in less time than the journalist spent on his article, express a far wiser opinion on Eliot or Rilke; but objective detachment forbids him to utter a value-judgment. It seems as if that perpetual taking stock of what was written before us were paralyzing creation—and criticism. Too few of our bibliographies are selective and critical. They should boldly proclaim: "There are fifty books on this subject. Avoid reading forty-six out of fifty; they are worthless. Here is why."

2) The second occupation of a self-respecting scholar is the editing of texts: it is a commendable task of abnegation, and a very useful one for our successors. To be sure, establishing the text of classical and medieval writers, of Chaucer and Shakespeare, was an indispensable and invaluable task. American classics were long treated as poor relations which could be neglected. But the practice has now been carried so far that some learned editions, instead of elucidating the text, accumulate pseudo-sources, parallel passages from other authors, pedantic quotations, and actually make our understanding and enjoyment of literature impossible. The simplest love song dashed off by Catullus or Herrick appears as a mosaic of borrowings. Too little, if anything, is said of the esthetic value of the poem and of the reasons why the annotator considers it a masterpiece or a third-

rate work. The labor spent on editing is often disproportionate to the value of the text, and misrepresents the spontaneous flight of fancy from which a certain poem sprang, by turning it into a patient task of combination. Yeats's humorous lines should be recited aloud yearly by scholars:

> Bald heads, forgetful of their sins,
> Old, learned, respectable bald heads
> Edit and annotate the lines
> That young men, tossing on their beds,
> Rhymed out in love's despair
> To flatter beauty's ignorant ear.

3) Excesses of the genetic method have lured scholars into looking for sources almost exclusively in previously published works. Sheer common sense should tell us that many works of the past merely do not exist for us, because we are blissfully unaware of their existence. Common sense might add that the deepest influences we undergo are not necessarily those of books, but of the conversation of our friends, the smile of a woman, the contemplation of a city street or of a cloud at sunset, the sight of a picture in a studio, or a reverie started by a piece of music. These sources cannot be measured or defined; but criticism might try to weigh imponderables by a qualitative scale, instead of falling back upon the very few and often unimportant elements which can be measured. The study of sources, which requires only extensive library facilities, wide knowledge, and a retentive memory, has been practiced on such a scale for fifty or sixty years that it has made scholars distrustful of the new. They are reluctant to admit that there are such things as altogether new irruptions in a literary tradition, revolutionary creations *ex abrupto* and, for all practical purposes, *ex nihilo*. Moreover there is a simultaneous, if mysterious, polygenesis of themes and of ideas.

4) The biographical or personal heresy has been slightly less harmful to criticism; yet it has misled scholars into relating the life of a writer with minute, often colorful details, while neglecting the only reason that made that life important: his works. Any

insignificant revelation in the life of Van Gogh, Rimbaud, or Shelley is deemed valuable by the scholar who hopes to rival in success the popular biographies by Ludwig and Maurois; Byron's love affairs are related in several thrilling chapters, but the estimate of his poems is dismissed in a few pages. The professor who lectures on Gauguin rejoices to tell of his sudden transformation from banker to Bohemian artist and then of his "romantic" adventures in Tahiti. But long after his death, a good criticism of Gauguin as a painter has still to be written. Sainte-Beuve, who was one of the chief sinners in overemphasizing the biography of writers at the expense of close study of their works, has had too many followers who are not equipped with his subtle gifts as an analyst of souls.

At the same time, the notion of evolution has been too lavishly carried into our studies. Scholars have become obsessed by chronology: they place every poem, every picture, at its precise day of composition in the life of the artist and discover in it a progress beyond the artist's previous achievements. Every biography thus ascends toward a climax and sadly follows the decline toward old age and death. Changes are all rationally explained. Evolution becomes a conscious process groping toward the final causes of riper fulfilment or more perfect art. Existence is symbolized by a harmonious curve. Chance is banished; so is common sense, which should teach us that writers often compose their works at a certain date because they are prompted to do so by some random demand, express at forty a mood which they experienced at thirty, or an idea which occurred to them at thirty-five and has remained buried in their minds ever since. The time has come to revolt against the excessive study of the origins and youth of artists inherited from the last century and against our slavish emphasis on time as measured by the succession of months and years. Many of the greatest men do not evolve after twenty-five or thirty: their inner life feeds on a latent wealth of emotions and thoughts accumulated during childhood and adolescence. They delve alternately into the depths of their ego or borrow from its more superficial layers, according to circumstances or their shifting moods, but not following an evolutionary and continuous pattern.

5) The invasion of scholarship by sociology has already been lamented in our preceding chapters. Great literature creates life more than it imitates it; Balzac thought he was depicting the French society in which he lived (1830 to 1850), while only under the Second Empire did France mold itself according to his prophetic vision. English women under Queen Elizabeth were no more like Desdemona or Cordelia than the average Russian is like Stavrogin or French peasants like those of Zola. Little is learned by studying novels and plays in order to write on the bourgeoisie, social problems, family traditions, feminist ideas, as reflected in literature. Even less has been revealed by ambitious studies of the conditions in which a work of art is brought out and a book manufactured: the history of printing or of book publishing can be at times a helpful handmaid to the history of literature, but the natural order should not be reversed. In the beginning was the word! Professors of literature attracted by sociological interpretations act as if the recent vogue for "social studies" had made them ashamed of their own calling; they try to justify literature, like the dealer in cigarettes or the grocer who presents his trade as a social service.

6) Several of us have expressed our anxieties at the manner in which "psychological criticism" has recently lured some of the most acute minds of our generation. At the source of so much mental energy expended on tenuous hairsplitting, there lurks, we fear, defeatism. Those psychologists and logicians refuse to treat literature as a set of qualitative values; they refuse to feel and to judge. They direct all their ingenuity to an attempt at dismantling the mechanism of literary works already accepted and labelled as great. They have not helped us appreciate recent poetry more lucidly or even revaluate the poetry of the past. What is worse, one looks in vain through the writings of subtle and "philosophical" minds, like I. A. Richards, William Empson, Kenneth Burke, and the younger men who have adopted their terminology, for *one* sensitive article of criticism. They are con-

tent with telling us how criticism should proceed and how a poem should be dissected. Their elaborate analyses retain very little in common with literature; they remain without effect on readers and on writers alike. Adolescents may be temporarily seduced by the seven types of ambiguity to be discerned in a sonnet by Shakespeare or by an explanation of the "Ode on a Grecian Urn" on the intellectual, emotional, and sexual planes which treats the poem as "a viaticum" that leads into the oracular equation of Beauty with Truth.[26] Once they have divested those exegetic attempts of their intimidating words, they wonder whether true philosophical interpretations of things of beauty require such paraphernalia and whether these English and American critics are not behaving in the presence of psychology and literature "as sailors and soldiers who had lately learned to think." [27]

7) But the deadliest sin of scholars, whether their scholarship be historical, philosophical, sociological, or symbolically logical, is their manner of writing. Their jargon for initiates betrays an ominous callousness to beautiful style, an inability to experience a work of art except through the help of external methods of dissection, and, graver still, a total lack of concern for communicating their impressions to their readers. Richard Blackmur, Georges Poulet, Lucien Goldmann cultivate barbaric and obscure inelegance. The detachment of scholars is admirable after a fashion. But it is also an abdication on their part. Howard Mumford Jones once called them "the uninfluentials." [28] While they play their "elaborate private game," the public continues to pay twenty times more attention to a half-educated book reviewer or an ob-

[26] See Kenneth Burke's article "Symbolic Action in a Poem by Keats," *Accent*, IV (Autumn 1943), 30–42. The ridiculous and scholastic vogue for rhetoric and figures of speech and for categories or "modes," which seems to revive the worst features of Greek and Latin grammarians, keeps many sophisticated students in America from feeling freshly and from thinking independently.

[27] The phrase, in which my text has substituted "to think" for "to read," is Emerson's in his chapter on English literature in *English Traits*.

[28] See the *Saturday Review of Literature*, November 11, 1941, and a previous article, *ibid.*, September 6, 1941, on "The Limits of Contemporary Criticism."

viously "inspired" advertisement than to the opinion of a professor. The academic world means the world of the dead for them. In the dust of their libraries and with the help of their scientific labelling, scholars continue to fulfill their function as it has been mockingly defined: "To read books that nobody had ever read, in order to write a book that nobody will ever read."

Can scholars do no better? I entertain such a lofty opinion of their potential ability that I think no group of men in any profession equals them in intelligence, discrimination, devotion, and integrity. They incarnate some of the virtues which the world of tomorrow will need most urgently for the salvation of the humanities: reverence for what was best and what is most alive in the traditions of the past; detachment from the political passions of the day and refusal to accept money or success as a criterion of value, insistence on critical spirit, not as the destroyer of faith, but as essential to the building up of a true and honest faith which supplements or transcends reason but does not blindly spurn it.

Colleges and universities are the precious nurseries in which a better humanity and a better world may be slowly evolved in the face of dire threats outside. Teachers and scholars of literature, that is to say students of the record of man's most intense and varied experience, are in a position to achieve much. They must display more courage as intellectual leaders of the youth, and not merely curators of the legacy of the past. We submit that their chief fault has been their humility.

They have allowed themselves to be awed by the quantitative methods of science: they have worshipped facts; they have accumulated data. Judgment or appreciation they have left to posterity, that is to say to men probably less well equipped but bolder than they.

They have stifled their personality when they should have intensified it. They could not but acknowledge that an intuition of Hazlitt on Shakespeare, of Lamb on Webster, of Pater on "Shakespeare's English Kings," of Eliot on Dryden, of Gide on

Baudelaire had penetrated more deeply into the secrets of genius than big volumes of well-established but irrelevant facts. But they have added with excessive modesty that only those demigods called critics could venture such free intuitions and that their disciples had first to learn how to refrain from having or expressing their personal reactions.[29]

They have behaved like the last Puritans of the modern world: they have been afraid of pleasure. Whenever literary works could be reduced to a certain intellectual content, they have been moderately successful in explaining ideas, structure, and objective correlatives. In the presence of a symphony, a painting, a poem, they have either balked or failed. Of too few of the scholars of our century would the words used by T. S. Eliot in praising the late W. P. Ker be justified:

He was a great scholar who was also a great humanist, who was always aware that the end of scholarship is understanding, and that the end of understanding poetry is enjoyment, and that this enjoyment is gusto disciplined by taste.[30]

They have been afraid of the present and even more afraid of adventure. It was so much easier to announce that none of the living writers were worth the scholar's attention! It was so much safer to explore Chaucer's French and Italian sources or to bow before immortal Shakespeare—the same Shakespeare who branded security as "mortal's chief enemy" (*Macbeth*, III, v, 32) and asked what pleasure we find in life "to lock it from action

[29] Robert Graves tells jokingly in his book on *Poetic Unreason* (London: Palmer, 1925), p. 48, how an Oxford don reprimanded an undergraduate for "temperamentalism" in these terms: "I understand from Professor Y. that your literary judgments are a trifle summary, that in fact you prefer some authors to others."

[30] T. S. Eliot, Ker Memorial Lecture at Glasgow, published in the *Partisan Review*, November–December 1942, p. 451. Elsewhere, in an essay written before he mellowed into a broad and undogmatic critic, T. S. Eliot asked his contemporaries "to return again and again to the critical writings of the seventeenth and eighteenth centuries, to remind ourselves of that simple truth that literature is primarily literature, a means of refined and intellectual pleasure" ("Experiment in Criticism," *Bookman* (New York), November 1929, p. 227).

and adventure" (*Cymbeline*, IV, iv, 3). But the scholar's past also
was adventure in its day; and we may not be able to enjoy it
truly in its boldness unless we occasionally take some risk with
the present. "The scholar who tells us that he understands Dryden but makes nothing of Hopkins or Yeats is telling us that he
does not understand Dryden," as Allen Tate once asserted. Many
years ago, Henry A. Beers, a Yale professor who was also a man
of letters, lamented the fact that American colleges were ceasing
to be centers of literary influence; he gently warned his colleagues of their responsibility. They play for safety, and lose
their influence on the youth.

It is much safer to praise an old book than a new. . . . The old book
has been duly labelled. Contemporary merit is uncertain as yet; authorities have not stamped it with their approval. A dull man gets a
certain advantage over a clever man, if he is able to compare him, to
his disadvantage, with some much cleverer man who is already dead.
. . . Some day his successors will be lecturing their classes on the
books now coming out, just as he is engaged in expounding and interpreting authors whom time has made classic. But scholarship has a
Philistinism of its own and is not always liberal in its recognition of
fresh talents.[31]

While scholars, in their self-effacing discreetness, refuse to entertain or to express an opinion on the literature of their day,
other men, less honest or less modest, and often far less competent than the scholar, move into the place left vacant. They are
the journalistic critics or the book reviewers. The best among
them are honorable; their criticism succeeds in being spontaneous
and apparently instantaneous, yet penetrating and discriminating;
they judge with courage, do not mince their words of censure,
use adjectives of praise without nauseating banality and have pre-
served some of the most valuable attributes of a true critic: common sense, wit, and a pungent style. Why do so few professors

[31] Henry A. Beers, "Literature and the Colleges," *Points at Issue* (New
York: Macmillan, 1904), pp. 44–45. The sentence by Allen Tate quoted
above is from *Reason in Madness* (New York: Putnam, 1941), p. 115. On
the faults of book-reviewing, see the Appendix.

try to rival them? Why should their book reviews usually be encumbered with pedantry, timidity, turgid style, involved circumlocutions which thinly disguise their reluctance to judge or their absence of judgment?

We lamented the slow death of the old literary essay, the small space granted literary articles in the monthly and quarterly magazines, the regrettable confusion of values which leads many serious minds to revere a best seller because success in all its forms commands respect and because it is undemocratic to scorn what the majority likes. But book reviewing can become an instrument of culture, as the longer essay was for our fathers. The very brevity of a book review has its advantages. Its effect upon living literature can be great. In other countries (in the *Times Literary Supplement,* in the *Observer* and the *New Statesman,* in *La Nacion, Il Corriere della Sera,* in several Swiss and Austrian papers) some of the most influential criticism appeared in daily or weekly newspapers. That criticism is comparatively independent of the political slant of the paper and of publicity. It is frequently written by professors, or by men with a literary education who seem to avoid the most sickening formulas of American reviewers. The new book is not invariably praised, but it is discussed, and it sells all the more for having aroused some controversy.[32] A critic's function is after all to arouse interest, debate, and life around a work.

If scholars are too busy to write for "popular" papers and reviews, there must be a most regrettable flaw in American education, since the men who could and should spread culture and mold opinion are prevented from doing so by too heavy teaching or administrative tasks. If they have no taste left for contempo-

[32] Mr. Ralph Thomson, in an article on "The Popular Review and the Scholarly Book," published in *The English Institute Annual, 1940* (New York: Columbia University Press, 1941), expressed his wish that professors attempt more book-reviewing, and quoted some of the formulas current in America in 1935 to praise books now already forgotten, "one of the greatest novels of our time," "a book for the ages," "a true American epic," "the most important novel since *Moby Dick*" (of *Of Time and the River*), "a book that no civilized man can afford to miss" (of Briffault's *Europa*).

rary works or no time or curiosity for them, let the boldest among them deplore it and teach their students to step in where scholars fear to tread. A little less creative writing and a little more book-reviewing might be taught in colleges: quick reaction, keen sensitiveness, gusto, and brilliance of style are not necessarily incompatible with the academic virtues of balanced judgment, fairness, and solidity. More students, hence more alumni and alumnae, would think by themselves if they had been taught in college to formulate their opinions, to analyze and organize their impressions after reading a new book, listening to a concert, a play, or a movie. The teacher should be the first to demonstrate by his own living example that the habit of analysis and meditation has not killed freshness of enjoyment and freedom of imagination in him. A fine American scholar, George Edward Woodberry, wrote some decades ago a sentence which should still serve as a motto to scholars of the present day: "The secret of appreciation is to share the passion for life that literature itself exemplifies." [33]

Such appreciation should be easy for a country in which "dynamism," vitality, and enthusiasm are not only revered words but qualities actually possessed by many. Traditions are respected in America, but without any hidebound fetishism. The past is studied with respect, but the future arouses fervent hopes of accomplishments higher than those of past ages. The faith in equalitarian democracy should not and does not conflict with the belief in leadership and pioneering enterprise. Material facilities are abundant and have been made generously available to all those who try to improve man's welfare. It is certainly important that millions should be spent on studying cancer and infantile paralysis, on improving nutrition and education, on building spacious museums and efficient libraries. It is gratifying to find that money is always forthcoming to anyone who undertakes a Chaucer bibliography or an index to Shakespeare's images. Eventually, however, American civilization of 1930 or 1970 may be judged by its

[33] G. E. Woodberry, *The Appreciation of Literature* (New York: Baker & Taylor, 1907, p. 26.

artists and its writers, by the younger brothers of Rembrandt, Beethoven, Keats, and Balzac now alive in a country of one hundred and ninety million inhabitants. The cultural level of the public may be measured by the amount of recognition they will have given to such geniuses and by their degree of affinity with them. Nothing may prove more disappointing to our successors than the low estate of our literary criticism, than the scant means of interpreting great contemporary works provided by the leading magazines and the scholarly journals of America in 1960 or 1965. An infinitesimal fraction of the sums we devote to medical, psychological, space, or educational research would be enough to found and maintain literary reviews in which honest criticism might be attempted. The benefit to American culture, to American prestige, and—the word is not too big—to mankind, would be immense.

An American scholar remarked recently that "Harvard meant a great deal to American literature one hundred years ago; now it means about as much as the New York subway." [34] It is clear that the most vigorous writing done in America today is no longer accomplished by graduates of Harvard, Yale, and Princeton; it is not even being done in the East, or by graduates of universities at all. It is equally clear that the best American colleges, with their expert and carefully selected faculties, more numerous and more remarkable than ever before, play a very small part in molding the critical opinion on contemporary letters, arts, and life. We submit that they could again become influential and serve their country, living literature, criticism, and even scholarship far better than they do; they would also enhance their own prestige and increase their effect on youth. Their knowledge of the past should be brought to bear on the understanding of the present and on the shaping of the future. Courage, decision, adventure, imaginative vision have often been the qualities of American leaders in the fields of industry, politics, education, architecture. Let scholars recapture those virtues, let critics display them

[34] Wilbur Schramm, quoted in *Literary Scholarship: Its Aims and Methods* (Chapel Hill: University of North Carolina Press, 1941), p. 211.

more boldly. A better space-age world is being depicted in rosy
hues by our current prophets: they envisage it as the golden age
of television, automobiles, bathtubs, refrigerators, and gadgets of
all kinds "plastically" produced by the miraculous chemistry of
tomorrow. But literature, painting, music are also entitled to a
place in that brave new world. Long hours of leisure are contemplated, which will have to be wrested from boredom; they should
be filled by more enjoyment of the culture of the past, by more
creative energy in the higher and more disinterested branches of
man's activity. Scholars have a duty to the public in what is called
by its detractors, and occasionally by its admirers, a "mass age,"
and that is to lead adventurously, not to resign themselves with
humility to seeing the present regularly by-pass them. Critics
have the duty of continuing to be the lifeblood of any vigorous
creation. Both scholars and critics might thus help the public to
fulfill its own duty, which is, not to ignore, discourage, and silence the creators who live among them, but to try and rise to
their level in a manner worthy of them. As Walt Whitman said,
"To have great poets there must be great audiences too." [35]

[35] Walt Whitman, "Ventures, on an Old Theme."

APPENDIX, BIBLIOGRAPHICAL NOTES,
AND INDEX

APPENDIX

What Is Wrong with American Book-Reviewing? [1]

"BEFORE we have an American literature, we must have an American criticism," James Russell Lowell once pronounced. A rich and original American renaissance in literature, however, was taking place even as Lowell, Emerson, Poe, Hawthorne, Thoreau, Melville, and others were writing. A hundred years later, American literature, of the two great literatures in English, had become the more rigorous and influential abroad. At the same time, foreign observers of America, and not a few Americans themselves, watched with wonder or dismay the stupendous growth of criticism in the United States. France alone among the European lands presented a similar sight; and contemporary American criticism ignored the recent French critical thinking about as complacently as the French remained unimpressed by our "new criticism," practical or theoretical. It was a miracle that in neither country did the plethora of disquisitions on the goal and meaning of literature, on a reborn and proud rhetoric, on how to dissect a novel or how to read a page of verse, succeed in drying up the energy of creators or in dampening their uncritical audacity. Since 1945 the British, always prone to some patronizing condescension when judging the labor of American professors and quick to deride the inelegant jargon of the specialists in literary dissection, have often deplored the fact that their former colony has become a beehive of ponderous critics, addicted to the un-English but earnest sport of juggling general ideas.

[1] This essay, complementing the developments which precede, was published in *Daedalus* (*Journal of the American Academy of Arts and Sciences*) in XC (1961), 128–144. It is reproduced here with the kind permission of the editors of *Daedalus*.

In the United States today we do indeed live in an age of criticism, at least in academic circles. The number of articles, pamphlets, and books published on Hemingway, Faulkner, Joyce, Yeats, Eliot, even on Proust, Rilke, Mann, and Beckett, is truly staggering. They are read mostly by other professors and by awestruck students. Attempts have been made, often with dubious results, to attach poets in residence and superannuated novelists to some colleges so as to foster "creative writing." Their Socratic function is to answer the questions aimed at them by young Platos titillated by the sacrosanct word "creativity." In truth, however, 95 per cent of our courses in American, English, or foreign literatures and in composition teach solely criticism. The mountain of so-called critical essays perpetrated within a decade by the five million students in American colleges, not to mention the high-school teenagers, would rise higher, if less majestically, than the Grand Tetons. Curiously enough, the authors of these essays turn after graduation to the pursuit of happiness on Wall Street, Madison Avenue, or Sunset Boulevard; they manufacture gadgets, bring forth a progeny, husband their funds in order to send their sons and daughters to colleges, where they will in turn write critical essays every two weeks: very few ever practice the art of evaluating the literature or the art of their times. Not many can be said to retain a critical attitude toward the books which they will occasionally open, toward the plays they will watch, or toward the half-veiled persuaders in their midst. If prosperous and encumbered with a wealth which they would rather not sacrifice to a rapacious income tax office, they occasionally assist universities in founding a review devoted to more criticism. The number of such scholarly journals has easily doubled in the last ten years with the founding of periodicals issuing from such universities as Texas, Wisconsin, Louisiana, Wayne State, Minnesota, Boston, Chicago. The quality of the essays published, while very unequal, is sometimes high. The difficulty lies in the dearth of readers. Since doctors and analysts have not yet taken to prescribing the reading of scholarly criticism to restore sleep to insomnia-ridden patients or to untie oedipal knots, most serious magazines in America vie with one another for the shrinking time of normal readers. Our reading public has not grown in proportion to the increasing literate population of this country. We may legitimately take pride in our paperback era, which has placed all the classics (and more and more of the books published up to five years ago) within the reach of millions. Not only reprints of "safe" volumes but also originals have been enterprisingly published in this form and have attracted or created their audience.

Nevertheless, it is true that many new works of genuine significance remain unnoticed or hardly read. This country has a population approximately three times greater than any of the four most advanced countries in Western Europe, and a much larger proportion of that population is "exposed" to a college education. Yet important new books, even those of political or sociological import, certainly many volumes of fiction, drama, poetry, and speculative or critical thought, seldom find more than four or five thousand purchasers; the corresponding figure would be higher in Britain, France, or West Germany, each with less than a third of our population. It is too easy to brand the cinema or television as the culprits—they are to be found elsewhere. It is even more fallacious to imagine the average Englishman or Frenchman as innately more endowed with fastidious taste than is the American. The novels encountered in many middle-class homes or in lending libraries in Britain seem far from edifying to the literary critic, and the success of Françoise Sagan and of similar "prodigies" in France testifies to the gregariousness of the French or to their uncritical response to publicity, rather than to their taste. Something is deeply wrong, not so much with the American reading public itself as with its guides and mentors.

"The critic" (in the singular) is but an abstract entity, and the multifarious functions of criticism can only be fulfilled by several divergent minds. Unanimity in any acclaim for a book (whether or not by a Nobel Prize winner), a play, a concert performer, or an artist, even if he has become as venerable as Picasso or Chagall, should arouse suspicion. It can only be a sign of conventionality, of intellectual laziness, or timidity. The worst that can happen to any department of literature is to have achieved such a unity of methods and views among its members that dissent no longer stimulates the students, and their critical sense becomes dulled by dogma.

Some critics are at their best when evolving a theory of literature in general, debating standards or a system of esthetics, attempting to link specific works with a broad genre, or a national tradition, or a philosophical approach. They seldom review books other than those also offering a theory of criticism. The novels that appear (perhaps of an ephemeral interest) do not seem worth their while; in any case, general theories seldom provide criteria with which to evaluate new works. One hardly expects a profound philosophical mind like that of Heidegger, Blanchot, or Poulet, Kenneth Burke or Northrop Frye or William Wimsatt to condescend to reviewing new novels or to entice uninitiated readers into the deceptive arcana of current production. All except the unhappy few who do not pursue pleasure in literature stand in awe of them. Their influence, which will be lasting and deep, acts chiefly through the universities.

Other critics set themselves the task of reappraising the works of the past, which yield a new meaning every twelve or fifteen years to each new generation. They are unusually perspicacious readers; they bring to their reading the enrichment afforded by their knowledge of the historical background, of minor writers, of sources and influences. They project into the past, in order to arouse it to life, the concerns of their own age, their romantic anguish, their Freudian or Jungian psychology, their obsessions with symbols, their Marxist or existentialist doctrines. The very trend of their loaded questions brings forth answers with which their predecessors, probably less complex, had not been rewarded. Many of these critics are college professors who, when lecturing on Sophocles or Racine or Wordsworth to demanding audiences of young students, have to discover new layers of meaning in these classics. They are so accustomed to dealing with the three or four score of great authors who have survived the shipwreck of time that they cannot be expected to evince much patience with the untried works of their own age. A forgivable professional idiosyncrasy often leads those critics to use the remarks of other critics as a springboard so as to convince those peers or rivals of their mistakes or limitations, and to utilize that springboard to plunge into the mysteries of the work under discussion, or to soar more boldly. They revel in judging anew what has already been judged many times. Thus, *Oedipus Rex*, a few lines of Virgil or of Dante, the same scene in *Hamlet* or *Phèdre*, the same "anniversary" by Donne or the same "ode" by Wordsworth or poem by Yeats or quartet by Eliot are endlessly tortured by those critics. They resemble actors and singers who must be tested by their interpretations of the celebrated monologues or arias which brought fame to their predecessors. Book-reviewing for these eternal reappraisers of the past or those sedulous high priests of the classics can but be a secondary and perfunctory occupation.

Unlike these two groups of writers on literature, the theoreticians and the reappraisers of the classics, who have world enough and time, and who publish their leisurely essays when and as they wish (their main source of income is usually derived from some other profession), book reviewers are pursued by deadlines. They are not free to expand their judgments or to expound theories apropos of the new book, treated as a text or as a pretext. Space is limited to so many words; quotations are frowned on; obscure or overly literary language is taken to be a pedantic effort to puzzle the average reader, who in this country is not credited with much epicurean delight in words. The number of new books accumulating on the desk of the reviewer, sometimes sent to him directly by the author himself with a hyperbolic dedication, is staggering. Even if he is conscientious enough to read them through and not just to skip, he seldom enjoys the chance to reread and either confirm or contradict his first impression. One of the crucial questions which conscientious critics must keep asking themselves is thus forbidden the reviewer: "Does the charm of this new book, its power over me, wear out? Or do I

perceive new complexities, a hidden depth, which had first passed
unnoticed? Was its interest due to timeliness or to circumstances
which will fail to touch my successors or my children? Has the
virtue I discerned in this volume been felt equally by other readers, and is it likely to fire still others in diverse lands, or is it devoid of any widespread or universal appeal?"

Criticism, and the criticism of contemporary literature in particular, can hardly ever hope to scale impressive heights. Music
critics are the most maligned (by composers), and perhaps they
deserve it. Art critics are hardly more assured of survival, at least
if they have devoted themselves solely to apportioning praise and
blame to their contemporaries. Joshua Reynolds, Roger Fry,
Lionello Venturi, André Malraux, Henri Focillon, or Erwin
Panofsky survive by the vast portion of their work that is devoted to the past or to theoretical writing. Sainte-Beuve's *Port-
Royal* is a lasting and admirably scholarly monument of erudition
and psychological insight, but it looks back two hundred years.
The truly great critics are the creators: Goethe at times, Balzac
on *La Chartreuse de Parme,* Hugo on Balzac, Baudelaire on Wagner and on *Madame Bovary,* Mallarmé, and Thomas Mann. But
we admire them for portraying themselves, even if involuntarily,
rather than their models. Moreover, these novelists and poets
were never subjected to the drudgery of having to assess the current production and of commenting on writers for whom they
entertained scant esteem.

In America imaginative writers have seldom been inclined to
state their views on literary technique (Henry James excepted)
or to judge the work of their contemporaries. John Dos Passos or
Thornton Wilder could have done it superbly, but have chosen
otherwise. T. S. Eliot renovated our stock of critical ideas in the
Twenties and occasionally proved acutely perceptive on books of
that decade; he erred signally at other times and prudently with-
drew some prefaces or articles from his reprinted works.

It is a great misfortune that there are all too few nonacademic
critics of the first order in the United States. Our important

monthlies, for all their excellence in commenting on politics at home and abroad, fail or do not care to succeed in giving their readers an adequate view of what happens in the world of books, even less so in the world of art and music. (Records alone, tersely described, detain their attention.) Their comments on current books amount to little more than enumerations and shallow opinions which cannot tempt many readers. Equally regrettable is the small space granted to the criticism of books in the *New Yorker,* which could have wielded an incalculable influence as the guide of sophisticated taste in America: space for such criticism is niggardly allowed at the very end of each number, while it is allotted over-generously to long profiles squeezed between two columns of advertising. *The New Republic* and *The Nation* have had their vicissitudes in the last three of four decades. At different phases, however, they have provided the very best, the most discriminating and the most prophetic view of literature in America. *Commentary* and the *Partisan Review* (although it has not fulfilled its promises of becoming the broad, lively, and well-written review of America) have grouped outstanding critical talent; still, their influence on literary opinion at large is limited, and at present probably shrinking. The United States is perhaps too vast a country for any one critic to become an oracle or a trusted counselor. If any two men in our mid-century were qualified to play that role, they would be Edmund Wilson and Alfred Kazin. The collections of reviews by the former, even more perhaps than his books on *Axel's Castle,* on the historians who preceded and prepared Lenin's arrival at "the Finland Station," and on Turgenev, have stood the test of time. Alfred Kazin's *Contemporaries* (1962) contains in my opinion the fairest, shrewdest, and wisest criticism of a decade. A note of plaintive severity creeps into some of the articles, many of which appeared in *The Reporter,* the remonstrating tone may irk those readers who would prefer to be amused. But the critic has read widely and not in English alone, has felt intensely, has reflected, and he has had the courage to choose between the good and the bad, between the good and the less good, and to state his reasons for his opinions. The last essays in that volume, *The Critic's Task*, are in every way worthy of the very best British critics of our age.

It is unfortunate that criticism of such high quality, well-written, urbane, and thoughtful at the same time, should reach relatively few readers and wield small influence on the general public. Few of our weeklies (*Time* magazine or *Newsweek*, for all their merits, do not attempt much literary criticism) reach more than a few thousand persons. Our monthlies are lucky when, by dint of active publicity, they print a few tens of thousands. Yet over a million young people every year enter our colleges and universities. They take courses in English, often in a foreign language, and presumably are inspired with a little zest for reading and some desire to understand the world around them; and literature is probably the best means at our disposal to understand other people and ourselves. I would even contend that many a divorce and many an estrangement in young married couples caused by naïvety, clumsiness, and lack of imagination and of thoughtfulness in the American male might be avoided if young people had gained a little more vicarious experience of life, a little more appreciation of sentiment, a better preparation to face the discords of wedlock, through the reading of novels and plays. The yearly crop of half a million university graduates should provide a sizable public for the reading of books; once these students had learned to want to read books of some merit. A statistical inquiry (if a truthful one could be made) would show, we fear, that the graduates who read one book a month are a sad minority. Someone is at fault if our leisure, which is increasing for all but the managerial groups in our society, is not utilized more profitably.

Mass media have been blamed; but these are not the contrivances of diabolical obscurantists, intent on obliterating all power of attention in us so as to convert us into ready purchasers of a soap, a brush, a watch, or a cosmetic. The guilty ones are those who form the passive elements in the audience. In other countries the radio has become a vehicle of book-reviewing as effective as the press and at just as high a level. The typically American habit, now adopted by the British, of having all the reviews of a new book appear the same week in all the weeklies, and on the same day in the dailies, probably constitutes a handicap to the diffusion of that book. Massive publicity that quotes excerpts from the reviewers sells a novel by Bellow or by Ellison or Irwin Shaw; but it quickly passes on to another new book, and the previous one sinks into semi-oblivion. The readers who buy a novel as soon as it appears are not many. Staggered reviews, followed by more elaborate ones in the monthlies and the quarterlies, would probably serve the authors better. Among the purchasers of books, even more than among purchasers of automobiles or of shelters, there is a resistance to the pressure of publicity which our persuaders would do well to take into account. The present writer has heard far more buyers of *For Whom the Bell Tolls, East of Eden,* and lately *A Ship of Fools* protest angrily against the claims put forward by publicity and by reviewers, claims which these readers failed to find worth their money and their time; they swore they would not be taken in a second time.

The lament most often heard in university circles in America is that we do not have in this country a *Times Literary Supplement* and that *The New York Times* weekly book section fails to come up to the famed British weekly. In truth, the comparison is not a fair one. The *T. L. S.* reaches some fifty thousand readers, a sizable fraction of them outside Britain, in particular among American college professors. *The New York Times* addresses itself to twenty-five times that number of purchasers. The *T. L. S.,* like *Le Monde* in France and corresponding highbrow papers in Zurich or Milan, is published in a country where the interest in literature is lively and widespread. Readers of such newspapers are on the whole informed and curious about the new books and plays discussed at dinner parties or in cafés. They have received substantially the same kind of education, done the same required reading in philosophy, history, and literature for the matriculation, the French baccalaureate, or the corresponding and equally standardized examinations in Germany or Italy.

For varied reasons, things are managed otherwise in this country, much vaster and more diverse geographically, less standardized and far more anarchistic, or stubbornly individualistic, in its education. Criticism of literature or art, reviews of books on music or the philosophy of history, appeal less to the American than to the European. The average American is convinced that his ilk is not interested in books published in a foreign tongue; the French press shares that conviction. But British weeklies readily review volumes in French, German, or even Russian, and are not afraid of quoting French in the text. American periodicals, except for scholarly journals, review foreign books only when they are published here in translation.

Even so, the record of book-reviewing in *Le Monde, Le Figaro, or L'Express* is not exemplary. A great many errors of judgment have been committed by the critics of *Le Monde* when it was called *Le Temps* (by Paul Souday, André Thérive, and much earlier by Anatole France) and by its recent reviewers. The tone of the criticism is academic, often sanctimonious. New novels are relatively neglected (new poetry even more so) under the pretext that they accumulate too fast. Preference goes to works dealing with ideas or with past literature re-examined. In most French periodicals, the reviewer is regularly the same man, entrusted with the weekly article on books, and thus well established in his fortress, but also able to compare one work to another and to propose ranks or to discriminate.

Finally, the *mores* of literary life differ. For better or worse, continental critics, and some British in the livelier periodicals like *The New Statesman* or *Encounter*, often enjoy being sarcastic, ferocious, sometimes vicious and patently unfair. The *homo americanus* is probably the most goodnatured, the least cantankerous, of the human race. If a critic of contemporary books, he is wary of hurting authors, or perhaps he is not sure enough of himself to heap derisive obloquy on a new work. After all, many critics in the past who dealt thus with art and literature have since been proved ludicrously wrong.

The Times Literary Supplement is in many ways an admirable weekly of literary information and thoughtful criticism. It is pleasantly written, varied, lively; it covers books appearing in several languages and in several countries; it touches on art, the history of music, biography, philosophy, religion, travel, sports. Still, it is not above reproach. The scattering of interests is often excessive, the titles of many articles are not only too far-fetched and smart but also deceptive. Many of the editorial comments on the middle page are platitudinous and inconsequential. A note of complacency or superciliousness has often marred articles dealing with American scholarly works (literary, sociological, historical). Its reviews of new novels, often grouped at random under one heading, are frequently hasty and amateurish. It has committed serious errors in failing to hail as significant many of the books published in the Twenties or Thirties (by Joyce, Lawrence, Pound, Eliot) which are now esteemed as classics. A picture of British fiction or drama drawn since 1920 from the articles in *T. L. S.* with a thirty-year retrospect would make us laugh today, as would a similar picture of American literature from *The New York Times* or of French literature from *Le Temps* or *La Revue de Paris.* In any case, it is unlikely that we could have a *T. L. S.* in America, even if some foundation financed the undertaking, without its falling into the hands of academic critics.

The regret most often voiced by observers of literary life in America is that the weeklies supposedly devoted to literature have progressively moved away from the promises of their titles and have granted more and more space to advertising, to brief articles on phonograph records, schools, politics, and other sundry topics. That is notoriously the case with the *Saturday Review.* Many American intellectuals frown on it as a magazine of popularization for the culture vultures of the female sex, to be placed conspicuously in the sitting room next to TV magazines and the latest from the Book of the Month Club. It is far from perfect, to be sure, but many of its reviews are discriminating and inform readers honestly and wisely on the content of a book. That is more than one can say for a number of reviews in certain European periodicals for the literary elite, in which the critic hardly pays any attention to the new volume under review, which he considers a mere springboard for expressing his own ideas. He is fond of admonishing the unfortunate author on how he should have written his book to please the reviewer. "Do not speak while I interrupt you" is not too unfair a caricature of the conversation of an average Latin when he wields a critic's pen. The most serious flaw in the *Saturday Review* is the lack of a clear editorial policy, the dearth of substantial articles by the editorial board that evaluate books according to firm critical standards. The American editor is wary of playing the role which many Europeans expect so-called intellectuals to fulfill—that of doing the thinking of the lay reader for him.

The flaws of *The New York Times* are just as glaring. While it too is heterogeneous, concentrating daily on one book and therefore excluding comparative evaluations of other novels or biographies of the same category, the articles by Orville Prescott, Charles Poore, and others are often (in my own opinion) comparable to the most trenchant reviews of current productions in European periodicals of wide circulation in London, Manchester, or Paris. But those reviews are tucked away on a page which only the determined reader eventually reaches, after leafing through plentiful news on local and foreign politics, sport contests, transcripts of statesmen's speeches, and much else. "All the news that's fit to print" also means a surfeit of news, which passes on to the reader the burden of discriminating, selecting, assimilating. Courses on how to read a newspaper should be offered in every American school.

The Sunday book section has rich possibilities; it does not often fulfill them, in the opinion of the literary reader or of many authors who are irked that their books are not noticed, while others which they deem inferior (and which perhaps are) receive attention. One should bear in mind that such a Sunday supplement is not destined primarily for the highbrow; it seldom pioneers into avant-garde territory, which will perhaps be the regular fare of readers twenty years from now. It aims at informing the general reader who comes to that section after having sated his appetite for news with some two hundred pages of diverse reading matter, or having pondered over the stock market or the descriptions of the previous Saturday weddings. It is to be lamented (perhaps some day that plague of the none-too-well-hidden persuaders may be averted from us) that the advertising of books which hardly belong to literature and which promise a well-adjusted sex life or peace of mind through subscription to a book club or the contemplation of Goya, Van Gogh, or Picasso should be granted so much space, while book reviews often have to be emasculated to retain their cramped box. It is equally deplorable that the reviews are short, lacking in continuity and unity of point of view, and that there are far too few articles of general interest (like the excellent long articles in the Sunday magazine section on a political, economic, or demographic subject), and that few discussions of the biographies, the essays or poems of a whole season ever appear.

The general editor's proverbial iron hand in a velvet glove is probably deficient in iron. The choice of books to be reviewed impresses one as arbitrary; shorter notices, which might fill the gap when certain books of value cannot receive a full review, would be a felicitous alternative. The style of a motley company of reviewers (many not native Americans) is edited so as to become drearily uniform; rare words, which might humiliate the casual reader who has no Latin and whose vocabulary has shrunken since college are driven out; flamboyance in style seems to be dreaded by those who reign in editorial offices. Finally, many of the reviews are too lenient or else noncommittal. The reviewer is reluctant to say outright that a book is bad or mediocre, either from fear of a publisher who is also an advertiser or from excessive kindness. "A book's a book, although there's nothing in it," Byron once mocked. Some American reviewers seem to have adopted that motto.

It may be that in time the pressure of readers and the constructive criticism of professors or recent graduates who earnestly wish advice on what to read and on who are the worthwhile writers of their time, will remedy some of the deficiencies of *The New York Times* or other Sunday book reviews. Meanwhile, it would be unfair to forget that many excellent ones have appeared in those columns, reviews that are easily comparable to those in the best foreign periodicals; and that not a few readers have been drawn to difficult recent works by those weekly sheets, far more so relatively than by the reviews in *Harper's* or the *Atlantic* or *Time* magazine. In my opinion, the only constructive solution does not lie in launching a new weekly made up only of reviews of volumes of a literary, historical, philosophical, or artistic character. Such a publication simply would not attract enough subscribers to be effective. Too few people today, even in Europe, are interested in literature as such, excluding political, social, even scientific topics and excluding current events. America is too vast, the readers' interests are too conflicting, the reluctance to sever literature from life, even from politics and sociology, is too ingrained for any such weekly journal of pure criticism to succeed.

Diversity should remain an essential feature of current criticism in America. No academy will ever claim to dictate to public taste, as has been attempted with indifferent success in Paris or Leningrad. New magazines must continue to crop up and to vituperate against the more staid and venerable ones. Their reviewers may be university dons, but they may also be men and women who care deeply for literature, who write with vigor and warmth; they need not have learned their trade in college courses in criticism or have been impregnated by the *Criterion* or the *Kenyon Review*. The less academic they are, the better. Only by improving the book-reviewing in *The Nation, The New Republic, Commonweal, The Reporter,* and in other weeklies where criticism is already quite good, and by persuading the monthlies that their own criticism should and could be better, and by inciting the public, hence the editors, to ask for better literary, art, and music criticism can it be hoped that American discrimination in those matters will greatly improve. A good beginning might be a gathering, under the sponsorship of some foundation, of some eighty publishers, editors, and literary critics of America, comparable to a similar international gathering in Europe in 1962 that proved a source of fruitful reflection to many. The American Academy of Arts and Sciences would serve the cause of American culture if it could procure the funds and the leadership for a three-day convention, from which a clearer awareness of what is right and wrong with our book-reviewing might emerge.

The eventual gains would accrue to the public, which desperately wants to be guided through the labyrinth of publications, for it has been led to eye with suspicion both advertisements and the banal uncommitted reviews. The gains would also benefit the authors themselves. In no other great country today do the makers of literature work in such isolation; in no country are they so averse to the affluent society which surrounds and supports them. Even the vituperations of Flaubert, the Goncourts, or Zola against the bourgeoisie and the Philistines fail to equal the wrath against business pursuits, big money, movie magnates, "decent" family life, or well-meaning average women which has envenomed almost all American novels and plays from Dreiser, Lewis, and O'Neill down to Mailer, Styron, Updike, and our young authors, who are less angry than suffering. This almost unanimous hostility on the part of imaginative writers—and lately of the social critics of our organization men, our suburbanites, and the new villains of our age, the Madison Avenue "brainwashers"—is a grave flaw in our culture. Through college courses and paperbacks, it is permeating the young with pessimism or with cynicism. It would take no more than a serious recession to turn their disaffection into a mire like that into which some of their predecessors sank during the Thirties. Yet American writers are better rewarded in terms of royalties, lecturing opportunities, and movie rights than any others in the world. Money has never been enough or even primarily what they wanted. They lack circles of critics and fervent devotees of literature who would criticize them intelligently, help them see their creations with some detachment, discriminate between their good work and their failures, interpret them to themselves and to the audience of the young for which all artists yearn.

Do these potential intermediaries between the writers and their work, between the writers and their natural allies who could break the isolation to which they feel doomed, exist anywhere in the United States? The answer is emphatically a positive one. They exist in the colleges and universities, which wield today as much if not more power in this country than the academies and *cénacles* did once in older lands, or than the Catholic Church enjoyed in medieval times in its tax-exempt domains and its monasteries with their enormous spiritual influence. Professors of literature and "American studies" have some leisure; they are decently rewarded, and as humanists, they are fortunate in that they want chiefly to be left alone; hence they need fewer funds than do their colleagues in the sciences or the social sciences, whose research now tends to be oriented by their sources of support. They are asked to lecture to culture addicts of all ages and of either sex. They have in the classroom a captive audience whom they can attempt to indoctrinate, and into whom they should instill an eagerness to read and to think long after twenty-one or twenty-five.

Academic critics, however, appear to shy away from any book-reviewing which is not destined for their scholarly journals and which therefore does not deal with other works of scholarship. Occasionally some of them will venture to appraise recent poetry, even more seldom recent fiction, in the *Sewanee Review,* the *Kenyon Review,* the *Virginia Quarterly Review,* or the *Yale Review.* But their articles on current imaginative literature are tucked away in some obscure columns so as not to obtrude into the really substantial part of the periodical devoted to more serious pursuits. Future authors of dissertations will one day stand aghast at the distorted view of American literature at its liveliest (1919–1939) which will emerge from the criticism in our quarterlies during those two decades.

Most professors of literature—at the very time when they are multiplying articles to show condescendingly how Milton, Keats, Browning, Hardy, Melville, or Hawthorne were unacknowledged or misunderstood by their contemporaries—refuse to discriminate from among the productions of today and to mold the public taste. Their timidity stems from their clinging to the literary standards evolved from their studies of the past. Even more than lawyers, they cherish precedents. Their notions of beauty, greatness, profundity, structure (none of which is susceptible of an easy definition) were attained by the dissection of the few novels, plays, and poems of earlier ages which have been decreed as classics. Yet new works, also some day to rank among the classics—that is, volumes studied in the classroom (as those of e. e. cummings, Wallace Stevens, Tennessee Williams, Nathanael West, Saul Bellow, even perhaps Jack Kerouac and J. D. Salinger are studied today)—are original only if they differ from the works bequeathed by the past. Their authors translate their own vision of life in a language that is fresh; and they should be appraised, not in terms of their conformity with antecedent masterpieces, but on their own terms.

It is up to the reviewer to enter into their universe and to judge the revolutionary author according to his own laws. It is no paradox to submit that the academic reviewer should forget his familiarity with the past when confronted by new works; in all fairness he should never crush the new novel, the new painting, the new music, by comparison with three or more centuries of fiction, art, and music in several lands. His task is that of a discoverer. His attitude should be one of open-mindedness and freshness. Naturally, nine-tenths or more of what is modern today is doomed to oblivion, as has always been the case; but which nine-tenths? The reviewer may be emboldened to say, even if he is later proved wrong. Audacity is part of a critic's armory.

Recently the most eager among the young critics of America evolved a set of concepts and criteria which they imparted to their students only to find the latter applying them dogmatically and mechanically. These bellicose "new" critics easily cowed into acquiescence many of their overawed enemies among the old fogies on the faculty, but they did not preserve themselves from their well-meaning friends and students. Unwittingly, the latter have caricatured them. They learn in college what the criteria of tragedy are according to Aristotle—which is about as reasonable as appealing to Euclid or to Hippocrates in judging the geometry or the medicine of today. They then decide who among the moderns is tragic (no term of praise has become more prestigious in our age of anxiety) and who is not. They pull out of their schoolboy's satchels a few rulers, imposingly termed irony, ambiguity, and paradox, and they promptly measure recent poems and novels with their inflexible and humorless instruments. They worship order, which is decreed to be organic structure. No metaphor has proved more misleading than that which likens a literary work to an organism with no superfluities, no waste, no discordance.

In truth, however, waste abounds in any human body, and even more in any spirit. Contradictions with oneself, as some psychologists assert, are the very mark of the civilized person. At the source of a work of art there often lie passion, disorder, chaos. The artist creates in order to find, or to force, some order into that chaos and to reach some clearer insight into his darkness. Nevertheless, that striving for order is seldom totally successful; and the best in many a writer is not his attempt to turn into a literary engineer and build up a structured but cold and mechanical masterpiece for the critic to take to pieces at his heart's content; it lies in the lived experience of chaos, in the passionate formlessness which impelled him to create and seek a form. Formlessness (notwithstanding our subtlety, which insists on reducing it to a hidden structure perceptible only to the new critic) is the virtue of most great novels of the last two centuries, as well as of the second part of *Faust*, or *A Season in Hell*, or Claudel's poetry and Proust's fiction, in fact, almost all the modern American works which have any vitality. In the pregnant lines of Wordsworth's *Prelude* (I, 341–43), dear to some of our humanists who are overly jealous of their engineering colleagues, the adjectives "dark" and "inscrutable" are the key words, often forgotten:

> . . . There is a dark
> Inscrutable workmanship that reconciles
> Discordant elements, makes them cling together
> In one society.

Our new critics have concentrated on analyzing the works of the past, through what a young British author (who has little liking for them) has branded as "a form of necrophily." [2] They have, he says, "transferred their own dullness to something that was originally exciting." Their favorite sport of hunting out metaphors and symbols has naturally led them to prefer fiction. In the latter some vulgarity often must prevail, and this is synonymous with vitality; squeamish critics would reduce it to genteel old maidishness or ascribe it to profound intentions. Yet Balzac, Dickens, Whitman himself, Dostoevski, Zola, H. G. Wells, and most American novelists of the present age have shown not a little vulgarity. Many of them were in part hacks, writing fast to appease creditors and leaving a good deal to chance. The critic would be well advised to accept them, as well as their successors who at first appear to them as vulgar (as Céline, D. H. Lawrence, Henry Miller, Norman Mailer), as they are. Only thus might he hope to exercise some influence on them if he began by accepting the impulse toward adventurousness and passionate self-assertion which caused them to create. The critic's function is certainly not to praise indiscriminately. Few artists value such praise. Their egotism is less inflated than we might believe. They are grateful for honest dissent and for discerning appraisals of their achievement which point to flaws and denounce failures. After all, the role of a critic is not to bury a new work or to praise it, but to arouse discussion about it, to enhance our enjoyment of literature, and to impart pleasure to others. T. S. Eliot himself—the oracle of many of our analysts of literary structure and of our

[2] Anthony Cronin, "A Massacre of Authors," *Encounter*, VI, no. 19 (April 1956), 25–32.

ingenious critics who add their own subtlety to that of a poet in order the better to marvel at it—did not balk at using the noble word "enjoyment." In *The Sacred Wood,* he rightly defined the aim of literary study as that of helping us return to the work "with informed perception and intensified, because more conscious, enjoyment." We need critics and reviewers who will not fear to be adventurous, to enlighten the public, to formulate judgments of value, and to write with zest and style. They will easily be found if we bridge the artificial gulf between the academics and the nonacademics in America.

Bibliographical Notes

A VOLUME like the present one, which draws illustrations from several literatures over several centuries of their evolution and occasionally from the arts and music, rests on a good deal of varied research and obviously owes much to previous works of literary history and art criticism. It would be an idle display of pedantry to list all the books on Greek, English, American, French criticism which have been consulted and utilized in some degree. Volumes and articles which were found especially helpful in preparing Part One have been regularly mentioned in the text or in the footnotes (e.g., on the criticism of Shakespeare, Wordsworth, Shelley, Meredith, Hawthorne, Whitman, Stendhal, Hugo, Baudelaire). References to them will be found in the Index under the writers whom they concern. French works are published in Paris unless otherwise noted.

General works on the HISTORY OF CRITICISM in England, France, and occasionally in other countries have naturally been consulted. On criticism among the ancients, the two most convenient volumes in English are those of J. D. Denniston (1924) and W. Rhys Roberts (1928). More recent and important works are those of J. W. H. Atkins, *Literary Criticism in Antiquity* (Cambridge and London: Cambridge University Press, 1934) (Vol. I, Greek; Vol. II, Graeco-Roman), William Wimsatt and Cleanth Brooks, *Literary Criticism: A Short History* (New York: Knopf, 1957), and René Wellek's monumental *History of Modern Criticism* (5 vols.; New Haven: Yale University Press, 1955–1968). On AMERICAN CRITICISM or on the place of American criticism in American literature, the more important works are:

Auden, W. H., Norman Foerster, John Crowe Ransom, Donald H. Stauffer, and Edmund Wilson. *The Intent of the Critic.* Princeton: Princeton University Press, 1941.

Babbitt, Brownell, Eliot, Spingarn, and others. *Criticism in America: Its Function and Status.* New York: Harcourt Brace, 1924.

Foerster, Norman. *American Criticism: A Study in Literary Theory from Poe to the Present.* Boston: Houghton Mifflin, 1928.

Kazin, Alfred. *On Native Grounds.* New York: Reynal and Hitchcock, 1942.

Wilson, Edmund. *The Shock of Recognition.* New York: Doubleday Doran, 1943.

Zabel, Morton D. *Literary Opinion in America.* New York: Harper, 1937. (An anthology of fifty critical essays.)

On the GENERAL PROBLEMS treated in Part Two, the most valuable works have been found to be:

Baldensperger, Fernand. *La Littérature: Création, succès, durée.* Flammarion, 1913.

Hazlitt, Henry. *The Anatomy of Criticism: A Trialogue.* New York: Simon and Schuster, 1933.

On the judgment of MUSICAL CRITICS on composers who were their contemporaries, interesting views have been expressed by:

Mueller, John H., and Kate Hevner. *Trends in Musical Taste.* Bloomington: Indiana University Publications, 1942.

Newman, Ernest. *A Musical Critic's Holiday.* New York: Knopf, 1923.

Rolland, Romain. *Musiciens d'aujourd'hui.* Hachette, 1908.

——. *Voyage musical aux pays du passé.* Édouard-Joseph, 1919.

Stravinsky, Igor. *Poétique musicale.* Cambridge: Harvard University Press, 1942.

On the question of OBSCURITY AND OBSCURISM IN LITERATURE, treated in Chapter V, a few essential bibliographical references may be listed here:

Brooks, Cleanth. "What Does Modern Poetry Communicate?" *American Prefaces,* I (Autumn 1940), 18–27.

Daiches, David. *The Place of Meaning in Poetry.* Edinburgh: Oliver & Boyd, 1935.

Eastman, Max. *The Literary Mind: Its Place in an Age of Science.* New York: Scribner, 1931.

Eliot, T. S. Preface to *Anabasis,* a poem by St. John Perse, translated into English. New York: Harcourt, Brace, 1938.

Falls, Cyril. *The Critic's Armoury.* London: Cobden Sanderson, 1924.

Graves, Robert. *Another Future of Poetry.* (Hogarth Essays, XVIII.) London: Leonard and Virginia Woolf Press, 1926.

—— and Laura Riding. *A Survey of Modernist Poetry.* London: Heinemann, 1927.

Lewis, Cecil Day. *A Hope for Poetry.* Oxford: Blackwell, 1936.

MacNeice, Louis. *Modern Poetry: A Personal Essay.* London: Oxford University Press, 1938.

Mornet, Daniel. *Histoire de la clarté française.* Payot, 1929.

Muhlfeld, Lucien, "Sur la clarté," *Revue Blanche,* II (1896), 73–82.

Peyre, Henri. "Obscurity in Recent French Poetry," *Romanic Review,* XX, no. 2 (April–June 1929), 131–136.

Picard, Roger. "Obscurisme et clarté dans la littérature française," *French Review,* December 1942, pp. 107–114.

Proust, Marcel. "Contre l'obscurité," *Revue Blanche,* II (1896), 69–72. Reprinted in *Chroniques* (Gallimard, 1927), pp. 137–144.

Read, Herbert. "Obscurity in Poetry," *In Defence of Shelley and Other Essays* (London: Heinemann, 1936), pp. 145–163.

Sitwell, Edith. *Poetry and Criticism.* (Hogarth Essays, XI.) London: Leonard and Virginia Woolf Press, 1925.

Sparrow, John. *Sense and Poetry: Essays on the Place of Meaning in Contemporary Verse.* New Haven: Yale University Press, and London: Constable, 1934.

Thibaudet, Albert. *La Poésie de Stéphane Mallarmé.* New ed.; Gallimard, 1926.

——. "Le Fantôme de l'obscurisme," *Les Nouvelles Littéraires,* February 4, 1928.

Valéry, Paul. "Lettre sur Mallarmé," *Variété II* (Gallimard, 1930), 211–235.

——. "Remerciement à l'Académie Française" (June 23, 1927), *Oeuvres complètes,* V (Gallimard, 1935), 9–45.

——. "Je disais quelquefois à Mallarmé," "Questions de poésie," "Commentaires de charmes," *Variété III* (Gallimard, 1936).

Vandérem, Fernand. "De l'obscurité et de la clarté en littérature," *Revue de France,* November 1 and December 1, 1927, pp. 153–164 and 534–544; January 1, 1928, pp. 143–162.

The most important bibliographical references for Chapter VI, THE SEARCH FOR STANDARDS AND THE MYTH OF POSTERITY, are:

342 *Bibliographical Notes*

Abercrombie, Lascelles. *The Idea of Great Poetry*. London: Secker, 1925.

Bennett, Arnold. *Literary Taste and How to Form It*. London: Doran, n.d.

Birrell, Augustine. "Is It Possible to Tell a Good Book from a Bad One?" *Essays and Addresses* (New York: Scribner, 1901), pp. 198–226.

Brownell, W. C. *Standards*. New York: Scribner, 1917.

Dowden, Edward. "The Interpretation of Literature," *Transcripts and Studies* (London: Kegan Paul, 1896), pp. 237–268.

France, Anatole. *La Vie littéraire*. Calmann Lévy, 1888–1892. Vol. I, "M. Alexandre Dumas et son discours"; Vol. II, preface; Vol. IV, preface.

——. *Le Jardin d'Épicure*. Calmann Lévy, 1895. Pp. 219–221.

Kellett, E. E. *Fashion in Literature: A Study of Changing Taste*. London: Routledge, 1931.

Lanson, Gustave. "L'Immortalité littéraire," *Hommes et livres* (Lecène et Oudin, 1895).

Mordell, Albert. *The Shifting of Literary Values*. Philadelphia: The International, 1912.

Paulhan, Jean. *Les Fleurs de Tarbes ou la terreur dans les lettres*. Gallimard, 1941.

Schopenhauer, Arthur. *Essays*, trans. Bailey Saunders. New York: Burt & Co., n.d. Vol. IV, *The Art of Literature*. Also Ann Arbor: University of Michigan Press, 1960.

Scrutinies. Collected by Edgel Rickword. London: Wishart, 1931. Vol. II.

Sichel, Edith. "Some Suggestions about Bad Poetry," *Essays and Studies by Members of the English Association*, I (Oxford and London: Oxford University Press, 1910), 136–167.

Stapfer, Paul. *Des Réputations littéraires: Essais de morale et d'histoire*. Vol. I, Hachette, 1895; Vol. II, Fishbacher, 1901.

"Towards Standards of Criticism." Selections from F. R. Leavis, *The Calendar of Modern Letters* (London: Wishart, 1933).

A selective bibliography of references for the chapters on CRITICISM IN GENERAL and on BOOK-REVIEWING, in their relationship to scholarship and to the public, would include, in English and in French:

Alvarez, Alfred. *Stewards of Excellence.* New York: Scribner, 1958. Published in Great Britain as *The Shaping Spirit* (London: Chatto and Windus, 1958).

Babbitt, Irving. *Literature and the American College.* Boston: Houghton Mifflin, 1908.

——. "Humanist and Specialist," *The Spanish Character and Other Essays* (Boston: Houghton Mifflin, 1940), pp. 183–197.

Barthes, Roland. *Essais critiques.* Seuil, 1964.

——. *Critique et Vérité.* Seuil, 1966.

Barzun, Jacques. *The Energies of Art.* New York: Harper, 1956.

Beers, Henry A. *Points at Issue.* New York: Macmillan, 1904.

Benn, M. B. "The Problem of Truth in Poetry," *A.U.M.L.A.* (New Zealand), no. 25 (May 1966), pp. 57–67.

Bonnefoy, Yves. "Critics, English and French," *Encounter,* XI, no. 1 (July 1958).

Canby, Henry S. "A Prospectus for Criticism," *Definitions* (New York: Harcourt Brace, 1922).

——. "The American Scholar and the War" (address), *Publications of the Modern Language Association,* LVII, no. 4 (December 1942).

Cargill, Oscar. *Toward a Pluralistic Criticism.* Carbondale: Southern Illinois University Press, 1965.

Cazamian, Louis. *Criticism in the Making.* New York: Macmillan, 1929.

Cecil, David. *The Fine Art of Reading and Other Literary Studies.* London: Constable, and New York: Bobbs Merrill, 1957.

Chambers, E. K. "The Study of English Literature," *A Sheaf of Studies* (London: Oxford University Press, 1942).

Chinard, Gilbert. "Literature and the Humanities," *The Meaning of the Humanities,* ed. Th. Meyer Greene. Princeton: Princeton University Press, 1938.

Crane, Ronald S. "History vs. Criticism in the Study of Literature," *English Journal,* XXIV (October 1935), 645–667.

——. *The Language of Criticism and the Structure of Poetry.* Toronto: University of Toronto Press, 1954.

Croce, Benedetto. *La Critica letteraria: questione teoriche.* Rome: Loescher, 1894.

——. *Nuovi Saggi di estetica.* Bari: Laterza, 1920.

Dallas, E. S. *The Gay Science.* London: Chapman and Hall, 1866.

344   *Bibliographical Notes*

Darrel, Abel. "Intellectual Criticism," *American Scholar*, XII, no. 4 (Autumn 1943), 414–428.

Diéguez, Manuel de. *L'Écrivain et son langage*. Gallimard, 1960.

——. "Jean-Pierre Richard et la Critique thématique," *Critique*, no. 193 (June 1963).

Doubrovsky, Serge. *Pourquoi la Nouvelle Critique?* Mercure de France, 1966.

Du Bos, Charles. *Approximations*. Coll. éd.; Fayard, 1965.

Edgley, R. "The Object of Literary Criticism," *Essays in Criticism*, XIV, no. 3 (July 1964), 221–236.

Eliot, T. S. "The Perfect Critic," *The Sacred Wood* (London: Methuen, 1920).

——. "The Function of a Literary Review," *Criterion*, I (July 1923), 420.

——. "Experiment in Criticism," *Bookman* (New York), November 1929, pp. 225–233. Reprinted in *Tradition and Experiment* by several authors (Oxford and London: Oxford University Press, 1929).

Elton, Oliver. *The Nature of Literary Criticism*. Manchester: Manchester University Press, 1932.

Evans, Ifor. "The Limits of Literary Criticism," *Essays and Studies by Members of the English Association*, XVIII (Oxford University Press, 1933), 24–52.

Farrell, James T. *A Note on Literary Criticism*. New York: Vanguard, 1936.

Ferguson, De Lancey. "Should Scholars Try to Think?" *American Scholar*, XI, no. 2 (Spring 1942), 208–219.

Fernandez, Ramon. "De la Critique philosophique," *Messages* (Gallimard, 1926).

Feuillerat, Albert. "Scholarship and Literary Criticism," *Yale Review*, XIV (1925), 309–324.

Foerster, Norman. *The American Scholar*. Chapel Hill: University of North Carolina Press, 1929.

Frank, Joseph. *The Widening Gyre*. New Brunswick: Rutgers University Press, 1965.

Frye, Northrop. *Anatomy of Criticism*. Princeton: Princeton University Press, 1958.

——. *Fables of Identity: Studies in Poetic Mythology*. New York: Harcourt, Brace and World, 1964.

Gardner, Helen. *The Limits of Literary Criticism.* New York: Oxford University Press, 1956.

———. *The Business of Criticism.* New York: Oxford University Press, 1959.

Génette, Gérard. *Figures.* Seuil, 1966.

Gosse, Edmund. *Questions at Issue.* London: Heinemann, 1893.

Gracq, Julien. *Préférences.* Corti, 1966.

Guérard, Albert. *Preface to World Literature.* New York: Holt, 1940.

Guérard, Albert, Jr. "Criticism and Commodity," *The New Republic,* December 8, 1941.

Holloway, John. *The Charted Mirror.* London: Routledge and Kegan Paul, 1960.

Hough, Graham. *The Dream and the Task: Literature and Morals in the Culture Today.* London: Duckworth, 1963.

Jarrell, Randall. *Poetry and the Age.* New York: Knopf, 1953.

Jones, Howard Mumford. "Literary Scholarship and Contemporary Criticism," *English Journal,* November 1934, pp. 740–757.

———. "The Limits of Contemporary Criticism," *Saturday Review of Literature,* September 6, 1941.

———. "The Uninfluentials," *Saturday Review of Literature,* November 11, 1941.

———. "Literary History and Literary Plenty," *Saturday Review of Literature,* October 31, 1942.

———. "Scholarship and Democratic Faith," *University Review* (Kansas), Autumn 1942, pp. 12–18.

Kazin, Alfred. *On Native Grounds.* New York: Reynal and Hitchcock, 1942.

———. "The Useful Critic," *Atlantic Monthly,* CCVI, no. 12 (December 1965), 73–80.

Krutch, Joseph Wood. *Experience and Art: Some Aspects of the Esthetics of Literature.* New York: Harrison Smith, 1932.

Leavis, F. R. "What's Wrong with Criticism," *Scrutiny,* September 1932, pp. 132–140.

Levin, Harry. "Criticism in Crisis," *Comparative Literature,* VII, no. 2 (Spring 1955), 144–155.

———. *Contexts of Criticism.* Cambridge: Harvard University Press, 1957.

——. *Refractions: Essays in Comparative Literature.* Oxford University Press, 1966.

Lippmann, Walter. "Education without Culture," *Commonweal,* January 17, 1941. Reprinted as "Education vs. Western Civilization," *American Scholar,* X (1941), 184–193.

Literary Scholarship: Its Aims and Methods. By Norman Foerster, John McGalliard, René Wellek, Austin Warren, and Wilbur Schramm. Chapel Hill: University of North Carolina Press, 1941.

"Literature and the Professors," by Cleanth Brooks, Arthur Mizener, Sidney Cox, Hade Saunders, and Lionel Trilling, *Kenyon Review,* Autumn 1940, 403–442.

"Literature and the Professors," by John Crowe Ransom, Allen Tate, Joe Horrell, Wright Thomas, and Harry Levin, *Southern Review,* VI (Autumn 1940), 225–269.

Lowes, John Livingston. "The Modern Language Association and Humane Scholarship," *Publications of the Modern Language Association of America,* XLVIII (1933), 1399–1408.

Lucas, F. L. "Criticism," *Life and Letters,* November 1929, pp. 433–465.

MacCarthy, Desmond. *Criticism.* London and New York: Putnam, 1932.

MacLeish, Archibald. "The Irresponsibles," *A Time to Speak* (Boston: Houghton Mifflin, 1941).

Muir, Edwin. *Transition: Essays on Contemporary Literature.* London: Leonard and Virginia Woolf Press, 1926.

Murry, John Middleton. "The Function of Criticism," *Aspects of Literature* (London: Collins, 1920), pp. 1–14.

——. "A Critical Credo," *Countries of the Mind* (London: Collins, 1922), I, 237–246.

Nadal, Octave. *À Mesure haute.* Mercure de France, 1964.

Nathan, George Jean. *The Testament of a Critic.* New York: Knopf, 1931.

Nicolson, Marjorie. "What's Wrong with the Scholars?" *Saturday Review of Literature,* April 15, 1944.

Peyre, Henri. *Literature and Sincerity.* New Haven: Yale University Press, 1963.

Picard, Raymond. *Nouvelle Critique, nouvelle imposture.* Pauvert, 1965.

Picon, Gaëtan. "Metamorphose de la Littérature," *La Table Ronde,* no. 17 (May 1949), pp. 754–775.

———. "Critique et Lecture," *L'usage de la lecture* (Mercure de France, 1960).

———. "D'une esthétique contemporaine," *Cahiers du Sud,* no. 361 (June–July 1961), pp. 339–364.

Pottle, Frederick. *The Idiom of Poetry.* Ithaca: Cornell University Press, 1942.

Poulet, Georges. *Études sur le temps humain.* Plon, 1950.

———. *La Distance intérieure.* Plon, 1952.

———. *Les Métamorphoses du Cercle.* Plon, 1961.

Pound, Ezra. *Literary Essays,* ed. T. S. Eliot. Norfolk: New Directions, 1954.

Pound, Roscoe. "Scholarship and Democratic Leadership," *American Scholar,* Spring 1942, pp. 220–227.

Raleigh, Walter. "A Note on Criticism," *On Writing and Writers* (London: Edwin Arnold, 1926).

Ransom, John Crowe. *The New Criticism.* Norfolk: New Directions, 1941.

Read, Herbert. "The Attributes of Criticism," *Reason and Romanticism* (London: Faber & Gwyer, 1926), pp. 1–30.

———. *Collected Essays in Literary Criticism.* London: Faber & Faber, 1938.

Richard, Jean-Pierre. *Littérature et sensation.* Seuil, 1954.

Rouzaud, Maurice. *Où va la critique?* Éditions Saint Michel, 1929.

Smith, David Nichol. *The Function of Criticism.* Oxford and London: Oxford University Press, 1909.

Sollers, Philippe. *L'Intermédiaire.* Seuil, 1963.

Spingarn, J. E. *Creative Criticism.* New York: Holt, 1917.

Spitzer, Leo. "History of Ideas vs. Reading of Poetry," *Southern Review,* VI, no. 3 (Winter 1941), 584–609.

Starobinski, Jean. *L'Oeil vivant.* Gallimard, 1961.

Swinnerton, Frank. *The Reviewing and Criticism of Books.* London: Dent, 1939.

Tate, Allen. "The Present Function of Criticism," *Reason in Madness* (New York: Putnam, 1941).

———. "Is Literary Criticism Possible?" *Sewanee Review,* September–October 1952, pp. 546–557.

Teeter, Louis. "Scholarship and the Art of Criticism," *English Literary History (ELH)*, V (September 1938), 173–194.

Thibaudet, Albert. *Physiologie de la Critique*. Nouvelle Revue Critique, 1930.

Thomson, Ralph. "The Popular Review and the Scholarly Book," *The English Institute Annual, 1940* (New York: Columbia University Press, 1941), pp. 130–143.

Tindall, William Y. "Scholarship and Contemporary Literature," *The English Institute Annual, 1940* (New York: Columbia University Press, 1941), pp. 42–60.

Trilling, Lionel. *The Liberal Imagination*. New York: Macmillan, 1948.

——. *The Opposing Self*. New York: Macmillan, 1955.

——. "English Literature and American Education," *Sewanee Review*, LXVI, no. 3 (Summer 1958).

Tucker, T. G. *The Judgment and Appreciation of Literature*. Melbourne: Melbourne University Press, 1926.

Turnell, Martin. "Literary Criticism in France," *Scrutiny*, VIII (1939), 167–183 and 281–298.

Wain, John. *Interpretations*. London: Routledge and Kegan Paul, 1956.

Warren, Robert Penn. *Selected Essays*. New York: Random House, 1951.

Wellek, René. "Literary Theory, Criticism and History," *Sewanee Review*, LXVIII, no. 1 (January–March 1960), 1–19.

——. *Concepts of Criticism*. New Haven: Yale University Press, 1964.

Wimsatt, William. *The Verbal Icon: Studies in the Meaning of Poetry*. Lexington: University of Kentucky Press, 1954.

Woodberry, George Edward. *The Appreciation of Literature*. New York: Baker & Taylor, 1907.

——. *Two Phases of Criticism, Historical and Aesthetic*. Gambier, Ohio: Kenyon College Lectures, 1914.

Worsfold, W. Basil. *Judgment in Literature*. London: Dent, 1900.

Young, C. M. "The Technique of Criticism: Classical," *Essays and Studies by Members of the English Association*, XXIII (1938), 70–78.

Index

Abercrombie, Lascelles, 288
Adams, Henry, 72
Addison, Joseph, 13, 37, 206, 252
Aeschylus, 30, 31, 199, 253, 276
Akenside, Mark, 284
Alcott, A. B., 73, 76
Alfieri, Vittorio, 130
Alvarez, Alfred, 288
Ameipsias, 31
Ampère, J. J., 90
Anderson, Sherwood, 84
Annual Review, 42
Annunzio, Gabriele d', 279
Apollinaire, Guillaume, 127, 128, 256
Aragon, Louis, 10, 108, 129, 212, 222
Aratus, 200
Argonne, Bonaventure d', 95
Aristarchus, 29
Aristophanes, 31, 276
Aristotle, 6, 29, 31, 200, 226, 276, 289, 336
Armstrong, Walter, 241
Arnauld, Antoine, 97
Arnold, Matthew, 4, 8, 54, 56, 62, 63-64, 67, 71, 77, 90, 99, 132, 150, 169, 253, 271, 279
Asselineau, Charles, 112, 113
Athenaeum, 53, 54, 55, 164
Atlantic Monthly, 85, 86, 297, 332
Aubignac, Abbé d', 292
Aubigné, Agrippa d', 14, 266
Auden, W. H., 7, 60, 201, 238
Audiberti, Jacques, 222
Augier, Émile, 141
Augustus, 275
Ausonius, 184
Austen, Jane, 45, 53, 247, 253, 257, 266
Austin, Alfred, 77
Autran, Joseph, 131
Aymé, Marcel, 129

Babbitt, Irving, 61, 82, 132, 183
Babcock, Robert W., 34
Babou, Hippolyte, 112, 113, 114
Bach, J. S., 12, 163, 175, 258, 264, 267
Bach, P. E., 163
Bachelard, Gaston, 20
Bacon, Francis, 6, 13, 33, 94, 155
Bagehot, Walter, 67
Bainville, Jacques, 159
Baldwin, James, 295
Balzac, Honoré de, 9, 14, 55, 56, 72, 75, 79, 80, 82, 93, 106, 107, 109, 110, 115, 126, 135, 136, 139, 140, 142, 143, 148, 157, 158, 167, 168, 170, 171, 173, 177, 184, 208, 232, 234, 235, 237, 242, 249, 253, 259, 261, 271, 290, 308, 315, 324, 337
Banville, Théodore de, 112, 113, 114
Baour-Lormian, Pierre, 101, 102
Barbey d'Aurevilly, Jules, 102, 104, 106, 108, 110, 111, 112, 114, 139, 206
Barbier, Auguste, 131
Barbusse, Henri, 122
Baring, Maurice, 59, 158
Barrès, Maurice, 141
Barrow, Isaac, 38
Barthes, Roland, 21, 24, 288
Batteux, Abbé, 98
Baudelaire, Charles, 7, 12, 18, 25, 60, 62, 64, 72, 78, 80, 82, 92, 93, 96, 106, 110, 112-118, 119, 129, 130, 135, 137, 139, 140, 141, 142, 148, 150, 153, 157, 175, 176, 184, 185, 186, 187, 205, 219, 221, 229, 239, 240, 243, 245, 258, 259, 261, 262, 264, 265, 269, 270, 280, 291, 324
Bayle, Pierre, 95, 96, 169
Bazille, Frédéric, 272
Beauvoir, Roger de, 139
Beckett, Samuel, 320
Beddoes, Thomas L., 45, 266

THE MESSENGER LECTURES

This book in its original form consisted of lectures delivered at Cornell University in the Spring of 1943, namely, the Messenger Lectures on the Evolution of Civilization. That series was founded and its title was prescribed by the late Hiram J. Messenger, B.Litt., Ph.D., of Hartford, Connecticut, who directed in his will that a portion of his estate be given to Cornell University and used to provide annually "a course or courses of lectures on the evolution of civilization, for the special purpose of raising the moral standard of our political, business, and social life." The lectureship was established in 1923.

Fl